Communications in Computer and Information Science   1574

Antonia Moropoulou · Andreas Georgopoulos ·
Anastasios Doulamis · Marinos Ioannides ·
Alfredo Ronchi (Eds.)

Trandisciplinary Multispectral Modelling and Cooperation for the Preservation of Cultural Heritage

Second International Conference, TMM_CH 2021
Athens, Greece, December 13–15, 2021
Revised Selected Papers

 Springer

Editors
Antonia Moropoulou (iD)
National Technical University of Athens
Athens, Greece

Andreas Georgopoulos (iD)
National Technical University of Athens
Athens, Greece

Anastasios Doulamis
National Technical University of Athens
Athens, Greece

Marinos Ioannides (iD)
Cyprus University of Technology
Limassol, Cyprus

Alfredo Ronchi (iD)
Polytechnic University of Milan
Milan, Italy

ISSN 1865-0929   ISSN 1865-0937 (electronic)
Communications in Computer and Information Science
ISBN 978-3-031-20252-0   ISBN 978-3-031-20253-7 (eBook)
https://doi.org/10.1007/978-3-031-20253-7

This Springer imprint is published by the registered company Springer Nature Switzerland AG
The registered company address is: Gewerbestrasse 11, 6330 Cham, Switzerland

Preface

Innovative scientific methodologies and challenging projects marking future trends in the protection of cultural heritage have initiated through a holistic approach, merging competence from the scientific fields of architecture, civil engineering, surveying engineering, materials science and engineering, information technology, and archaeology, a universal conversation among scholars, heritage professionals on restoration and conservation, stakeholders, industry representatives, and policy makers. The combined utilization of digital documentation technologies with innovative analytical and non-destructive techniques; numerical, computational; and 3D techniques; and archaeometric and archaeogene methods supports the development of a transdisciplinary multispectral modeling methodology towards the sustainable preservation of cultural heritage. Innovation is enhancing and revealing a critical dimension of the preservation of cultural heritage along with social participation and communication.

The National Technical University of Athens' interdisciplinary "Protection of Monuments" team (A. Moropoulou, M. Korres, A. Georgopoulos, C. Spyrakos, and C. Mouzakis), scientifically responsible for the rehabilitation of the Holy Aedicule in the Church of the Holy Sepulchre in Jerusalem, and the Technical Chamber of Greece, in collaboration with international and Greek Authorities, successfully organized the 2nd International Conference on "Transdisciplinary Multispectral Modeling and Cooperation for the Preservation of Cultural Heritage: Recapturing the World in Crisis through Culture" (TMM_CH 2021), which has held during December 13–15, 2021, in Athens, Greece, and discussed modern trends in the original agora of our technological and democratic roots.

The conference was organized by the National Technical University of Athens (NTUA) in cooperation with the Technical Chamber of Greece, under the patronage of H.E. the President of the Hellenic Republic, Katerina Sakellaropoulou, inaugurated by H.E. the Vice President of the Government of the Hellenic Republic, Panagiotis Pikrammenos, with benedictions bestowed by His All Holiness, Ecumenical Patriarch, Bartholomew I of Constantinople and His Beatitude Archbishop Hieronymus II of Athens and All Greece.

Distinguished scientists and representatives of the National Geographic Society, the Cultural Heritage Finance Alliance (CHiFA), the International Council of Monuments and Sites (ICOMOS), the International Committee for Documentation of Cultural Heritage (CIPA), the Organization of World Heritage Cities (OWHC), the European Society for Engineering Education (SEFI), the European Construction Technology Platform (ECTP) and the Hellenic Construction Technology Platform (HCTP), the International Federation of Surveyors (FIG), the World Monuments Fund (WMF), AHEPA Hellas, the Grand Priory of Greece at the Sovereign Military Order of the Temple of Jerusalem, the UNESCO Chairs on "Digital Cultural Heritage" and "Culture, Tourism, Development", and other major international and European organizations, associations, networks, universities, and research centers in the field of cultural heritage preservation, participated in the international Steering and Scientific Committees, and addressed the conference at the opening session.

At the 1st TMM_CH conference, which was held with great success in October 2018 at the Eugenides Foundation in Athens, with the attendance of 350 delegates from 22 countries, the emblematic rehabilitation of the Holy Aedicule of the Holy Sepulchre in Jerusalem was presented as an exemplary application, in the field of monuments' protection, of interdisciplinary and multispectral collaboration, as an outcome of innovation in both research and implementation, with emphasis on technological advancements, not only intersecting all the scientific fields of engineering and natural science but also initiating an ongoing dialogue with the humanities, such as archaeology, theology, sociology, diplomacy, and tourism.

The 2nd TMM_CH conference focused on the latest developments in research and innovation and the identification of novel trends to build an interdisciplinary approach to conservation and holistic digital documentation of cultural heritage. The utilization and reuse of monuments, historic cities, and sites forms the framework for the sustainable preservation of cultural heritage, in accordance with the principles of a circular economy, in terms of the respect and protection of values, materials, structures, architecture, and landscape, with an informed society able to participate effectively in the policies that will design and implement the new strategies required.

Innovative knowledge transfer through practice and education is continuing the venture for the rehabilitation projects in the Church of the Holy Sepulchre, joining the National Technical University of Athens and La Sapienza University of Rome with the Bezalel Academy of Science and Arts in Jerusalem, in cooperation with Israeli Antiquities Authority, the Hellenic Research Institute of Alexandrian Civilization, and PerpetielSI SRL, through the Erasmus+ Strategic Alliance EDICULA "Educational Digital Innovative Cultural Heritage related Learning Alliance".

The issues discussed within the 14 sessions and 14 panel discussions at TMM_CH 2021 were as follows:

1. The Holy Sepulchre rehabilitation project: an emblematic source of innovation;
2. Resilience to climate change, natural hazards, and pandemic risks - biosafety;
3. Novel educational approaches for the preservation of cultural heritage;
4. Preserving compatibility, the materiality and integrity of structures, and architectural authenticity;
5. Advanced nondestructive and structural techniques for diagnosis, redesign, and health monitoring;
6. Earthquake and structural rehabilitation;
7. Archaeology, archaeometry, and archaeogene;
8. Bridging heritage stakeholders, science, and industry;
9. Transdiciplinary dialogue for world heritage at risk: the exemplary Hagia Sophia;
10. Digital heritage: a holistic approach;
11. Green and blue deals for local and regional sustainable development: revealing and preserving cultural and natural assets for isolated areas development with social participation;

12. Green deal and blue deals for sustainable development of isolated areas: sustainable land management and rural and urban development through preserving, reusing, and revealing cultural heritage;
13. Historic cities and centers: new Reuse and preservation strategies applying a circular economy; and
14. Recapturing the world in crisis through culture.

Sharing knowledge, experiences, and recommendations about sustainable cultural heritage approaches and practices, at a moment of great risk and a time of renewed possibilities, has reorientated conversation to explore the current conditions and contours of the world in crisis, recapturing itself through culture and relaunching development.

The TMM_CH 2021 conference was held at the Eugenides Foundation in a hybrid format. Due to the pandemic both onsite and online attendance was facilitated for oral presentations, in compliance with governmental directives against COVID-19. All sessions and panel discussions were accessible for the registered conference participants using the unique link in their personal conference ticket. The opening session and all panel discussions, as addressed to the general public, were livestreamed with free access via the conference's YouTube channel and website.

The 2nd TMM_CH Conference was highly anticipated, attracting researchers from all over the world. It was held with great success, despite the pandemic, with the physical presence of 150 delegates and online attendance of 500 delegates in real time.

Striving to ensure that the conference presentations and proceedings were of the highest quality possible, we only accepted papers that presented the results of various studies focused on the extraction of new scientific knowledge in the area of transdisciplinary multispectral modeling and cooperation for the preservation of cultural heritage.

In total, 310 contributions were submitted, and 124 papers were accepted for oral presentation and publication (representing the work of 377 authors from 33 countries) after peer review and consequent revision, with a rate of acceptance equivalent to 40%. A single-blind peer review process was employed with each paper receiving, on average, three reviews. Accepted papers were published in this Springer proceedings volume and in Special Issues of scientific journals in the field of cultural heritage preservation.

The interdisciplinarity in the preservation of cultural heritage requires holistic documentation with the fusion of the various disciplines' data on 3D models. Computer-aided design and advanced computer science methodologies support an interdisciplinary synthesis of the preservation state assessment, i.e. the evaluation of the rehabilitation achieved in respect of the integrity of materials and structures, throughout the design of the restoration of authentic architecture. In parallel, new technologies can be used to enhance research and education and communicate the reuse and exploration of cultural and natural assets, providing, through tourism, external economies to sustain local and regional development in a circular way.

Hence, 24 papers presented at the 2nd TMM_CH conference, integrating all of the aspects above, are published in this book, Transdisciplinary Multispectral Modeling and Cooperation for the Preservation of Cultural Heritage, within the Springer Communications in Computer and Information Science (CCIS) series.

We would like to acknowledge all the people who made the conference possible and successful: the organizers as listed at the beginning of this preface; the sponsors, the Public Power Corporation, the AEGEAS Non-Profit Civil Company, the Bank of Greece, Dalkafoukis House Ltd., Attica Bank, TITAN Cement Group, and Eurobank; the media sponsor, BCI Media Toronto, and the media support by DNA Sequence Ld, PerpetielSI SRL, and Boussias Media Group; the Eugenides Foundation for the kind offer of the venue for the conference; the partners of the Erasmus+ Strategic Alliance EDICULA "Educational Digital Innovative Cultural Heritage related Learning Alliance", coordinated by NTUA, for the co-organization of Panels 1 and 3, as an EDICULA Innovation Session and EDICULA Educational Session, respectively; the organizers of "Researchers' Night at the National Technical University of Athens 2021" for the co-organization of Panels 11 and 12 as Researcher's Night post events according to the action's special theme "Green Deal"; the partners of the research program RESPECT, "An exemplary information system and methodology for the integrated management, analysis, and dissemination of digital cultural heritage data coming from the rehabilitation of the Holy Aedicule", coordinated by NTUA, PA 2014-2020, for the co-organization of Panel 10; and the partners of the research program AEI, "Sustainable development of less developed areas by creating new tourism resources and products through analysis, documentation, modeling, management, and preservation of the cultural preserve using ICT applications", coordinated by NTUA, PA 2014-2020, for the co-organization of Panels 11 and 12.

The conference would not have been possible without the commitment of NTUA's interdisciplinary team for the "Protection of Monuments"; the full cooperation of the TMM_CH editors of this volume; the scientific support of the international Steering Committee and the Scientific Committees; and the support of the Executive Organizing Committee and the Technical System Providers; as well as the valuable assistance of the CCIS team at Springer, to whom we are most grateful. We are very proud of the result of this collaboration and we believe that this fruitful partnership will continue.

The 3rd TMM_CH conference has already been announced and will take place during March 20–23, 2023.

February 2022   Antonia Moropoulou

Organization

President – General Chair

Antonia Moropoulou   National Technical University of Athens, Greece

Steering Committee Chairs

Berbers Yolande   KU Leuven, Belgium and European Society for
Engineering Education (SEFI), Belgium
Burnham Bonnie   Cultural Heritage Finance Alliance, USA
D'Ayala Pier Giovanni   International Scientific Council for Island
Development (INSULA – UNESCO), Belgium
Georgopoulos Andreas   National Technical University of Athens, Greece,
and International Council of Monuments and
Sites (ICOMOS), France
Gravari-Barbas Maria   Paris 1 Panthéon-Sorbonne University, France
Hiebert Fredrik   National Geographic Society, USA
Ioannides Marinos   Cyprus University of Technology, Cyprus
Korka Elena   Ministry of Culture and Sports, Greece
Leissner Johanna   Fraunhofer Institutes, Germany
Minaidis Lee   Organization of World Heritage Cities, Canada
Oosterbeek Luiz   Polytechnic Institute of Tomar, Portugal, and
International Council of Philosophy and
Human Sciences (CIPSH), Belgium
Rodriguez-Maribona Isabel   European Construction Technology Platform
(ECTP), Belgium
Žarnić Roko   University of Ljubljana, Slovenia
Ronchi Alfredo   Polytechnic University of Milan, Italy
Stasinos Giorgos   Technical Chamber of Greece, Greece
Stylianidis Efstratios   Aristotle University of Thessaloniki, Greece, and
International Committee for Documentation of
Cultural Heritage (CIPA), France

Steering Committee

Achniotis Stelios   Cyprus Scientific and Technical Chamber
(ETEK), Cyprus
Aesopos Yannis   University of Patras, Greece
Amditis Angelos   National Technical University of Athens, Greece

Anagnostopoulos Christos	University of the Aegean, Greece
Anagnostopoulos Dimosthenis	Harokopio University, Greece
Anastasiadis Spiros	University of Crete, Greece
Andrade Carmen	International Centre for Numerical Methods in Engineering, Spain
Androulidaki Amalia	Ministry of Culture and Sports, Greece
Antonatos Alexandros	Hellenic Society for Non-Destructive Testing, Greece
Arabiyat Abed Al Razzaq	Jordan Tourism Board, Jordan
Arakadaki Maria	Aristotle University of Thessaloniki, Greece
Aravossis Konstantinos	National Technical University of Athens, Greece
Athanasiou Stefanos	University of Bern, Switzerland
Avgerinou-Kolonias Sofia	National Technical University of Athens, Greece
Avgeropoulos Apostolos	University of Ioannina, Greece
Avni Gideon	Israel Antiquities Authority, Israel
Avramides Yiannis	World Monuments Fund, USA
Babayan Hector	National Academy of Sciences, Armenia
Badalian Irena	Church of the Holy Sepulchre, Israel
Bafataki Vicky	"Giuseppe Sciacca" Foundation, Italy
Bakogiannis Efthimios	National Technical University of Athens, Greece
Baruch Yuval	Israel Antiquities Authority, Israel
Benelli Carla	Church of the Holy Sepulchre, Israel
Botsaris Pantelis	Democritus University of Thrace, Greece
Caradimas Costas	National Technical University of Athens, Greece
Caristan Yves	European Council of Academies of Applied Sciences, Technologies and Engineering (Euro-CASE), France
Chatzarakis E. George	School of Pedagogical and Technological Education, Greece
Chetouani Aladine	University of Orleans, France
Cholakian Paul	Grand Priory of Greece at the Sovereign Military Order of the Temple of Jerusalem, Greece
Chondrokoukis Grigorios	University of Piraeus, Greece
Coccossis Harry	University of Thessaly, Greece
Constantopoulos Panos	Athens University of Economic and Business, Greece
Corradi Marco	University of Northumbria, UK
Correia Mariana	Gallaecia Higher School, Portugal
D'Ayala Dina	University College London, UK
Daktylidis Michail	Panhellenic Association of Engineers Contractors of Public Works, Greece
De Vries Pieter	Delft University of Technology, The Netherlands
Della Tore Stefano	Polytechnic University of Milan, Italy

Di Giulio Roberto	University of Ferrara, Italy
Dimakopoulos Vassilios	University of Ioannina, Greece
Distefano Salvatore	University of Messina, Italy
Drdácký Miloš	Institute of Theoretical and Applied Mechanics, Czech Academy of Sciences, Czech Republic
Erdik Mustafa	Bogazici University, Turkey
Farouk Mohamed	Bibliotheca Alexandrina, Egypt
Floros Andreas	Ionian University, Greece
Forde Michael	University of Edinburgh, UK
Forest Emmanuel	Bouygues Group, France
Gómez-Ferrer Bayo Álvaro	Valencian Institute for Conservation and Restoration of Cultural Heritage, Spain
Grekas Aristarchos	National and Kapodistrian University of Athens, Greece
Groysman Alec	Association of Engineers, Architects and Graduates in Technological Sciences, Israel
Hamdan Osama	Church of the Holy Sepulchre, Israel
Ioannidis Charalambos	National Technical University of Athens, Greece
Ioannou Ioannis	University of Cyprus, Cyprus
Kallithrakas-Kontos Nikolaos	Technical University of Crete, Greece
Kalogirou Christiana	Ministry of Shipping and Island Policy, Greece
Kampanis Nikolaos	Foundation for Research and Technology Hellas, Greece
Karadimas Dimitris	Vision Business Consultants, Greece
Karapiperis Christos	American Hellenic Progressive Association (AHEPA), Greece
Kastanas Nikos	Independent Cultural Marketing Advisor, Greece
Katsifarakis Konstantinos	Aristotle University of Thessaloniki, Greece
Keane Kathryn	National Geographic Society, USA
Kollias Stefanos	National Technical University of Athens, Greece
Kordatos John	Worldwide Industrial and Marine Association, Greece
Koundouri Phoebe	Athèns University of Economics and Business, Greece
Kremlis George	Espoo Convention, Belgium
Kriari Ismini	Panteion University of Social and Political Sciences, Greece
La Grassa Alessandro	CRESM, Italy
Lee-Thorp Julia	University of Oxford, UK
Lianos Nikolaos	Democritus University of Thrace, Greece
Loukopoulou Politimi	International Council of Museums (ICOM), Hellenic National Committee, Greece

Maistrou Eleni	Society for the Environmental and Cultural Heritage, Greece
Masi Alessia	Sapienza University of Rome, Italy
Mataras Dimitris	University of Patras, Greece
Mavroeidi Maria	International Committee for the Conservation of Industrial Heritage (TICCIH), Greece
Mavrogenes John	Australian National University, Australia
Menychtas Andreas	BioAssist SA, Greece
Mitropoulos Theodosios	Church of the Holy Sepulchre, Israel
Mouhli Zoubeïr	Association de Sauvegarde de la Médina de Tunis, Tunisia
Nakasis Athanasios	ICOMOS, Greece
Neubauer Wolfgang	Ludwig Boltzmann Institute for Archaeological Prospection and Virtual Archaeology, Austria
Nobilakis Ilias	University of West Attica, Greece
Nounesis George	National Centre for Scientific Research "Demokritos", Greece
Ntroutsa Eirini	Erasmus+ Hellenic Agency (IKY), Greece
Padeletti Giuseppina	Italian National Research Council, Italy
Panayiaris George	University of West Attica, Greece
Papageorgiou Angelos	University of Ioannina, Greece
Papakosta Kalliopi	Hellenic Research Institute of Alexandrian Civilization, Egypt
Papi Emanuele	University of Siena, Italy
Pappas Spyros	ARGO - Hellenic Network in Brussels, Belgium
Paraskevopoulos Marios	University of Leicester, UK
Petridis Platon	National and Kapodistrian University of Athens, Greece
Philokyprou Maria	University of Cyprus, Cyprus
Pissaridis Chrysanthos	ICOMOS, Cyprus
Potsiou Chryssy	National Technical University of Athens, Greece
Pressas Charalambos	University of West Attica, Greece
Prodromou Elizabeth	Tufts University, USA
Providakis Konstantinos	Technical University of Crete, Greece
Rydock James	Research Management Institute, Norway
Salakidis Antonios	PerpetielSI SRL, Romania
Sali-Papasali Anastasia	Ionian University, Greece
Santos Pedro	Fraunhofer Institutes, Germany
Sela Wiener Adi	Bezalel Academy of Arts and Design, Israel
Skianis Charalambos	University of the Aegean, Greece
Skriapas Konstantinos	PERRAIVIA Network, Greece
Soile Sofia	National Technical University of Athens, Greece

Sotiropoulou Anastasia	School of Pedagogical and Technological Education, Greece
Spathis Panagiotis	Aristotle University of Thessaloniki, Greece
Stamoulis Georgios	University of Thessaly, Greece
Stavrakos Christos	University of Ioannina, Greece
Tapinaki Sevi	National Technical University of Athens, Greece
Touliatos Panagiotis	Frederick University, Cyprus
Tournikiotis Panayotis	National Technical University of Athens, Greece
Tsatsanifos Christos	Pangea Consulting Engineers Ltd., Greece
Tsiampaos Kostas	National Technical University of Athens, Greece
Tsimas Pavlos	Independent Journalist, Greece
Tucci Grazia	University of Florence, Italy
Tzitzikas Yannis	University of Crete, Greece
Tzitzikosta Aikaterini	Hellenic National Commission for UNESCO, Greece
Varvarigou Theodora	National Technical University of Athens, Greece
Vergados Dimitrios	University of Piraeus, Greece
Nenad (Amvrosije) Vesić	International Scientific Committee for Places of Religion and Ritual (PRERICO), ICOMOS, France
Vlachoulis Themistoklis	Ministry of Culture and Sports, Greece
Ward-Perkins Bryan	University of Oxford, UK
Zacharias Nikos	University of Peloponnese, Greece
Zervakis Michael	Technical University of Crete, Greece
Zouain Georges	GAIA-Heritage, Lebanon

Scientific Committee Chairs

Korres Manolis	National Technical University of Athens, Greece and Academy of Athens, Greece
Georgopoulos Andreas	National Technical University of Athens, Greece and ICOMOS, France
Mouzakis Charis	National Technical University of Athens, Greece
Spyrakos Constantine	National Technical University of Athens, Greece
Favero Gabriele	Sapienza University of Rome, Italy
Baruch Yuval	Israel Antiquities Authority, Israel
Turner Mike	Bezalel Academy of Arts and Design, Israel
Aggelis Dimitris	Free University of Brussels, Belgium
Delegou Ekaterini	National Technical University of Athens, Greece
Doukas Haris	National Technical University of Athens, Greece
Doulamis Anastasios	National Technical University of Athens, Greece
Ioannidis Charalambos	National Technical University of Athens, Greece
Konstanti Agoritsa	National Technical University of Athens, Greece

Kyriazis Dimosthenis	University of Piraeus, Greece
Lampropoulos Kyriakos	National Technical University of Athens, Greece
Liritzis Ioannis	University of the Aegean, Greece
Osman Ahmad	Saarland University of Applied Sciences, Germany
Zendri Elisabetta	Ca' Foscari University of Venice, Italy

Scientific Committee

Abuamoud Ismaiel Naser	Hashemite University, Jordan
Achenza Maddalena	University of Calgary, Canada
Adamakis Kostas	University of Thessaly, Greece
Agapiou Athos	Cyprus University of Technology, Cyprus
Aggelakopoulou Eleni	Acropolis Restoration Service, Greece
Alexopoulou Aleka	Aristotle University of Thessaloniki, Greece
Apostolopoulou Maria	National Technical University of Athens, Greece
Argyropoulou Vasilike	University of West Attica, Greece
Asteris Panagiotis	School of Pedagogical and Technological Education, Greece
Avdelidis Nikolaos	Cranfield University, UK
Bakolas Stelios	National Technical University of Athens, Greece
Balas Kostas	Technical University of Crete, Greece
Bettega Stefano Maria	Higher Institute for Artistic Industries, Italy
Betti Michele	University of Florence, Italy
Biscontin Guido	Ca' Foscari University of Venice, Italy
Boniface Michael	University of Southampton, UK
Bounia Alexandra	University of the Aegean, Greece
Boutalis Ioannis	Democritus University of Thrace, Greece
Boyatzis Stamatis	University of West Attica, Greece
Bozanis Panayiotis	University of Thessaly, Greece
Cassar Jo Ann	University of Malta, Malta
Cassar May	University College London, UK
Castigloni Carlo	Polytechnic University of Milan, Italy
Cavaleri Liborio	University of Palermo, Italy
Chamzas Christodoulos	Democritus University of Thrace, Greece
Chiotinis Nikitas	University of West Attica, Greece
Chlouveraki Stefania	University of West Attica, Greece
Christaras Basile	Aristotle University of Thessaloniki, Greece
Daflou Eleni	National Technical University of Athens, Greece
De Angelis Roberta	University of Malta, Malta
Demotikali Dimitra	National Technical University of Athens, Greece
Dimitrakopoulos Fotios	National and Kapodistrian University of Athens, Greece

Dritsos Stefanos	University of Patras, Greece
Economou Dimitrios	University of Thessaly, Greece
Efesiou Irene	National Technical University of Athens, Greece
Exadaktylos George	National Technical University of Athens, Greece
Facorellis Yorgos	University of West Attica, Greece
Firat Diker Hasan	Fatih Sultan Mehmet Vakif University, Turkey
Formisano Antonio	University of Naples Federico II, Italy
Foudos Ioannis	University of Ioannina, Greece
Frosina Annamaria	Centre for Social and Economic Research, Italy
Fuhrmann Constanze	Fraunhofer Institutes, Germany
Ganiatsas Vassilis	National Technical University of Athens, Greece
Gavela Stamatia	School of Pedagogical and Technological Education, Greece
Ghadban Shadi Sami	Birzeit University, Palestine
Gharbi Mohamed	Institute of Technological Studies of Bizerte, Tunisia
Hadjinicolaou Teti	International Council of Museums (ICOM), Hellenic National Committee, Greece
Iadanza Ernesto	University of Florence, Italy
Izzo Francesca Caterina	Ca' Foscari University of Venice, Italy
Kaliampakos Dimitrios	National Technical University of Athens, Greece
Kapsalis Georgios	National University of Ioannina, Greece
Karaberi Alexia	National Technical University of Athens, Greece
Karagiannis Georgios	Ormylia Foundation, Greece
Karellas Sotirios	National Technical University of Athens, Greece
Karoglou Maria	National Technical University of Athens, Greece
Katsioti-Beazi Margarita	National Technical University of Athens, Greece
Kavvadas Michael	National Technical University of Athens, Greece
Kioussi Anastasia	Ministry of Culture and Sports, Greece
Komnitsas Konstantinos	Technical University of Crete, Greece
Konstantinides Tony	Imperial College London, UK
Konstantinidou Helen	National Technical University of Athens, Greece
Kontoyannis Christos	University of Patras, Greece
Kourkoulis Stavros	National Technical University of Athens, Greece
Koutsoukos Petros	University of Patras, Greece
Kyvellou Stella	Panteion University of Social and Political Sciences, Greece
Lambropoulos Vasileios	University of West Attica, Greece
Liolios Asterios	Democritus University of Thrace, Greece
Lobovikov-Katz Anna	NB Haifa School of Design and Technion - Israel Institute of Technology, Israel
Loukas Athanasios	University of Thessaly, Greece

Lourenço Paulo	University of Minho, Portugal
Lyridis Dimitrios	National Technical University of Athens, Greece
Maietti Federica	University of Ferrara, Italy
Mamaloukos Stavros	University of Patras, Greece
Maniatakis Charilaos	Water Supply and Sewerage Company of Hersonissos Municipality, Greece
Maravelaki Pagona-Noni	Technical University of Crete, Greece
Marinou Georgia	National Technical University of Athens, Greece
Maroulis Zacharias	National Technical University of Athens, Greece
Matikas Theodoros	University of Ioannina, Greece
Mavrogenes John	Australian National University, Australia
Medeghini Laura	Sapienza University of Rome, Italy
Milani Gabriele	Polytechnic University of Milan, Italy
Miltiadou Androniki	National Technical University of Athens, Greece
Mohebkhah Amin	Malayer University, Iran
Nevin Saltik Emine	Middle East Technical University, Turkey
Oikonomopoulou Eleni	Independent Architect, Greece
Ortiz Calderon Maria Pilar	Pablo de Olavide University, Spain
Osman Ahmad	University of Applied Sciences in Saarbrücken, Germany
Ouzounis Christos	Aristotle University of Thessaloniki, Greece
Pagge Tzeni	University of Ioannina, Greece
Paipetis Alkiviadis	University of Ioannina, Greece
Panagouli Olympia	University of Thessaly, Greece
Pantazis George	National Technical University of Athens, Greece
Papagianni Ioanna	Aristotle University of Thessaloniki, Greece
Papaioannou Georgios	Ionian University, Greece
Papatrechas Christos	Institute of Geological and Mineral Research, Greece
Pérez García Carmen	Valencian Institute for Conservation and Restoration of Cultural Heritage, Spain
Perraki Maria	National Technical University of Athens, Greece
Piaia Emanuele	University of Ferrara, Italy
Polydoras Stamatios	National Technical University of Athens, Greece
Prepis Alkiviades	Democritus University of Thrace, Greece
Psycharis Ioannis	National Technical University of Athens, Greece
Rajčić Vlatka	University of Zagreb, Croatia
Saisi Antonella Elide	Polytechnic University of Milan, Italy
Sapounakis Aristides	University of Thessaly, Greece
Schippers-Trifan Oana	DEMO Consultants BV, The Netherlands
Seligman Jon	Israel Antiquities Authority, Israel
Smith Robert	University of Oxford, UK

Stambolidis Nikos	University of Crete, Greece
Stavroulakis Georgios	Technical University of Crete, Greece
Stefanidou Maria	Aristotle University of Thessaloniki, Greece
Stefanis Alexis	University of West Attica, Greece
Tavukcuoglu Ayse	Middle East Technical University, Turkey
Theodorou Doros	National Technical University of Athens, Greece
Theoulakis Panagiotis	University of West Attica, Greece
Thomas Job	Cochin University of Science and Technology, India
Tokmakidis Konstantinos	Aristotle University of Thessaloniki, Greece
Triantafillou Athanasios	University of Patras, Greece
Tsakanika Eleutheria	National Technical University of Athens, Greece
Tsilaga Evagelia-Marina	University of West Attica, Greece
Tsilimantou Elisavet	Ministry of Infrastructure and Transportation, Greece
Tsoukalas Lefteris	University of Thessaly, Greece
Tzannini Evgenia	National Technical University of Athens, Greece
Van Grieken René	University of Antwerp, Belgium
Van Hees Rob	Delft University of Technology, The Netherlands
Varum Humberto	University of Porto, Portugal
Vayenas Dimitris	University of Patras, Greece
Vintzilaiou Elissavet	National Technical University of Athens, Greece
Vlachopoulos Andreas	University of Ioannina, Greece
Vogiatzis Konstantinos	University of Thessaly, Greece
Vyzoviti Sophia	University of Thessaly, Greece
Xanthaki-Karamanou Georgia	University of Peloponnese, Greece
Yannas Simos	Architectural Association School of Architecture, UK
Zachariou-Rakanta Eleni	National Technical University of Athens, Greece
Zervos Spyros	University of West Attica, Greece
Zouboulakis Loukas	National Technical University of Athens, Greece

Executive Organizing Committee

Lampropoulou Antonia	National Technical University of Athens, Greece
Sinigalia Maria	National Technical University of Athens, Greece
Psarris Dimitrios	National Technical University of Athens, Greece
Konstanti Agoritsa	National Technical University of Athens, Greece
Roumeliotis Stergios	National Technical University of Athens, Greece
Manitsa Theodora	Technical Chamber of Greece, Greece

Technical System Providers

Cosmolive Productions
BOUSSIAS Media Group

The Conference Venue was a Kind Offer of

Eugenides Foundation

Contents

Scientific Innovations in the Diagnosis and Preservation of Cultural Heritage

Scientific Architecture of the Educational Toolkit of the Project EDICULA

Antonia Moropoulou, Kyriakos Lampropoulos[✉], Ioannis Rallis,
and Anastasios Doulamis

National Technical University of Athens, Iroon Polytechniou 9, 15780 Zografou, Greece
{amoropul,klabrop}@central.ntua.gr

Abstract. A major challenge worldwide is to promote cultural heritage protection as a lever for the enhancement of the society's identity and the integration of 'culture as an enabler for sustainable development'. The EDICULA "Educational Digital Innovative Cultural heritage related Learning Alliance" is a Strategic Partnership for Higher Education in Erasmus+ that aims to provide new knowledge in the field of cultural heritage protection that breaks the boundaries of science and engineering and be integrated in education. The EDICULA address this through the tow educational toolkits for the general public and for more restricted audience such as scientists and stakeholders. An educational framework to advance scientific transdisciplinary synthesis developed based on the interdisciplinary collaboration among the sectors of applied sciences in the protection of monuments with humanities disciplines using XR technologies, to develop. The architecture of the EDICULA toolkits emphasize the instrumentalization of this transdisciplinary collaboration through education, with the various universal educational tools and the experience from the emblematic rehabilitation of the Holy Aedicule of the Holy Sepulchre acting as common base.

Keywords: EDICULA · Cultural heritage · Educational platform

1 Introduction

The protection of Cultural Heritage (CH) assets is a comprehensive, interrelated and often contradicting collection of decision making processes, activities and assessment procedures. The EDICULA (Educational Digital Innovative CUltural heritage related Learning Alliance) project [1] is an innovative approach that fuses the interdisciplinary collaboration among the sectors of applied sciences in the protection of monuments with humanities disciplines using Extended Reality (XR) technologies, to develop an educational framework to advance scientific transdisciplinary synthesis. The innovation of the EDICULA project is that it emphasizes that this transdisciplinary collaboration can be instrumentalized through education, with the various universal educational tools and the experience from the emblematic Holy Sepulchre rehabilitation acting as common base.

The EDICULA project taking as a starting point the emblematic rehabilitation of Holy Sepulchre [2–4] aims to promote cooperation between Universities, stakeholders

A. Moropoulou et al. (Eds.): TMM_CH 2021, CCIS 1574, pp. 3–16, 2022.
https://doi.org/10.1007/978-3-031-20253-7_1

and SMEs in the field of CH protection and to fuse the interdisciplinary and innovative research in the rehabilitation of the Holy Aedicule, its context and setting, to trans-cut with the history of architecture in Jerusalem. EDICULA aims to create immersive and interactive educational material by using Augmented Reality (AR) technologies. It will also reform the curricula of the three participating postgraduate programs, develop a Teacher's course for higher education teachers that promotes transdisciplinary scientific synthesis as a key element for innovative education, organize hands-on and immersive experience multiplier events and special conference sessions.

EDICULA aims to develop an open e-courses platform that addresses key issues in the rehabilitation, protection and sustainability of CH, and disseminates valuable knowhow and experience both to the wide audience as well as to CH stakeholders, scientists and professionals. The fundamental characteristic of this platform is that it will promote a holistic approach for transdisciplinary documentation, without, however, becoming too complicated. The key issues addressed relate to the enhancement of the educational aspects of engineering innovation; the emergence and establishment of transdisciplinarity as a fundamental trend in the protection of monuments; the capabilities of multi-modelling methodologies for multi-discipline management and analysis of knowledge; the capabilities of Augmented Reality (AR) and Virtual Reality (VR) to effectively diffuse information for social responsibility and awareness.

These key issues set the basic challenges for a purposeful design of this toolkit. Due to the wealth of knowledge and expertise, as well as the wide range of the thematic subjects that are relevant to the protection of Cultural Heritage, such a platform cannot aim to become just a detailed depository of knowhow and data; regardless how feasible this could be. Instead, the selection of its thematic subjects and the way they will be presented to the users of this toolkit, must be governed by the educational needs such a platform aims to address. The EDICULA educational toolkit consists of two modules:

- EDICULA-4-all educational toolkit, addressed to the wide audience (open access), including basic level of information. It supports only a limited number of scientific data, can be transferred in life-long learning and school education, demonstrating the effectiveness of transdisciplinarity in fusing science into general knowledge.
- EDICULA+ educational toolkit, which is the advanced module (registered access), addressed to scientists and experts in the field of protection of monuments with a relevant background. It provides knowledge with more scientific details and encompasses advanced information, relevant studies, scientific papers, data and metadata of the knowledge gained by the consortium in the emblematic restoration of the Holy Sepulchre. It can be transferred to professional and university courses for architects, archaeologists, conservators, students in arts and other relevant engineering disciplines, demonstrating the need for a new teaching framework that promotes cooperation and utilizes complementarity between diverse disciplines

2   Methodological Approach for the Architecture of the EDICULA Educational Toolkit

The careful design of the architecture of the educational toolkit emerges as the initial crucial step for its successful development. Important issues that drive its development include: the target groups that the EDICULA toolkit will be addressed to; the content (thematic areas) of the EDICULA toolkit; the toolkit-to-user information presentation approach and educational aspects; the semantics and ontology of the toolkit content and its management; the Artificial Intelligence (AI) module for classification of different data and metadata; and the technical requirements for the creation and operation of this educational toolkit.

The architecture of the educational toolkit will conform to the following fundamental prerequisites: (i) provide flexibility through its e-learning platform, enabling easy navigation and immediate access to all main categories and activities of the toolkit; (ii) no previous knowledge in cultural heritage or its rehabilitation is required to assess EDICULA-4-all; (iii) EDICULA+ will provide an easy sequential learning progress, divided into basic and advanced modules, enabling the end-users to experience a learning procedure. The following presents the development stages for the EDICULA educational toolkit.

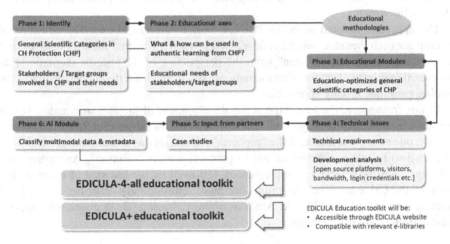

Fig. 1. Development stages for the EDICULA educational toolkit

The architecture of the two toolkits is such that platform will include lectures and virtual laboratories, videos, lecture notes, and other types of educational material. However, it has been recognized that the diversity of types, size and presentation specifications of the aforementioned educational material and media, despite its desired advantages, inevitably creates diverse technical requirements that the architecture of the educational platform must identify, evaluate, integrate and conform to. Moreover, an AI module will aid and facilitate classification of multimodal data and metadata for data storage and retrieval, in a more reliable and transferable approach, compared to the conventional subjective and expert oriented methodology.

3 Development of the Thematic Nodes of the EDICULA Toolkits

The protection, rehabilitation and the enhancement of the sustainability of Cultural Heritage assets is a comprehensive, interrelated and often contradicting collection of decision making processes, activities and assessment procedures. As clarified above, the EDICULA Toolkits, in both their forms, do not aim to function as a one-stop depository of all the wealth of use cases and the vast array of activities related to the subject. This is indeed a huge undertaking and does not actually offer a significant educational value. Instead, the toolkits aim to introduce the users in the process of understanding the complexity of the protection of Cultural Heritage and provide them with the appropriate training to address the related challenges.

Although the toolkits cannot and do not need to cover all potential use cases and CH related activities, they still need to be structured around a core collection of typical processes and activities for which characteristic use cases and educational material can be provided, as a guide for further elaboration and as a starting point for the users. This collection of thematic nodes largely defines the extent and complexity of the toolkits and the interrelation of its modules. Many thematic areas are interdisciplinary and trans-cut various subjects. The challenge, thus, is how to describe subjects that are relevant to many thematic areas, without reverting either to focused and specific analyses or to extensive interlinking.

The approach adopted in the EDICULA toolkit is a hybrid one: The educational material for each thematic subject is developed in such a way that the user realizes that the technique or process is "seen" from the perspective of the specific thematic area, however, it may be relevant for other thematic areas – through a different perspective – for which appropriate linking is provided.

In this framework, the first stage of the development of the thematic nodes was to decide upon the main pillars (groups). These groups follow the general flow of activities. Initially, one needs to understand the "problem". Based on this understanding, decisions then need to be taken, whether or not to proceed with a "solution". An appropriate "solution" must be sought and implemented, followed by the last step of ensuring the future of the CH asset. The four pillars are more appropriately described as 1st level thematic nodes (1st level TN): (A) Analysis of the CH asset; (B) Decision making; (C) Interventions; (D) Sustainability.

3.1 Analysis of the CH Asset

The analysis of the CH asset takes into account the structure itself, the surrounding environment, time and values. A historical building or a monument must be seen as the result of a continuous process of history imprinting upon its structure and of an unavoidable interaction with its natural and anthropogenic environment. Also information about them is not readily available, but instead needs to be "extracted" from them through many complementary approaches. These approaches are presented in the toolkits through a series of 2nd level thematic nodes.

Specifically, while envisioning a general timeline-type approach, the archaeological study is a typical thematic area relevant to the analysis of the CH asset. It regards archaeological excavations, archaeological surveys and conservation activities related to archaeological sites. The archaeological issues will be presented with emphasis on Technology and with use cases and educational material for conservation activities.

In a similar manner, historical documentation will focus on the technology of archiving, organization of libraries (digital libraries and scientific publications) and the latest advancement of Information Technology. Historical Documentation is an important element in the analysis of a CH asset, but the process of searching, retrieving and utilizing historical documentation is valid for other relevant scientific disciplines in general.

An important part of the analysis of the CH asset is its architectural analysis. This can be approached in three main groups: (a) Historic cities; (b) historic buildings and monuments; (c) cross-cutting digital technologies for documentation and modelling. The architectural analysis of architectural is an important thematic area, useful for other engineering disciplines too, e.g. the constructional analysis and documentation, which can be approached through the perspective of architecture. Obviously all these thematic areas are interlinked with other thematic nodes, such as Diagnosis or Structural analysis – assessment, which approach the same subject from other perspectives.

Geometric documentation a thematic node with an intense IT content, will cover subjects of passive and active methods of data acquisition, advanced processing of data and the latest advancements in the creation of geometric documentation products.

Materials are studied in the toolkit through a series of interlinked roles they play in a CH asset. Materials can function as building elements in a structure. They can also have a decorative role. But materials also interact with the environment, creating new decay products and damage to the CH asset. This interaction with the environment necessitates the study of the various categories of restoration materials, the main consolidation, strengthening, conservation and protection materials and techniques, and of course the emerging role of smart and advanced materials and techniques. The various categories of materials, understandably regard a vast number of materials and relevant information, which need not and will not be covered in its entirety. Materials science is an extensive scientific discipline that requires in-depth understanding of its interaction with other disciplines. The EDICULA educational toolkit does not envision achievement of such a full analysis, neither it is required for all target groups (especially the wide audience). Therefore, the selected materials and applications of technological advancement will constitute the principal tool in understanding the often-underestimated role that the materials play in the operation and sustainability of our built environment, including CH. The trans-cutting, interdisciplinary importance of non-destructive testing (NDT) for assessment and evaluation of materials and interventions will be presented through use cases and relevant educational material.

The five aforementioned thematic nodes effectively largely focus on the CH asset itself. However, as in any ordinary structure or infrastructure, the environment is a crucial factor that influences the operation and state of the CH asset. The various environmental loads acting upon the CH asset include the atmospheric pollution, water interaction, earthquakes, climate change and anthropogenic impact, in correlation with risk assessment and management and assessment of their impact on CH assets.

Supporting all these, an important technology-intensive thematic node regards diagnosis. This refers to a methodological study of the decay and damage. Decay refers to the identification, classification and documentation of decay patters, their mapping with NDTs, modeling of the decay and evaluation of the susceptibility of materials to decay factors. Also, it includes identification of damage patterns, its mapping by NDTs and identification and evaluation of their causes and mechanisms. Diagnosis provides the necessary information to assess the preservation state of the CH asset and to assess the environmental impact, both with a strong mapping and data-management character.

Similarly, the analysis and assessment of the structural behavior of the CH asset is crucial, obviously related to the asset itself and its interaction with the environment, and includes analytical structural and assessment methods (laboratory testing and structural assessment), structural health monitoring technologies, numerical approximation methods and an array of techniques utilized for earthquake engineering.

The CH asset, however, is not only a tangible entity, but equally important it carries values. This thematic issue, regards issues of authenticity and compatibility of past interventions. The assessment of the CH asset is concluded by addressing subjects relevant to knowledge-based digital infrastructure. This is a critical component of advanced assessment campaigns, as exemplified by the experience from use case of the rehabilitation of the Holy Aedicule, due to the need to fuse, manage and present large amounts of multi-spectral and multi-modal data. To some extent, this thematic node reflects the emerging need for efficient state-of-the-art user-interface, with emphasis on 3-D representations, virtual reality and augmented reality.

3.2 Decision Making

Decision making is a poly-parametric process that involves many stakeholders in CH. It builds upon the knowledge gained from the previous thematic nodes and can be broken up into five general categories. The first one regards all the relevant studies (architectural, structural, materials and interventions, other). These form the "input" elements, in a condensed form, for the decision making process, i.e. whether to intervene or not. Another thematic node, regards the legislation framework, to which any decisions must adhere to.

An important 2nd level TN regards the various categories of stakeholders: Ministries and national bodies, regional and local authorities, society/wide public, religion stakeholders, private entities and persons, NGOs, and the scientific and technical communities, all of which create a complex matrix of responsibilities and interest. Moreover, the socio-economic and technical framework needs to be described, that highlights how cultural heritage is perceived by Society, how it is related with Tourism and local development (especially historic cities) and how all relevant activities can be financed. Also, thematic nodes need to be included that describe the role and limitations of Science and Technology that often drive any relevant decisions. Finally, the EDICULA toolkit analyzes how CH is protected in areas of conflicts and how cooperation challenges with relevant authorities and stakeholders can be addressed.

3.3 Interventions

The third 1st level TN compiles and describes all the necessary steps for implementing any interventions required and decided upon from the two aforementioned thematic nodes. The initial stage of such a comprehensive array of task regards, obviously, the design of interventions. This 2nd level thematic node covers all relevant issues ranging from the organization of the worksite and in-situ laboratories and workshops, the logistics of materials and equipment, human resources, detailed planning and detailed pre-description of all necessary stages. These are presented through real use –cases, such as the rehabilitation of the Holy Aedicule.

The integrated governance of such projects is discussed, since these are thematic subjects not often well understood, despite their importance. Similarly, risk management and contingency planning of the actual interventions works must be taken into account, to cope with real-world uncertainties. Following the careful planning, the next stage in typical CH projects is the design, implementation, assessment and comparative evaluation of pilot-scale works. The use-case of the Holy Aedicule rehabilitation is a characteristic example, which underlines the importance of pilot works in the optimization of interventions prior to their actual implementation.

Another thematic area regards the main issues related to the implementation of interventions. Obviously, with such a large variety of CH use cases it is not feasible, nor desirable to describe in detail all potential interventions. However, these can be categorized in intervention aiming to assure structural integrity, to reveal and preserve the values, and to enhance the sustainability of the CH asset. Digital depositories are described as the latest essential tool for the documentation of works.

It is important for all target groups to realize that CH protection does not end upon implementation of any designed interventions. In fact, the assessment and evaluation of interventions, both during their implementation as well as after the finalization of work, is equally important and a crucial element in decision making. To this end, criteria for assessment and evaluation must be set, regarding the compatibility, performance, authenticity and integrity that can often shift necessary decisions to alternative interventions approaches. The joint importance of in-situ utilization of advanced NDTs and conventional testing will be underlined, as well as the concurrent validation of the response of the retrofitted structure by modeling.

In fact, as experience from a variety of use cases has shown, the actual implementation of interventions can lead to the revealing and preservation of values. New findings are revealed and documented during the implementation of works, or during parallel or post-works analysis of new data. These require optimization of interventions to ensure preservation of values, which in turn require comprehensive risk analysis for the preservation of values, as well as design, implementation and documentation of relevant mitigation & protection measures. Communication strategies must be adopted to effectively disseminate such findings to the media and to the society.

3.4 Sustainability

CH assets must be preserved for future generations, and in this context they differ from ordinary buildings and infrastructure which are designed and operated within predefined lifetimes. Therefore, the concept of sustainability is of utmost importance and entails a series of activities. Foremost are the activities that regard monitoring of the CH asset, where critical parameters are set and monitored, through permanent sensors and instrumentation or through regular scientific surveys. Similarly, monitoring of the environment can provide crucial information that can influence the state of preservation of the CH asset or its behavior to environmental loads. In addition, in certain cases, maintenance of the CH assets is performed through a strategic planning that includes preventive and regular maintenance schemes, prioritization procedures and interaction with the Society. In an analogous approach, environmental management can provide "solutions" for interventions to the CH asset's environment to minimize or control the impact. It should, however, be realized that sustainability is not an issue of the CH asset or its environment, but it is an issue on how Cultural Heritage is perceived and coexist with the Society. In this framework, dissemination and communication activities play an important role nowadays, and enhance the dialogue between Science, relevant authorities and the Society, ensuring a bilateral effective integration of cultural heritage in the socio-economic development. A typical example, which will be addressed in the EDICULA toolkit is the role of Tourism. Moreover, sustainability is indirectly and long-term enhanced through Education. By ensuring that the right professionals are taking the right decisions, and by ensuring that the general public understands the importance and the challenges involved in the protection of our CH, Education can emerge as the fusion tool for all this knowledge.

4   The Generic Core and the Thematic Nodes

The architecture of the two EDICULA toolkits is derived from the generic core, which comprises the list of the thematic components and the structured table of generic features, using the "functional, data, enabler" attribute, and the mutated relevant project features. A critical step in the definition of the architecture, thus, is to define the components' features, using certain rules. As described above the thematic components can distinguish four groups of thematic components: the natural environment, the man-made environment, the disciplines involved and the interventions required or implemented.

The generic core comprises all the thematic components and their features. Each thematic component has one or more generic features. An example of a generic component is "nondestructive testing", and a "child" generic feature "thermographic analysis". The granularity of components and features is relevant to the total number and the overall complexity of the educational toolkits. It should be clarified that a generic feature belongs to one and only one thematic component. As mentioned earlier, although certain thematic subjects (e.g. a technique) are relevant to many thematic components, it should always be "approached" from the perspective of these specific thematic components, in order to maximize its educational value and learning "footprint" to the specific target groups.

A generic feature has attributes that provide information about it and help to classify it. A very important step for the development of the architecture is the definition of "functional, data, enabler" attributes. A feature can be of one and only one of the following three types:

- A functional feature is a package of functionality relevant to the component to which it belongs. As an example, a Microsoft PowerPoint presentation of thermographic analysis is a functional feature of the thermographic analysis component.
- A data feature refers to how the component uses data. An example is the classification of different data and metadata.
- An enabler feature refers to the technical elements that enable the component. An example is the educational software that supports the preparation and packaging of a short introduction to thermographic analysis

A functional feature addresses the needs of a specific user group and is always linked to at least one enabler feature which enables it, i.e., makes it available for use to the users. Each functional feature must be described with emphasis on what the user does, what are the results, if any, and whether it is linked somehow to other functional features, forming in a sense a "chain", or a "set". Examples of functional features are lectures and virtual laboratories, videos, lecture notes.

Two types of data will be included in the toolkits: Static and dynamic data. Static data do not change as the toolkit gets used, i.e., as the user groups use the available functional features. Dynamic data, on the other hand, are generated using the toolkit, i.e., are the result of the users using one or more functional features. A data feature may be related to one or more functional features. There may be data features that are not directly related to functional features, but to the overall use of the toolkit. An example is user authentication data. Each data feature requires an enabler feature which enables it, i.e., makes it available to the toolkit environment.

Enabler features comprise what we might call the "technology" layer of the toolkit. There are two groups of enabler features. One group is derived from the functional and data features. It is the group that "enables" these features. The other group is not linked to functional and data features. An example is the enabler that manages the user sessions. This enabler is independent of functional and data features. The definition of the generic core requires that at least one project core is also defined. The project core is analyzed, and the results feedback the definition of the generic core.

5   The Effect of Users' Requirements on the Toolkit Architecture

The composition of the user groups of the EDICULA-4-all and the EDICULA+ educational toolkits is highly dependent on the user's needs and ambitions. The motivation to exploit these educational toolkits and benefit from their educational content does not rely only on issues of accessibility. Obviously the general public has different expectations and learning capacity compared to more specialized groups of users such as CH students, professionals and experts. It is readily apparent that the social, educational, scientific and knowledge background of a user are crucial parameters that need to be taken into account, and addressed by the architecture of both toolkits. The challenge is how to categorize such a diverse variety of users, without resorting to exclusion issues or without ending in users losing their interest to use the educational toolkits either as a result of too much information or as a result of too little information.

The categorization of users takeo into account that, fundamentally, the motivation to learn does not necessarily "coincides" with a user's intellectual or learning capacity. For example, we should not arbitrarily assume that a user loosely categorized as general public (e.g. a merchant, a lawyer etc.), i.e. a person not directly related to the field of CH protection, that he or she may not have the intellectual or learning capability to process, analyze and synthesize specialized information more focused on CH issues. Conversely, a specialized user (e.g. a conservator, an archaeologist) may find useful the general information provided to the so-called "general public", as he or she may want to start understanding the field of CH protection from perspectives other than his or her expertise. On the other hand, the flow of information should be somehow tailored to the user's needs and intellectual capacity, since the unrestricted "overflowt" with information may end up emerging as an educational barrier to many users regardless of their intellectual capacity.

The categorization of users, should also be flexible. The educational toolkits, through their architecture, should allow the user to "navigate" between user categories, as required, not only through accessibility regulators but also through levels of educational contents. The following users groups have been defined:

General Public: Admittedly, this term is rather difficult to define, since it refers to citizens with a wide variety of social and intellectual skills. It basically refers to all citizens that do not have specialized knowledge in the field examined, e.g. CH protec-tion. However, being such a generic term, it still refers to users with different needs and educational background. The general public needs to become aware that the so-cial and educational value of European CH can actively contribute to job creation, economic growth and social cohesion. The essential requirement for the EDICULA-4-all educational toolkit, is therefore to be effective in raising awareness of the im-portance of Europe's CH through education, including activities to support skills de-velopment, social inclusion, critical thinking and youth engagement. The general public can be defined through two sub-groups:

- active citizens with basic interest in CH protection, who require basic information, with easy-to-understand terminology and user-friendly platform-user interfaces to allow them to "navigate" through various CH protection thematic areas.
- citizens with an economic interest in CH protection who want to utilize the EDICULA-4-all educational toolkit to become more acquainted with the issues related to CH protection from the perspective of business or economic opportunities.

Students. This is a very important wide-ranging sub-group of users with challenging educational needs. It includes students from elementary school up to post-graduate students. Understandably the educational needs and intellectual capabilities depend on their educational level. However, the common issue for students of all levels is how to make CH protection, through the EDICULA-4-all educational toolkit, a useful instrument for their educational development. In fact, students will form the future experts and professionals in various fields and especially in the field of CH protection. Interdisciplinary and transdisciplinary cooperation of scientific and professional fields is a vital element and key enabler in CH protection and rehabilitation, and the vast experience from this field is diffused to the students through the educational toolkits. In addition skill development as well as a hands-on experience of all students is a prerequisite especially for those who will engage as professionals with cultural heritage related issues. The Youth today is very familiar with IT, especially AR, often much more compared to the general public. The educational toolkit exploit this "skill" focusing on media more familiar to the students, such as videos, AR or VR applications, or narrative-type diffusion of information.

Experts and Professionals in CH-Related Stakeholders: The protection of CH is a complex and wide-ranging process for Society that is entrusted to various "stakeholders". CH assets are managed by Ministries of Culture, or corresponding regional authorities.

Often, however, central responsibilities overlap with those of local authorities, such as municipalities or prefectures. A complex bureaucratic environment is unavoidably developed with often contradicting and unproductive interweaving boundaries of responsibilities. Furthermore, many stakeholders are staffed by personnel not fully trained on CH protection but rather apply ad-hoc their respective field of expertise. Stakeholder groups also include private owners and institutions which due to their limited human resources, may face acute diminishing of relevant expertise. Due to their varying level of skills, educational and scientific backgrounds, as well as the varying needs of members of this group, the toolkits are characterized by a dynamic flexibility, in the sense of providing the necessary information with the most appropriate user-optimized level of analysis.

Academic Personnel and Teachers: This group of users refers to those responsible for teaching the students and aid them utilize for their own studies the lessons obtained in the field of CH protection. This group includes elementary and high schools teachers, professional schools trainers and University-level professors. Obviously the scientific and educational background is varying but to some extent it addresses the needs of the respective level of students. The terminology and the educational content of the toolkits need to be adjusted accordingly. The educational level also influences the compilation and character of educational material that the teachers, trainers and professors need to utilize. A more pictorial and simplified type of educational material is required for elementary school teachers, not because they cannot understand the issues discussed, but because it is easier and more effective to transfer this type of information instead of asking them to analyse complex data and prepare their own educational material for distribution to their students. As the educational level is increased, the information is less generic, more focused, more detailed and requires more critical synthesis for the teacher/professor, while offering more opportunities to ensue different directions. The academic personnel have more flexibility in integrating in their courses the experience in the field of CH protection, as presented through the EDICULA educational toolkits. In fact a Teacher's course will be organized as part of the EDICULA project. The wider availability and accessibility of the EDICULA toolkits enables them to support such a transformational process for other courses.

Researchers: The final group of users includes all researchers, whether these are affiliated to Universities or academic institutions, or whether they are employed in CH-related organizations such as Museums, but are not directly involved in decision-making processes for CH assets. These users are linked with Innovation and Research, at theoretical or experimental levels. The EDICULA + toolkit, which is mainly relevant to Researchers, functions as the basis for Research in the field of CH protection, by providing a compact depository of relevant information with emphasis on IT, digitalization of techniques and data management, organization challenges of complex projects and a synthetic way of thinking. The interdisciplinarity of the field becomes evident through the educational material of the EDICULA + toolkit, bringing together expertise from a variety of relevant scientific fields. Even more important, the scientific dialogue, as expressed by the Case Studies includes in the toolkit is a legacy for all Researchers utilizing this toolkit and a prerequisite for effective and open-minded Research.

6 The Presentation Layer

The term "presentation layer" does not strictly refer to the toolkit-user-interface, in the sense of how the user sees the toolkit in front of his or her computer screen, but rather in the organization of the hierarchy of the toolkits' various components. Obviously, the general organization is driven from the selected thematic nodes, which structurally display a hierarchy in the subjects discussed. Also, as described earlier in the relevant section, these thematic nodes follow a typical "course of actions", i.e. some form of step-by-step procedures. Therefore, fundamentally, the thematic nodes already exhibit some form of hierarchy and drive a presentation approach that is incremental and evolutional. The role of the presentation layer is even more important, when the issues discussed in the thematic nodes is presented through specific projects. In these cases, the presentation layer acquires a central role, as it needs to allow the user to understand, analyze and dynamically learn from complex projects. These projects are characterized by a strong "interventions" character, although it is the role of the Educational Toolkits to highlight the processes required prior- and post- interventions that ensure an effective and sustainable solution to the issues involved.

In order to understand this, it should be reminded that a Cultural Heritage area may have many Sites. A prime example in the EDICULA is the Old City of Jerusalem. Each site of an area may have been the subject of one or more projects, as is the case with the Church of the Holy Sepulchre, in which many past and ongoing projects have been implemented. For example, the rehabilitation of the Holy Edicule is a project of the Holy Sepulchre site. In this project the general object hierarchy "Area-Site-Project" is transformed to an Instance Hierarchy "Old City of Jerusalem – Church of the Holy Sepulchre – Rehabilitation of the Holy Aedicule". In these cases, it is more effective to approach the projects through an "area – site – project" hierarchy, rather than through analyses of the various disciplines and thematic nodes, as described in detail in the preceding sections.

7 Technical Requirements

Platform Goals: The main objective of the learning platform is to provide an easy-to-use set of tools to course creators in order to enable them to design their course as they originally intended and not have to make any major alterations in order to upload it into the platform (Fig. 1). Along with this, a set of different activity types had to be available for them to perform the different activities found within their courses, such as regular course content, forums for discussion, quizzes and multiple choice and content submission for assignments and other tasks.

The courses allow different user groups. Courses can either be taken by individual learners or groups of multiple users depending on the course creators' preferences, the type of activity being taken and the learning outcomes as defined by the course. The configuration and design of the EDICULA-4-all learning platform was implemented keeping in mind that the courses being made available for this project include asynchronous and synchronous methodology. The web-based educational material hosted on the public website of the EDICULA project allows sharing the results with the general public, interested users and with the EDICULA partners and beneficiaries. The dissemination of project results and scheduled events will be highly served by web-based means and mechanisms.

Learning Analytics: Another main objective of the EDICULA-4-all e-learning platform is the recording and visualisation of different learning analytics during the duration of a course. These analytics are then to be used as metrics for both the determination of the success of a course model and also evaluation of the platform as a whole. The platform needs to be able to record these different analytics without any additional work on the course creators' part to make sure that consistency will be kept for the evaluation of the courses. Different learning analytics tools record a whole range of data from the different activities and courses found within the educational platform.

EDICULA e-Learning Requirements: The e-learning environment is a web-based environment which contains the corresponding educational material for adults' education on Internet use. With this, the participating users educate, train and assess their knowledge on ICH topics, or contribute with training material on these topics. The requirements based on the main objectives of the e-learning environment fall into the thematic nodes described in the previous section.

8   Conclusions

The EDICULA educational toolkit departs from being a simple depository of information or a collection of pre-set lectures, videos and other educational material. By adopting a cultural heritage oriented architecture it manages to address challenging requirements and to serve the needs of a wide audience. The thematic nodes selected function as the core of the educational character of the toolkits, but their cross-linking nature, the interdisciplinarity they introduce and the way they are presented (AR, VR, e-learning) evolves them into crucial flexible and adaptable educational elements for further reading, study and analysis. This work demonstrates that the field of Cultural Heritage can be a useful starting point for educational needs, providing case-studies, methodologies and technological achievements relevant to other scientific fields and the society. More important, it highlights another important aspect of the field of CH protection, namely its educational character.

Funding. This work was part of the Project EDICULA "Educational Digital Innovative CUltural heritage related Learning Alliance" which has received funding from the European Union's Erasmus+ under the Project Code: 2020-1-EL01-KA203-079108.

References

1. Project EDICULA: Educational Digital Innovative Cultural heritage related Learning Alliance. Co-funded by the Erasmus+ Programme of the EU. http://edicula.eu/. Accessed 28 July 2021 (2020-2023)

2. Moropoulou, A., et al.: Faithful rehabilitation. Civil Eng. – The Am. Soc. Civil Eng. **87**(10), 54–61, 78 (2017)
3. Moropoulou, A., et al.: The project of the rehabilitation of holy sepulchre's holy aedicule as a pilot multispectral, multidimensional, novel approach through transdisciplinarity and cooperation in the protection of monuments. In: Moropoulou, A., Korres, M., Georgopoulos, A., Spyrakos, C., Mouzakis, C. (eds.) TMM_CH 2018. CCIS, vol. 961, pp. 3–25. Springer, Cham (2019). https://doi.org/10.1007/978-3-030-12957-6_1
4. Moropoulou, A., Lampropoulos, K., Apostolopoulou, M., Tsilimantou, E.: Novel, sustainable preservation of modern and historic buildings and infrastructure. The paradigm of the Holy Aedicule's Rehabilitation. Int. J. Architectural Heritage **15**(6), 864–884 (2019). https://doi.org/10.1080/15583058.2019.1690076

The Protection of Natural and Cultural Heritage Monuments, Museums and Archives from Risks: Bridging Artificial Intelligence, Risk Assessment and Stakeholders

Elena Korka[1], Dimitrios Emmanouloudis[1], Kalliopi Kravari[1(✉)], Nikolaos Kokkinos[2], and Katerina Dimitriadi[1]

[1] Hellenic Committee of the Blue Shield, Athens, Greece
ekorka@otenet.gr, demmano@for.ihu.gr, kkravari@ihu.gr,
info@hellenicblueshield.com
[2] International Hellenic University, Thessaloniki, Greece
nck@chem.ihu.gr

Abstract. The issue of the risks of World Cultural and Natural Heritage Monuments, museums and archives and how we can protect them is becoming more and more imperative over the years. The current work, aims to present the role of the Hellenic Committee of the Blue Shield in Greece on the one hand and a novel practical methodology on the other, which consists of risk assessment techniques and edge technologies such as Artificial Intelligence and the Internet of Things. The article presents the holistic and easily adaptable new methodology, called INBO, while the involved intelligent agent technology and its contribution on how it saves monuments and human lives is discussed. This methodology will improve the way in which first responders and monument managers, even visitors, react to and handle risky or emergency situations. INBO enables the right prognosis along with smart decisions that will help prevent potential damage to the Cultural and Natural heritage without human loses. In other words, the proposed smart awareness and management solution, based on accurate information and the right knowledge, will be able to automatically make or propose the right actions and decisions. Furthermore, a high-level procedure is provided in the context of the methodology is presented.

Keywords: Artificial intelligence · Risk assessment · Heritage protection

1 Introduction

Wars and conflicts, in general, have always been a serious threat to the integrity of cultural heritage. Unfortunately, this threat in most cases leads to the destruction of a significant part of the moveable and immoveable, tangible and intangible cultural heritage: monuments, religious sites, museums, libraries, archives, etc., thus depriving humanity of its common values and irreplaceable goods [1]. Although the practice of looting, transporting and destroying cultural goods has existed since ancient times, the

© The Author(s), under exclusive license to Springer Nature Switzerland AG 2022
A. Moropoulou et al. (Eds.): TMM_CH 2021, CCIS 1574, pp. 17–28, 2022.
https://doi.org/10.1007/978-3-031-20253-7_2

phenomenon became terrifying in the twentieth century, with the two World Wars causing disastrous consequences for cultural assets, even though humanity should have been much wiser. The use of long-range weapons, air bombardment, and the ever-growing technology, which was put to the service of the armed forces, has created a serious multidimensional threat. During the First World War, entire cities were flattened, and this led to the disappearance of remarkable monuments and historical sites, while World War II gave the final blow and enriched beyond imagination the list of destroyed or lost cultural treasures. Unfortunately, the century we live in still counts many such losses in various areas of the world given the fact that cultural heritage has been targeted, looted and destroyed, in many cases without having the possibility to record and document these actions, by extremists and non-state actors making the attacks against cultural heritage a threat to modern societies [2, 3].

Ever since the beginning of the last century, however, many countries, in their effort to codify the law of war and identify war crimes against humanity decided to deal with these issues at two international conferences in the Hague in 1899 and 1907. The second and most important conference culminated all these efforts in the text of the Convention on the Protection of Cultural Property in the Event of Armed Conflict, adopted in 1954. The Convention underlines that the damages caused to the cultural assets of a people harm the cultural heritage of the whole of mankind, given that each people have its own contribution to world culture. That is why the Member States of the Convention are committed to providing protection to the various categories of cultural goods taking general but also specific measures. [4].

One of the many actions that ensued from the Hague Convention is the symbol of the Blue Shield, established as an emblem for the protection of historic sites in the event of war operations, being the cultural equivalent of the Red Cross. The aim of this label is to protect a site in case of an attack during armed conflict. The need for the dissemination and the establishment of this symbolic protection signage has led to the creation of a global network, in which organizations supporting museums, libraries, archives, monuments and sites are involved at a national level. This network is supervised by the Association of National Committees of the Blue Shield (ANCBS), established in 2008 and based in The Hague [5].

Acknowledging the importance of the role of International Blue Shield's network in regard to the protection of cultural property not only during warfare, but also in the event of Natural disasters, an effort was initiated in 2018 to establish a Hellenic Committee of the International Blue Shield, a process which was successfully completed in January 2020. The statutory objectives of the Hellenic Committee of the Blue Shield correspond to the global demand for action in order to develop and coordinate knowledge and measures, wherever possible, which prevent or mitigate damage before it can occur. The founding members of the Committee are prominent experts from various disciplines (lawyers, archaeologists, academics, architects, conservators, civil engineers, officers of armed forces and defense etc.), who are involved in raising awareness, educating and building capacities in terms of respect, protection and safeguarding of Cultural heritage and cultural goods, risk mapping and prevention, as well as disaster management [6].

In recent decades in Greece the number of disastrous natural phenomena has increased (floods, fires, earthquakes and others), causing both social and economic problems and adverse effects on cultural heritage. Therefore, the Hellenic Committee of the Blue Shield cooperates with members of local, national and regional networks of NGOs, as well as national bodies and academic institutions in order to optimally protect cultural heritage in emergencies. By bringing together all stakeholders, we can make a significant contribution to capacity-building, nationally and internationally, as well as confront disasters so that our precious cultural reserves can be transferred in the best possible way and according to international standards to the future generations. Furthermore, the work of our national committee will strengthen at the level of an NGO, Greece's role and contribution to the implementation of international conventions for the preservation of cultural heritage, especially in this particular geographical area, which is very rich in cultural assets, that have, however, already suffered or are at risk from man-made and Natural disasters [6].

Natural and man-made disasters lead to hundreds of casualties and significant catastrophic consequences, affecting world Cultural and Natural heritage sites. Many of these Monuments are at risk due to even moderate Natural or man-made hazards, given the structural vulnerability created over the course of their hundreds or even millennia of existence. To this end, novel approaches that could assist on protecting them is undoubtedly imperative. The current work designs, develops and presents INBO, a methodology that brings together artificial intelligence, risk assessment techniques and even stakeholders. More specifically, the article clarifies the added value of the approach focusing on the intelligent agent technology that acts a virtual alter ego of our world without the limitations of the human factor. The article is organized as follows, Sect. 2 presents an overview of the INBO methodology, Sect. 3 presents the valuable agent technology and the INBO system while Sect. 4 discusses a turnkey educational procedure that can help people involved in the management of a monument/archaeological site to be better trained and prepared. Finally, Sect. 5 summarizes the added value of the article with some final remarks.

2 The INBO Approach

The variety of dangers along with the vulnerability of Cultural and Natural heritage sites that have plagued for centuries or even millennia, reveals a need for novel approaches that could protect them. In this context, the INBO approach, developed by members of this team, brings forward a holistic and easily adaptable methodology that combines edge technology with risk assessment techniques. The main purpose of INBO is to prevent potential damage to the Cultural and Natural heritage sites by enabling the right prognosis leading to timely and smart decisions. Following this methodology, first responders, heritage stakeholders, as well as visitors will be able to improve the way, in which they react and handle the provided information.

Actually, INBO is a three-stage methodology that includes an INDEX and an IT Booklet, (INDEX + BOOKLET = INBO) which allows both monument monitoring and real-time emergency response. Figure 1 depicts the main stages of the methodology. The first stage aims at the monument studying. The second stage reproduces the site purposes of public awareness. The third stage monitors and manages the site using Artificial Intelligence (AI) technologies, such as the Intelligent Agents and the Internet of Things (IoT). This holistic smart awareness and management approach will be able to automatically make or propose the right actions and decisions, supporting managers and stakeholders.

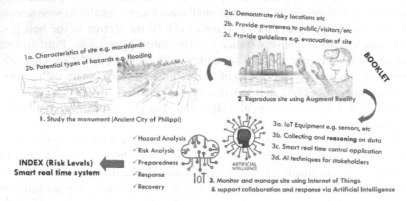

Fig. 1. The overview of the INBO methodology

2.1 INDEX

As already mentioned, the first phase of the methodology includes the development of an INDEX for each Monument. This stage will identify, record, classify and prioritize the dangers that threaten a Monument or an Archaeological site. To this end, an appropriate questionnaire will be shared to site managers and responsible stakeholders. The first page of the questionnaire is presented below indicatively (Fig. 2). This questionnaire will collect data related to natural hazards, such as hurricanes, lightning, flash floods, landslides etc., natural-human induced hazards, such as agro and forest fires, man – made hazards, such as air, water pollution, and technological risks, such as IT Protection Systems failure. Upon the completion of the questionnaires, referred to a specific heritage site, INBO methodology proceeds with the analysis. For this purpose, specific AI techniques are used such as expert systems and inference services provided by intelligent agents. Next, based on these metric findings, the group of experts in Natural and Technological Risks will prioritize the dangers that threaten the site, in terms of importance and size. Finally, a multi-criteria analysis will provide a general assessment of the current site state and a forecast about the size and frequency of each risk.

The aforementioned INDEX is proposed to be uploaded on a platform that will be supported by the Blue Shield. There, it will be real-time updated through the continuous flow of incoming answers from questionnaires, as well as the analysis outcomes of these answers. Beyond the assessment and forecast results, the platform will also provide brief guides (Behavior Codes) for visitors and site stakeholders that will contain instructions for protection and/or survival from all the important and most frequently occurring risks of Natural and Technological Disasters. For purposes of better understanding, the advice offered through these Guides will be supervisorial enhanced with the help of technologies such as augmented reality (AR) videos and animations. This way, stakeholders and visitors will be better prepared and more familiar with what they should do in case of the Monument, the Archaeological site, and the wider area or even their life is threatened.

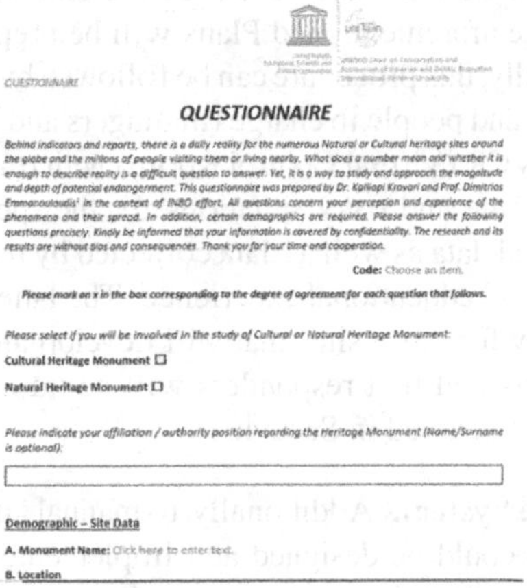

Fig. 2. Part of the INBO questionnaire

2.2 IT BOOKLET

The second phase of the methodology includes the development of a two-stage IT Booklet, where initially with the use of augmented and virtual reality the Monument will be reproduced, providing awareness to the public and visitors, as well as stakeholders. This part will demonstrate risky locations while evacuation plans will be provided. Next, the Internet of Things and Artificial Intelligence will support the design and development of a smart real-time control application that will enable monitoring and management of the Monument using appropriate equipment and software [7]. This part will include the appropriate IoT equipment, collecting and reasoning on data, smart real-time applications, and AI techniques for stakeholders.

This phase, actually, concerns only those heritage sites that are interested in receiving assistance from the team of experts through Risk Management Plans, Preparedness, and Awareness Plans, Evacuation Plans, Automation solutions, and so on. For this purpose, the team will be prepared for each case by taking into account the relevant material of the site that comes out from the first phase while new information will be collected and extracted. Additionally, the collection of various case studies will allow, through a selection of typical cases and with the consent of the stakeholders, the development of a general-purpose manual guide (Booklet). This guide will provide knowledge, information, and potential solutions to countries and sites that could not possibly afford a tailor-made study upon suggestions. Of course, this Booklet will be uploaded to the aforementioned platform while a help desk will be available for further assistance.

In other words, this phase includes both informative and practical steps. Making decisions and proposing protection along with response systems for each specific site is the kernel of this phase. To this end, at the start of this phase, additionally to the INDEX material, the team sends to those in charge of the protection and operation of the heritage site, specific instructions for the collection of material such as satellite images, photos, drawings, 3D illustrations, and so on, of the site. Based on the INDEX and the receiving material, the aforementioned Plans will be prepared and sent back to the people in charge. Optionally, this procedure can be followed by an educational part. More specifically, stakeholders and people in charge (managers and security gards) can follow a training seminar in the VCR (Virtual Control Room) with (tailor - made) scenarios that will focus on most important and risky situations for the specific Monument. For this purpose, both pre-collected data as well as data collected by the site itself will be used in order to provide a high-level educational experience. The latter is a new service that can be provided by VCR only for those sites that will develop an IoT real-time ecosystem in-situ, hence stakeholders and first responders will be trained at their own site case; more about these will be discussed in Sect. 4.

INBO Smart Real-Time System. Additionally, to manual guides and training services, a smart real-time system could be designed and implemented in-situ using intelligent technologies and IoT sensors. This system is actually a custom-made implementation of the aforementioned IT Booklet. Whether or not the people in charge will decide to implement the team's recommendations depends, among others, on economic, social, and topological factors. Figure 3 presents the main technologies that are involved in the proposed system. Of course, some of them could not be used in specific cases, i.e. perhaps there is no need for robotics and so on. What exactly will be used is the result of IT Booklet study. Yet, all system cases will have five (5) modules, namely Hazard Analysis, Risk Analysis, Preparedness, Response and Recovery. It is out of the scope of this article to analyze each of these modules and technologies; hence this article discusses further mainly on the preparedness and response modules.

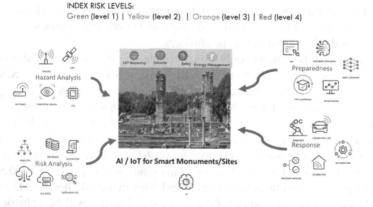

INDEX RISK LEVELS:
Green (level 1) | Yellow (level 2) | Orange (level 3) | Red (level 4)

Fig. 3. INBO Smart real-time system main technologies

For purposes of better understanding, mention the following example. An INBO smart real-time system is up and running for a site. One night the Risk Analysis module upgrades Risk to level 3 (Orange), which means that there is a potential threat. Hence, this module informs the next one, the Preparedness module, which on its turn monitors the situation analysing incoming data and proposes real-time possible response scenarios. For instance, it demands vehicle charging at night in order to be ready in case that the situation worsens while automated notification is sent to first responders, e.g. fire fighters, and stakeholders, e.g. civil protection, providing recommended action plans. This will be done by sending automating request to vehicles and charging station/building. Suppose that later that night the Risk level is upgraded to 4 (Red – Alarm). As a result, the Response module supports the decision making, proceeds with automated actions, supports stakeholders, e.g. fire station, by giving instructions and guidelines on how they should act and where they should operate. Despite the specific IoT sensors or machine learning technique, the question that arise here is how these smart communication and decision making is done. The answer is that INBO uses a core component, the agent technology which enables automation, intelligence and trustworthiness based on reasoning.

3   Intelligent Agents and INBO System

The INBO system, as discussed, is a novel approach that uses symbolic artificial intelligence, in order to provide real-time risk assessment, early warning and decision-making methods that will be fed with data from the aforementioned modules and established IoT sensors [9, 10]. The connecting link of the system is the intelligent agents which create a human-like artificial intelligence environment without the need for supervision, which will represent every aspect of the site. Intelligent Agents (IAs) are a well-studied technology, using special software actually, that offers plenty of properties (Table 1), especially autonomy, reactivity, proactivity and communication ability. The notion of autonomy means that an agent exercises exclusive control over its own actions and state. Reactivity means sensing or perceiving change in their environment and responding while all agents have the ability to communicate with other entities, such as human users, other agents, or objects.

Table 1. Intelligent agents' properties

Autonomy	Migration
Adaptability	Learning
Social ability (Collaboration/ Coordination/Interaction)	Reactivity
Persistence (execution)	Proactivity
Communication ability	Mobility

Furthermore, agents have the ability to plan and set goals, to maintain beliefs, to reason about their actions and others, including humans, and learn from past experience and machine learning techniques. In INBO, each agent has its own roles and responsibilities, yet all agents acting on the environment form a dynamic and meaningful community. Hence, although designing and building agents is not trivial, information systems based on intelligent agent technology are inevitable when strategic advantage, in cases such as heritage protection, is needed.

What is even more important for bridging artificial intelligence, risk assessment, and the various stakeholders is the ability of agents to think and, therefore, act like humans. Think of a multi-agent system as a virtual social community, which is the reflection of a real human community, where all entities (human or virtual), services and devices are assigned with an extendable list of characteristics C and preferences P based on the risk assessment studies. Yet, this is not enough, each agent is equipped with a specific logic. For our case, this is defeasible logic (DL) that introduced by Nute [11]. DL is a simple and efficient rule based nonmonotonic formalism that deals with incomplete and conflicting information. More specifically, DL has the notion of rules that can be defeated; hence it derives plausible conclusions from partial and sometimes conflicting information. These conclusions, despite being supported by the currently available information, could nonetheless be rejected in the light of new, or more refined, information. This property is of great importance in cases such as those studied by INBO methodology where emergencies could happen while a great number of agents have to interact (Fig. 4).

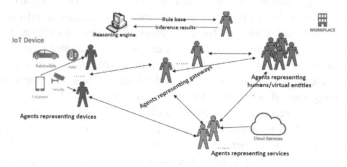

Fig. 4. INBO system entities

DL in contrast with traditional deductive logic, allows the addition of further propositions to make an existing belief false, making it non-monotonic, pretty much like the way human brain acts [11]. Hence DL, being a non-monotonic logic, is capable of modeling the way intelligent agents, like humans, draw reasonable conclusions from inconclusive information, leading to more realistic conclusions and assessments similar to human reasoning. DL can be and it is adapted in a variety of applications such as decision making and negotiation cases. For instance, DL was successfully applied for knowledge representation and reasoning about which task to perform next [8]. It can be used even in order to provide a formalism for specifying authorization policies of a dynamic system.

Figure 5 depicts a case of emergency in a museum. Suppose that suddenly a fire breaks out in a closed hall. The first security guard is outside far away checking an incoming vehicle, the other is in the security room. As soon as, the latter releases that a fire emergency occurs, moves towards that hall. Unfortunately, soon the fire extends to the adjacent hall where there are visitors and significant historical findings. The security guard is panicked, he forgot to call the fire department, and the situation is now out of control while the second lifeguard is still outside without a clue about what happens inside. Meanwhile, the fire protection and alarm system are off because the maintainer forgot to turn it on after last week's repair. The situation seems struggling, and a tragedy is a soon-to-be reality.

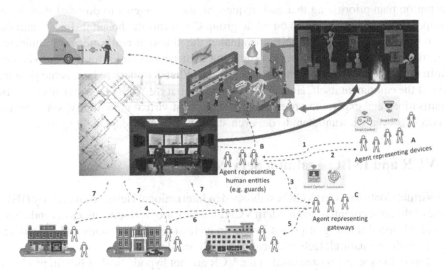

Fig. 5. Transaction emergency example

Now, let's take a look at what INBO can do (lower point of Fig. 5). As already mentioned, agents are special intelligent software that can communicate and act upon goals. Hence, here, there are plenty of agents that control a variety of IoT sensors and devices such as cameras or automatic door mechanisms. Additionally, there are agents that are representing all potential human museum roles, e.g. guards, managers and etc. Each of these agents has a knowledge base that transforms it to a role expert, something like a virtual alter ego that knows how to react, remaining calm and avoiding mistakes. Furthermore, there are more agents that represent gateways, these agents allow INBO agents to communicate with external systems even if they are not so smart. In this scenario, we suppose that the fire station, the police and the hospital of the area have also some agents. Yet, it is not necessary even a mobile phone would be enough for INBO agents to send an alarm message to these stakeholders.

In this context, let's look at the scenario from the beginning. As soon as, the "device" agents (group A) detect the first fire, inform the appropriate "human" agents (group B), e.g. the virtual guard in charge (line 1). On its turn, that expert agent reasons upon the data and extracts the conclusion that the hall must be sealed and the fire station should be informed. Hence, sends a message request to the appropriate agents of the group A to close the door, activate the fire extinguishing system and play a voice message to visitors at the adjacent halls to move calmly outside the building (line 2) while another message is sent to the appropriate gateway (group C) asking it to inform the fire station (line 3), which is done immediately (line 4). Meanwhile, human security guards are informed with alerts to their smart wearables, or whatever equipment they have, with specific instructions for action (red lines). Unfortunately, even if the door was closed and the system was activated, the fire extended. Now, new data are sent from group A to group B agents. The latter evaluate the situation; fire fighters are on their way getting the appropriate instructions (line 7) while guards have specific plans. Yet, the new hall that is on fire has a number of remaining visitors. Hence, they extract an updated evacuation plan prioritizing that hall, requesting the rest agents to do what they have. Group A activate alarms and so on while group C informs the hospital (line 5) and the police (line 6). All-in-all, the INBO evaluated the situation real-time, communicated with the appropriate stakeholders coordinating their actions and informed the visitors, eliminating the human factor without time waste. What is important here is the policies and not the equipment itself. Hence, it is important to have synergies with stakeholders, organisations and experts in order to prepare the best virtual community, since agents can do whatever, we want them to do, even state laws can be adapted by agents.

4   VCR and INBO Training Service

The Virtual Control Room (VCR) established in International Hellenic University (IHU) is one of the most complete and modern VCR all over Europe. It specializes in fundamental and advanced training of professionals on control room operations and emergency responses during natural, technological or natech accidents.

Most of the scenarios examined in the VCR are not hypothetical or fiction products, but rather the result of long-term interviews with field operators and control room operators in order to reproduce accurately, efficiently and effectively dangerous incidents. This is particularly beneficial to the trainees for being well acquainted with what-if fact-scenarios of our developed comprehensive database, and coping with difficult circumstances, often more difficult than they actually were. To that end, trainees have the opportunity to test and understand their limits in a highly secure environment; on the other hand, the organization and the stakeholders to be informed about the suitability and readiness of their staff.

The VCR of IHU comprises a pair of rooms that is set up as a Trainer/Trainee system. The Trainee Room is an emulated modern control room environment that allows both training and competency assessment of procedures and emergency response situations, with audio-visual recording and printed monitoring of the operators' performance. The Trainee Room of the VCR is equipped with real interfaces and prerecorded CCTV videos from real Monuments, museums and archaeological sites (Fig. 6). In addition to the CCTV invigilation, the control room operators (trainees) can communicate through two-way radios with other trainees in the role of security officers on the archaeological field and through the VCR telephone center with the crisis management dispatch center. Moreover, the trainees learn how to properly use the fire protection system and to manage the alarm system of the site in a virtual reality environment. The VCR can be also interconnected with INBO system in order to handle and reproduce data in real time from

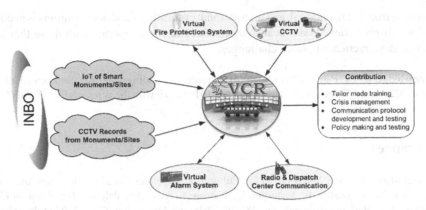

Fig. 6. The contribution of virtual control room connected with INBO system

the actual Monument or Archaeological site. Thus, stakeholders and first responders will have the opportunity to experience a high-level educational procedure and be trained with real data from their own sites online. The latter service can be provided only for "smart" Monuments and Archaeological sites equipped with INBO system. The VCR Trainee Room consists, among others, of console-workstations, alarm panels, CCTV camera system, VOIP telephone system etc.

All the control room operators' (trainees) responses are fully monitored from a separate room where the instructors control the training process and assess competence. The Trainer Room views the Trainee Room through a one-way window. The trainers may use the process simulation system to inject incidents or to emulate operating sequences and eventually to assess trainees' performance.

The VCR embedded with INBO comprises a state-of-the-art environment for tailor-made training on the field of world Cultural and Natural heritage Monuments protection. The specific virtual environment can significantly improve first responders' preparedness in case of crisis during a Natural or man-made disaster, develop and test effective communication protocols between operators and stakeholders, and even contribute in new policy making and testing dedicated in Monument/site protection.

5 Conclusions

This article presented the work of the Hellenic Committee of the Blue Shield and how it can promote cooperation of all stakeholders to optimally protect cultural heritage in emergencies. It also discussed upon INBO, a two-phase methodology that consists of an INDEX and an IT Booklet. INBO realizes an intelligent-based approach where both technical and practical guidelines and tools support the protection of Monuments and human lives. It limits the common disadvantages of the existing distributed human-based approaches, by considering the agents as a social network acting in the environment on behalf of humans. Yet, although this broad methodology provides valuable edge technologies, it needs the synergy of organization and stakeholders in order to provide accurate policies, prioritizing the needs of all involved stakeholders. In this endeavor, assistance from local, national, and international committees and organizations is needed, since we firmly believe that it is absolutely necessary to cooperate with those that face the everyday practical or policy challenges.

Acknowledgements. Part of this research has received funding from the European Union´s UCPM-2020-KN-AG under grant agreement No 101017819 with the acronym RESISTANT.

References

1. Viejo-Rose, D., Stig Sørenson, M.L.: Cultural heritage and armed conflict: new questions for an old relationship. In: Waterton, E., Watson, S. (eds.) The Palgrave Handbook of Contemporary Heritage Research, pp. 281–96. Palgrave Macmillon. CrossRefGoogle Scholar, Basingstoke, UK (2015)
2. Cunliffe, E., Muhesen, N., Lostal, M.: The destruction of cultural property in the syrian conflict: legal implications and obligations. I. J. Cu. Property **23**(1), 1–31 (2016)
3. Carcano, A.: The criminalization and prosecution of attacks against cultural property. In: Pocar, F., Pedrazzi, M., Frulli, M. (eds.) War Crimes and the Conduct of Hostilities: Challenges to Adjudication and Investigation, pp. 78–97. Edward Elgar. Google Scholar, Cheltenham, UK (2013)
4. UNESCO: Convention for the Protection of Cultural Property in the Event of Armed Conflict with Regulations for the Execution of the Convention (1954)
5. International Committee of the Blue Shield: The Seoul Declaration on the Protection of Cultural Heritage in Emergency Situations (2011)
6. Hellenic Committee of the Blue Shield: Statutes (2019). Available in Greek at https://hellen icblueshield.com/en/statutes/. Last accessed 04 July 2021
7. Astorga González, E.M., Municio, E., Noriega Alemán, M., Marquez-Barja, J.M.: Cultural heritage and internet of things. In: 6th EAI In. Conf. on Smart Objects and Technologies for Social Good, pp. 248–251. Association for Computing Machinery (2020)
8. Kravari, K., Bassiliades, N.: StoRM: a social agent-based trust model for the internet of things adopting microservice architecture. SIMPAT Journal **94**, 286–302 (2019)
9. Khan, I., Melro, A., Oliveira, L., Amaro, A.C.: Internet of things prototyping for cultural heritage dissemination **3**, 20–35 (2020). https://doi.org/10.34624/jdmi.v3i7.16212
10. Whitmore, A., Agarwal, A., Xu, L.D.: The internet of things—a survey of topics and trends. Inf. S. Front. **17**(2), 261–274 (2014). https://doi.org/10.1007/s10796-014-9489-2
11. Nute, D.: Defeasible Logic. Springer-Verlag: Web Knowledge Management and Decision Support. In: 14th Int. Conf. on Applications of Prolog, pp. 151–169 (2003)

Developing an H-BIM-Ready Model by Fusing Data from Different Sensors

Dimitrios-Ioannis Psaltakis[1], Maria Fostini[3], Stavros Antonopoulos[3],
Athena-Panag iota Mariettaki[2], and Antonios Antonopoulos[3(✉)]

[1] LANDMARK Athens, Attica, Greece
Support@landmark.com.gr
[2] Dipl.-Architect, Marousi, Greece
athenamariettaki@gmail.com
[3] ALL3D, Athens, Greece
info@landmark.com.gr, info@all3d.gr, info@metrisiltd.gr

Abstract. Cultural heritage objects are vulnerable to natural and man-made disasters. Thus it is necessary to have their complete geometric documentation. It is also necessary to organize all the tangible and intangible information, which concerns each object.

This work will explore the possibility of digitally documenting a building by fusing data from different sensors. Based on the digital documentation, a 3D model will be developed, which will be the basis for the further implementation of H BIM.

Keywords: BIM · Digital documentation · Terrestrial laser scanning · Mobile laser scanning · Photogrammetry

1 BIM and H-BIM

1.1 BIM in the New-Build Construction Sector

British standard PAS 1192–2:2013 defines Building Information Modeling (BIM) as "the process of designing, constructing or operating a building or infrastructure asset using electronic object oriented information. Regardless of the formal definition, most experts agree that BIM describes a process, rather than a specific software or even a digital object (model). BIM refers to a framework for ""sharing structured information"" between project stakeholders. In technical terms, BIM can be described as object-based parametric modeling, a digital technology with origins in mechanical systems design. The modeling process involves the assembly of 'intelligent' parametric objects into a visual representation of a building or facility. The use of parametric components, which consist of geometric definitions and associated data and rules", are central to BIM philosophy. Various types of information, including materials, properties, cost, structural and environmental performance, are integrated in a structured way within the building model, which constitutes a digital information system. It is therefore evident

A. Moropoulou et al. (Eds.): TMM_CH 2021, CCIS 1574, pp. 29–39, 2022.
https://doi.org/10.1007/978-3-031-20253-7_3

that BIM differs from CAD and 3D modeling software, which are mostly limited to the digital representation of geometric information. A BIM model, empowered by the information attached to building components, operates like a virtual diagram of how the actual building is expected to perform.

1.2 BIM for Heritage - HBIM

BIM. is applied worldwide in the new-build construction sector for a number of years while BIM for Heritage (HBIM) is a relatively new topic in academic research. HBIM as a shared system of building information, which includes both geometric and non geometric information. Building components (walls, doors, windows, furnishings) are represented geometrically with the required level of detail both in 2D and 3D inter-connected views. Non-geometric information is also represented in the model: materials, color, etc. This is particularly important in the field of cultural heritage, where non geometric information can include both tangible and intangible values. Each HBIM platform has a set of different types of information (attributes) pre-programmed in the software, but new properties can easily be added in accordance with specific project needs. All this information is structured and object-oriented, namely information is always linked to the building element it logically refers to.

At present information depending on archaeological sites and historic buildings is represented as a collection of drawings, reports, documents, various datasets and files of 2D or 3D CAD Software, provided by different scientists, each working with his own Datum, standards and tools. This information is dispersed in different places, da databases and archives. Parts of the information for a single object after some years are lost or useless.

HBIM is a type of historic asset information model that:

- Represents the appearance of existing historic fabric using high-quality digital survey point clouds.
- Offers a framework for collaborative working multi-disciplinary teams.
- Incorporates all qualitative and quantitative information of a build, including physical and functional characteristics.
- Intergrades intangible characteristics of the build.

2 Digital Documentation

""*Digital documentation*"." is the digital surveying of an object as it is found (as build). There are a lot of digital documentation applications ranging from the ""simple visualization"" to the 3D models development that are then used in planning, repair and reconstruction projects etc.

During the digital survey procedure there are a lot of points measured on every single surface of an object that describe the topology of every surface as a dense total of points with known XYZ coordinates. This sum of points is also known as «Point cloud». These points that «Point cloud» is composed from, also have in many cases one sort of information regarding the color of the point (RGB Value), a fact also very helpful during the visualization procedure, since this allows the 3D models true color creation.

The Point cloud Is the information carrier of all the available information for an object, and it can be used for a great variety of different purposes, such as the detailed production of 2D drawings (views, floor plans, sections, etc.), the creation of 3D models, the visualization, Building Information Modeling (BIM) etc. Digital documentation can be applied to various objects, ranging from tiny ones (millimeter), to huge areas of interest. The scale of the object, the level of Detail-LOD and the level of Accuracy (LOA), are the main elements to be considered when choosing the appropriate method.

Chart in Fig. 1 shows the methods used for 3D digital survey with respect to the size of the object and the LOD (detail level).

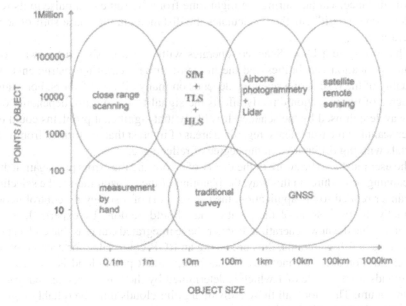

Fig. 1. 3D survey methods with respect to the size of the object and the LOD (detail level)

2.1 Structure from Motion Photogrammetry (SfM)

Until recently, Photogrammetry was used mostly for large scale objects and it was not suitable for small ones; overall costs were very high due to the need for airplanes or helicopters, expensive photographic instruments and expensive technical support (including data analysis and software).

The last few years, a number of technological and market developments have changed photogrammetry significantly. UAVs allow accurate photography at a very low cost. Digital cameras have evolved to provide excellent accuracy at very low cost. Finally, the development of SfM (Structure from Motion) and associated logistical support (software and analytical methods) makes it possible to develop accurate 3-D representations of objects, which is a point cloud, similar to the one produced by Laser Scanning.

The scale and Datum of point cloud is ensured through a GCP network (Ground Control Points), which should be measured with an accuracy at least at par with the expected accuracy of the photogrammetric capture.

2.2 Terrestrial Laser Scanning (TLS)

Laser scanner is an instrument that sends a laser light beam to the surface of an object and receives reflection of this beam, calculating the distance from the object. A mirror on the scanner is rotating and captures, along vertical lines, whatever is on an almost spherical surface around it. Two calculation methods are used in order to measure the distance between the instrument and the object. The ""Time of Flight"" method calculates the distance, via measuring the flight time from the route of a pulse to its return, and the ""Phase shift"" method, calculates the distance via the phase shift of sending and returning.

Whatever system Laser Scanners operates with, the user should be aware of the specific application capabilities and the limits of these measuring instruments. Thus, the quality of the results of a scanning depends on many different factors. For example, the degree of the reflection directly affects the signal-to-noise ratio, depending on the laser wavelength used by the scanner. It is likely that significant problems could occur in laser scanning measurements, regarding areas of interest that are formed from various materials with big differences in the degree of reflectance.

The user must also be aware of the theory of errors and the errors propagation during the Scanning procedure. In this way, the planning of the measurements, the selection of the scanner related to the application, the use (or not) of a surveying control network, and finally the processing of the point cloud, should be done by experts. It is worth mentioning that the new generation Scanners have integrated cameras that collect photos and generate a full panorama, thus producing an RGB color value for each point of the point cloud. For each Scanner position an independent point cloud is created. These point clouds have a scale of 1 which is determined by the Laser Scanner, but each has its own Datum. Therefore, all these individual point clouds must be reliably registered together to obtain the desired Datum.

The desired point cloud Datum is achieved through targets measured by classical surveying methods. These points are recognized by the Scanner software and their coordinates are used by the editing software to place point clouds on the Datum.

2.3 Mobile Laser Scanning (MLS)

The mobile scanners (LiDAR) that are placed on a mobile base (such as a car, an airplane, a trolley) operate in a different way. Every single moment, the position of the mobile scanner is usually calculated with the use of GPS and other inertial systems, and subsequently, the coordinates of the points of the area of interest are being calculated. Apparently the precision of the final coordinates cannot be as high as the precision that the terrestrial laser scanners could reach. So these instruments are not particularly interesting for digital documentation.

One subcategory of these scanners, which is particularly interesting for digital documentation work, is the SLAM mobile laser scanner. This scanner is light-weight and can be held by the user, while he is walking through the area of interest. The technology that is used is Simultaneous Localization and Mapping (SLAM). The SLAM algorithms utilize information from sensors to compute a best estimate of the device's location and a map of the environment around it. More specifically the SLAM technology works as below:

1. The SLAM algorithm utilizes data from a Lidar sensor and an industry grade inertial measurement unit (IMU).
2. The IMU is used to estimate an initial position and create a point cloud from which 'Surfels' are extracted to represent the unique shapes within the point cloud. The trajectory is then calculated for the next sweep of data using the IMU and 'Surfels' extracted again in the same way.
3. The two sets of Surfels are then used to match the point clouds together and subsequently correct and smooth the trajectory estimation. Following this iterative process, the final point cloud is recreated based on the new smoothed best estimate trajectory. In order to further optimize the trajectory and limit any IMU drift, a closed loop is performed such that the start and finish environments are accurately matched together.

The whole procedure is fully automatic and the user cannot control the quality of the end-results, but by following some guidelines, the best possible results can be achieved.

This category of scanner is particularly interesting for H-BIM applications, as it can be applied inside buildings, completely autonomously without the need for external support (e.g. GPS) to determine the location of the scanner.

3 Fusing Data Collected from Various Digital Documentation Methods

The results of all three methods of digital documentation are point clouds, which describe parts of the same object and usually with many common areas. Roofs and parts of walls are usually captured with SfM photogrammetry, exterior walls and interior of the building with TLS and hard-to-reach areas with MLS. So these individual point clouds should be registered, i.e. to have a common Datum.

When trying to fuse point clouds produced by different methods, it should be clear that the results will not be homogeneous in terms of accuracy. Thus, while TLS and SfM can, if used properly, give accurate measurements well below cm, the MLS measurement method can at best give accuracy greater than cm.

3.1 Cloud to Cloud Registration (ICP – Iterative Closest Point)

The most common method for registering point clouds is the ICP which is usually referred to as Cloud to Cloud registration. In this method a point cloud is pre-aligned on a "fixed" point cloud manually, via location sensors or with use of pre-alignment algorithms. Then the shortest distance between one point to another is calculated and the registration parameters are calculated. This procedure is iteratively repeated until the final solution is computed.

A prerequisite for this method is that there must be overlapping regions in the point clouds and preferably scattered throughout their extent. Also important in the application of this method is the choice of the "fixed" point cloud, which must be the one with the greatest accuracy.

3.2 Point to Point Registration (Artificial Targets)

Another common method for registering point clouds is the use of artificial targets. Spherical or planar checkerboard targets are placed at various positions indoors and outdoors. The centers of the targets are determined and the point to point correspondences are established.

The location and number (at least 3) of the targets in each point cloud are very important. Targets should be evenly distributed in the overlapping region and not in a straight line. At least 3 targets, preferably more, should be in each point cloud.

If the targets are used for transforming into a desired Datum, then they should be measured with high accuracy, using traditional surveying methods, i.e. Total station, to ensure that their accuracy is proportional to that of TLS. Thus, the application of forced centering and the correction with the Least Squares Adjustment of the results are required, in order to ensure the quality of the target network. Capture methods using RTK GNSS are obviously excluded.

4 Digital Documentation and H-BIM.

Completing the process of digital documentation, we have available - a faithful digital copy of the object, which is a point cloud. This is especially important for cultural heritage sites, but it is not enough, since the digital copy-Point cloud does not allow engineers of different specialties to process it with their usual digital tools, i.e. the various software packages. It should be noted here that the amount of information that results from digital documentation is too large and difficult to manage. So it seems that it will be too late to develop technical tools-Software, which will allow the immediate, reliable technical processing of point clouds. Thus, in order to be able to edit the object with the usual tools of software-software packages, it is necessary to transform point cloud into a three-dimensional model, with the necessary simplifications and generalizations, which will be H-BIM ready, that is and editable by the relevant Software packages (Revit, Archicad, etc.).

5 Applications

The fusing of various methods with the application of the Target Network was applied to the digital documentation of a single-storey building of the interwar period. The methods used were:

- *SfM photogrammetry,* for the surrounding area, the roof and the exterior of the building. The photo was taken with two Drone to DJI MAVIC PRO 2 with Hasselblad 20 MP camera and the DJI 1000S with SONY NEX5N 16 MP camera. The photo was taken at Nadir with intersecting courses with the drone MAVIC PRO 2 and oblique with the DJI 1000S around the building.
- *TLS,* using Z?+?F Imager 5016, around the building and inside, where it was possible.
- *MLS,* using the GeoSLAM ZEB-REVO, inside the building, with full coverage of all spaces.

For the fusing of point clouds produced by the above methods, a network was established, the points of which were implemented by forced centering on the outside and inside of the building. The targets were captured from the points of this network.

The individual point clouds were compared in their common areas, before their registration.

Fig. 2. Fusing of SfM and TLS point clouds

In Fig. 2 shows part of the point cloud, resulting from the fusing of point clouds by SfM and TLS.

The calculation of the differences of the two point clouds, gave the histogram of Fig. 3, where it seems that in the vast majority the points of the two point clouds from TLS and SfM have differences less than a centimeter.

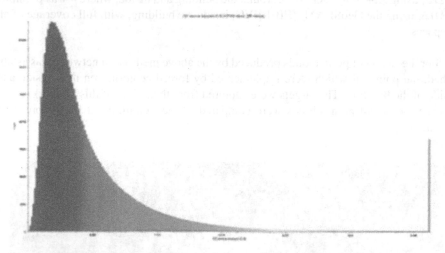

Fig. 3. Coordinate differences between SfM and TLS point clouds

In Fig. 4 shows part of the point cloud, resulting from the fusing of point clouds by MLS and TLS.

The calculation of the differences of the two point clouds, gave the histogram of Fig. 5, where it seems that in the vast majority the points of the two point clouds from TLS and SfM have differences of less than 2 cm.

After completing Fusing and checking the results, the H-BIM ready Model was created in Revit environment, which was delivered to the study team for further processing as shown in Fig. 6.

Fig. 4. Coordinate differences between HLS and TLS point clouds.

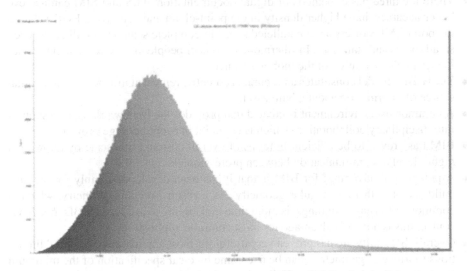

Fig. 5. Coordinate differences between HLS and TLS point clouds

Fig. 6. Section of the 3D model in Revit environment

6 Conclusions

- There are three basic methods of digital documentation. TLS and SfM can achieve better accuracy, have higher density in the point-cloud and can give a RGB value to the points. MLS offers an unparalleled speed in complete scanning of all areas, even small rooms and staircases. Furthermore, objects or people in the environment are not hindering the operation of the mobile scanner.
- The H-BIM model constitutes an accurate geometric representation as well as a digital source of information about a built asset.
- A common data environment is created that provides the framework used to support interdisciplinary collaboration, which is essential in every heritage project.
- BIM has proven to be efficient in terms of overall cost and timescale by allowing a higher level of communication between professionals.
- A potential disadvantage for BIM is that it has been developed mainly for the new build sector with more regular geometry. As a result irregular geometry, which is common in Heritage buildings, is more time-consuming to produce the 3D model. Of course, this is not a disadvantage for most common applications.
- Overall, BIM software has proven very useful for most applications. Potential limitations to irregular geometries can be overcome by clear specification of the minimum level of detail and accuracy, sufficient for each application.

References

1. Buhrow, T.: Genauigkeitsuntersuchungen von Laserscanner Messungen Am Beispiel des I SiTE 3D Laser Imaging Systems, Diplomarbeit, unverntlicht, Berlin (2002)
2. Historic England: 3D Laser Scanning for Heritage, 2nd edition (2011)
3. Kontogianni, G., Georgopoulos, A.: Exploiting Textured 3D Models for Developing Serious Games. ISPRS XL-5/W7 **57**, pp. 249–255 (2015)
4. Antonopoulou, S.: BIM for heritage: parametric modeling for contemporary conservation practice. MSc Diss. (unpubl.). University of Edinburgh (2015)
5. Raymond, C.: Real-world comparisons between target-based and targetless Point-cloud registration in FARO Scene, Trimble Real Works and Autodesk Recap, unpubl. Dissertation. University of Southern Queensland (2015)
6. Doulamis, A., et al.: 5D modeling: an efficient approach for creating spatiotemporal predictive 3D maps of large-scale cultural resources. ISPRS Ann. Photogramm. Remote Sens. Spatial Inf. Sci (2015)
7. Historic England: Traversing The past: the total station theodolite. In: Archaeological Landscape Survey, 2nd edn. Historic England, Swindon (2016)
8. Ossello, A., Rinaudo, F.: Cultural heritage management tools: the role of GIS and BIM. In: Stylianidis, E., Remondino, F. (eds.) 3D Recording Documentation and Management in Cultural Heritage. Whittle Publishing, Dunbeath (2016)
9. Remondino, F., Nocerino, E., Toschi, I., Menna, F.: A critical review of automated photogrammetric processing of large datasets. ISPRS XLII-2/W5 **25**, 591–599 (2017)
10. Historic England: Photogrammetric Applications for Cultural Heritage (2017)
11. Psaltakis, D., Kalentzi, K., Marietta, A., Antonopoulos, A.: 3D survey of a neoclassical building using a handheld laser scanner as basis for the development of a BIM-ready model. In: 1st International Conference TMM-CH, Athens (2018)

Technical Museum Nikola Tesla in Zagreb - Survey and Documentation for the Enhancement of Structural Performance After Recent Earthquakes, Maintenance and AR and VR Applications

Vlatka Rajčić[1]([✉]) [ID], Marco Medici[2] [ID], and Federico Ferrari[3] [ID]

[1] Department of Structures, University of Zagreb, Zagreb, Croatia
vrajcic@grad.hr
[2] Department of Architecture, University of Bologna, Viale del Risorgimento 2, Bologna, Italy
[3] Department of Architecture, University of Ferrara, Via Della Ghiara 36, 44121 Ferrara, Italy

Abstract. The paper presents the survey, documentation, and enhancement experience of the Tesla Museum in Zagreb. A hybrid methodology, now consolidated, was used for the survey of the architectural complex. which uses a laser scanner integrated with photogrammetry techniques, both aerial and terrestrial for the detail of artifacts. The collected data served as a basis for the creation of BIM-based models architectural and structural, then enriched by the technologies offered by the platform INCEPTION to aggregate the additional documentation collected towards the creation of models H-BIM. The latter then allowed their exploitation, through appropriate analysis for seismic reinforcement of the structure, for the maintenance of the building but also through optimizations, in immersive environments of virtual and augmented reality, for the enjoyment of the value of the architectural work and the artifacts contained herein.

Keywords: Survey · Documentation · H_BIM · Seismic retrofitting · Maintenance · VR · AR

1 Framework and Scope of Investigation

The survey, documentation and enhancement of the spaces and the layout of the technical museum Nikola Tesla in Zagreb (TMNT) is part of the case studies of the INCEPTION project [1], with the aim of enhancing and developing communication tools to be used at inside the museum, to strengthen the understanding of the museum itinerary and the role of the museum in the economic, urban, and historical-political development in Croatia. Since two earthquakes happened in Zagreb 2020 with a mag- nitude of 5.5 on the Richter scale occurred in Zagreb, on Sunday, March 22, 2020, and another one with a magnitude of 6,3 on the Richter scale occurred 40 km from Zagreb on 29th December 2020., survey was used primarily for seismic retrofitting and mainte- nance plan.

A. Moropoulou et al. (Eds.): TMM_CH 2021, CCIS 1574, pp. 40–51, 2022.
https://doi.org/10.1007/978-3-031-20253-7_4

To this end, the INCEPTION platform was used as an aggregator element of all specific information, through BIM-based 3D models, used for verification and for structural analysis of the building (FEM model) as well as an aid to decision making strategies in terms of maintenance and for web-mobile applications of virtual reality (VR) or augmented (AR) for tourism-information, dissemination and cultural marketing purposes.

2   The History of the Complex

The complex in which the technical museum Nikola Tesla in Zagreb (TMNT) is located today (Fig. 1), originally known as the Zagreb Fair on Savska Street, was built based on a project by Marijan Haberle and Hinko Bauer, already almost completely com- pleted in 1939.

Since 1909, with a series of pavilions, created as a venue for trade fairs, Zagreb has been enriched with architectural structures of interest, among which the French pavilion stands out.

After the First World War, it is evident that the Assembly area is used as an instrument of cultural diplomacy, with the aim of proving the capacity and economic strength of neo-Yugoslavia.

Fig. 1. Airial view of the complex of the former Zagreb Fairground realized based on the project by Marijan Haberle and Hinko Bauer. The French pavilion, the student center and the technical museum Nikola Tesla Museum are highlighted. The picture below shows the "square" at the entrance to the Museum with the four pavilions.

In this sense, in 1946 the Assembly area was renamed the Zagreb Fair [16] and the decision was made to expand the 13,400 square meters of exhibition space, which proved insufficient.

In 1949, in 8 months, the architect Marijan Haberle built new pavilions for 8,000 square meters, at 39 Savska Street in front of the original nucleus, today the Student Center (Fig. 2). The main building, which replaces a tram depot, has an innovative wooden supporting structure.

The larger structure (pavilions A and B), with a partially curved L-shaped layout, is positioned in depth, while another pavilion closes the intersection (pavilion C) creating a square as access and placing another small pavilion (D) inside.

A prefabricated bridge to cross Savska street (connection to the old part) and a vertical column of 30 m, with urban relevance and an advertising-commercial declination, should have completed the project but were not realized.

After 1950 these last pavilions were transformed into the Museum of Science and Tech- nology when the Fair was fully re-functionalized for commercial purposes. More pre- cisely, from 1954 to 1959 the Fair was moved to a new location, while the museum was officially opened in 1963 and from 2016 it was named after Nikola Tesla [2].

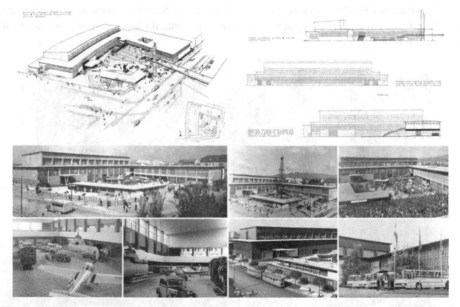

Fig. 2. Drawings of architect Marijan Haberle project vision and historical photos of the Museum, including the one of the opening days. In the perspective, it is worth noting the prefabricated steel bridge for the crossing of Savska street (as a connection to the former Fair) and the vertical column of 30 m in steel tubes, both never built. The rhythm of the façades is highlighted by the seriality of the module used by the designer.

3 The Main Structure of the Museum: Characteristics and Uniqueness

The load-bearing structure of the main pavilion (Pavilion A) represents the most inter- esting element: the designers decided to use a reticular structure completely made of wood, despite the availability of technologies such as reinforced concrete and steel, in vogue at the time.

The external dimensions (Fig. 3) are between 81.27 m of the east facade and 87.75 m of the west facade, with a width of 25.40 m, reaching a height of 19.74 m, for a total area of 2,137 m². The main load-bearing system consists of 15 truss frames with a span between 6.8 and 7.3 m. The main frames are interconnected with 11 secondary trusses with a span between 1.6 and 3 m. The columns, connected to a complex grid, define the vertical supporting structure with N shaped bracing.

The main beams divide the hall into three naves, fixed on the structure and the columns of the facade, which act at the same time as a support for the wooden grid windows on 40 × 95 cm modules.

The structure is never visible, since the entire interior has been designed with wood paneling and finishing formwork that cover it: hence the need to develop a few informative paths aimed at enhancing the structure itself.

Pavilion B is designed to support offices and administrative premises, while Pavilion D, also made of wood except for the central part with Sljeme stone walls, hosts the bookshop.

Pavilion C is intended for services and is characterized by the large span of the covered area and the balanced shape/volume ratio.

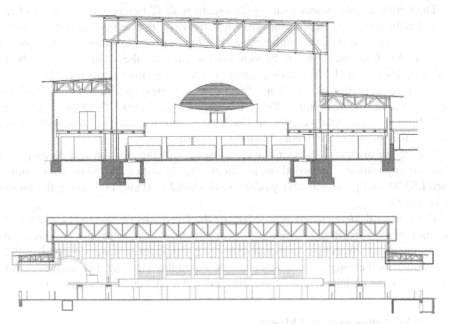

Fig. 3. Cross section and longitudinal section of the main Hall A

4 Survey Methodology and Documentation

The complexity, both in terms of historical-architectural and functional-expository value, required a survey and documentation methodology that could, on the one hand, integrate multiple data acquisition methods and tools and allow their aggregation and subsequent reuse. For this reason, we opted for the realization of BIM-based models that could be used both for the documentation, management and structural verification of the building and for the realization of AR and VR applications. Several acquisition techniques, integrated with each other, have been chosen according to specific purposes following the guidelines identified in the survey protocol developed within the INCEPTION project [9].

4.1 The Survey

For the survey of the architectural complex a hybrid methodology has been used, now consolidated, which makes use of terrestrial laser scanner and aerial photogrammetry [12], recorded through topographic network. A FARO LS330 was used to survey the interiors of Pavilion A and the exterior of the entire complex, while a drone, DJI Mavic 2 Pro, was used for the survey of the roofs and the parts in elevation hidden by spokes or vegetation in collaboration with University of Ferrara [10].

The terrestrial laser scanner survey (254 scans with 12 mm residual error) has been rec- orded directly on the existing topographic network (with external and internal control points), realized for structural monitoring. The land survey, together with the control points visible from the drone (n. 5) were used to improve the accuracy of the photo-modelling alignment (1,500 processed images) and reduce drift errors (Fig. 4).

For the construction of the Virtual Tour of the complex, specific for off-site related applications, 123 high resolution 360° spherical photos (10,000 × 5,000px) acquired in HDR through Ntech iStar were taken. The Virtual Tour was then realized with 36 images and then populated with contextual information.

The survey of the artefacts, inside the museum, for the creation and development of an AR application was carried out by integrating the data acquired by laser scanner (Faro LS330) and photogrammetry (Canon 5D Mark2 - 50 mm f1.4) using flat targets for re- cording.

The structural survey that we carried out by the University of Zagreb [14] starts from the study of the verified project and historical documents and integrates the direct survey by means of inspections and endoscopy or by indirect and non-destructive techniques such as thermography, ultrasound, resistographs, etc. The data collected were then used for the definition of the three-dimensional model and its enrichment.

4.2 3D Modelling and BIM Models

The architectural H-BIM modelling of the TMNT has been realized with Autodesk Revit 2018, with a LOD suitable [3] for the insertion of all the information deriving from the surveys and investigations carried out, structured with an information organization that can be used by the Museum staff, in place of the existing 2D CAD, for management and maintenance purposes, and can be updated and implemented to record future interventions.

The BIM model of the structure, also produced in Revit in collaboration with the Uni- versity of Zagreb [15], posed the challenge of recreating the complex geometry of the structure, hidden from view, from documents, surveys and investigations carried out. Most of the structural elements have been modelled using the available geometrical parameters, to simplify the realization of both the geometries and the properties of the individual elements and/or groups, which is fundamental to allow changes over time, should new or more correct information from on-site measurements be available, such as verifications and punctual analysis.

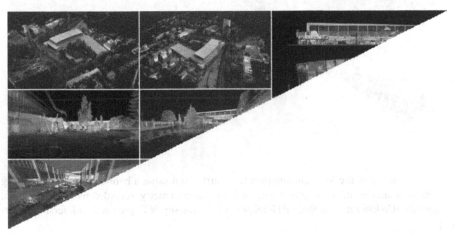

Fig. 4. The survey of the Museum complex was carried out using a hybrid methodology, using the terrestrial laser scanner integrated with aerial photogrammetry, recorded using topographic strongholds. (Collaboration in INCEPTION project: University of Zagreb and University of Fer-rara)

5   The Semantic Enrichment of the BIM Model and the Population with Attached Documentation

BIM models have been realized (architectural and structural) according to the IFC 2 × 3 standard, so that the single elements are correctly classified once loaded on the INCEPTION platform [11], where converted into TTL [6], they can be further enriched semantically or with attachments of different types (PDF, structural reports, thermo-graphic, images, 3D detail models, etc.), linked to the individual elements of the model (Fig. 5).

In the same way, the information already contained in the IFC model is automatically transferred to the INCEPTION platform, such as the material, the technical properties of the element, the function (load-bearing element, external closure, internal partition etc.) or the construc- tion/maintenance phase [4]. To compare, several concepts of 4D viewer can be observed [17–20].

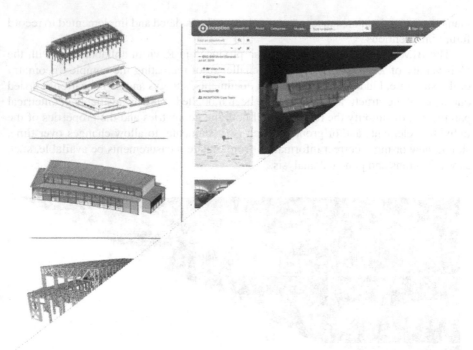

Fig. 5. The survey of the Museum complex was carried out using a hybrid methodology, using the terrestrial laser scanner integrated with aerial photogrammetry, recorded using topographic strongholds. (Collaboration in INCEPTION project: University of Zagreb and Uni-versity of Ferrara)

6 Results and Applications of AR/VR for the Fruition of the Documented Contents

Starting from the survey and the BIM model, three-dimensional models have been developed for the creation of virtual (VR) or augmented (AR) reality applications [Parrinello et al. 2016]. In most cases they were re-processed, optimized and redefined using simple surfaces or NURBS, using Rhino or Sketchup [Ausonio et al. 2018]. This has allowed simplifications, where necessary, to solve the problem of the computer weight of the model or scene, one of the major limitations in the use of these technologies.

In the configuration of the models, it was of fundamental importance the a priori defi- nition of the storytelling that the AR/VR communication would develop.

The topological structure of the models has been redefined, according to perceptual factors, working on the textures to obtain an effective geometric reduction. The use of the texture baking, has allowed a simplification of the volumetric structure, integrating the effect of light into the texture itself. Using Twinmotion, a VR off-site navigation experience of the complex has been achieved, making it possible to use and enhance the hidden load-bearing structure (Fig. 6).

The demonstration development of an AR app for smartphones enhances the structure on-site, dynamically overlapping it in real time, inside the large room. The same app

Fig. 6. Using the Twinmotion (Unreal Engine) platform, an off-site virtual reality navigation experience has been realized on the architectural complex of the museum in relation to its supporting structure. The image also shows the different levels of deepening of the architectural model necessary for the immersive realization of the VR scene (done by the partner team from University of Ferrara)

integrates the increased use of three artifacts on display, identified with the museum's curator: a Tesla coil, a prototype electric car from the Croatian company Dock-In and a late nineteenth century steam engine. The recognition technology used is based on

Fig. 7. For the application of AR augmented reality, some objects were chosen with the curator to be enhanced with this technology inside the museum, including one of Tesla's coils and an electric car prototype made by a Croatian company. The image also displays the function of the app that enhances the structure by superimposing it, dynamically and in real time, inside the great room. The development was carried out in the Unity environment

Vuforia's algorithms for development in Unity. The objects in the museum collection thus be- come access points for the enjoyment of aggregated content, directly and dynamically taken from the INCEPTION platform (Fig. 7).

The same logic of on-the-fly retrieving of the contents on the platform has been adopted for the Virtual Tour of the museum and its collection. A raster-based product made from 360° photos, loaded on the platform and spatially connected to the BIM model. The Virtual Tour was designed primarily for use via web browser, all-in-one VR head- set or mobile devices (Fig. 8).

Fig. 8. The Virtual Tour of the museum was created from 360° spherical photos, acquired during the survey campaign, and was mainly designed for use via web browser, all-in-one VR headset or mobile devices

7 Conclusions and Future Developments

The complex, built in 1949 as a temporary structure, was built at a time when cross-laminated timber was almost unknown, making this building a project of absolute interest, where ambition and audacity of the designer still impresses today. The imposing wooden structure is a valuable example of Croatian post-war architecture, and in 2005 it was included in the protected cultural heritage.

Despite this, the architecture of the Tesla Museum was still poorly investigated before this project. The modern BIM surveying and modelling techniques implemented have not only made it possible to understand, preserve and manage the artefact but have also become the basis for communicating this value. New media such as the web and virtual reality and augmented reality tools therefore become lexical tools for dialogue and storytelling for the new generations, opening to subsequent reuse in a logical cross-generational communication and cultural transfer.

Acknowledgements. We would like to acknowledge the EU project H2020 INCEPTION. The presented paper is a compilation of the work of several INCEPTION project partners. Their contribution is gratefully acknowledged.

References

1. European project "INCEPTION - Inclusive Cultural Heritage in Europe through 3D semantic modelling", concluded in May 2019 and funded by the European Commission under the Horizon 2020 Program, Research and Innovation Action under Grant Agreement No. 665220.
2. Technical Museum website in Nikola Tesla: <tmnt.hr/hr-hr>
3. Referable to a LOD F/G provided for by the Italian legislation UNI 11337-4:2017 for works of historical-architectural interest.
4. A specific set of properties allows you to extend the IFC 2x3 standard and include component nomenclatures according to the Getty vocabulary, through specific addressing of the INCEPTION platform via links.
5. Elena, A., et al.: Potenzialità dei software Free e/o Open Source per la modellazione, gestione e fruizione di entità 3D. In Geomatics Workbooks, n. 14 - FOSS4G-it (2018)
6. Bonsmar, P., et al.: Handling huge and complex 3D geometries with Semantic Web technology. IOP Conference Se- ries: Materials Science and Engineering **364**(1), 12–41 (2018)
7. Stefano, B., Gianfranco, R., Filippo, S., Pamela, M.: Augmented Reality for Historical Storytelling. The INCIPICT Project for the Reconstruction of Tangible and Intangible Image of L'Aquila Historical Centre. In Proceedings **1**, 1083 (2017)
8. Cadelano, G., et al.: Improving the Energy Efficiency, Limiting Costs and Reducing CO_2 Emissions of a Mu- seum Using Geothermal Energy and Energy Management Policies. In Energies **2019**(12), 3192 (2019)
9. Roberto, D.G., et al.: Integrated data capturing requirements for 3D semantic modelling of Cultural Heritage: the INCEPTION protocol. In: Int. Arch. Photogramm. Remote Sens. Spatial Inf. Sci., XLII- 2/W3, pp. 251–257 (2017)
10. Francesca, F., Manuela, B., Andrea, M.: Survey Methodologies, Research and Technological Innovation for a Case of Medieval Archaeology: Torre Melissa in the province of Crotone. In DisegnareCon **10**(19), 6–1 (2017)
11. Federica, M., et al.: Docu- mentation, Processing, and Representation of Architectural Heritage Through 3D Semantic Modelling: The INCEPTION Project. In: Cecilia, B., Cettina, S. (eds.). Impact of Industry 4.0 on Architecture and Cultural Heritage. Hershey, PA: IGI Global, pp. 202- 238 (2020)
12. Francesco, N., Fabio, R.: UAV for 3D mapping applications: a review. In Applied geomatics **6**(1), 1–15 (2014)
13. Sandro, P., Francesca, P., Monica, B.: La 'migrazione' della realtà in scenari virtuali: Banche dati e sistemi di documentazione per la musealizzazione di am- bienti complessi. Musei virtuali dell'architettura e della città. In Disegnarecon **9**(17), 14–1 (2016)
14. Vlatka, R., Dean, Č, Mislav, S.: Reconstruction of the technical Museum in Zagreb. In Advanced Materials Research **778**, 919–926 (2013)

15. Vlatka, R., Mislav, S., Jure, B.: In Situ Advanced Diagnostics and Inspection by Non-destructive Techniques and UAV as Input to Numerical Model and Struc- tural Analysis - Case Study. In: Antonia, M., Manolis, K., Andreas, G., Constantine, S., Charalambos, M. (eds.) Transdisciplinary Multispectral Modeling and Cooperation for the Preservation of Cultural Heritage. TMM_CH 2018. Communications in Computer and Information Science, vol 962. Springer, Cham (2019)
16. Dubravka, V.: The Zagreb Fair as a Generator of New Zagreb's Planning. Journal of Planning History.Author, F.: Article title. Journal **2**(5), 99–110 (2016). (2020)
17. Doulamis, A.D., et al.: A 4D Virtual/Augmented Reality Viewer Exploiting Un- structured Web-based Image Data. VISAPP (2) (2015)
18. Doulamis, N., et al.: Modelling of static and moving objects: digitizing tangible and intan- gible cultural heritage. Mixed reality and gamification for cultural heritage. Springer, Cham, pp. 567–589 (2017)
19. Johnson, P.S., et al.: Online 4D reconstruction using multi-images available under Open Access. ISPRS Annals of the Photogrammetry, Remote Sensing and Spatial Information Sciences (2013)
20. Protopapadakis, E., Doulamis, A.: Semi-supervised image meta-filter- ing using relevance feedback in cultural heritage applications. International Journal of Her- itage in the Digital Era **3**(4), 613–627 (2014)

Digital Heritage a Holistic Approach

Mapping Ancient Athens: A Digital Map to Rescue Excavations

Anna Maria Theocharaki[✉], Leda Costaki, Wanda Papaefthimiou, Maria Pigaki, and George Panagiotopoulos

Dipylon Society for the Study of Ancient Topography, Athens, Greece
theocharakiannita@gmail.com, lcostaki@otenet.gr,
wanda.papaefthimiou@gmail.com, pigaki@survey.ntua.gr,
g.panag@metal.ntua.gr

Keywords: Rescue excavations · Urban archaeology · Historical topography · Cartography · Space use

1 Introduction

The project *Mapping Ancient Athens* is about systematizing the archaeological documentation of 160 years of rescue excavations in Athens. Besides the well-known sites and monuments, the huge archaeological resource of Athens is rarely visible in daily life, and now *Mapping Ancient Athens* has made it freely accessible by digital media, opening up new horizons in disseminating archaeological information to the general audience. Thus, one can wander through time and space to correlate the various archaeological features, unconnected at first glance, and compose, unexpectedly, one's own narrative. At the same time, it aims to highlight the tremendous work of 240 Greek archaeologists who undertook the excavation, research, preservation, and publication of archaeological evidence for the benefit of future generations.

This paper presents an original project conceived by the Dipylon Society, a non-profit organization for the study of ancient topography, as it stemmed from a research gap, and describes the key points of the methodology that was developed for its implementation.

2 A Key Issue of the Historical Topography of Athens

Our knowledge of the built environment of ancient Athens is mainly based on ancient texts, inscriptions, and the physical remains brought to light by the archaeological excavations. There are numerous publications for standing monuments in large archaeological sites, such as the Acropolis, the Kerameikos, the Agora, the Olympieion. However, what do we know about the other Athens, the invisible one, where human activity has unfolded for four thousand years? Where, for example, were the most densely populated neighborhoods, and which streets crossed them? Where did the potters and the coppersmiths set up their workshops? Were their homes close to these workshops? Or, how do the ancient streets relate to the current road network?

An inexhaustible resource of knowledge about the fabric of the ancient city is well preserved beneath layers of later deposits; rescue excavation findings come to light daily, and yet, many areas of the city are still unexplored. Rescue excavations take place prior

A. Moropoulou et al. (Eds.): TMM_CH 2021, CCIS 1574, pp. 55–65, 2022.
https://doi.org/10.1007/978-3-031-20253-7_5

to any private or public technical work in Athens; on private plots before constructing a new building or in public squares for the construction of underground car parks, or in narrow trenches for laying cables and pipes along the city streets; but also for large public urban infrastructure projects, such as road widenings, uneven junctions and, more recently, the metro and the tram.

As the ancient city lies beneath the modern [1], the relationship between fragmentary surviving remains is not easily recognizable. The main reason for such disconnection derives from the fact that sites have been excavated at random, [2] making it difficult to restore a possible history of the area. Theodora Karagiorga [3], honorary head of the Athens Ephorate of Antiquities, characteristically conveys her experience from the rescue excavation carried out at Lenormant Street in the years 1984-1985: "The most important thing is that we were not able to verify the results of the excavation in one section with those in another, because, by the time the excavation of one section was completed, the remains of the previous one no longer existed."

The historical topography of Athens has been at the center of research for more than a century. Scholars have traditionally focused on identifying standing monuments or locating those known only from ancient sources. For example, there is a plethora of studies on the identification of monuments that Pausanias described during his visit to Athens. But what is the urban environment wherein the famous monuments were included? Treatises on the development of ancient Athens published by Judeich [4] and Travlos [5] constitute seminal works on the documentation and synthesis of existing knowledge at their time. Yet, new evidence has since been published.

Despite the serious efforts in recent years regarding individual aspects of the topography of Athens, such as streets [6], city walls [7], cemeteries and development of habitation areas [8], or other specialized topics [9], there is a lack of a complete study encompassing the entire archaeological documentation published so far combined with historical maps and complementary historical evidence. The main reason for this is largely due to the difficulty in fully managing and integrating all archaeological data in their spatial context. Besides, it would certainly take many generations of archaeologists to index and map an uninterrupted history of centuries with conventional non-digital means. Dipylon Society addressed this issue by designing and implementing an interactive web map.[1] Technology and geographic information systems have helped to render the spatial dimension of archaeological data as accurately as possible.

3 Brief Description of the Project

The digital platform _Mapping Ancient Athens_ classifies and organizes on the modern urban cadastral map spatial and descriptive data for all the hitherto fragmented immovable finds brought to light by the rescue excavations. These finds are for the most part no longer visible, having been removed, reburied in situ or preserved in inaccessible basements of modern buildings. Hundreds of rescue excavations have been conducted over the years, with archaeological records creating a space-time puzzle.

---

[1] Dipylon is a non-profit organization for the study of ancient topography and the cultural environment through interdisciplinary research in Archaeology, History, Informatics, and Cartography; https://dipylon.org/en/.

Mapping Ancient Athens is the first complete archaeological resource of published immovable antiquities which indexes and registers in a bilingual geospatial database (Greek/English) 670 drawings, 1,400 bibliographical references, and information data from 1,473 excavation sites. Archaeologists, cartographers, surveyor engineers, and specialists in databases and geographic information systems, as well as artists, have collaborated for four years on a project of high complexity. This project was an effort to glimpse into the momentarily visible part of the history of Athens by highlighting every minimal trace and connecting it to others in the area; a path is slowly being opened for a better understanding of history.

4 Methodology

The project brought together specialists from different fields and disciplines as it provided the platform for the exchange of knowledge and collaboration. Particularly, there was a transfer of knowledge between cartography and archaeology: the cartographer had to understand archaeological stratigraphy and the archaeologist had to understand ideas, concepts, and methods governing cartography. Gaps or inaccuracies in documentation had to be bridged or amended and often solutions were found through collaboration of disciplines. Perhaps the greatest challenge was to "transcribe" vague descriptive data into measurable values and searchable fields. There were thus often juxtapositions between archaeology, history, and cartography, but thanks to effective interdisciplinary teamwork, suitable solutions were found. The map offers the ability to construct a narrative out of scattered and disparate material, making archaeology once again a vibrant source of inspiration.

4.1 Project Area

The map covers a surface area of about 6,7 km² and includes the modern urban space within the Themistoklean (5th cent. BC) and the Valerian Walls (3rd cent. AC), as well as a 500 meters-zone outside the ancient fortifications (Fig. 1).

4.2 Descriptive Data

The cartographic project covers 160 years of archaeological documentation and includes all the immovable antiquities discovered by rescue excavations. The multitude of archaeologists involved in archaeological interventions of different eras formed a huge volume of complex data, largely uneven.

Descriptive Data Indexing. Archaeological evidence documented by excavators at various times in Athenian archaeology had to be systematized for the information data to become manageable. The main source of information about the rescue excavations of Athens is kept in the valuable excavation reports of archaeologists published annually by the Archaeological Service in the *Archaiologikon Deltion*. In addition, an effort was made to extract archaeological content from all the excavation reports that have been published from the middle of the 19th century until today, which include conference proceedings, monographs, and articles in various academic journals (*PAE, AAA, AE, Hesperia, BCH, AJA*, etc.) (Fig. 2).

Fig. 1. The 6.7 km^2 project area, including the ancient fortifications.

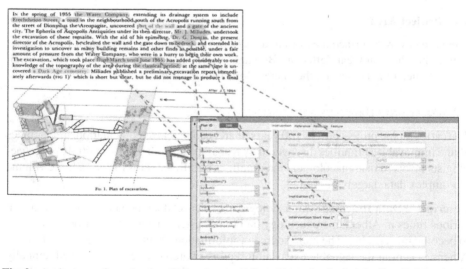

Fig. 2. An instance from the descriptive data workflow. From the *Archaiologikon Deltion* (top) to the database entry (bottom).

A bilingual vocabulary of semantic terms was created to classify archaeological records. It is compatible with acknowledged thesauri and dictionaries for cultural heritage documentation, such as Art and Architecture Thesaurus (AAT), the Forum in International Standards in Heritage (FISH), and the Dictionnaire méthodique de l'architecture grecque et romaine.

Classification of Descriptive Data. The selected classification is divided into two categories, the typological and the chronological. The typological classification concerns the uses of space. It is divided into twelve classes: public space, religion/cult, education, transport, fortification, water supply/drainage, health/welfare, domestic space, production, commerce, funerary space, and unknown use. Each class has its subcategories; for example, archaeological features listed under the class of "production" may be associated with any of the following categories: brick-making workshops, fullery, olive processing workshops, pottery workshops, etc.

As far as the chronological classification is concerned, the specific dating for each feature has been systematized in wider periods and sub-periods of history, which were finalized in eleven periods of general significance, as established in the historiographical tradition (Neolithic, Bronze Age, Geometric, Archaic, Classical, Hellenistic, Roman, Late Roman, Byzantine, Ottoman, Modern Greece). Undated remains have also been listed under a twelfth class to be searchable on the digital map.

4.3 Spatial Data

Excavations indexed in the geospatial database span 16 decades in a constantly evolving city. It was thus important to collect and use historical cartographic backgrounds that reliably capture the city's image at different times (Fig. 3).

Cartographic Backgrounds. Multiple backgrounds, such as historical maps, topographic diagrams, photogrammetric maps, and aerial photographs, were collected and, where appropriate, digitized and joined the Hellenic Geodetic Reference System EGSA '87. The main backgrounds used in the project were the following: the 1925 and the 1936 topographic diagrams (Municipality of Athens), the 1974 topographic maps that were photogrammetrically produced (Ministry of Public Works), and, finally, the 2009 orthophoto maps and the 2019 cadastral diagrams (National Cadastre and Mapping Agency of Greece).

Locating Excavation Sites. Locating the excavation sites was mainly based on the published plans that accompanied the excavation reports of the *Archaiologikon Deltion*. These cases of published plans amount to only 35% of the total excavation sites. Finding the exact location of an excavated site without a published plan was not an easy task. The site location process presented various difficulties, especially when the only indication for the excavated area was the modern address specified in the title of the excavation report.

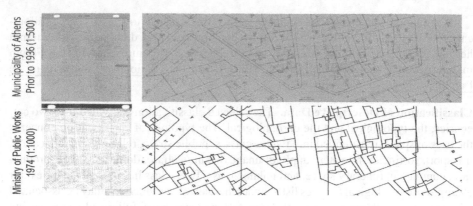

Fig. 3. Example of superimposed cartographic backgrounds.

A persistent effort has therefore been made to resolve issues such as unclear addresses. For example, there were many cases where the description of the location of the plot had the following wording: "... we excavated a property at the intersection of X and Y streets ...". Such a description is unclear since either one of the four corners of the intersection could coincide with the excavated site (Fig. 4). In that case, a thorough search was done for data possibly existing in other sources, such as building permits (e.g., owner name, building construction time), telephone directory information, and a general internet search.

Georeferencing and Vectorizing Excavation Plans. Georeferencing the plans has often been a laborious task due to the lack of information required, such as the scale or clear boundaries of a property. The main steps for georeferencing and vectorizing excavation plans were the following: 1. Locate the excavated plot in the modern urban fabric and enclose it in a polygon. 2. Georeferencing the plan (move, scale, rotate). 3. Vectorize the georeferenced plan. 4. Enclose the excavated remains (features) in polygons (Fig. 5).

4.4   Platform Development

The implementation of the webGIS platform consists of three distinct parts, the development of the database, two middleware applications, one to handle spatial data and one for the non-spatial data, and the web client application. Only open-source tools and software have been used to develop the platform, using the latest stable versions during the development period. The basic structure and interaction of the various components of the platform are given in Fig. 6.

The PostgreSQL database with the PostGIS extension has been used to manage the data. The database consists of several tables for each archaeological entity, as well as separate tables for the spatial data, when applicable. Data management is carried out through customized forms, while the spatial data are uploaded to the database through the QGIS software [10].

Fig. 4. Example of an unclear description for the location of the excavation site.

The NodeJS and the ExpressJS tools have been used for web client communication with the database. An appropriate Application Program Interface (API) has been developed to run queries in the database via HTTP calls. The queries are mainly used for filter functions and the creation of lists or detailed forms for the archaeological entities, in which the participation of spatial data is not necessary.

The Geoserver software has been used to generate the mapping services from the database. Geoserver provides flexibility in the mapping visualization as well as the management of spatial data. The production of the cartographic services is done by joining tables (spatial and non-spatial data) in the Geoserver environment. Web Feature Services (WFS) or Web Mapping Services (WMS) are provided according to the spatial detail of the data. Spatial data with high detail, like the cad layer, are provided with the WMS format, while less detailed data like the sites are given in WFS format to offer better mapping renders and more interactive functionality.

The Angular framework and the Angular Materials, Openlayers, as well as several other libraries, have been used to develop the front-end web client of the application. The OpenLayers library is responsible for managing and visualizing spatial data, and the application tools related to the styling of spatial entities, map navigation functionality, etc. All other controls and functions have been developed through the Angular framework in TypeScript, HTML, and CSS programming languages. Examples of these functions are widgets, data management, and dynamic calculations for filters, lists, and forms. It is noted that most of these functions are performed in parallel with the cartographic

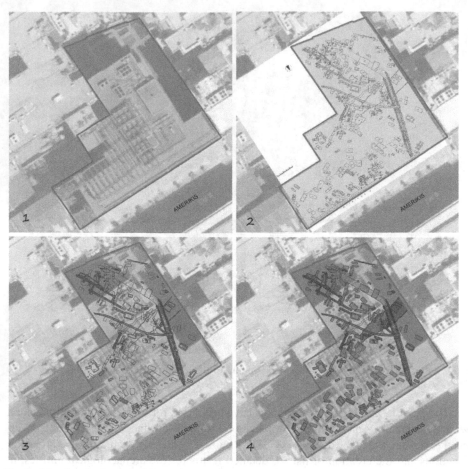

Fig. 5. The four basic steps followed for the treatment of the spatial data of the excavated plot at 3 Amerikis Street, Athens.

functionality (e.g., filters and their representation on the map). Finally, for the graphical design of the application, the Angular Materials library has been used, which offers numerous design options for theming, widgets, layout, etc.

The online digital platform organizes and classifies spatial and archaeological data in the modern urban cadastral map of Athens. It provides the ability to search for different types of space use featuring classified immovable antiquities with the greatest possible accuracy, combining them with their dating (e.g., "show me where Hellenistic houses or Roman baths were found"). Class subcategories of space use, periods of excavation years, names of archaeologists involved in rescue excavations, infrastructure bodies, and types of excavated sites can be retrieved, among other search types, from the advanced menu.

Navigating the digital map is possible in three main ways: first, by selecting one or more uses of space (see "Explore: use of space" at the top row of symbols); second, by

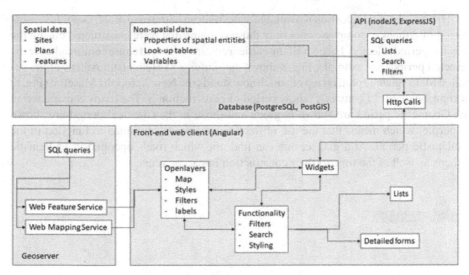

Fig. 6. Basic structure and interaction of the various components of the WebGIS platform.

selecting one or more historical periods of the city (see "Explore: period at the bottom of the map) and, thirdly, by selecting one of the addresses of the indexed excavation sites (Fig. 7; see address at the top of the map). In addition, the color-coding is selected on the layers' menu at the top right (Fig. 8; see layer "Features") to indicate colored features either concerning the use of the space or concerning the period of construction.

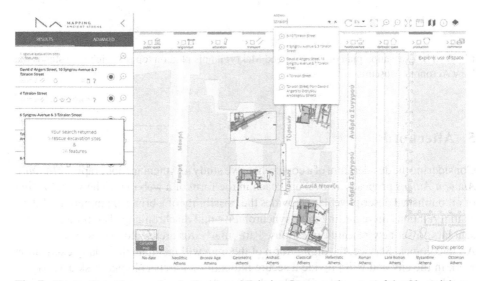

Fig. 7. Excavations along and on both sides of Tziraion Street, to the west of the Olympieion.

Historical period selection is available at the bottom of the map. Each major historical period of Athens encompasses not only those remains that were constructed during the specific period selected, but also all the earlier remains whose lifetime continued over the selected period. For example, Fig. 8 shows the remains of Hellenistic Athens at the so-called Makrygiannis plot, on top of which now stands the New Acropolis Museum (Fig. 8, at right, see layer "Features", "show period of construction"). The roads constructed in the Geometric period are shown in green and those in the Classical period are shown in purple, which means that the use of these earlier roads continued to function in the Hellenistic period. At a glance, one can find out which roads operated in Hellenistic Athens as well as the time of their construction in earlier years.

Fig. 8. The excavation plan of the so-called Makrygiannis plot, on top of which now stands the New Acropolis Museum.

5   Afterword

Considering the desideratum of a comprehensive study in Athenian topography, *Mapping Ancient Athens* proposes a novel approach in the form of a web map. The visualization of all published descriptive data provides the possibility of a broad examination of their spatial relationship regarding their synchronicity and diachronicity. The project invites scholars to set new research questions. Particularly for archaeologists working in the Archaeological Service, the digital form of the map will facilitate their daily excavation work in the city and will provide a secure indication of archaeological risk assessment for future construction works. Besides, the digital map will disseminate archaeological information to non-academic audiences and generate community values based on cultural heritage. Knowledge of a shared past on a neighborhood level creates a sense of belonging, and by making this knowledge easily available we hope to disseminate the principles of heritage protection and preservation in a historical city that suffers from vandalism, graffiti on monuments, and very low respect for public spaces. Within the framework of the current memorandum of cooperation with the Ephorate of Antiquities of the City of Athens, the project will, hopefully, be enriched with the addition of unpublished excavation plans.

Finally, the ultimate goal is to expand the mapped area; first, towards the northwest, including the area of the Academy, the location of the ancient gymnasium and Plato's philosophical school; and, at a later stage, towards the southwest, to cover the whole area traversed by the Long Walls, all the way to the sea and the ancient ports of Phaleron and Piraeus.

Acknowledgements. *Mapping Ancient Athens* was funded by the Stavros Niarchos Foundation (lead donor), The Packard Humanities Institute, and the Aegeas Non-Profit Civil Company. We wish to acknowledge and thank all the partners who have contributed to the project, which has been made possible thanks to the permissions granted by the Greek Ministry of Culture.

References

1. Parlama, L., Stambolidis, N.C.: The City Beneath the City: Antiquities from the Metropolitan Railway Excavations, Athens N.P. Goulandris Foundation, Museum of Cycladic Art; New York (2000)
2. Katsianis, M., Lampraki, S., Theocharaki, A,M., Pigaki, M., Costaki, L., Papaefthimiou, E.: Reconnecting a Fragmented Monument through Digital Mapping: the City Walls of Athens. Studies in Digital Heritage **2**(2), 177–195 (2018). https://doi.org/10.14434/sdh.v2i2.24440
3. Karagiorga-Stathakopoulou, T.: Δημόσια ἔργα καὶ ἀνασκαφὲς στὴν Ἀθήνα τὰ τελευταῖα πέντε χρόνια. Horos **6**, 87–108 (1988)
4. Judeich, W.: Topographie von Athen. Munich (1931²)
5. Travlos, J.: Pictorial Dictionary of Ancient Athens (German Archaeological Institute). Praeger Publishers, New York (1971)
6. Costaki, L.: The *Intra Muros* Road System of Ancient Athens. PhD dissertation. University of Toronto (2006)
7. Theocharaki, A.M.: The Ancient Circuit Walls of Athens. De Gruyter, Berlin, Boston (2020). https://doi.org/10.1515/9783110638202
8. Dimitriadou, E.M.: Early Athens. Settlements and Cemeteries in the Submycenaean, Geometric, and Archaic Periods, Los Angeles (2019)
9. Greco, E.: Topografia di Atene: Sviluppo urbano e monumenti dalle origini al III secolo d. C. 5 vols. Paestum, Italy: Pandemos (2010–2015)
10. Lampraki, S., Vakkas, T.: Mapping Ancient Athens: From the Fragmented Archaeological Data to the Digital Map. In: Archeologie. Temi, Contesti, Materiali. Dipartimento di Studi Umanistici – University of Naples Federico II, pp. 73–83 (2021)

Vra Core 4.0 Metadata Standard for the Facades of the Historic Houses of Athens (19th – Early 20th Century)

Athina Kremmyda[1](✉), Konstantina Siountri[1,2], and Ioannis Anagnostopoulos[1,3]

[1] "Digital Culture, Smart Cities, IoT and Advanced Digital Technologies", Track "Digital Culture", Department of Informatics, University of Piraeus, Piraeus, Greece
athina.krem@gmail.com, {ksiountri,janag}@unipi.gr
[2] Cultural Technology and Communication Department, University of the Aegean, Mytilene, Greece
ksiountri@aegean.gr
[3] Computer Science and Biomedical Informatics Department, University of Thessaly, Lamia, Greece
janag@dib.uth.gr

Abstract. The development of technology and the continuous production of information through research in culture have created the need to store a large amount of new and existing digital data. The digital storage of information relating to cultural heritage is possible with the use of structured databases, with related information for their safe preservation over time and the easiest access to them. This paper presents a research project on the collection of information about the characteristics of the facades of the Athenian houses from the 19th until the beginning of the 20th century. The information was divided into three periods for their classification, the Neoclassical period (19th – early 20th century), the Eclectic period (mid-19th century – early 20th century), and the Interwar period (early 20th century – 1940). The metadata standards were created to manage and exchange cultural information using the library of Congress in the US and the XML markup global language that is readable both by humans and computers. Moreover, the hierarchical classification of information enables architectural features to be used also in other platforms e.g. such as HBIM (Historic Building Information Modeling), GIS, or three-dimensional models etc. During the research of the external characteristics of the Athenian houses from the 19th to early 20th century, the existing databases on Internet, for the buildings that are dated on the period which is being considered (19th – early 20th century), were examined. Nevertheless, each of them had different characteristics e.g. the information was organized either on a map using pins or in images, based on chronology, accompanied by texts in the Greek language. As a solution to the aforementioned problem, the present work, which was a master's thesis in the framework of the "Digital Culture" program of the University of Piraeus, aims to identify the main architectural characteristics of each period and create metadata in the English language so that they can be interoperable and used with other related vocabularies.

Keywords: Data bases · Metadata · Vra Core 4.0 · XML

A. Moropoulou et al. (Eds.): TMM_CH 2021, CCIS 1574, pp. 66–78, 2022.
https://doi.org/10.1007/978-3-031-20253-7_6

1 Introduction

Databases are collections of records and files which are developed to serve a specific purpose, according to the needs of a specific research field. For that reason, there are many differences between the existing databases, even though the common goal is to store information in a digital environment, not only for its preservation over time but also for the ability to process and retrieve it.

Database's data are accompanied by metadata, which are not independent but refer to other information about specific objects [1]. Metadata serve as entries for editing and they are stored in separate files that are linked together as subcategories beside the main categories. In addition, metadata information is created by a specific format according to a defined syntax [1].

Many of these existing databases on Internet are made by crowdsourcing. The term crowdsourcing was introduced by Howe in 2006 in an article in Wired magazine. It consists of the word crowd and the term outsourcing [2]. Regarding to the cultural sector, the reasons why volunteers offer their work without financial impact are the contribution to society, the satisfaction of a good act, the appreciation for the cultural organization and its work, the enjoyment, and entertainment, the pleasantly spent of time, the development of individual skills, the acquisition of knowledge / learning about a particular subject, the practice of creativity and the confidence they feel as a result from their offer. Moreover, it is about social or professional reasons, such as socialization and collaboration with other people [3].

For example, in the "Ancient lives" project, volunteers recorded ancient Greek texts found in fragments from the Oxyrhynchus Papyri collection [3]. Similar work was carried out in the "Megalithic Portal program", which aims to record and protect Europe's megalithic monuments, according to information which was provided by volunteers [3]. Another example is the collection, recording, and classification of information in the "Historypin program", in which people share their stories about a place. These stories are posted on the website, and anyone can search for them on a map where pins are located per area [3].

In Greece, "Monumenta" is a program carried out with the help of volunteers who study the monuments of Athens since the 19th century. Other similar programs are the "Neoclassical Heritage Archive" and the "Interesting Architecture of Athens", where research through crowdsourcing was used. Both programs are based on providing information through google maps. Everyone can share photographs and information about a building and its location by pining on the map and adding the information in a blog where an external link lead. These data are available to everyone, even if they do not participate in the survey.

Six databases were found on the internet regarding the buildings of Athens, dating from the 19th to the beginning of the 20th century. As mentioned, there are the bases of "Monumenta", "Neoclassical Heritage Archive" and "Interesting Architecture of Athens". In addition, there is the "Archive of Modern Monuments- modmov" and the "Archeology of the city of Athens", which include information about the location, images, and texts in the Greek language for the buildings of 1880–1940. The "modmov" database, contains 1300 addresses of the Interwar period buildings (1920–1940), placed with pins on a map.

These are important surveys that provide images, texts, and other information about Greece's tangible cultural heritage, from the 19th to the 20th century. However, in its of it, a manual would be useful for the reasons of better user experience, since several people are interested in the architectural heritage, but they are not technologically trained and informed to easily understand how each database system works. In addition, translating the texts in the English language would allow the worldwide use of information.

Based on this problem, this research focused on the creation of a structured vocabulary with the aim of more accurate documentation and interoperability of the recording systems of the architectural facades of the Athenian historical houses. To achieve that, the characteristics of the facades of the Athenian houses from the 19th to the beginning of the 20th century were studied by each period (Neoclassical, Eclectic and Interwar). The information was searched through the relevant literature and the internet, e.g., through social media, digital libraries, websites, and databases. In addition, the size of the houses, the masonry, the openings, the roof ending, and the balconies of the houses were separated groups of research. The conclusions are about the creation of all the elements that characterize the facades of the Athenian houses by period (Neoclassical, Eclectic and Interwar).

2   State of the Art

The external characteristics of the houses which were studied, dated to Neoclassical, Eclectic, and Interwar period. Neoclassicism appeared in Europe in the 18th century. Some of its characteristics are the following: plasticity, elaborate decoration, pilasters, friezes, railings with scenes from nature, mythology, etc. [4]. Eclecticism appeared in the middle of the 19th century. This style combined elements of different periods in one building. Some of the architectural styles that Eclecticism includes are the Art Nouveau (an international movement developed between 1890–1910 and distinguished for the sophistication of forms mainly from elements of nature) [5] and the Beaux Arts (architectural style taught at École des Beaux-Arts in Paris from 1830 to the end of the 19th-century). This style introduced new, modern materials such as iron and glass [5]. From 1920 to 1940, the Interwar period, the elements of the facades of the houses were affected by the German school of Bauhaus (1913–1933, founded by W. Gropius -1883–1969) and they are simple constructions, in contrast to the impressive classicist elements and the intense exterior decorations of the previous years (early 19th – early 20th century). Also, is obvious the emphasis on the functionality of the living space based on the studies of Le Corbusier (1887–1965) for the best living conditions of people in urban centers [5].

From the study of the historical Athenian houses several data emerged about the size of the buildings, the architectural decoration, the openings, the balconies, the masonry, and the roof ending.

Furthermore, the houses of Neoclassical architecture (Figs. 1 and 4) were built according to the model of the urban mansion from Germany that is a one-story house whose facade divided into three sections (base, middle part, and crown) [6]. In their exterior masonry isodome system was used at the base of the building. Later, (late 19th century) was observed to the surfaces of the wall, the addition of slightly protruding pillars under of which an entablature ended in a cornice. The crown of the building was richly decorated (balusters, cornices, etc.) while in some cases ended in a pediment. Concerning the architectural decoration of the houses was simple and designed to give them prestige ('pulled' mortar, framing openings with pilasters, etc.) until 1880. After 1900, buildings were richly decorative. The decoration of balconies was also important, included corbels (a structural piece, jutting from a wall to carry the weight of the balcony) with various decorations, per period (engraved helix, acanthus leaves, etc.). Railings were decorated with geometrical shapes, or themes imported from Europe, mythology, and nature (Figs. 2 and 3) [6].

Fig. 1. Neoclassical, one - story house whose façade divided into three sections (base, middle part, and crown) and its openings are framed with pilasters (Athens, Greece)

Fig. 2. Neoclassical balcony with corbels and railings decorated with mythological scenes (Lysiou 7 Str., Athens, Greece

Eclecticism (Figs. 5 and 6) appeared in Greece at the end of the 19th century, while in Europe it had already appeared since the middle of the same century [4]. The rhythm is distinguished by the rich decoration and the use of elements of various rhythms such as Baroque (renaissance elements) and Baux Arts (symmetry) etc. At the beginning of the 20th century, the population growth, and the reduction of space in the town of Athens led to the construction of larger buildings with two or three floors with apartments. The use of the isodome system at the base of the buildings, such as in the neoclassical houses (early 19th century), continued, while the horizontal engraving of the walls and the curved transition of their surfaces were also observed [6]. The facade of the houses in this period was richly decorated with corbels, garlands, wreaths, etc. (Figs. 7 and 8) However, since 1928 there has been a decongestion of buildings from the dense decoration and there were created harmonious compositions. Around 1900, there were added more balconies in the facades of the buildings. Railings were influenced by Baux Arts and corbels helix had an "antitectonic form", and gradually, in the early 20th century corbels stopped being used [6].

The Interwar period (Figs. 9 and 10) lasted in Greece from 1920 until 1940. In this period were built ground floor houses, two or four-story houses, as well as apartment buildings which consisted of three to six floors [7]. The use of new materials such as reinforced concrete appeared in buildings construction. Influences from the Bauhaus and the architecture of Le Corbusier are the basic elements of modern architecture through

Fig. 3. Davari house – one story house whose façade divided into three sections (base, middle part, and crown) and its openings are framed with pilasters (Athens, Greece)

Fig. 4. Neoclassical, one - story house whose façade divided into three sections (base, middle part, and crown) and its openings are framed with pilasters (Athens, Greece)

Fig. 5. Eclectic house richly decorated with garlands, wreaths, and blind windows (Athens, Greece)

Fig. 6. Eclectic house with two entrances, framed windows and roofing decorated with balusters and decorative vases (Athens, Greece)

Fig. 7. Livieratos mansion – richly decorated façade with corbels, garlands, wreaths etc. (Athens, Greece)

Fig. 8. Mitarakis mansion – richly decorated façade with corbels, garlands, wreaths etc. (Athens, Greece)

the 1920–1940 period. The simplicity of the facades of the Athenian houses in this period is an element that emphasizes their geometric shape. A new type of balcony in the Interwar period was, closed rectangular, polygonal, or curved protrusions on the facades of homes (11, 12). In addition, the architects of this period built semicircular balconies to give plasticity in the facades of the houses. The railings were metal, linear, and straight but were also used geometric patterns in variations [7] (Figs. 11 and 12).

This information was the metadata of Athenian houses from 1880 to 1940, that would not have been created if there was not a diligent study over the buildings of the specific chronological period. In this work, the metadata concerning the architectural features of the facades of the houses in Athens was coded in the XML markup language, which produces codifications even for complex metadata. Nevertheless, before the encoding, metadata was described according to the VRA Core 4.0 metadata standard [1].

3 Methodology

The VRA Core 4.0 (Visual Resources Association) data model, created in 1996, is used to digitally describe works or images (sculptures, paintings, architecture, books, etc.), and it is managed by the Library of Congress in the United States [1]. This version offers the use of elements, sub-elements, and attributes.

Firstly, the 19 elements that can be used to describe works, images or collections are collection/work/image, agent, cultural Context, date, description, inscription, location, material, measurements, relation, rights, source, state Edition, style Period, subject, technique, textref, title, and worktype. In combination with these, the XML attributes, data Date, extent (the part of the Project, Collection, or Image being analyzed), href (hyperlink), pref (preferred value, the specific value of the item or sub-element), refid (unique code link to internal identifiers), rules (description template), source (information source), vocab (vocabulary) and xml: lang (entry language) enrich the description

Fig. 9. The Antonopoulos Flats or Blue Building (deep blue and warm sienna on its external walls) has influenced by Modern Architecture. The closed and semi-outdoor areas that architect K. Panayotakos designed, give a plasticity to the building. (Arachovis 61 & Themistokleous 80 Str., Athens, Greece)

Fig. 10. Interwar architecture. Building with a closed rectangular balcony on its façade. (P. Ioakeim 51 Str., Athens,Greece)

of the element or sub-elements [1]. The Vra Core Image Elements optical items were not included in the information. The proposal for the creation of three-dimensional models of houses was made in a theoretical context, which will be analyzed later.

More specifically, the elements Work, Collection, or Image refer to a work, collection, or image that is analyzed in the database. The id attribute refers to its unique identity, refid attribute its unique code, and source attribute the space in which the elements Work, Collection, or Image are located. The element Agents refers to the name of the person who created the Work, Collection, or Image, while the attributes name, culture, date (earliest Date - latest Date), role, and attribution give further information about the creator 's culture, date of birth, status and capacity. The element Cultural Context refers to the cultural context with which the Work, the Collection, and the Image are connected. The date is added in the element Date and more details are given by the attributes earliest and latest Date. The element Description allows the description in text format. In addition, the element Inscription refers to an inscription, date, description, or shape about the Work, Collection, or Image. In the attributes author, position and text can be included more information about the name of the person who creates it, where the inscription is located, and if any text has been preserved. Location is indicated in the element Location. The attributes name and refid refer to the name and the code of the location. Construction Material is an element where can be made references about the construction material and proportions of Work, Collection, or Image. This element includes the attributes, type, and refid while in the element Measurements can be added more information about the type,

Fig. 11. Polygonal protrusions on the facades of block of flats (Athens, Greece)   **Fig. 12.** Rectangular protrusions on the facades of block of flats (Athens, Greece)

the unit, and extent. In the case in which Work, Collection, or Image relates to other, it is declared through the element Relation and the attributes type and refid. The Copyrght of the Work, Collection and Image include the attributes notes, rights holder, and text. The bibliographical references included in Sources in combination with the source name and unique code (refid). If there is information about the version or status of the Work, Collection, or Image, it refers to the State Edition, with the attributes type, num, and count. Style Period describes the period which is represented. The element Subject is about the description that has been given to the upper element (Work, Collection, Image) and Technique is the process of executing it. The Textef element indicates the reference that has been made for the Work, Collection, or Image, in text format, source and refid. Finally, the element Title, refers to the title that has been given to the upper element and Worktype to its specific type [8].

The Getty Research Institute dictionary was used to attribute unique identities (refid) to elements. This dictionary is certified with ISO (International Organization for Standardization) and NISO (National Organization for Standardization) and includes terminology and information about people, places, cultural objects, art, and architecture in different languages, with a specific identification number (id) for each condition [1]. Linked Open Data is one of the five vocabularies and is widely used in the world of cultural heritage. This is the AAT (Art & Architecture Thesaurus) where there is information about art and architecture, the TGN (Getty Thesaurus of Geographic Names) where information about historical places, cities, empires, etc. is mentioned, and the ULAN (Union List of Artists Names) which contains information about people and organizations related to the arts [9]. The structure of these vocabularies is hierarchical, and their subdivision is the facet. For example, "neoclassical architecture" is found in the Styles and Periods facet.

These elements were not used in total to describe the external characteristics of the Athenian facades. The work1 element was used to describe the characteristics of the Neoclassical period, the work2 element of the Eclectic period, and the work3 element of the Interwar period. The refid feature of the historic houses 300008064 emerged from a search of the Getty Research Institute dictionary in the Art and Architecture Vocabulary (AAT). The Cultural Context element was used to declare the Cultural Context, i.e., Greece, as the place where the studied buildings are located. The refid code of Greece 300389734 was found in the Vocabulary for Geographical Names (TGN) of the Getty Research Institute. The chronological period of works 1,2,3 was stated with the Date and the attributes earliest Date-latest Date (early 19th – early 20th century, late 19th century – early 20th century, early 20th century – 1940). In the Description, the data for the size of the buildings, the openings, the balconies, the architectural decoration, and the crown were mentioned. The City of Athens was declared as Location and in type, vocab, and refid elements of the subdivision, information was added stating that it is a geographical place with code 7001393 in the Getty Thesaurus of Geographical Names. Through the study of the architectural features, were studied the Materials used in constructions, the unique refid code of which, was searched in the Getty dictionary. The element Technique contains information about the techniques in each period e.g. artificial coating. Neoclassical, Eclectic, and Interwar architecture with the code 300021477, 300056522, 300264736 were mentioned in the Style Period. The work type was added to the Work Type element, i.e., the neoclassical, eclectic, and interwar dwellings. In addition, the attributes for the statement of the information's Source and Copyright were added (Fig. 13).

4 Utilization of the Metadata

The classification and description of the characteristics according to the Vra Core 4.0 metadata standard is possible to be used in other digital systems e.g., in Building Information Modeling (BIM), in the Geographic Data System (GIS), or in a 3D model database.

Building Information Modeling (BIM) is a platform that allows the creation and storage of data for the construction of a building, which in recent years in the field of tangible cultural heritage has been developed to the Historic Building Information Modeling (HBIM). Furthermore, HBIM can be used as a database for architectural monuments and a significant contribution to the restoration, representation, and connection to other cultural monuments [10]. Autodesk Revit software is used to design the monuments, which are added to "Families", i.e., to groups of elements with a standard set of parameters and a similar graph, which can be customized. For example, the balconies of neoclassical houses had corbels in various forms and with various common elements, as shown in Figs. 14, 15, 16 and 17. Therefore, if the corbel in Fig. 14 is designed and added to the "Family corbel (a structural piece, jutting from a wall to carry the weight of the balcony) there is not necessary to be designed the balcony in Figs. 15, 16 and 17 again. The existing drawing of the corbel in Fig. 14 will be customized according to the new data (e.g., reducing the size of the helix).

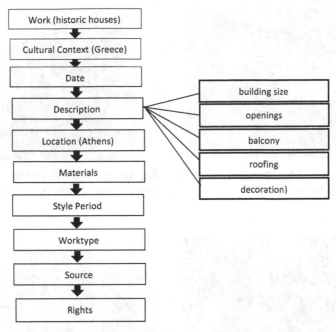

Fig. 13. The Elements of Vra Core 4.0 that were used

Although there are many different methods for creating 3D models such as laser scanner or photogrammetry, they have different characteristics. For example, these methods are used either for small or for largescale cultural objects and, they can be very expensive. A 5D model creation could improve the management and production cost of 3D models. This is because a 5D model contains the dimensions of the cultural object, the date of its creation and its characteristics. Therefore, 5D modelling is a process that includes the 3D model, categorized according to its dimensions and other characteristics, such as balconies, corbels etc., and its "*spatial-analysis*". Eventually, cultural object's information is connected and accessible everywhere and from everyone [11].

The houses that are saved in HBIM could possibly be added to a map, through which will be provided information about their location and their external characteristics. Firstly, a list of the building address, postal code, current condition, etc. should be created. The locations of the buildings could be separated into geographical zones to be easy to organize and find them per area [12]. Athens geographical information is available online (google maps, ArcGIS, etc.). Subsequently, buildings should be photographed in their current condition or scanned with a laser scanner, that can convert their images into 3D models. Finally, the geographic information system would be included information about the location of the houses and the HBIM model information which would be provided with an external link [12].

Saving information in digital form is important and useful in research. The 3D technologies could be used in the storage, processing, and retrieval of information about a cultural object [13]. For a database creation, the objects should be separated into groups and decided the form of the database. Usually, a relational database template

Fig. 14. Balcony with corbels with engraved helix. (Athens, Greece)

Fig. 15. Balcony with corbels with engraved helix. (Athens, Greece)

Fig. 16. Balcony with corbels with engraved helix. (Athens, Greece)

Fig. 17. Balcony with corbels in elliptical shape (Athens, Greece)

(data organized into correlated tables that can be modified) is used. The determination of which audience will be using it (e.g., researchers, citizens) is also important for the adaption of the user experience of the database [14]. VRML (Virtual Reality Modeling Language) and Javascript could be used for the creation of a database with 3Dscenes. In this way, the historical and morphological data of houses could be visually edited by the user. For example, as the external characteristics of the houses in Athens have been organized, could be imported into a similar database. In this way the images of the buildings would be maintained during the time in case of their destruction [14].

Game software could be used for the creation of virtual museums, where the 3D Athenian houses from HBIM platform could be added. This software provides many capabilities, such as 3D object visualization, good graphics, interaction with the object or space, etc. [15] The data could be added also by Europeana which contains over 50 million digitized objects and Google images, which support open data technologies or social media that are useful tools for the virtual restoration of a cultural object, since they contain a large variety of images [16]. In the Unity platform, 3D or 2D games can be created, since this platform provides a rich library of items that could be downloaded and used for the creation of the digital museum and many features such as artificial intelligence systems, music, image effects, etc. The "Syntesis Museum" was created with data provided by open technologies [14].

5 Conclusions

In the present work, the study and classification of the characteristics of the facades of the neoclassical, eclectic and interwar houses of Athens were presented and analyzed. The available literature and resources from the internet such as websites, databases, etc. were used. For their organization, the VRA Core metadata model in version 4.0, that created in the XML markup language, was used. The VRA Core 4.0 refers to a specific Project, Collection, or Image and includes 19 elements and 10 XML attributes to describe elements and subcomponents that used in combination with the Getty Research Institute Vocabularies for the art, architecture (AAT), and geographic locations (TGN).

Metadata translated into the English language to be useful worldwide, as it was observed that in most databases for the Athenian houses, from the 19th until the early 20th century, the official language is Greek. Some of the information of the databases collected by crowdsourcing.

Since the metadata is organized, an HBIM platform could be created. In this platform, can be included information about the historic buildings as also their three-dimensional model. This information could be linked to a geographical system by an external link.

The 3D models could be imported into a database created with the VRML (Virtual Reality Markup Language) and Javascript language. As a result, information about Athenian houses could be digitalized. In addition, open data could be used for museum creation in Unity 3D or 2D platforms.

In the future, this research will focus on the creation of a database in which the location, the three-dimensional illustration, and the provision of information of the characteristics of the facades of the houses in Athens, from 1830 to 1940 will be provided. Moreover, further study on this subject would be interesting to extend to all the houses of Greece during the chronological period 1830–1940, apart from the creation of the database for the facades of the houses in Athens.

Acknowledgements. The publication of this paper has been partly supported by the University of Piraeus Research Center (UPRC).

References

1. Metadata: Retrieved from Repository Kallipos. https://repository.kallipos.gr/bitstream/11419/1682/1/02_chapter_3.pdf (2015)
2. Holley, R.: Crowdsourcing and social engagement: potential, power and freedom for libraries and users. In: Specific Rim Digital Library Alliance (PRDLA) Annual Meeting, Auckland, New Zealand (2009)
3. Sylaiou, S., Lagoudi, E.: Utilizing crowd intelligence: crowdsourcing applications in cultural heritage. In: 1st CAA GR Conference, pp 179–185. Rethimno (2014). https://doi.org/10.13140/RG.2.1.2213.3529
4. Biris, M, Kardamitsi-Adami, M: Neoclassical Architecture in Greece. Melissa, Athens (2001)

5. Wikipedia: Retrieved from https://el.wikipedia.org/wiki/%CE%92%CE%AC%CF%83% CE%B7_%CE%B4%CE%B5%CE%B4%CE%BF%CE%BC%CE%AD%CE%BD%CF% 89%CE%BD (2020–21)
6. Biris, M.: Athenian Architecture: 1875–1925. Melissa, Athens (2003)
7. Roussi, V.: The houses of the interwar period in Attica: urban, suburban, country house. National Technical University of Athens, Athens. http://hdl.handle.net/10442/hedi/30337 (2011)
8. Vra Core 4.0 Element Description: Retrieved from https://www.loc.gov/standards/vracore/ VRA_Core4_Element_Description.pdf (2007)
9. Harpring, P.: Getty vocabularies and LOD introduction. https://www.getty.edu/research/tools/ vocabularies/cidoc_getty_vocabs_lod.pdf (2014)
10. Quattrini, R., Malinverni, E.S., Clini, P., Nespeca, R., Orlietti, E.: From TLS to HBIM. High quality semantically-aware 3D modeling of complex architecture. The International Archives of the Photogrammetry, Remote Sensing and Spatial Information Sciences **XL-5/W4**, 367– 374 (2015). https://doi.org/10.5194/isprsarchives-XL-5-W4-367-2015
11. Doulamis, A., Doulamis, N., Ioannidis, C., Chrysouli, C., Grammalidis, N., Dimitropoulos, K., Potsiou, C., Stathopoulou, E.-K., Ioannides, M.: 5D modelling: an efficient approach for creating spatiotemporal predictive 3D maps of large-scale cultural resources. ISPRS Annals of the Photogrammetry, Remote Sensing and Spatial Information Sciences **II-5/W3**, 61–68 (2015). https://doi.org/10.5194/isprsannals-II-5-W3-61-2015
12. Prizeman, O, Jones, BC, Parisi, M, & Pezzica, C (2018) How can century-old architectural hierarchies for the design of public libraries be re-interpreted and re-used? 481- 494. doi: https://doi.org/10.1108/JCHMSD-08-2017-0051
13. Brumana, R., et al.: HBIM feeding open access vault inventory through GeoDB HUB. In: Ioannides, M., et al. (eds.) EuroMed 2018. LNCS, vol. 11196, pp. 27–38. Springer, Cham (2018). https://doi.org/10.1007/978-3-030-01762-0_3
14. Tsirliganis, N., Pavlidis, G., Koutsoudis, A., Papadopoulou, D., Tsompanopoulos, A., Stavroglou, K., Loukou, Z., Chamzas, C.: Archiving cultural objects in the 21st century. J. Cult. Herit. **5**(4), 379–384 (2004). https://doi.org/10.1016/j.culher.2004.04.001
15. Kiourt, C., Koustsoudis, A., Arnaoutoglou, F., Petsa, G., Markantonatou, S., Pavlidis, G.: A dynamic web - based 3D virtual museum framework based on open data. Atena's Research Center, Greece. (2015). https://doi.org/10.1109/DigitalHeritage.2015.7419589
16. Doulamis, A., Voulodimos, A., Protopapadakis, E., Doulamis, N., Makantasis, K.: Automatic 3d modeling and reconstruction of cultural heritage sites from twitter images. Sustainability **12**(10), 4223 (2020). https://doi.org/10.3390/su12104223

The Value of 3D Modeling of Cultural Heritage Monuments with the Method of Digital Photogrammetry for Use in Augmented Reality Applications

Anastasia Lampropoulou(✉) ⑩ and Spyros Siakas ⑩

University of West Attica, Agiou Spyridonos, 12243 Egaleo, Greece
{alampropoulou,sthsiakas}@uniwa.gr

Abstract. Nowadays, the need to digitize cultural heritage sites and present them to the public in original and easily accessible ways is very important. The advantages are many both in times when Museums and archeological sites are open, and in times of forced closure such as the Covid-19 pandemic. As a result, there is more motivation and interest from the spectators, young and old, easy access and from remote areas, the ability to travel the collection outside the museums. Also due to the limited space of the museums there are exhibits that remain in warehouses and are not exhibited in the collections. The digital documentation enables the enrichment and display of a large volume of exhibits virtually. The dynamics of Photogrammetry with the rapid and continuous evolution of software and the ability to utilize them by many specialties gives rise to this study. The basic premise is that with simple media such as a compact camera and the right software, 3D exhibits such as the funeral masks and personal belongings of the 18 21 fighters can be reproduced, many of which are in storage. The conjuncture of 200 years since the beginning of the Greek Revolution gave even greater impetus to the investigation of ways of presenting them using AR Technology.

Keywords: Photogrametry · Cultural Herritage · Monuments digitization · Blender · Model decimation · Distance exhibition · Augmented Reality · Pandemic period

1 Introduction

In the course of the University of West Attica "3D environment design" and due to the celebration of the 200th anniversary of the Greek E-revolution of 1821, it was decided to create a series of works on this subject. The models were created with Blender software on the one hand and digital Photogrammetry on the other. For the Photogrammetry procedures, cooperation was concluded with three major museums: the National History Museum and the Athens War Museum and Tripoli department. The result was the creation of models of the funeral masks of the fighters of 1821 and other objects. Many of them were stored and inaccessible to the public. These specially processed models would have

A. Moropoulou et al. (Eds.): TMM_CH 2021, CCIS 1574, pp. 79–84, 2022.
https://doi.org/10.1007/978-3-031-20253-7_7

the potential to be utilized in an Augmented Reality application for public presentation and educational use.

The advent of the pandemic during the development of the project demonstrated even more strongly the need to digitize the cultural heritage and highlight it through digital applications. New needs emerged in areas such as education and culture. The result was a shift to distance education, both formal and informal during this period. Museum education that is identified with aesthetic education [1] had already begun to change form and move in a digital direction. In this way the Museum experience began to have the potential to become more attractive through the interactivity of the learning environment [2]. Museums today are exhibition spaces but at the same time provide education in various ways [3]. The use of augmented reality is nowadays more and more frequent, since museums use the advantages it provides [4]. A cultural institution or artists can use this technology to highlight their exhibits with greater originality [5]. To achieve this it is necessary to create the three-dimensional models of the exhibits that will then be utilized in this direction.

1.1 Purpose and Research Questions

Based on the above, the purpose of the work is to create accurate copies, using the method of Photogrammetry, of the funeral masks and objects of the fighters of 1821 for their digital presentation in the application of Augmented Reality. Sub-objectives were: to select the appropriate programs based on their fidelity, speed and possible free availability, to use simple media such as a compact camera, existing lighting and museum media, free software for further processing in order to include them into an AR application. Research questions that arose after the aforementioned targeting were the following:

- In what ways can Photogrammetry help highlight cultural heritage remotely even during a pandemic period?
- What are the quality parameters that will make possible the efficient process of collecting the digital material to import them into a photogrammetry program?
- What are the quality characteristics for a model produced by Photogrammetry to be imported in an AR application?
- How important is the role of the Blender program in this process in the final production of the model to be utilized?

1.2 Methodology

For this purpose, bibliography was utilized and a case study was created in the museum that controls and utilizes the above conditions. Action research with on-site photography work in museums, problem identification and solution by simple means are the dominant element in this study.

2 Using Digital Photogrammetry for Cultural Heritage Reconstruction

2.1 Benefits of 3D Modeling with Digital Photogrammetry

In addition to the use of design programs to create 3D models, the technique of Photogrammetry is increasingly used. The process of digital photogrammetry can be described as an input-processing-output system that requires the appropriate hardware and software. By taking photos from at least two different positions, so-called "visual contacts" can be developed by each camera as points on the object to be represented [6].

Any digital camera can be used to take pictures. 3D model reconstruction methods based on SFM (structure from motion) algorithms also require overlapping images with angular displacement [7]. In this way the photos are connected in order to create a point cloud, which with the appropriate processing turns into a grid (mesh), and then into a three-dimensional object. At the end, the color, materials and texture are added, information that is in the collected photos.

The most obvious reasons for the importance of 3D modeling of monuments are: their precise documentation for restoration in case of destruction, the creation of valuable educational resources for students and researchers, the visualization from a point of view that is impossible to access from the world due to either of size or accessibility, interaction with objects without the risk of damage and finally virtual tourism especially in a period when museums are closed such as the pandemic period [8].

2.2 Photogrammetry in the Museum with Simple Tools

Photograsmetry consists mainly of three phases [9]: the preparation where practical issues such as photography issues are defined, the digital capture of photographs by simple means [10] and finally the processing of data by photogrammetry software. In relation to the present work, which aims to utilize the models from a toy machine, we add the stages of reducing the number of triangles/polygons [11] and reducing the file size of the uv map produced by the photogrammetry program.

Fig. 1. Funeral mask of Nikitaras, National and Historical Museum of Greece

Based on all the above, the preparation included the permission of the museums for the Photography and specifically of the National Historical Museum and the War

Museum respectively. In it, the objects that would be photographed were precisely determined. This request was also accompanied by a visit to the museums to determine the available conditions. A simple Nikon Coolpix compact camera, a table provided by the museums for the placement of objects and the lighting in the room were used for the photography. A very important role was played by changing the white balance of the camera for better control of the glosses that existed. A patterned cloth (Fig. 1) was placed on the table as a base, to facilitate the operation of the algorithm in distinguishing object background as there was movement around the subject for taking photos.

2.3   Combining Photogrammetry with Blender

After the capture of the pictures the Reality Capture and 3df Zefyr programs were used for the reconstruction of the models and comparative evaluation of the performance. Both programs delivered reliable models (Fig. 2), with Reality Capture having an advantage over costume models in the performance of details and a difference in the speed.

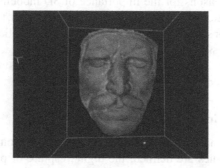

Fig. 2. Phptogrametered model of Funeral mask of Theodoros Kolokotronis

However, today there is a great evolution and improvement in 3df Zefyr and these differences are smoothed out. After the export of the models it was necessary to reduce the number of triangles. Blender and the decimate modifier tool were used for this purpose. This program also made it possible to intervene in micro imperfections that arose in the event of an excessive reduction of the triangles that might be deemed necessary. This was very important to maintain the uniformity of the model and its fidelity compared to the original. It was also very important to reduce the volume of the uv map file. The above two steps lead to efficient utilization of phogrametered models by gaming machines.

2.4   Types of Digital Presentation of Photogrametered Models

Many forms can be used for the presentation of the 3D models. A very significant tool is Sketchfab. There the models can be uploaded and can represented in many ways including VR and annotation tools. Simple manipulations such us rotate and scale can give the user the freedom to see the object from many aspects. A link is provided for each model and also embedded code. With the use of QR codes the access is possible from printed forms such as posters, brochures etc. Further more AR applications that use image targets can be used from museums for more enhancing results that gives to the users more interesting learning experiences [4] and also gives flexibility to the exhibitions inside or outside the museum with physical or digital ways.

3 Conclusion

In conclusion, we can say that digital Photogrammetry is a valuable tool that can be used to highlight Cultural Heritage Monuments through interactive, expansive applications with success. It makes it possible to overcome the limitation of the physical space of museums and to highlight the cultural heritage treasures that are stored or not even in the period of violent closure such as the period of the pandemic. Photogrametry programs can be used simply and produce satisfactory results. Simple tools as compact digital cameras, the existing lighting with white balance regulation can give very good results. Futher work with free programs like Blender can giveeven more excellent results.

To create models that will be used in gaming machines and Augmented Reality applications, necessary steps are: preparation, capturing photos, inserting them in the photogrametry program, reducing triangles/polygons, reducing the volume of the uv map file in an image editor. Utilizing the Blender program gives great possibilities both for the stage of reducing polygons in an easy way and in the further processing of the model.

4 Further Prospects

For the close future is critical point, the use of the produced models in an organized user friendly mobile app. The combination of printed media with many different forms with the use of mobile phones or tablets will give an additional pedagogical value to the monuments and museums.

References

1. Νικονάνου, Ν., Μπούνια, Α., Φιλιππουπολίτη, Α., Χουρμουζιάδη, Α., Γιαννούτσου, Ν.: Μουσειακή Μάθηση Και Εμπειρία Στον 21ο Αιώνα. Ελληνικά ακαδημαϊκά συγγράμματα και βοηθήματα. www.kalipos.gr (2015). Last Accessed 9 Apr 2021
2. Günay, B.: Museum concept from past to present and importance of museums as centers of art education. Procedia - Social and Behavioral Sciences **55**, 1250–1258 (2012)
3. Μανώλη, Β.: Ψηφιακά παιχνίδια σε ιστοσελίδες ελληνικών μουσείων για μαθητές Δημοτικού Σχολείου. Κόρινθος, Πανεπιστήμιο Πελοποννήσου. http://korinthos.uop. gr/~hcicte10/proceedings/70.pdf (2010). Last Accessed 20 Nov 2017
4. Billock, J.: Five augmented reality experiences that bring museum exhibits to life. https://www.smithsonianmag.com/travel/expanding-exhibits-augmented-reality 180963810/AR features allow visitors to explore historical spaces and artifacts in new ways (2017). Last Accessed 20 Apr 2021
5. Αναγνωστοπούλου, Α.: Η χρήση της Επαυξημένης Πραγματικότητας (AR) σε εφαρμογές eLearning, Μελέτη περίπτωσης: Ίδρυμα «Κωνσταντίνος Γ. Καραμανλής» (Ι.Κ.Κ.), Τμήμα Γραφιστικής και Οπτικής Επικοινωνίας 3D Animation, Πανεπιστήμιο Δυτικής Αττικής **1**(1) (2020)

6. Haming, K., Peters, G.: The structure - from - motion reconstruction pipeline, a survey with focus on shortimage sequences. Kybernetika, 46(5), 926- 937 (2010)
7. Bemis, S., Micklethwait, S., Turner, D., James, M.: Ground-based and UAV-Based photogrammetry: A multi-scale, highresolution mapping tool for structural geology and paleoseismology. J. Struct. Geol. **69**, 163e178 (2014)
8. El-Hakim, S.F., Beraldin, J.-A., Picard, M., Godin, G.: Detailed 3D reconstruction of large-scale heritage sites with integrated techniques. IEEE Computer Graphics and Applications **24**(3), 21–29 (2004). https://doi.org/10.1109/MCG.2004.1318815
9. Pavlidis, G., Koutsoudis, A., Arnaoutoglou, F., Tsioukas, V., Chamzas, C.: Methods for 3D digitization of cultural heritage. J. Cult. Herit. **8**(1), 93–98 (2007)
10. Λαμπροπούλου, Α.: Η αξιοποίηση της 3D σχεδίασης και της φωτογραμμετρίας στη δημιουργία παιγνιωδών εκπαιδευτικών δραστηριοτήτων. Open Journal of Animation, Film and Interactive Media in Education and Culture [AFIMinEC] **1**(1) (2020)
11. Liu, B., Davis, T.: Game asset considerations for facial animation, CGAMES 2013. In: The 18th International Conference on Computer Games, pp. 159–163 (2013)

IASIS-Integrated Cultural Heritage Management System: A Christian Monastery, a Muslim Mosque and a Contemporary State Administrative Building, Ioannina: Digital Approach

Athina Chroni[1]([⊠]) [iD] and Andreas Georgopoulos[2] [iD]

[1] Hellenic Ministry of Culture and Sports-General Directorate of Antiquities and Cultural Heritage, Postdoctoral Research Associate-National Technical University of Athens, 20, Paramithias Street, 10435 Athens, Greece
athina.chroni@gmail.com

[2] Laboratory of Photogrammetry-National Technical University of Athens, 9, Iroon Polytechniou st., 15780 Athens, Greece
drag@central.ntua.gr

Abstract. Under the perspective of exploring and restoring the cultural context of the Byzantine and Post-Byzantine era of Ioannina city and a cultural heritage-open access approach, the 3D digital abstractive rendering for certain landmarks of Ioannina city's afore-mentioned periods has been the stepping stone for further developing *IASIS*, an integrated system for documenting, protecting and highlighting cultural heritage in the framework of the related Postdoctoral Research Project, the digital products of which are available via a participatory interactive web-based platform [34], a virtual museum [36] and QR coded interactive labels set in the city's public space, with the support of the Municipality of Ioannina.

Ultimate goal, to activate, primarily, the local community in the direction of participation in matters of culture and cultural heritage preservation via innovative, open-access software and methodologies, through a user-friendly interface and an open-culture mentality, thus reinforcing and restoring the democratic dimension of culture.

The specific paper forms the second part of *Hagia Paraskevi* Christian Byzantine Monastery-*Namaz Giyah* Muslim Mosque-*Perifereia* Hellenic Republic Administrative Building cultural landmarks' integrated management, i.e., the landmarks' digital approach and dissemination of scientific information to people's and scientists' community, in the framework of *IASIS* Postdoctoral Research Project.

Keywords: Cultural heritage · Documentation · Digitization · GIS · Photogrammetry · 3-D Modelling · Open sources · Ioannina

---

Implemented by Athina Chroni, Dr. Archaeologist, supervised by Professor Andreas Georgopoulos, Laboratory of Photogrammetry-National Technical University of Athens

1 Introduction

1.1 Application Method – Tools of the Digital Project

Main aspect of the specific Postdoctoral Research Project, i.e., *IASIS*, has been the implementation of free data sources and software, thus complying with the *values-based approach* model of cultural heritage management, emphasizing the values attributed to cultural heritage by different interest groups of people.[1] [3] The scientific research project has been articulated on the following components, each one representing the related work phase and methodology implemented in a successive procedure:

- Extensive documentation based on historiographic, bibliographic and archaeological data combined with cartographic and topographic data, as well as with optical depictions such as engravings, paintings, postcards, terrestrial and aerial photographs, of the oldest possible date they can be traced, the afore-mentioned crosschecked with the contemporary city's remote sensing imagery[2]. For the implementation of the specific work phase extensive bibliographic research was carried out making use of online library platforms, commercially available bibliography and published archaeological data, respecting the principles of *copyright*, in accordance with the appropriate references, remote sensing imagery as well.
- Implementation of a GIS for achieving flexible, multi-layered management of the varied data as well as laying the foundations for a web database. The *QGIS* free software has been implemented. [41]
- 3D digital representation of the selected landmarks, overlayed on an image product including always the air view of the modern city, in order to render the sense of each landmark's interaction with the urban web and figure out the alterations of the urban fabric, aiming also at a more recognizable view of the city from the part of the end users. The *Sketchup* free software has been implemented. [43]
- Development of an online virtual museum, an online website and an online city audio tour platform proposing cultural routes in the city, based on the research's cultural and scientific axis, aiming at rendering *IASIS* project userfriendly and opening up to the people's community. The *Artsteps*, the *WIX* and the *izi.travel* free platforms have been respectively implemented. [30, 37, 48]
- QR coded interactive labels set at the specific sites, where the landmark buildings used to stand and have been now 3D digitally developed, under the intention to achieve more interaction of the project with the local community and thus fulfil the role of active portals to *IASIS* virtual environment. The *QR Code Generator* free platform has been implemented. [42]

---

[1] The *values-based approach* cultural heritage management model emerging in the western world from the 1980s onwards; it was accompanied by the development of the *post-processual archaeology theory* [3,35].

[2] The Directorate of Environment and Urban Planning-Municipality of Ioannina [31], the Hellenic Cadastre [46] and the British School at Athens [44] contributing related data for free.

It should be noted that the cultural sites' documentation has formed the basic concept of the research project, while their consequent 3D digital rendering has formed the medium for visualizing cultural data and, thus, achieving its communication to the public.

1.2 The Site Selected: Deconstruction of the Cultural Palimpsest

The site where nowadays Ioannina's modern landmark of *Perifereia*[3] Hellenic Republic Administrative Building and *Pyrros* Central Square, at a most neuralgic spot of the city center, selected for the present paper, represents a multiple landmark's site, translated to a "cultural palimpsest", deployed as following:

- *Hagia Paraskevi* Christian Byzantine monastery dated, approximately, in the year 528 as estimated. Status: destroyed between the years 1431 -1584,[4] as estimated. [1, 2, 5, 25, 33]
- *Namaz Giyah* Muslim *metzit*, at its first stage/*mosque*, at its last phase, dated in the years 1431–1584,[5] as estimated. Status: destroyed approximately in 1930. [1, 2, 12, 15, 18, 24, 25, 32]
- The afore-mentioned religious buildings' cemeteries. Status: destroyed. [1, 2, 12, 15, 18, 24, 25, 32]
- *Perifereia* Hellenic Republic Administrative Building, constructed in 1935. Status: existing. [40]

2 *Hagia Paraskevi* Christian Monastery, *Namaz Giyah* Muslim Mosque, *Perifereia* State Administrative Building: Form and characteristics

2.1 Form

Hagia Paraskevi Christian Monastery

Given that the Ottomans, when having conquered Ioannina in 1430, did not have the right to reside in the Castle, [25] according to *Sinan Pasha Decree*, the site of Hagia Paraskevi monastic building complex would have been an ideal choice for the newcomers:[6] located at the suburbs of the city, on a hill, offering thus panoramic view of the greater area, in case of danger, and being, probably, enclosed by a wall, it would ensure protection, offering, at the same time, residency, i.e., the monastic cells, a site for praying and, outside the wall, a site for a burial area. The monastic building complex's typology[7] would be

---

[3] "Perifereia" for the Greek word "Region".

[4] Taking into account the existing documentation, the afore-mentioned time range could be further limited to the years 1480–1579.

[5] The dating corresponding to the destruction of the former Christian religious building.

[6] Taking into consideration Lambridis' citation and the Ottoman State's official report, as well as crosschecking with the description of Namaz Giyah Muslim mosque's greater area by Evliya Celebi, visiting Ioannina in 1670 [12, 18, 24].

[7] Fulfilling the Muslim religious building complexes typology [23].

similar to the one of *Kaisariani* Christian monastery, (Fig. 1) of the 11th century, given that Christian monastic complexes followed a rather stable typology through time.[8]

Given that Namaz Giyah's plan view[9] is depicted in Melirrytos (& Christides) urban plan of 1916–1918 and accepting that the *katholikon* of the monastery might have become, in the years 1431–1584, the main prayer site of Namaz Giyah, originally a *metzit*,[10] then we might assume a continuity in form between the two religious buildings, i.e., that Hagia Paraskevi's *katholikon* also had a square plan view, not including a narthex, which, in case there might be one, it should have been located probably at the *katholikon*'s western side (later on, the *narthex*, if really having existed, becoming the *porch* of the Muslim religious building).

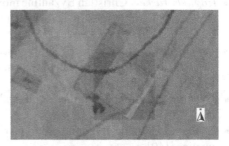

Fig. 1. *Kaisariani* Monastery, Attica, Greece, 11th century. Sketch by Barsky (Christian Orthodox monk and traveler from Kiev.), 1745. [Imagery source: © 21]

Fig. 2. Screenshot from GIS developed for *IASIS* project. Layering of *Moni Latomou* plan view, [27] (Moni Latomou, Thessaloniki, Greece, first half of the 5th century) with the urban plan of Ioannina/1916–1918/Implemented by Melirrytos (& Christides)-Signed by Melirrytos. [Imagery source: Digital processing by Athina Chroni. © 7, © 31]

Considering the estimated dating of Hagia Paraskevi as already cited, it is very probable that the *katholikon* of Latomou Monastery, in Thessaloniki, dated in the first half of the 5th c. A.D. having a square wooden dome and a square plan view as well, [7, 20, 27] might have been the prototype for the *katholikon* under question. (Fig. 2).

Namaz Giyah Muslim Mosque
According to official Ottoman documentation, Namaz Giyah religious building complex covered an area of 15 acres, and was located at the homonymous district of Ioannina,

---

[8] Monasticism officially appears from the middle of the 2nd c. AD., while from the first half of the 4th c. AD. the organized character of monks' commune is required. The Byzantine monasteries were enclosed by a perimetric wall, the shape of which depended on the related site's geomorphology [19].

[9] A square plan view for the prayer hall building and a rectangular plan view for the porch at its western side in Melirrytos (& Christides) urban plan of 1916–1918 [31].

[10] Keeping, nevertheless, the rest of the religious building complex's structural units.

the most prominent one. The building complex included a place of prayer, a *meddresse*, a cemetery, a spot for placing the dead and a courtyard. The full name of the *waqf* is cited as "Deferdar Mustafa Efendi" [24].

Fig. 3. Namaz Giyah Muslim mosque. View from the northeast. Left: Postal card of unknown date and publisher. [Imagery source: Private collection] Digital processing by Athina Chroni, indicating spatial correlation with the urban web of the contemporary city of Ioannina. Right: Photograph by Ernest Hébrard, dated app. 1920. [Imagery source: © 28]

Studying Melirrytos' (& Christides') map,[11] it becomes clear that the Muslim mosque, having succeeded the Christian monastery, keeps the square plan view. In its first phase, as a *metzit*, probably no transformations might have occurred, while in its next phase, as a *mosque*, after 1617,[12] it is very probable that changes might have occurred concerning the roof and the interior.

As depicted in postcards and photographs of the beginning of the 20th century, (Fig. 3) the mosque in its last phase had a four-sided tiled roof, covering the square plan view prayer hall building, the four Byzantine columns, still supporting, most probably, the mosque's porch. The minaret was placed at the southwestern corner of the mosque, following the prevailing mosque typology.[13]

Cemeteries of Hagia Paraskevi Christian Monastery and Namaz Giyah Muslim Mosque
For reasons of hygiene, the cemeteries of the monasteries, as well as those of the cities, were situated *extra muros*[14] and were usually bordered by a low wall.[15] [19].

---

[11] Under the consideration that the specific map has a high degree of accuracy.

[12] In the Muslims' group praying (*namaz*) it is necessary for the *imam* to be visible and audible by all the participants [23]: a dome resting on crossed arches, as probably originated in the Christian religious building, would be unfunctional for the Muslim ritual, rendering, thus, obligatory a reconstruction of the building.

[13] The architecture of the mosque is completed by the minaret, which in most mosques of Ioannina is located at the SW corner of the main prayer hall building, so that its volume protrudes outwards [24]. The typological development of the surviving mosques of Ioannina plan view, as well as those whose composition has been read with certainty, always follows the same standards [24].

[14] Outside the walls.

[15] The same principles also applying for the Muslim cemeteries [23].

Lambridis' description on Namaz Giyah cemetery is quite clear.[16] [18] The greater area of the cemeteries around Namaz Giyah mosque is clearly depicted in Jean-Denis Barbié du Bocage's map, dated in the beginning of the 19th c.[17] Namaz Giyah's one of the three cemeteries was situated where nowadays the contemporary *Pyrros* square of the modern city, opposite *Perifereia* State Administrative Building. [1, 9, 11, 14, 18, 29] The old age of the specific burial site is emphasized by Aravantinos. [1].

Fig. 4. Left: View of Namaz Giyah mosque and eastern cemetery from the south. The green-coloured area indicating the site of Namaz Giyah mosque, former Hagia Paraskevi monastery, and the yellow-coloured area indicating the site of one, out of three, respective cemeteries. Digital processing by Athina Chroni. Copper engraving by C.R. Cockerell (sketch) και J. Smith (engraving), 1820. [10] [Imagery source: © 22] Right: View of Namaz Giyah mosque and eastern cemetery from the south. Yanina. Palace of Ali Pacha. Sketch by R. Cockerell, engraving by T. Higham, 1832. [Imagery source: © 8] Digital processing by Athina Chroni.

Fig. 5. Ioannina. 12/13 May 1849. E. Lear, Watercolor and sepia ink over graphite on tan paper with watermark. View of Namaz Giyah eastern cemetery from the south. The yellow-coloured area indicating the site of one, out of three, Namaz Giyah's cemeteries, where originally, probably, Hagia Paraskevi's cemetery. [Imagery source: © 38] Digital processing by Athina Chroni.

Optical depictions of the end of the 19th century, further complete fragments of Namaz Giyah's mosque and cemetery puzzle. It is in the specific cemetery to the east of the mosque, where, generally, all the Ottomans[18] used to be buried, being the official Muslim cemetery until 1923. [9, 14] If we accept that the Muslim religious building complex had been developed where formerly the Christian monastery building complex, then we should also accept a spatial coincidence for the respective cemeteries as well. (Figs. 4 and 5).

---

[16] Lampridis' description confirms that the site of the pre-existing cemetery, i.e., of Hagia Paraskevi, was not walled. The phrase "and the contents of each one remained intact" could be assumed to indicate earlier existing tombs, perhaps of the Christian cemetery which, probably, were not destroyed by the newly arrived Ottomans [18].

[17] In 1811–1815, according to Kanetakis [11].

[18] Only everyday people [16].

2.2 Characteristics

The comparative study (Fig. 6) of the destroyed Namaz Giyah mosque in relation to Fethiye mosque still standing at the SE Acropolis of the Castle of Ioannina, [4] in the GIS environment already developed for *IASIS* project, proved morphological identification, resulting from the following data:

- An, almost, square plan view of the prayer hall building.
- Location of the minaret at the SW corner of the prayer hall building.
- Location of the mihrap towards Mecca.
- Location of a porch at the prayer hall building, antidiametrically to the mihrap.

Concerning the orientation, in the Muslim mosque, the eastern wall is considered to be the one that is perpendicular to the theoretical axis that connects the mosque with Mecca, and not necessarily with the east. [24] On this wall is situated the *mihrap*, a niche in the wall, colorfully decorated. [26] This niche is showing the direction to Mecca [45].[19]

Regarding the length and the width of the mosque's prayer hall building,[20] the respective data have been derived from Mellirrytos' (& Christides') urban plan/1916–1918 digital processing in the environment of the GIS developed for *IASIS* project. Mellirrytos' (& Christides') urban plan clearly depicts the mosque's prayer hall building, the porch, a secondary building and the site of the main cemetery to the east. Also, the altitude map curves of the specific hill site. (Fig. 7) As a result, the specific urban plan becomes the link between the modern era and the Byzantine and Post-Byzantine era of Ioannina, the study of which confirms Smyris' citation on Namaz Giyah's porch dimensions. [24].

Regarding the height of Hagia Paraskevi *katholikon*, no assumptions should be made, except if we accept a continuity in form with the mosque's prayer hall. The height of the four Byzantine columns, i.e., 2.00 m, as cited by Lambridis [18] does not permit us to assume that they supported a dome or a roof, unless it was a building of a limited height.

Regarding the height of Namaz Giyah's prayer hall building, the minaret's height, formed a reference point.[21] (Fig. 8) Comparative study of Kanetakis' vertical view of

---

[19] In Greece, the mosques that emerged from the transformation of pre-existing Christian churches do not apply with this axis (to the southeast in Greece) and are oriented towards the east, following the Christian religious buildings orientation towards the east. In this case, the mihrap of the Muslim mosque does not coincide with the niche of the Christian church's chancel, and is located to the right [23].

[20] Representing also Hagia Paraskevi's *katholikon*, under the continuity-in-form-assumption.

[21] Given the fact that:

- According to Smyris, "the typological development of the plan view of the mosques of Ioannina, always follows the same type." [24]

- The research project of Kombou et al. on the typology of the 17 Muslim mosques of Ioannina confirmed that the minaret in each one of 10 of the afore-mentioned mosques had a height of 20.00 m minimum to 24.10 maximum [13].

 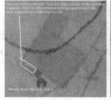 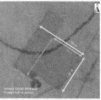

Fig. 6. Screenshot from GIS developed for *IASIS* project. Layering of the ortho imagery 2015 with the urban plan of Ioannina/1916–1918/Implemented by Melirrytos (& Christides)-Signed by Melirrytos. We should admit as proper orientation the one of Fethiye mosque, given that the building surviving until now represents the last construction phase of the mosque, as implemented in the framework of Ali Pasha's building program of the southeastern citadel of the Castle of Ioannina. The slight deviation concerning the orientation between the two Muslim mosques, is probably due to the continuity of form of Namaz Giyah mosque from the previous Christian monastery. [Imagery source: © 46, © 31] Digital processing by Athina Chroni.

Fig. 7. Screenshot from GIS developed for *IASIS* project. Vector layering of metrics indications for Namaz Giyah mosque's building on the urban plan of Ioannina/1916–1918/Implemented by Melirrytos (& Christides)-Signed by Melirrytos. [Imagery source: © 31] Digital processing by Athina Chroni.

Fig. 8. Fethiye section plan d-d, by Kanetakis. [Imagery source: © 11] Digital processing by Athina Chroni.

Fethiye mosque[22] and Aspiotis' postal card, [47], crosschecked with Muslim religious architecture typology, led to the assumption that the height of Namaz Giyah mosque's minaret would not be lower than 20 m and not higher than 23.5 m. (Fig. 9).

3   3D Digital model Development

The optical product derived from the visibility activation of the georeferenced Mellirrytos' (& Christides') urban plan of 1916–1918 layered with the ortho image of 2015, has been chosen as the basic image to be imported in *Sketchup* software for developing the 3D model, thus ensuring the optical integration of the abstractively restored structural

---

[22] Located at the Castle's southeastern citadel [11].

Fig. 9. The square in which Ioannina was handed over to the Crown Prince Constantine. Postal card published by Aspiotis, in 1913. Photographic view of Namaz Giyah Muslim mosque from the northwest. It is clear that Namaz Giyah's prayer hall building and minaret follows the same building proportions as the one of Fethiye mosque's. [Imagery source: © 47] Digital processing by Athina Chroni.

Fig. 10. Sketchup software screenshot. Layering of the ortho imagery 2015 with the urban plan of Ioannina/1916–1918/Implemented by Melirrytos (& Christides)-Signed by Melirrytos. Left: Namaz Giyah prayer hall, porch, minaret and secondary building. Right: Cemetery area. [Imagery source: © 46, © 31] Digital processing by Athina Chroni.

volume in the city's urban web, permitting continuous comparative study between the past and the present urban web's status. (Fig. 10).

The 3D digital model has been developed under the reasoning of figuring out the interaction of the specific religious buildings' prayer hall[23] with the urban as well as with the natural environment, accepting the 3D model produced as representative for the prayer hall building of both religions, in successive chronological periods.

Concerning the cemetery site, only the area where nowadays the city's central square, i.e., the area to the east of the monastery's/mosque's site, has been 3D digitally implied. The tombs are implied by 3D rectangular vertical structures, their minimalistic approach representing tombstones for both religion's cemeteries.

---

[23] Being the unique part of the building complex providing adequate data for figuring out the location and the form of the building.

4 *IASIS* Website,[24] *IOANNINA 1430-1913* Virtual Museum,[25] QR Tagging

IASIS[26] website, (Fig. 11) furnishing cultural information data on the city, constantly updated, as well as being interactive with the people's community, fulfills the role of the portal to the project, giving also way out to a virtual museum.

Fig. 11. Screenshot of *IASIS* website. Designed and developed by Athina Chroni. [Imagery source: © 34]

Fig. 12. Screenshot of *IOANNINA 1430–1913* virtual museum. Designed and developed by Athina Chroni. [Imagery source: © 36]

A virtual museum has also been developed, where the visitor will have the opportunity to navigate in Ioannina city's cultural past. (Fig. 12) Text, image, sound and virtual walk-through-the-3D-digital-models mp.4 files, produced in the framework of this research project, are the virtual items of the exhibition, aiming to attract the viewer's attention, thus becoming an "open call" for a visit in the physical space of the modern city.

Under the perspective of reinforcing community participation and interaction with *IASIS* research project, QR coded interactive labels set at the specific sites, where the landmark buildings used to stand, become virtual portals to the digital products of the Postdoctoral Research Project, thus intervening in the physical urban web and succeeding to link the tangible with the intangible.

5 Conclusion

In the specific Postdoctoral Research Project Humanities and New Technologies have been combined for an integrated cultural heritage management.

Multiple scientific fields of New Technologies have been activated and fruitfully applied towards the direction of handling data, of various origin and quality, under the perspective of documenting, figuring out and, often, restoring cultural heritage assets,

---

[24] *IASIS*. https://athinachroni.wixsite.com/my-site-1, designed and developed by Athina Chroni.

[25] *IOANNINA 1430–1913*: https://www.artsteps.com/view/5feca5aafe659e68d58a48c8, designed and developed by Athina Chroni.

[26] *IASIS* acronym stands for **I**oannina **A**rchitectural & **S**ocietal **I**nfrastructure **S**tratification. [Fig. 11] The term *IASIS*, implying the concept of treatment/rehabilitation, constitutes an indirect reference both to the material as well as to the mental/emotional/psychological dimension of the research project's procedure.

thus preserving collective memory and cultural pluralism, fulfilling one more milestone: people's community (inter)active participation to the project, thus rendering each individual the defining component of the *locus*'[27] collective memory.

Given that the main objective of this research project was to explore the urban landscape at a specific period, the interaction of the destroyed landmarks' building complexes with the urban fabric and the related multicultural physiognomy of Ioannina in its Post-Byzantine period, the development of the digital model remained three-dimensional, the fourth dimension,[28] i.e., evolution over time, not included. Furthermore, the fifth dimension,[29] i.e., integrating information data, is fulfilled via the GIS developed in the framework of the specific project.

References

1. Aravantinos, P.: In: Vlastos, S.K. (ed.) Chronography of Epirus, vol. II. Publications, Athens (1856). Reprint: Koultoura Publications, Athens (2004)
2. Athenagoras: Neos Kouvaras. Epirotic Chronicles Magazine, Issue 4, Ioannina (1929)
3. Chroni, A.: Cultural heritage digitization & copyright issues. In: Proceedings of the 7th International Euro-Mediterranean Conference on Digital Heritage, ©Springer Nature Switzerland AG, ISSN 0302-9743, ISSN 1611-3349 (electronic), Lecture Notes in Computer Science ISBN 978-3-030-01761-3, ISBN 978-3-030-01762-0 (eBook), Library of Congress Control Number: 2018956722, Chapter 34, pp. 396–407. https://www.digitalmeetsculture.net/article/euromed-2018-proceedings-are-now-available/?fbclid=IwAR2nGI1eBUGlhcI0uIsObwKtd u41BOz9SSve1hMBaPYVyA83TZhgv9AuCE; https://www.springer.com/gp/book/978303 0017613?utm_campaign=bookpage_about_buyonpublisherssite&utm_medium=referral& utm_source=springerlink (2018)
4. Chroni, A., Georgopoulos, A.: Documentation and 3D digital modelling-the case of a byzantine christian temple and an ottoman Muslim mosque in Ioannina city, Greece. In: Proceedings of the 8th International Euro-Mediterranean Conference on Digital Heritage. ©Springer Nature Switzerland (2020)
5. Dakaris, S.: Ioannina, New Evroia. Monthly Inspection "Epirotiki Estia", Year A´, Issue Nr 6-October, Ioannina (1952)
6. Doulamis, A., et al.: 5D modelling: an efficient approach for creating spatiotemporal predictive 3d maps of large-scale cultural resources. ISPRS Annals of the Photogrammetry, Remote Sensing and Spatial Information Sciences, vol. II-5/W3, pp. 61–68 (2015)
7. Drandakis, N.: Byzantine Archeology, Volume I-Early Christian art up to the architecture of the years of Justinian, Issue II-The architecture of the 5th and 6th c. Publications "To Philologikon" Bookstore-V.G. Vassiliou, Athens (1976)
8. Finden, B.: Landscape and portrait illustrations to the Life and Works of Lord Byron, vol. II. Published by John Murray, London (31 Dec 1832)
9. Fotopoulos, K.: Giannina. Athens (1986)
10. Hughes, T.S.: Travels in Sicily, Greece and Albania. Printed for J. Mawman, London (1820)
11. Kanetakis, G.: The Castle: Contribution to the Urban History of Ioannina. Doctoral Thesis, Published by the Technical Chamber of Greece, Athens (1994)

---

[27] *Locus*: the latin word for "site", "location", defining "the place where something is situated or occurs" [39].

[28] 4D digital model [6].

[29] 5D digital model [17].

12. Kokolakis, M.: Evliya Celebi in Ioannina. Skoufas Magazine, Issue HD-1991/1, Ioannina (1991)
13. Kombou, M., Nikoloudi, D., Papantoniou, M.: Development of L.I.S. for the seventeen mosques of Ioannina and their representation in the modern city. Bachelor's Thesis, Supervised by Georgopoulos A. et al., National Technical University of Athens, Athens (2000)
14. Koulidas, K.: Ioannina that left. Ioannina (2010)
15. Koulidas, K.: The Muslim Vakif of the City of Ioannina. Publications of the Society on Epirotic Studies, Ioannina (2004)
16. Kourmantzis, G.: From the Byzantine to the Ottoman city (15th–18th century). In "Epirus, Society-Economy", Municipality of Ioannina, Ioannina (1987)
17. Kyriakaki, G., et al.: 4D Reconstruction of tangible cultural heritage objects from web-retrieved images. International Journal of Heritage in the Digital Era **3**(2), 431–451 (2014)
18. Lambridis, I.: Epirotic Studies. Volume II-Issue A': Description of the city of Ioannina. Vlastos-Varvarrigos Publications, Athens (1887)
19. Orlandos, A.: Monastery Architecture, No 64, 2nd edn. Publications of The Archaeological Society at Athens, Athens (1958)
20. Orlandos, A.: The Wood-roofed Early Christian Basilica in the Mediterranean Basin (in three parts). Publications of The Archaeological Society at Athens, No 36, Athens (1st Edition: 1952–1954, Repr. 1974. 2nd Edition in one vol. 1994)
21. Orlandos, A.: Medieval Monuments of the Plain of ATHENS and the Slopes of Ymittos-Pentelikos. Parnitha and Egaleo. Ministry of Education and Religions, Athens (1933)
22. Papastavros, A.: Ioannina of the 19th c. Dodoni-Odysseas Publications, Ioannina (2005)
23. Passadaios, A.: Polis (Constantinople) on the Bosporus-A Brief Systematic Guide. Publications of The Archaeological Society at Athens, No 96, Athens (1981)
24. Smyris, G.: The mosques of Ioannina and the urban planning of the Ottoman city. Epirotic Chronicles, vol. 34, Ioannina (2000)
25. Vranoussis, L.: On Historical and Topography of the Medieval Castle of Ioannina. Publications of the Society on Epirotic Studies, Ioannina (1968)
26. Xintaropoulos, S.: The orientation of the mosques in Argos and Nafplio. Bachelor's Thesis, School of Rural and Surveying Engineering-National Technical University of Athens, Athens (2008)
27. Xyggopoulos, A.: The katholikon of Latomou Monastery. Archaeological Bulletin of the General Ephorate of Antiquities and Museums, Athens (1929)
28. Yiakoumis H., Yerolympos A., Pédelahore de Loddis Ch.: Ernest Hébrard 1875–1933-La vie illustrée d' un architecte-De la Grece à l' Indochine. Potamos Publications, Athens (2001). ISBN 960-7563-74-3
29. Zygouris, T.: From Bernasconi to Hébrard- "Known" and Unknown Urban Maps of IOANNINA. Municipality of Ioannina-Zosimaia Public Library of Ioannina, Ioannina (2019)
30. Artsteps. https://www.artsteps.com/
31. Directorate of Environment and Urban Planning-Municipality of Ioannina. https://www.ioannina.gr/. Last Accessed 10 Jul 2021
32. Joseph and Esther Ganis Foundation. https://www.facebook.com/. Last Accessed 10 Jul 2021
33. Holy Metropolis of Ioannina. http://www.imioanninon.gr/main/?page_id=8. Last Accessed 10 Jul 2021
34. IASIS Website. https://athinachroni.wixsite.com/my-site-1. Last Accessed 10 Jul 2021
35. ICOMOS Australia-Burra Charter Archival Documents. https://australia.icomos.org/publications/burra-charter-practice-notes/burra-charter-archival-documents/. Last Accessed 10 Jul 2021

36. IOANNINA 1430–1913 Virtual Museum. https://www.artsteps.com/view/5feca5aafe659e6 8d58a48c8. Last Accessed 10 Jul 2021
37. Izi.travel. https://izi.travel/en. Last Accessed 10 Jul 2021
38. Lear Edward. Harvard University-Houghton Library. https://hollisarchives.lib.harvard.edu/ repositories/24/digital_objects/24431. Last Accessed 10 Jul 2021
39. Merriam-Webster Dictionnary. https://www.merriam-webster.com/dictionary/locus. Last Accessed 10 Jul 2021
40. Official Travel Guide of Ioannina. https://www.travelioannina.com/el/node/79. Last Accessed 10 Jul 2021
41. QGIS. https://www.qgis.org/en/site/. Last Accessed 10 Jul 2021
42. QR Code Generator. https://www.qr-code-generator.com/. Last Accessed 10 Jul 2021
43. SketchUp Make 2017. https://download.cnet.com/SketchUp-Make-2017/30006677_4-102 57337.html. Last Accessed 10 Jul 2021
44. The British School at Athens. https://www.bsa.ac.uk/. Last Accessed 10 Jul 2021
45. The Free Dictionnary. https://www.thefreedictionary.com/mihrab. Last Accessed 10 Jul 2021
46. The Hellenic Cadastre, www.ktimatologio.gr, last accessed 2021/07/10
47. Wikimedia Commons. Postal card Nr. 255. Published by Aspiotis in 1913. https://commons. wikimedia.org/wiki/File:Aspiotis_255.jpg. Last Accessed 10 Jul 2021
48. WIX. https://www.wix.com/. Last Accessed 10 Jul 2021

Conservation of Greek Neoclassical Facade Elements Through Their Integration in a HBIM Library

Elias Sakellaris[1](✉), Konstantina Siountri[1,2],
and Christos-Nikolaos Anagnostopoulos[2]

[1] Postgraduate Programme (M.Sc.) "Digital Culture, Smart Cities, IoT and Advanced Digital Technologies", Track "Digital Culture", Department of Informatics, University of Piraeus, Piraeus, Greece
{wpol18041,ksiountri}@unipi.gr, ksiountri@aegean.gr
[2] Cultural Technology and Communication Department, University of the Aegean, Mytilene, Greece
canag@aegean.gr

Abstract. The term HBIM (Heritage Building Information Modelling) refers to recording, modelling and managing monuments and buildings of cultural interest and so far gathers more academic interest than practical application. HBIM models of architectural elements can be fully parametric, meaning that typologies can be produced by them. Those elements can be integrated in digital libraries, which is a systematic way of capturing and storing architectural elements as "smart" data. In this paper, photogrammetry and laser scanning is used to capture primitive data of Greek neoclassical architecture elements. Subsequently, the way of designing, parameterizing and documenting of these elements is presented, through the creation of HBIM models. These models are integrated in a digital library consisted of neoclassical period typologies, ideal for their digital conservation. Additionally, the parameterization of a standard neoclassical facade which includes the library elements is investigated, based on the synthetic principles that define its architectural period. This research leads to conclusions in relation to the advantages of the HBIM methodology, setting the basis of a parametric HBIM library to be extended over other parts of the building or architectural periods.

Keywords: HBIM · Parametric design · Digital libraries · Scan-to-BIM · Heritage

1 Introduction

Building Information Modeling (BIM) has become a wide term for the parametric design of constructions, and it shows potential in applications of cultural heritage. A BIM for an existing or historical building can be used as a documentation and management tool for conservation work, renovations and building analysis [1]. The term Heritage Building Information Modeling (HBIM), defined as *"a novel solution whereby interactive parametric objects representing architectural elements are constructed from historic data,*

© The Author(s), under exclusive license to Springer Nature Switzerland AG 2022
A. Moropoulou et al. (Eds.): TMM_CH 2021, CCIS 1574, pp. 98–109, 2022.
https://doi.org/10.1007/978-3-031-20253-7_9

these elements (including detail behind the scan surface) are accurately mapped onto a point cloud or image-based survey" [2], which has been initiated at 2009 by M. Murphy, has been widely acclaimed between researchers in the field of cultural heritage (CH).

An ideal HBIM model must be very accurate in capturing the geometry of the existing building and provides all the necessary information to document its structure. The elements that constitute the building, so-called "families" in the most common BIM software, the Autodesk Revit, can be integrated into digital libraries, which are characterized by parametric reasoning and are semantically aware. This is therefore "smart" data that based on keywords are categorized and correlated based on architectural, constructional and historical information. There can be multiple advantages of these data, as they can be used for the integration and processing of time data, the analysis of the cost of interventions and the monitoring of the restoration and maintenance phases of the building.

In most BIM software programs, libraries are included with pre-defined parametric objects which are building parts like walls, doors, windows, slabs, beams, roofs etc., used to model the imminent building project. The user can choose the appropriate typology and edit its parameters in order to match the required dimensions and settings of its project. After combining these elements the model can be complete. Even with the wide contribution of users to create and upload in public sharing websites their own parametric objects there is lack of pre-defined parametric objects suitable for existing and historical buildings [1]. As a consequence, HBIM modelling requires many components to be created from scratch and this is a very time consuming process. Additionally, a BIM software allows information to enhance library objects, which is far more important in the field of CH, in regard with the historic background of each typology.

This research paper focuses on the creation of a database, but more in the sense of a library, which consists of architectural elements of neoclassical facades in Greece, with defined relationships that make them parametric. After the data acquisition, using aerial photogrammetry and terrestrial laser scanning, we select common neoclassical façade elements in order to model and parameterize them in a BIM environment. Those models are integrated as distinct entities in the library, setting the parameters of which one can edit them. This database will contribute to: a) the conservation of the elements implemented and the possibility to combine them in a range of typologies due to their parameterization and b) the creation of a neoclassical architecture facade template as a total of typology elements which obey the structure rules of symmetry, harmony and order.

The remainder of the paper is organized as follows. Firstly, related work of digital cultural heritage libraries is described. Subsequently, the methodology of modelling and parameterization of HBIM elements is analyzed, along with the methodology of creating a parametric neoclassical façade template based on elements of this library. Finally, the last section summarizes the conclusions of our work.

2 State of the Art

During 19th and early 20th century, many buildings of neoclassical architecture were constructed, most of which nowadays are listed. Those historic buildings are considered an important part of the Greek architecture and thus, they must be conserved in an organized and systematic way with technology holding an important role. Many attempts have been made for a database of neoclassical buildings including also the morphological elements and decorations found in their main facades [3]. Databases like these are excellent in order to define predominant features, while they can also be used to map the existence of specific architectural elements of a period in specific regions. However, the two-dimensional drawings that describe the geometry have low level of detail (LoD) in contrast to the three-dimensional models. Nowadays, there are advanced ways that make the digitization precise enough for conservation and this process can be set one step further with the hierarchical connection of each element of the database [4]. Additionally, the elements of a database can be treated as metadata that could be linked in the same database, or with elements from other databases and in this way interoperability is achieved [5].

The architectural elements of the neoclassical facades, ie. Doors, windows, balconies with porches and cornices are diverse, despite their obvious common elements, so it is difficult to design a formula that will summarize all their possible versions. Therefore, for the needs of this research, we will consider a common form from each category of façade elements. This work can be the basis for the future integration of many different elements of neoclassicism.

3   Analysis of HBIM Data Collection

The process of acquiring the primitive data is very significant for defining the geometry and especially in existing buildings of particular importance [6]. There are also additional steps regarding the configuration and preparation of the scan data and implementing the historic references. In BIM there are protocols for collaborative design processes that AEC industries use. Implementing BIM in Cultural Heritage (CH) monuments involves the following steps [7]:

a)   Historical-architectural-structural research
b)   Data collection (terrestrial laser scanning and aerial photogrammetry)
c)   Data processing (point cloud registration and configuration)
d)   Additional exports (mesh and texture)
e)   Separating every element from the rest of the building and modelling (in a BIM software)
f)   Implementation of metadata (as semantic components)

In the final step, after the model has become parametric and fully customizable, it can be saved as a component of an object library (Fig. 1), ideal for conservation.

Historical research is an integral part of any study of a historic structure, in order to identify and analyze its unique characteristics. The historical phases of the building over the ages are important and must become the basis of every documentation or restoration procedure. Additionally, the structural analysis which mainly concerns the identification and recording of construction materials is also prerequisite.

Creating an HBIM model requires metric information from all different parts of the structure as a first step. For the correct measurement, it is necessary to understand the object and all its structural components and there are several ways to collect dimensional data. Overtaking the traditional method of capturing building information, which is the use of conventional measuring tools such as tape measure, thread, spirit level and distance meter, there are now 3D digital survey techniques. These techniques are very fast, reliable, with excellent measurement accuracy and are performed without contact, which has a special value in sensitive monuments. Static terrestrial high resolution laser scanning can achieve the greatest accuracy among the methods and therefore it is very suitable to efficiently develop 3D models of heritage buildings, where precision is required for their documentation. Photogrammetry has been also established as a fast method of spatial data acquisition and can be completed using images captured with UAVs (drones). The advantage of using a drone is the ability to access inaccessible places, which are necessary for the complete recording of the object [8].

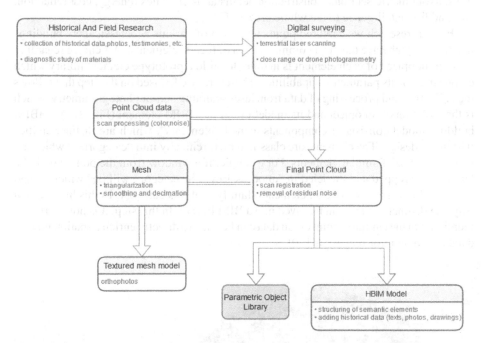

Fig. 1. The process of documenting data of cultural heritage in a library as parametric objects.

After the capturing of data, the additional point clouds of the scans and the drone need to be processed before modelled with a BIM software. During processing, the point cloud data are registered, aligned and merged into the same coordinate system. Handling scanned data involves removing residual noise and clearing the cloud of irrelevant information. The products of such a processing are the final point cloud, the mesh which results from the triangularization of the points and the texture which comes from the stitching of photos into the mesh. Finally, orthophotos can be exported from the final mesh, which are scaled and have accurate measuring information, capturing in detail the actual color of the monument and pathology information (cracks, alterations). For our research we will use only the final point cloud of various buildings for creating our HBIM models, setting it as background on the design interface.

4   Methodology

4.1   Modelling of Architecture Elements as Parametric Objects.

The HBIM methodology for historic monuments and sites tends to be established as the most rational and structured [9]. The final stage of the process is the creation of complete 3D models, which include details such as "smart data" on construction methods and material composition. In addition, HBIM automatically generates complete technical plans for maintaining the structure, including 3D documentation, orthographic projections, axonometric sections, construction details and schedules (energy, cost reduction, etc.), adding intelligence to the whole process [2].

For our research we captured point cloud data of various neoclassical era buildings in Athens which have the most common forms of facade elements. Our choice regarding the commonplace of each element is in order to build a prototype element library which emphasizes on its parametric capabilities. Therefore, we focused on the step that follows the collection and processing of data from laser scanning and/or photogrammetry, which is the isolation of an object and its modelling as an HBIM element (Fig. 2). An HBIM building model consists of components named "elements", which are distinct entities within the design. The elements are classified hierarchically into "categories" which are general groups of similar elements. For example, if a window from the point cloud of a building is cropped and modeled in Autodesk Revit, its category will be "window" and this specific window will be an element ("family") of this category. In this hierarchical way, the distinct models can be saved into a BIM library. In this step, it is noteworthy to mention that the captured point cloud data can be used to directly enrich a spatiotemporal database to monitor real estate [10].

Fig. 2. A window model of a Greek neoclassical façade as a result of the scan-2-BIM process, based on a photogrammetry point cloud

The basis of designing and configuring detail objects in BIM software is based on reference plains which are constraints of geometric value. It is necessary for an element to be consisted of many references which define it and make it fully customizable. Those constraints contribute in setting the architectural rules when the object is transformed in order to fit in a new building project. Additionally, it is possible to add formulas that automatically calculate dimensions of components that need to remain in proportions with others. Consequently, it is easy to create similar models which are actually the various typologies of this element.

Architectural elements in an HBIM project consist of sub-elements and their relations are distinct. In this way, a door is comprised of parts like the door panels, the jambs and a possible transom or glazing. Then, a sub-element may consist of another sub-element even lower in hierarchy, like the glazing railings (Fig. 3). This ontological approach contributes to the definition of a library with integrated relationships between each part. The position of each element in the hierarchy is distinct and when an element lower in hierarchy is configured, the element higher is been changed accordingly.

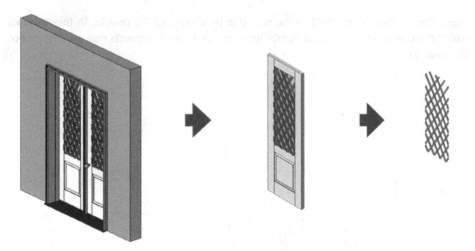

Fig. 3. Hierarchy of a door's components.

Some architecture elements like doors and windows of neoclassical era can be treated as compound objects. There are several architectural elements that must be combined to define e.g. a window opening [11], that we can insert in this case into three categories: window pane, opening's outline and shutters (Fig. 4). If parameters and constraints are set with the mindset of each constituent parts been interchangeable, then all those three sub-categories can be saved as parametric objects in the HBIM library. The different combinations of the sub-categories elements will result in a range of typologies regarding this window's category.

When it comes to sculptural details, the parameterization of the geometry is done by reducing these details to their primitive form [2]. In our case, we defined some classic profile shapes and then reproduced them over an axis in order to create the moldings (Fig. 5). Those profiles are stored as different elements and in case of a new

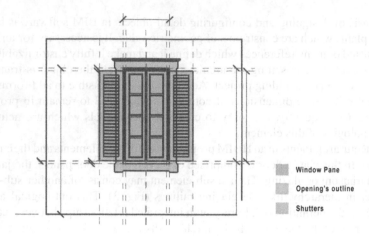

Window Pane

Opening's outline

Shutters

Fig. 4. Components of a window.

shape the molding can adjust to the new one by changing the profile. In this way, its parameterization provides great flexibility over typological elements that usually are not the same [12].

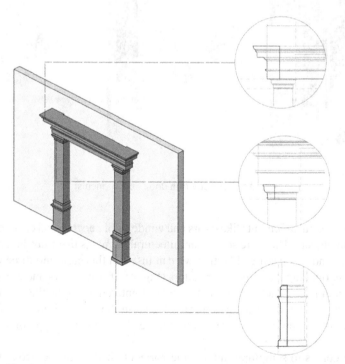

Fig. 5. Analysis of the shaping profiles of the cornices and the pillar.

One of the greatest advantages of BIM software is the possibility of linking information to each building component through parameters and these metadata are structured and easily accessible, thus enriching the database [13]. Metadata are organized into sections and those are: location (may be linked with GIS Data), dating, materials, identity, status (identification and decay), conservation state, cost list of parts, date and references. This information is dynamic, by the means that if someone updates it, it is updated in the database too and if it is parameterized to change a value in another parameter, this is done automatically. For example, if the material gets changed into a more specific one after some chemical research, its thermal values will be updated accordingly.

4.2 Using an HBIM Parametric Library to Create a Parametric Neoclassical Façade Template.

Additional features of the HBIM model are on the one hand the general geometric restoration of the model of the building under consideration, with as much fidelity to the structural elements as possible and on the other hand the enrichment by giving details that determine the identity of the monument under consideration. The architectural elements of the database may be implemented in the facade of a project but they will be not co-related regarding the architectural era. The relations between the facade elements of a particular architectural era, are distinct. Taking a step further and effectively utilizing the library requires one more step of parameterization in a different level. By deconstructing a building's ensemble, the synthetic principles on the basis of which it is formed can be identified. It is composed by many units that their spatial position is accorded to defined relations and investigating these relations leads to the parametric configuration of the building.

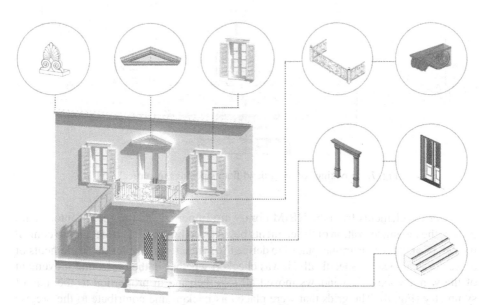

Fig. 6. Implementing Greek neoclassical elements in a parametric façade.

The horizontal separation of the building in "base", "core" and "top" is the basic synthetic rule of a neoclassical style architectural facade and every variant is based on it [14]. For the study, the most common of the typologies are chosen, in order to become a basic parametric facade template (Fig. 6). Also, in neoclassical architecture there is a wide variety of decoration elements, which we will not incorporate in the facade since they are secondary components.

The structure of the main façade in neoclassical architecture is defined geometrically with axes which are guides for the alignment of the walls, the position of the openings and the arrangement of the individual elements (balconies, eaves, etc.). In an HBIM model these axes can be bound to elements with dimensional parameters to control how they behave in modifications [15]. By "locking" some parameters, the principles of symmetry and harmony of a neoclassical facade will be maintained and the model will be a template for developing typologies in a possible study.

More specifically, these "locked" parameters are the following:

- Height of window sill
- Height of floor windows
- Vertical axis of windows and doors (Fig. 7)
- Horizontal axis of symmetry
- Vertical axis of symmetry
- Common type of floor windows
- Common type of ground floor windows

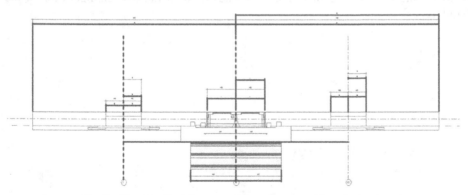

Fig. 7. "Locking" of the ground floor openings in vertical axis.

After the elements from the HBIM library are imported and the axes of interest are drawn, the parameterization of the elements begins step by step. It is necessary to control the behavior of the constraints placed to define the synthetic principles of the elements of a neoclassical facade. Specifically, it was checked whether in the horizontal movement of the window axis the windows moved all together and in proportion to the axis of symmetry (Fig. 8). The grids that were placed as background contribute to the precise placement of the axes based on the grid of the face.

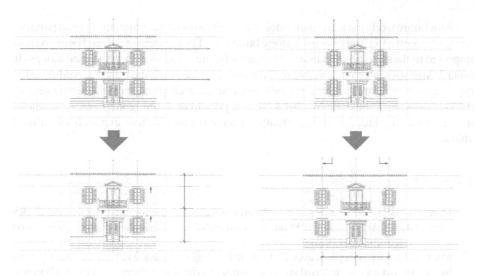

Fig. 8. The behavior of the elements during the displacement of the axes in height and width.

Respectively, in the vertical axis it was checked if the windows of the ground floor and the floor alongside with the rest of the top elements move all together in a vertical reposition and if the corresponding axis of symmetry is observed. It is important, by moving the axes, the façade to be enlarged accordingly, keeping constant the dimension between the last element such as a window and the corner of the building. In this way, the proportions, symmetry and harmony that characterize a face of the neoclassical period are ensured.

5 Conclusion

The product of the HBIM process is the creation of a complete three-dimensional model that contains detail beyond its surface, concerning its historicity and identity, its construction methods and its materiality over time. The level of detail that HBIM methodology offers, qualifies it as the best way of digitally conserve architectural elements of cultural value. This knowledge level in addition to the customizability that the parametric design offers, can lead to the creation of architectural element libraries to be used as a base to begin a new cultural heritage project. However, it is important to consider the principles that characterized architecture of a particular period, in order for the templates to be accurate.

Acknowledging the lack of heritage objects to be implemented in HBIM libraries, the need for such databases is imperative in order to emphasize in the conservation of CH elements with the use of advanced digital technologies. In addition, there is a wider aspect in this topic, as the HBIM library can be considered as a knowledge base developed by means of ontologies, in order to represent all the semantics needed for a comprehensive representation of the historical artifact [16]. This paper contributes in setting the basis of a parametric HBIM library and defining the kind of relation which the elements must have.

As a future work, the same methodology could be used to capture, model and parameterize elements of an inner part of historic buildings. The elements produced could be also imported to the same object library. Alternatively, the façade data may be used alongside inner house data to provide accurate information for a 3D Cadastre [17]. Additionally, typologies of other architectural periods could be researched and the parameterization of the elements would be done in other synthetic principles defining their era. As a whole, it is a promising direction in the attempt to organize architecture elements of cultural value.

References

1. Dore, C., Murphy, M.: Current state of the art historic building information modelling. ISPRS - International Archives of the Photogrammetry, Remote Sensing and Spatial Information Sciences, 185–192 (2017)
2. Murphy, M., Mcgovern, E., Pavía, S.: Historic building information modelling - adding intelligence to laser and image based surveys of european classical architecture. Historic Building Information Modelling - Adding intelligence to laser and image based surveys of European classical architecture. International Journal of Photogrammetry and Remote Sensing. **76**, 89–102 (2009)
3. Zerefos, S., Balafoutis, T.: A Database of Architectural Details: the Case of Neoclassical Façades Elements. BRAU4 Biennial of Architectural and Urban Restoration, Athens & Piraeus (2018)
4. Prizeman, O., Jones, C., Parisi, M., Pezzica, C.: How can century-old architectural hierarchies for the design of public libraries be re-interpreted and re-used? J. Cult. Herit. Manag. Sustain. Dev. **8**, 481–494 (2018)
5. Quattrini, R., Pierdicca, R., Morbidoni, C.: Knowledge-based data enrichment for HBIM: exploring high-quality models using the semantic-web. J. Cult. Herit. 1–14 (2017)
6. Zarogianni, E., Siountri, K., Michailidis, N. Vergados, D.: Pathology detection for HBIM application on a byzantine church in Axos village in Crete, Greece. In: International Conference on Cultural Heritage and New Technologie, Vienna, Austria (2019)
7. Volk, R., Stengel, J., Schultmann, F.: Building Information Modeling (BIM) for existing buildings - literature review and future needs. Autom. Constr. **38**, 109–127 (2014)
8. Castagnettia, C., Dubbinib, M., Riccic, P.C., Rivolaa, R., Gianninia, M., Capraa, A.: Critical issues and key points from the survey to the creation of the historical building information model: the case of santo stefano basilica. In: International Archives of the Photogrammetry, Remote Sensing and Spatial Information Sciences, XLII-5/W1, pp. 467–474 (2017)
9. Bruno, N., Roncella, R.: HBIM for conservation: a new proposal for information modeling. Remote Sensing **11**, 1–24 (2019)
10. Doulamis, N., Voulodimos, A., Preka, D., Ioannidis, C., Potsiou, C., Fritsch, D: An efficient framework for spatiotemporal 4D monitoring and management of real property. In: Proceedings of the High-Level Joint FIG/World Bank Conference on Sustainable Real Estate Markets—Policy Framework and Necessary Reforms, Athens, Greece, vol. 19 (2016)
11. Chevrier, C., Charbonneau, N., Grussenmeyer, P., Perrin, J.-P.: Parametric documenting of built heritage: 3D virtual reconstruction of architectural details. Int. J. Archit. Comput. **08**(02), 131–145 (2010)
12. Murphy, M, McGovern, E, Pavia, S.: Parametric vector modelling of laser and image surveys of 17th century classical architecture in Dublin. In: The 8th International Symposium on Virtual Reality, Archaeology and Cultural Heritage VAST, Brighton, Great Britain (2007)

13. Bacci, G., et al.: Hbim methodologies for the architectural restoration. the case of the ex-church of san Quirico All'olivo in Lucca, Tuscany. International Archives of the Photogrammetry, Remote Sensing and Spatial Information Sciences, XLII-2/W11, pp. 121–126 (2019)
14. Thanopoulos, N.: The Athenian Monumental Buildings of the 19th Century and of the Beginning of the 20th Century with an Investigation of the Constructional and Static Methodology (1834–1916). Stamoulis Publications, Athens (2007)
15. Lee, G., Sacks, R., Eastman, C.M.: Specifying parametric building object behavior (BOB) for a building information modeling system. Autom. Constr. **15**(6), 758–776 (2006)
16. Simeone, D., Cursi, S., Toldo, I., Carrara, G.: B(H)IM - Built Heritage Information Modelling: Extending BIM approach to historical and archaeological heritage representation. In: 32nd eCAADe Conference, Newcastle, Great Britain, pp. 613–621 (2014)
17. Potsiou, C., Doulamis, N., Bakalos, N., Gkeli, M., Ioannidis, C.: Indoor localization for 3d mobile cadastral mapping using machine learning techniques. ISPRS Annals of Photogrammetry, vol. 6. Remote Sensing & Spatial Information Sciences (2020)

The Use of Deep Learning in the Classification of Buildings at the Post-revolutionary City of Athens

Ioannis Kosmopoulos[1], Konstantina Siountri[1,2], and Christos-Nikolaos Anagnostopoulos[2(✉)]

[1] Digital Culture, Smart Cities, IoT and Advanced Digital Technologies, Track "Digital Culture", Department of Informatics, University of Piraeus, Piraeus, Greece
kosmopoulos@unipi.gr
[2] Cultural Technology and Communication Department, University of the Aegean, Mytilene, Greece
{ksiountri,canag}@aegean.gr, ksiountri@unipi.gr

Abstract. The building stock of a city is characterized by typological and structural inhomogeneity. In the urban web coexist many types of buildings of different historical periods e.g. Byzantine (medieval) temples, neoclassical (art nouveau, art deco), apartment buildings (interwar and postwar buildings), which have been built with different materials and styles.

Nevertheless, the "type" of such buildings (e.g. period-based, neoclassical, interwar and postwar buildings) is a repetitive recognizable organizational structure, which is perceived as part of a class of repetitive objects characterized by their common morphological features. Until nowadays, the recognition of the "type" was the result of collective mental mechanisms, which society processed through everyday construction experience. Today, the type pre-exists in the mind of the culture heritage (CH) researchers (architects, archaeologists, historians of art etc.) as a result of their special education. This paper focuses on the typological approach through the classification of data using methods of the field of Artificial Intelligence (AI), and more specifically Deep Learning. It is a process that may: a) lead to the comparative evaluation of the common and repetitive elements of different projects with architectural criteria, b) enable the huge classification of data in a short period of time, c) make possible the digital management of the available CH building stock and d) export useful conclusions that will contribute to the further study of the CH data in the future.

Keywords: Deep learning · Digital cultural heritage · Classification

1 Introduction

Deep learning has known a big development since the beginning of the century and is now a technique than generally proves to be faster and even more efficient than a human [1]. It is a part of a wide family of machine learning methods which are part of

A. Moropoulou et al. (Eds.): TMM_CH 2021, CCIS 1574, pp. 110–124, 2022.
https://doi.org/10.1007/978-3-031-20253-7_10

artificial intelligence, that uses methods based on artificial neural networks, giving them the ability to learn by themselves.

An artificial neuron is a mathematical and informatic model of a biological neuron that was introduced by Warren McCulloch et Walter Pitts in 1943 [2]. Recent studies showed that deep learning could simplify human's life even more i.e., automating diseases detection, better precision of diagnostics, self-driving vehicles etc. As far as it concerns speech recognition, a lot of commercial systems like Cortana (Microsoft), Alexa (Amazon), Siri (Apple) of even Now (Google) use deep learning on systems that are globally known and appear to be very effective for an everyday life use.

Since the beginning of the use of deep learning, it has been applied in a lot of different fields [3, 4], such as image captioning, natural language processing, choreographic learning [5], drug discovery and toxicology, medical image analysis, robotics or even self-driving vehicles. However, there are still a lot of applications where deep learning can be very useful.

Moreover, thanks to their architecture and to the fact that they are almost autonomous, these methods can be applied to a lot of other fields.

Today, most deep learning system are supervised, because it has proved to be more efficient than unsupervised systems. But it also means that, at least during the training of the system, human intervention is needed to make it work. The principle of these methods is to "train" a neural network to make it able to perform different tasks without human help. The nature of the input values can be different from one file to another: image, audio, video, etc. These values are duplicated in the input layer, which is the principal characteristic of deep learning systems. Machine learning systems only duplicate important features to the input layer while deep learning systems duplicate every single value of the input file. Because of this, this system is a bit more complex and needs several hidden layers to complete its operations. That is why it is called "deep" learning. [6, 7]. Joseph Redmon et al [8] proposed an end-to-end deep learning architecture, under the name You Only Look Once (YOLO), for detecting, locating and classifying custom objects, through computer vision techniques in digital images or videos.

This research paper focuses on the typological approach of cultural heritage (CH) buildings in Athens, after, the year of official recognition of the independent Greek state (1830), using Deep Learning methods, and more specifically the YOLO architecture. The classification of elements using the YOLO algorithm will contribute to a) the comparative evaluation of the common and repetitive architectural elements of different periods, b) a large-scale classification of CH data in a short period of time, c) the effective digital management of the CH building information and d) the export of useful conclusions for the further study of the CH data in the future, using advanced digital technologies.

The remainder of the paper is organized as follows: Firstly, related work on applying Deep Learning on Cultural Heritage is described. Subsequently, the case study of classification for architectural styles in Athenian buildings after 1830 is further analyzed, along with the methodology and the results of applying the YOLO algorithms on these buildings. Finally, the last section summarizes the conclusions of our work.

2 Related Work

In the literature, there is a restricted number of applications that use deep learning methods to classify cultural heritage (CH) objects, as the decision making in this field is a multi-criteria process, involving many parameters and stakeholders [9]. In the following research projects, the authors explore the applicability of supervised machine learning approaches to cultural heritage by providing a standardized pipeline for several case studies.

The ArchAIDE project [10] offers an artificial intelligence solution to simplify the classification of archaeological pottery. The research team provided images through their terminal devices to deep neural networks, which outputted five best classification labels and their context, although the final label was decided by humans (archaeologists). The training process was conducted in two phases with different datasets to avoid over-fitting scenarios. The image and the linked information were stored within an online database for future public access. The results for both shape and appearance classifications indicated a sufficient accuracy metric in both desktop and mobile apps using more than 820 images.

The Wooden Architectural Heritage project [11] focuses on the detection of cracks, damage, deformations and other material damage wooden constructions. With the use of the YOLO algorithm damages are detected in a short period of time and repaired. Consequently, the duration of the wooden heritage is extended, and its real-time protection is a reality. The training of the algorithm includes the construction of a huge amount of data with more than 1500 damages including beam cracks, fiber rupture, compressions of the column cover, etc. At the end of the training and testing of the model in test data, 90% detection accuracy is observed at each image in less than 0.1 s.

Underwater detection of entities [12] contributes to the successful revelation of underwater monuments, remnants of cities or civilizations, with the use of YOLOv3. Its use in this field is considered innovative since it can actively contribute to cultural heritage preservation, discovering objects that are not always visible to the human eye. Thus, computer vision enhances underwater exploration, bringing it to the surface. The data processed for the training was acquired from the official website Underwater Robot Picking Contest (URPC) which consists of 18,982 images. Subsequently, 4746 were used as a test set and the remaining 14,236 as a training set. The training process was completed at 30,000 repetitions as the accuracy of the model remains constant at 0.8 and did not change at all.

The architecture LODsyndesis [13] depicted a suite of scalable services acquiring data from the Linked Open Data Cloud. The authors proposed the need of addressing, integrating and linking the large amount of data that increases rapidly. The proposed methods of semantic indexing using different schemas and connectivity analytics between different datasets excel in finding all information about a specific entity and its provenance. Common difficulties including different models and representation of data, different Uniform Resource Identifiers (URIs) relating the same entity or different concepts, additional information and conflicting data were exploited by the LODsyndesis services. The URI discovery, fact checking, dataset discovery or enrichment and a global namespace finding describe the features of the aforementioned platform. Experimental results from the publication and the cultural domain confirmed connections of the British museum dataset and the Library of Congress.

As the relevant literature on the applications of machine learning in the general field of cultural heritage is limited, the applications related to the classification of historic buildings are even more constricted [14]. In the present research the experience from the aforementioned research projects is attempted to be transferred in the field of Greek architecture and its morphological and typological elements over time.

3 Classification for Architectural Styles in Athenian Buildings after 1830

In Athens, the construction of neoclassical buildings began mainly after 1836, (date that Athens becomes Capital of Greece) The characteristics of the Athenian Neoclassical style of the early 19th century were the plasticity and harmony in the volumes and the elaborate decoration (decoration with pediments, friezes and pilasters, balconies with corbels engraved in helix shape, railings with elaborate designs inspired by scenes from nature and mythology etc. [15].

At the same time, in the middle of the 19th century, a style appeared that combined the classic elements together with others, of different periods, such as the art nouveau style,[1] the Viennese secession,[2] the architectural style that was taught at the École des Beaux-Arts[3] and the neo-baroque style[4]. The style of Eclecticism was mainly applied on the Athenian buildings during the last decades of the 19th century and lasted until the beginning of the 20th century. It uses new, modern materials such as iron and glass and its main characteristic is the use of colors and light shading as well as and the excessive use of decorative elements (e.g., sculptures) [15].

After 1920, the development of industry and the need to house the working class and the refugees of the Asia Minor catastrophe of 1922, led to the massive construction of houses and apartment buildings. In the architecture of the interwar period, the influences from the German school of Bauhaus (1913–1933), founded by W. Gropius are evident, i.e. the simple constructions away from the impressive classical elements and the intense exterior decorations of the previous years (early 19th - early 20th century). Emphasis was also placed on the functionality of the living space, adapted to the needs of its inhabitants and based on the studies of Le Corbisier (1887–1965) - for the best living conditions of people in urban centers. The exterior surfaces were covered with artificial coating, closed polygonal, rectangular or curved bay windows appeared on the facades of the buildings and the use of new materials such as concrete, steel, etc was extended [16].

The multi-storey apartment buildings that began in post-war Athens and grew in numbers in the 1960s became a trademark of the city. These concrete made buildings are mainly aimed to house within the same construction a significant number of families, offering three- or four-room apartments. Smaller apartments are offered either on

---

[1] International movement developed in 1890-1910 and distinguished for the sophistication of forms mainly from elements of nature.

[2] Artist movement in Vienna of 1897, aimed at creating a style artist who would not be influenced by any artistic period.

[3] Movement that appeared in Paris from 1830 to the end of the 19th century.

[4] Movement that appeared in Italy in 1600-1750 and is strongly associated with painting.

the lower floors or on the uncovered side. A second feature of the apartment building concerns the relationship between public and private spaces. The public space is successfully diffused on the ground floors of the apartment buildings, which usually receive commercial use, while the general structure of the floor plans allows the conversion of the apartments into offices [17].

Between the periods of the above dominant morphological styles in the architecture of buildings there are transitional trends leading to pluralistic styles. The buildings of the late classicism are enriched with more elements of plastic decoration, which breaks the unity of the walls of the facade and tend towards eclecticism. Moreover, in the interwar period as many architects were reluctant to adopt the strict principles of the Modern Movement, create buildings that still have references to Eclecticism despite the use of new materials, the volume of the structures and the proportions of the built sections and the openings.

Taking into consideration the above styles such as neoclassical, interwar and postwar periods, and that the Eclecticism in most cases is combined with the Neoclassicism or the Modern Movement, for the purposes of this research we limit our classes in five categories (a) the neoclassical, (b) the neoclassical –eclectic, (c) the interwar-eclectic, (d) the interwar and (e) the postwar buildings.

4   Methodology

The primary objective of this research is to apply object detection techniques in the different architectural styles of the city of Athens. Notably, neoclassical, neoclassical-eclectic, interwar-eclectic, interwar, styles and apartments depict the building stock of the Athens city after the 19th century. Since the use of deep learning and especially the You Only Look Once (YOLO) algorithm is limited in the current bibliography, multiple experiments are conducted to exploit their potential.

A high-end workstation deploys the state-of-art framework, YOLO. Sufficient resources including a GPU Nvidia RTX 2080 Super were utilized to accelerate the training of the multi- class images. Notably, this end-to-end architecture excels in performing convolutional calculations with the parallel computing platform CUDA developed by Nvidia. Moreover, the open-cv module was enabled to permit faster data augmentations in each dataset. The configuration file includes the custom hyperparameter values including batch size, subdivision, height, width, momentum and learning rate. The batch size and subdivisions were set to 64 to avoid lack of memory issues since the weight and the height of the images were resized to 608 for the better accuracy and detection of the model. Filters were set after calculations with the number of the classes and classes after the number of the objects. Finally, momentum and learning rate acquired the values 0.494 and 0.001, respectively. Underfitting and overfitting scenarios were limited by stopping each training process at an early point. Table 1 depicts the aforementioned architecture.

The first approach included the distinguish of the neoclassical style based on its individual elements (Fig. 1). Due to insufficient resources, the dataset included only doors, balconies and windows excluding decorations like the gables or the friezes. As follows, the initial dataset consists of 977 images where 782 construct the training dataset and 195 the test dataset. The samples of the classes vary with different distances from the camera, angles, illumination, and combinations. In particular, most of them contain facades of the neoclassical buildings with most of the 3 classes. The training procedure is interrupted after 5000 iterations since the average loss was no longer decreasing dramatically. Figure 1 depicts the results of the detection based on the produced custom weights in random images of neoclassical buildings. Under certain circumstances, the custom weights excel in localizing and classifying the aforementioned classes. However, the distinguish between the different styles is not derived. The current approach detects doors, balconies, and windows in every architectural style even though the training dataset included only neoclassical elements. Consequently, the method of describing a building from its elements is abandoned in the current research since the same procedure should be repeated for every different architectural style and its main elements. The limited number of decorations in the current dataset that act as common references in neoclassical buildings, could address the aforementioned problem. However, the high confidence scores of the custom detection produce an encouraging outcome for the expansion of the study.

In the second place, the point of view of the building is changed. Since the elements that describe a building can be detected successfully, the whole building may be used as a new class. Specifically, this scheme is examined with 3 classes containing the neoclassical buildings, the interwar buildings (Fig. 2), and the apartments. At this point the eclectic styles, which concide with the late neoclassical and the early interwar styles are excluded from this approach. The new dataset included 956 images with the 3 new classes. It is noted that each image contains a façade or a different point of view of only one building. The same building may appear multiple times in the current dataset with a different distance from the camera or angle. However, the camera does not focus on specific elements or parts of the buildings but on the whole building instead. Notably, 765 images constructed the training set and 191 the test set. The second training procedure ends after 5500 iterations with a 1.13 average loss metric on the specific dataset. Figure 2 depicts the results of the detection. Therefore, the YOLO architecture is able to extract features from the dataset and convert them into bounding boxes to detect larger objects.

Finally, the eclectic buildings of the stock of Athens city is introduced in the current deep learning method. As Eclecticism is a transitional period at the beginning of the 20th century, new photos of the neoclassical-eclectic and interwar-eclectic styles were added to establish the final dataset. Each aforementioned class includes almost the same number of photos to train the model. More than 2365 photos were collected where 1896 constructed the training set and 469 the test set. The training procedure is interrupted after 7500 iterations to avoid over-fitting scenarios. At the 7500 iterations, the Mean Average Precision (mAP) metric is 76.67% whereas the average loss is 1.37. Figures 3 and 4 depict the results of the trained model. For example. Figure 5. Depicts the results of the custom weights. The full architecture of YOLOv4 was applied to detect the different types of buildings. Analytically, 161 layers were utilized including convolutional, shortcuts, routes and yolo layers. Based on the classes, the number of filters before each yolo layer was changed to 30, so the number of them is given by [18]

$$filters = (classes + 5) \times 3.$$

Fig. 1. Detection of elements on a Neoclassical Building

Fig. 2. Detection of an Interwar Building

The input size of the detector is 608 × 608 × 3, considering the width, the depth and the channels of the image, whereas the output before the yolo layer and the final detection and classification is 19 × 19 × 30. Table 1. describes the first 10 layers of the custom multi-layer YOLOv4 configuration.

Table 1. Network architecture

	Layer	Filters	Size	Input	Output
0	Conv	32	3 × 3/1	608 × 608 × 3	608 × 608 × 3
1	Conv	64	3 × 3/2	608 × 608 × 64	304 × 304 × 64
2	Conv	64	1 × 1/1	304 × 304 × 64	304 × 304 × 64
3	Route	1			304 × 304 × 64
4	Conv	64	1 × 1/1	304 × 304 × 64	304 × 304 × 64
5	Conv	32	1 × 1/1	304 × 304 × 64	304 × 304 × 32
6	Conv	64	3 × 3/1	304 × 304 × 32	304 × 304 × 64
7	Shortcut layer: 4				304 × 304 × 64
8	Conv	64	1 × 1/1	304 × 304 × 64	304 × 304 × 64
9	Route	8 2			304 × 304 × 128
10	Conv	64	1 × 1/1	304 × 304 × 128	304 × 304 × 64

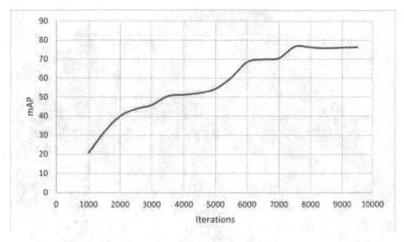

Fig. 3. Mean average precision diagram

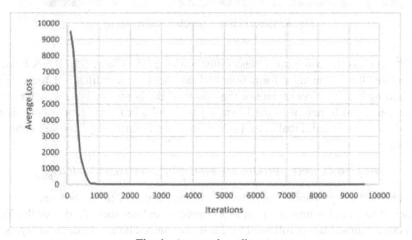

Fig. 4. Average loss diagram

4.1 You Only Look Once (YOLO) Architecture

You Only Look Once (YOLO) refers to an object detection system targeted for real time processing. The aforementioned system predicts the accurate location and type of an object. Object detection is addressed as a regression problem estimating bounding box coordinates and class probabilities. A single convolutional network predicts multiple type of objects at the same time by abandoning sliding window and region proposal techniques. Instead, YOLO considers the full image during training and testing, acquiring a global view about classes and their specific appearance. In the background, YOLO divides the input data into a S × S grid. Each object contains a center that is properly placed inside a grid cell. Only that grid cell is responsible for identifying the object. The grid cells predict B boundary boxes along with their specific confidence score and C conditional class probabilities. Notably, the confidence is defined as Pr(*Object*) *

Fig. 5. Detection of a neoclassical building

IOU^{truth} whereas the conditional class probabilities as Pr *(Classi|Object)*. A bounding box contains the following information such as the x: x coordinate of the center of the bounding box, y: y coordinate of the center of the bounding box, w: width of the bounding box and h: height of the bounding box and a box confidence score. During the prediction, the conditional class probabilities are multiplied by the individual box confidence scores,

$$\Pr(Class_i|Object) * \Pr(Object) * IOU_{pred}^{truth} = \Pr(Class_i) * IOU_{pred}^{truth}$$

which encodes the probability of class describing an object in the box and the fitting accuracy. The model is implemented as a convolutional network. Additionally, YOLO has 24 convolutional layers followed by 2 fully connected layers. Reduction layers with filter size 1×1 to reduce the dimensions of the features map are followed by 3×3 layers to extract features. The fully connected layers output the final probabilities and coordinates of the bounding boxes. Specifically, the final prediction is encoded as a (S, S, B* 5 + C) vector. Therefore, it applies a softmax unit to convert number scores into probabilities. Based on the ImageNet classification, the final convolution layer outputs a (7,7,1024) tensor which is flattened and by utilizing 2 fully connected layers, it output a (7, 7, 30) vector.

4.2 Dataset

The dataset photographs were retrieved by three ways. Firstly, camera shooting of buildings in the Municipality of Athens preceded the procedure. The photographs were taken for the entirety of the construction and for details, i.e. characteristic architectural elements of their facades. Also, several photos of the same building were taken from different angles in order to test the ability of the algorithm to predict the multiple inputs related to the same object. Secondly, screen shots from google street view were used, which also captured the buildings in question from different angles. Finally, images from the internet were used, both from crowdsourcing databases related to Athenian architecture (e.g. Archive of Preserved Buildings, ModMov etc.) as well as from relevant Pages on Social Media e.g. Athenian Modernism. The third case enabled us to have aerial images so that we could enrich the dataset with downloads beyond the street level.

The set of images was divided into different classes depending on the progress of the research. In the first phase, the photographs were divided by architectural element, mainly in buildings related to neoclassical constructions. In the second phase of research, the photographs were divided into neoclassical, interwar and post-war apartment buildings. In the third and final phase, the number of photographs was increased and was again divided into neoclassical (Fig. 6), neoclassical eclectic (Fig. 7) (including buildings of the late neoclassicism), eclectic-interwar (Fig. 8), interwar (Fig. 9) and post-war apartment buildings (Fig. 10).

Fig. 6. Neoclassical building   **Fig. 7.** Neoclassical eclectic building

Fig. 8. Eclectic-interwar building   **Fig. 9.** Interwar building

As we have already mentioned, several photos of the same building were used from different angles and positions from the camera to expand the previous dataset since

Fig. 10. Post-war apartment building

it composes a subset of the new one. In addition, the quality of the photos varied, as the internet images had low resolution. This differentiation did not caused problems in the progress of the research. On the contrary, this variety of quality was a challenge in order to test the performance of the algorithm. Also, photos with more than one building were intentionally added to the dataset (one main object in the foreground and more in the background or buildings in a parallel layout), as well as photos with elements that obstructed the full view of the building e.g. cars, trees, license plates, etc., in order to test the results. Buildings that had alterations due to damage or due to their newer use (e.g., change of windows and openings) were high in the images collection during both training and validation phase. This is explained by the fact that the recognition of the authentic typology of the Athenian buildings, which have undergone alternations, is one of the research requirements.

5   Results

After completing the training of the algorithm, two consecutive validation tests were performed from datasets of 500 photos from the interwar class and a dataset of 1000 photos from the 5 classes under consideration. The success rates were 78% and 76.2% respectively (Table 2). The outcome was considered satisfactory both in terms of quantity and quality.

More analytically, the algorithm gave a correct prediction to buildings that had been extensively alternated (e.g. the typology of the ground level has been lost due to its new use as seen in Fig. 11). Various elements or objects of the surrounding area (e.g. trees, cars, constructions, etc.), did not affect the result (Fig. 12–Fig. 13). In addition, pathology and damages of the exterior facades such as graffiti, damages of the coating, aging materials did not affect the exported results (Fig. 14). This also applies to the cases that involve various number of floors, because the algorithm recognizes the main architectural characteristics addressed to the main typological features of the respective class that had emerged from the overall training (Fig. 15). Finally, buildings constructed in more recent periods that share characteristics that derived from previous historical periods, gave also correct predictions (see Fig. 16).

Fig. 11. Neoclassical building with alternated ground floor

Fig. 12. Neoclassical building with trees in front of it

As far as the erroneous classification is concerned, we assume that it was due to specific reasons related to: a) distorted view of the façade as captured in the photos, b) low resolution of photographs, the architectural structure of specific buildings. As an example of the later we can mention a number of pre-war buildings with a very simple facade that resembled to post-war apartment buildings or newer buildings with curved elements that were quite similar to the inter-war contractions.

Fig. 13. Neoclassical building with metallic constructions in front of it

Fig. 14. Neoclassical building with bad condition of pathology

Fig. 15. One storey interwar building   **Fig. 16.** Newer building with characteristics
depicted from the past

Table 2. Confusion matrix

Classes	Neoclassical	Interwar	Apartments	Neoclassical-eclectic	Interwar-eclectic
Neoclassical	92/100	5/100	1/100	2/100	0/100
Interwar	3/100	88/100	9/100	0/100	0/100
Apartments	10/100	13/100	70/100	7/100	0/100
Neoclassical-eclectic	20/100	5/100	4/100	65/100	6/100
Interwar- eclectic	4/100	20/100	0/100	10/100	66/100

6   Conclusions

Monuments, by definition, have the ability to promote human memory and to function as a connecting link between the present and the past and reflect the overall history, social, economic, intellectual and artistic context of each era. However, our society today as a recipient of the tangible and the intangible cultural heritage can protect, degrade or destroy it. The preservation and management of cultural heritage presupposes awareness and understanding of the particular values of the "monumental wealth and digital tools can offer new, innovative and accessible methods that can contribute to this field.

Taking into consideration of the above, this study explored the classification of various buildings of the CH domain in the city of Athens. The advantages of the proposed method are (a) shorter time to classify structures with respect to manual methods and (b) the research over the applicability of Machine Learning methods on the building stock of an extensive area over more than 12 decades.

For future works, the authors aim to work further on different heritage buildings, improving the generalization of the classification of the five basic classes. In order to accomplish that, it will be necessary to increase the number of labeled images and exploit more complex machine learning algorithms. Finally, the use of these algorithms will be tested on photographs received from UAVs, in order to examine their contribution of this method to the registration of the tangible cultural heritage.

Acknowledgements. The publication of this paper has been partly supported by the University of Piraeus Research Center (UPRC).

References

1. Voulodimos, A., Doulamis, N., Doulamis, A., Protopapadakis, E.: Deep learning for computer vision: a brief review. Comput. Intell. Neurosci. **2018**, 1–13 (2018). https://doi.org/10.1155/2018/7068349
2. McCulloch, W.S., Pitts, W.: A logical calculus of the ideas immanent in nervous activity. Bull. Math. Biophys. **5**(4), 115–133 (1943). https://doi.org/10.1007/bf02478259
3. Li, D.: Artificial intelligence in the rising wave of deep learning. Retrieve on 27 Jul 2018. http://www.saebogota.unal.edu.co/DIRACAD/catedras/2018_I/mutis/docs/Sesion2/Artificial%20Intelligence%20in%20the%20Rising%20Wave%20of%20Deep%20Learning.pdf (2018)
4. Mitchell, F.: 10 Real-world examples of machine learning and AI. Retrieved on 27 Jul 2018. https://www.redpixie.com/blog/examples-of-machine-learning (2018)
5. Bakalos, N., Rallis, I., Doulamis, N., Doulamis, A., Voulodimos, A., Vescoukis, V.: Motion primitives classification using deep learning models for serious game platforms. IEEE Comput. Grap. Appl. **40**(4), 26–38 (2020). https://doi.org/10.1109/MCG.2020.2985035
6. Miikkulainen, R., et al.: Evolving deep neural networks. In: Artificial Intelligence in the Age of Neural Networks and Brain Computing, pp. 293–312. Elsevier (2019). https://doi.org/10.1016/B978-0-12-815480-9.00015-3
7. LeCun, Y., Bengio, Y., Hinton, G.: Deep learning. Nature **521**, 436–444 (2015). https://doi.org/10.1038/nature14539
8. Redmon, J., Divvala, S., Girshick, R., Farhadi, A.: You only look once: unified, real-time object detection. In: Proceedings of the IEEE Conference on Computer Vision and Pattern Recognition, pp. 779–788 (2016)
9. Kioussi, A., et al.: A computationally assisted cultural heritage conservation method. J. Cult. Heritage **48**(2021), 119–128 (2021)
10. Gualandi, M.L., Gattiglia, G., Anichini, F.: An open system for collection and automatic recognition of pottery through neural network algorithms. Heritage **4**(1), 140–159 (2021)
11. Liu, Y., Hou, M., Li, A., Dong, Y., Xie, L., Ji, Y.: Automatic detection of timber-cracks in wooden architectural heritage using YOLOv3 algorithm. The Int. Arch. Photogrammetry, Remote Sens. Spat. Inform. Sci. **43**, 1471–1476 (2020)
12. Yang, H., Liu, P., Hu, Y., Fu, J.: Research on underwater object recognition based on YOLOv3. Microsyst. Technol. **27**(4), 1837–1844 (2020). https://doi.org/10.1007/s00542-019-04694-8
13. Mountantonakis, M., Tzitzikas, Y.: LODsyndesis: global scale knowledge services. Heritage **1**(2), 335–348 (2018)
14. Kioussi, A., Doulamis, A., Karoglou, M., Moropoulou, A.I.: Cultural intelligence-investigation of different systems for heritage sustainable preservation. Int. J. Art, Cult., Des., Technol. **9**(2), 16–30 (2020). https://doi.org/10.4018/IJACDT.2020070102
15. Biris, M.Γ.: Athenian architecture 1875–1925, Melissa edn. Athens (2003)
16. Manos, Γ.: Athenian architecture 1875–1925, Melissa edn. Athens (2003)

17. Woditsch, R.: The Public Private House: Modern Athens and its Polykatoikia. Park Books Editions, Zurich (2018)
18. Laroca, R., et al.: A robust real-time automatic license plate recognition based on the YOLO detector. In: 2018 International Joint Conference on Neural Networks (IJCNN), pp. 1–10. IEEE (2018)

ICT and Digital Technologies. The New European Competence Centre for the Preservation and Conservation of Cultural Heritage

Emanuele Piaia(✉) ⓘ, Federica Maietti ⓘ, Roberto Di Giulio ⓘ,
and Ernesto Iadanza ⓘ

INCEPTION, Spin-Off of University of Ferrara, Ferrara, Italy
emanuele.piaia@unife.it

Abstract. Europe's cultural heritage sites are in danger, due to the increasing occurrence of disasters such as floods, earthquakes, and also because of man-made damage or the effects of climate change. In this framework, digital technology can help preserve the knowledge of threatened heritage artefacts, museums, monuments, documents and sites and make them accessible for citizens across Europe and for future generations.

In this direction, the European Commission has launched a call for the creation of a "Competence Centre" aimed at preserving cultural heritage through ICT technologies, as a transnational and interdisciplinary reference point. The project 4CH—*Competence Centre for the Conservation of Cultural Heritage* aims to design and define the overall architecture of a European Competence Centre on Cultural Heritage, which will operate proactively for the conservation and safeguarding of heritage. The project aims to initiate the implementation of the structure, organisation and services of the Competence Centre, which will operate as an infrastructure aimed at providing cultural, scientific, technological, financial, strategic and policy expertise and advice able to exploit the most advanced ICT, 3D and digital technologies.

Keywords: Cultural Heritage · Conservation · Digital technologies · 3D Documentation

1 Introduction

Europe's Cultural Heritage (CH) sites and historical documents, monuments and historic buildings across the Member States are increasingly under threat [1]. The increasing occurrence of disasters such as floods, earthquakes, fires, and pollution can sometimes cause irreversible damage to CH sites and historical assets or destroy entire areas together with the documents and monuments therein [2].

Apart from losing our heritage, the culture and creative sectors, and related industries such as tourism and hospitality [3] rely heavily on the appeal and conservation of cultural heritage sites, documents, and monuments.

A. Moropoulou et al. (Eds.): TMM_CH 2021, CCIS 1574, pp. 125–135, 2022.
https://doi.org/10.1007/978-3-031-20253-7_11

To address this scenario and following successful initiatives previously launched, the European Commission, under the H2020 Call-H2020-SC6-TRANSFORMATIONS-2020, proposed to set up a European Competence Centre (CC) aiming at the preservation and conservation of European CH using new state-of-the-art ICT technologies [4]. The term Competence Centre is used in different contexts to describe an infrastructure dedicated to knowledge organization and transfer, and may have different meanings according to focus area, scope, domain, and socio-economic framework, with different objectives, organisation, and operational mode.

In order to answer to the European Commission's challenge, a consortium composed by nineteen partners has proposed a new research program called: "4CH–Competence Centre for the Conservation of Cultural Heritage" which has been funded under Grant Agreement n.101004468-4CH. The research project started on January 1, 2021 and will end on December 31, 2023.

The 4CH consortium is led by three main partners: *Istituto Nazionale di Fisica Nucleare* (Coordinator); INCEPTION Srl (Scientific coordinator); PIN Scrl—*Servizi Didattici e Scientifici per l'Università di Firenze* (Technical Coordinator) and also includes leading institutions from academia, industry, Small Medium Enterprises (SMEs) and research centers with complementary expertise and broad geographical coverage of Europe.

2 Competence Centre Aims

The main aim of the 4CH project is to design and set up a CC on the Conservation of CH.

The Centre will offer knowledge (advice and support activities) and services to national and regional heritage agencies, CH institutions, professionals and citizens.

The main research actions of the 4CH project are:

- To promote state-of-the-art ICT solutions including 3D digitization, which have great potential for documenting, monitoring, mitigating, and preventing damage caused by natural degradation, human-related developments and disasters.
- To pave the way for the future work of the Centre by raising awareness among institutions and professionals about innovative ICT solutions, the positive benefits of high-quality digitization of heritage assets and sustainable exploitation of the cultural, social, and economic potential of the cultural heritage.
- To define the organizational framework and plan the activities of the future CC, designing and testing the infrastructure, tools, and services which the CC will provide.

To achieve the main goal, required by the European Commission, 4CH will pursue a sub-set of five related objectives (see Fig. 1):

1. "Establishing the methodological framework for the CC focusing on advanced digitization for preservation and conservation of Monuments and Sites". The objective is to design the methodological framework for the CC and the knowledge base needed to support work with the network of national, regional, and local cultural institutions. The framework will collect and relate experiences, skills and best practices,

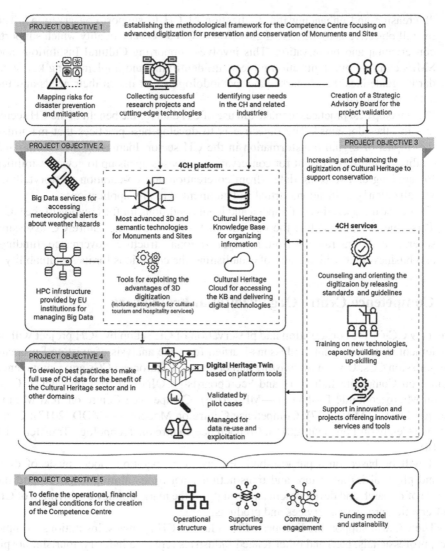

Fig. 1. Outline of the main objectives of the 4CH project in relation to the actions planned to achieve them.

innovative approaches, policies, and strategies for preservation and conservation of monuments and sites.

2. "To design and implement a Platform for the CC to support the collaboration among European CH Institutions". The objective is to create a CC Platform through which European CH institutions will be able to interact, access an interdisciplinary network of knowledge, providing advice and support. To enhance this task, an Advisory Board (AB) has been established including experts on CH, advanced technologies, and relevant industries.

3. "Increasing and enhancing the digitization of CH to support conservation". The overall objective is to increase digitisation of CH assets at a quality which supports conservation and preservation. This involves supporting Cultural Institutions and SMEs carrying out digitisation projects in identifying and implementing key standards, guidelines, benchmarks, and methodologies that match their needs and the solution required.
4. "To develop best practices to make full use of CH data for the benefit of the CH sector and in other domains". The objective is to develop best practices that maximize the impact of digital transformation in the CH sector. Increasing the volume and quality of digitized content for conservation purposes opens up to new possibilities for creating and re-using data—from co-creation and co-curation to storytelling, visualization, gamification, virtual and augmented reality applications.
5. "To define the operational, financial and legal conditions for the creation of the CC". This objective is to define the operational framework of the future CC assessing several conditions ranging from its organizational structure, governance, funding, and business plan with the aim of establishing the conditions for its sustainability.

3 Competence Centre Organizational Framework

The new CC for the conservation and preservation of CH set up by 4CH project will be implemented starting from the lessons-learned from the analysis of existing European Commission CCs. Up to now, existing and operational European CCs are: Competence Centre on Composite Indicators and Scoreboards—COIN (2016); Competence Centre on Microeconomic Evaluation—ME (2016); Competence Centre on Text Mining and Analysis—TMA (2017); Competence Centre on Modelling—MOD (2017); Competence Centre on Foresight (2018); Competence Centre on Technology Transfer—TT (2018).

It will be based on a purpose-built European cooperation model made of digital and physical infrastructure and trans-national networks, aiming to go beyond the sphere of research and development and to support the market/policy deployment of CH conservation processes, services and products.

The CC will support the European CH industry (CH agencies, institutions, companies, professionals, etc.) and other related industries (creative industry, tourism, hospitality etc.) in exploiting the added-value of CH digitization for preservation and conservation, overcoming existing hindrances by developing and acquiring new advanced skills.

Scope of the CC is also to bridge the gap between research and business, policy-making and finance, providing:

- "Counseling and orientation":

  - analyzing experiences, skills and best practices, past and ongoing research implemented so far in the European Countries;
  - mapping risks which can damage CH and technology that can help in avoiding them;

- creating and promoting of interdisciplinary networks and mapping user needs;
- releasing standards and guidelines for digitizing CH and managing preservation and conservation activities.

- "Training and capacity building":

  - creation and maintenance of training material for up-skilling using different modalities, both for distance learning and proximate learning;
  - sharing best-practices and promoting the use of released standards, guidelines and tools.

- "Supporting innovation and projects":

  - promoting innovative services and tools for the 3D digitization of Monuments and Sites;
  - facilitating access to finance, sharing knowledge about EU funds and national projects for innovation;
  - support innovative use and re-use by SMEs of data in edutainment and cultural tourism
  - working directly with the EU Commission policy Directorates-General, paving the way for new research.

The new CC will also collaborate with the existing European Centers, enriching the system of existing European CCs. It will be also integrated in the European Commission's Knowledge policy platform, and it will make use of the services provided by the Cybersecurity Industrial, Technology and Research one—as soon as it will be operative—regarding the protection of sensitive data.

Based on what has been introduced, the 4CH project is working to develop the organizational structure of the CC specifically with the drafting of the charter, in which roles, tasks, duties, reports, voting powers will be defined and designed.

The schema below is the conceptual map of the main governing bodies and the central and local units, operating inside and outside the CC, on which the 4CH will develop the CC organizational structure considering three main level (see Fig. 2).

The "first level", concerning a "governing board" with a decision-making and strategic role, would be in charge of compliance and consistency of objectives, financial matters, conflicts resolution. It would be composed by:

- "Founders": some partners from the 4CH Consortium and a few super-experts, one for each Thematic Department. Thematic Departments will be identified in the 4CH project;
- "Members": made of one delegate for each National Coordination Centre. The Governing Board would be supported by a Strategic Advisory Board (SAB), which would have the task of assisting and advising the CC in general. As main aim, the SAB would provide the Governing Board with matchmaking among mega-trend (socio-economic/global mission) and challenges linked to CC, contributing to define political and strategic orientations. SAB will include global recognized structures such as

UNESCO, ICOMOS, DOCOMOMO, and national consolidated institutions, such as Ministries, National Clusters, governmental institutions, heritage agencies, etc.

The decisions of the Governing Board are made operative thanks to the Executive Committee and its relevant Thematic Departments:

- The "Executive Committee" is composed by a group of selected members who run the CC, with operative duties. It includes a directorate and a management structure, in direct liaison with the Thematic Departments.
- The "Thematic Departments" will be identified within the project, based on most relevant topics for the CH preservation and conservation, including, among others, Sciences and Technologies, ICTs and 3D Technology, Training and Education, Policies and Strategies, Financial Department. Their role will be to provide support within their thematic axis, and to transfer the instances of the national task forces, guiding the research agenda. Their target will be stakeholders from the research and industrial communities and Member States, public administrations, management and conservation entities, academic actors, business players. The Departments will report to the Executive Committee and advocate with the National CH Coordination Centers.

The constellation of the CC will be completed with two supporting structures:

- The CH Cloud (digital), relying on the existing cloud structure.
- The High-Performance Computing centre (physical), relying on the HPCC infrastructure provided by the "Foundation Big Data and Artificial Intelligence for Human Development" and exploiting the services developed by the 4CH project.

The "second level" concerns the National CH Coordination Centers that will be the national structure in charge of the provision of services linked to Thematic Departments, complementing their expertise, by widening the know-how on CH. Each National CH Coordination Centers will be equipped with a task-force responsible for adapting and aligning contents from the Thematic Departments to specific national rules, policies, and laws. Each Member State participating in the CC will have its National CH Coordination Centre that will receive tools, guidelines, and directions from the Executive Committee. It will be responsible for pooling and connecting efforts and implementing locally, guidelines and directions in an efficient manner. A National Advisory Boards (NAB) will support each National CH Coordination Centre. NABs could be composed, for instance, by national technological clusters. They will have strategic role in the definition of services in terms of feedbacks and input on current trend in CH, and in the updating at European/national policy level; they will collect market and enterprise need as well as public administration requirements; they will provide inputs on technological innovations on national and global scale and share national technological roadmaps.

The "third level" regard the Member Countries interested in joining 4CH will promote the activities of the CC locally in order to recruit new members for the National CH Competence Community (Community). This Community is meant as a reticular structure including both regional and metropolitan, as well as local entities. It will involve entities—public and private institutions, professionals and SME, agencies, policymakers, decision makers and educational and training institutions—that are established within the EU or are linked with the EU matters, with CH expertise in the domains of research, development and/or training and education. The Community will contribute to collect both information and data about user needs, criticalities, frailty, and threats affecting the CH, and about local best practices, skills, and virtuous experiences. It can grow and up-scale according to the necessities of the CC and the relevance of the players involved.

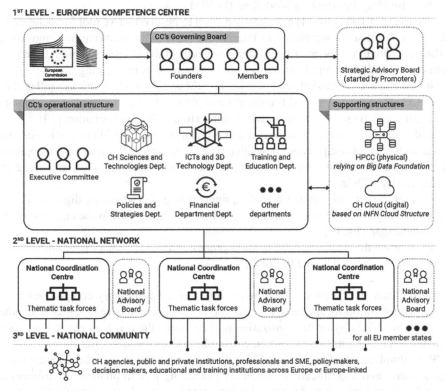

Fig. 2. Conceptual map of the main governing bodies and the central and local units, operating inside and outside the CC.

4   Cultural Heritage Digitization Process

In consideration of the CC aims, one of the main pillars of 4CH project is to promote the use of ICT solutions and digital technologies for 3D digitization process.

ICT and digital technologies can help preserve the knowledge of threatened heritage artefacts, museums, monuments, documents, and sites and make them accessible for citizens across Europe and for future generations [5, 6]. Moreover, online access to high quality holistically documented digital replicas (including storytelling) of artefacts, sites, documents, and monuments [7] may increase the appeal and promotion of a place, city or Member State, thus supporting the local tourism and hospitality industries [8].

The digitization potential is recognized also in the "Declaration of Cooperation on Advancing Digitization of Cultural Heritage" [9], signed by 27 EU Member States to join efforts in a European initiative on the 3D digitization of CH, re-use of digitized cultural resources to foster citizen engagement and innovative use in other sectors, and to enhance cross-sector, cross-border cooperation and capacity building.

If the 3D digitization defines a process for capturing reality, a complementary approach is represented by the use of modelling techniques and, in particular, the so-called Heritage Building Information Modelling (H-BIM).

The use of H-BIM [10, 11] has already proven to be an effective tool for technicians, offering a significant contribution to interpretive models for intervention. Innovations in the field should be aimed at the full-achievement of the Heritage Digital Twin [12], making the H-BIM model effective even for the continuous monitoring.

4CH recognizes the added value of using H-BIM and will include this as a pillar of the future CC, promoting a gradual transition from plain 3D scanning or photogrammetry, to sophisticated 3D solid models with rich contextual H-BIM information [13].

In detail, 4CH is working to implement a novel approach to 3D technologies integrated with an interdisciplinary knowledge base. It will propose an inclusive approach for time-dynamic 3D reconstructions of artefacts, buildings, and sites, achieving the Digital Heritage Twin.

3D digitization involves the use of equipment (e.g. 3D scanners, digital cameras) and proprietary software to convert the digital signals coming from the equipment into processable data [14, 15].

To improve the whole CH digitization process, the 4CH project is defining a dual approach to be adopted by the future CC:

- "Instrumental certification"—that means a test of the proprietary components by an independent authority and certify their compliance with quality requirements. In other words, the reliability of the digitization process needs the involvement of equipment manufacturers, contributing to an interdisciplinary certification procedure;
- "Procedural certification"—the 4CH will release guidelines for the data capturing procedures and a certification system for evaluating its compliance. Environmental conditions and the setup of the digitization campaign are also relevant for the quality of the outcome.

To these approaches are also added support tools such as:

- "Releasing guidelines" to improve the post-processing steps for the creation of 3D digitized model;
- "3D repository specification" to facilitate storing and accessing of 3D high quality scanned models that are usually much demanding in terms of size.

5　Conclusion

As introduced in this paper, the ambitions and expectations of the future CC are very high. At the conclusion of what has been described, it is relevant to summarize the expected positive impacts on the management, conservation, preservation and valorization of the CH.

The CC will increase the quality of preservation initiatives and create the condition for more effective strategies and programmes by the following actions:

- providing standards, guidelines and state-of-the-art tools for the initiatives of CH institutions, contributing to the development of the Knowledge Base;
- establishing links and connections between the existing networks of public and private institutions working on CH conservation;
- becoming a point of reference for transnational and interdisciplinary networking focused on the preservation of historic buildings, urban areas, monuments, sites and landscapes;
- promoting and encouraging the exchange and sharing of experiences, knowledge and best practices in the preservation of CH;
- promoting and supporting education and training programmes organized and implemented by local institutions (conferences, summer schools, workshops, etc.) and supplying on-line initiatives (e-learning, webinars, etc.).

Achievable impacts from 4CH, during the project, include also the construction of a "4CH Community" of prospective users of the CC, creating links and exchanges between existing networks of public and private institutions working on CH as the seed of the CC Community; defining criteria and parameters about the quality assessment of digitised monuments, sites and documents; establishing a dynamic repository on available new digital technologies for preservation and promotion of cultural heritage, arising from EU research projects; supporting on-going pilot projects or implementing new ones aiming at defining the basis and the methodology that the digitisation standards and guidelines, developed by the CC.

Summarizing, the CC, organized according to the 4CH criteria introduced, "will increase both the quantity and the quality of digitized sites and monuments" by: enhancing and sharing knowledge on digitisation; defining and promoting standards and guidelines; promoting protocols and criteria to validate the existing digital assets for their adaptation and reuse; promoting education and training on digitisation procedures, technologies and tools. The CC "will extend and strengthen the coordination between the players in CH": continuing to expand the Community started by 4CH to include all networks and players in the CH domain; involving the members of the CC community in existing networks and new networks in the CH and conservation domain; involving the AB, already set up during 4CH, formed by experts in all fields pertaining to CH preservation and exploitation.

Acknowledgement. The project is being developed by a Consortium of nineteen partners from thirteen European countries led by INFN—Istituto Nazionale di Fisica Nucleare (Coordinator), INCEPTION Srl (Scientific coordinator), PIN Scrl—Servizi Didattici e Scientifici per l'Università di Firenze (Technical Coordinator). The Consortium includes Fundacion Tecnalia Research & Innovation, Spain; Visual Dimension, Belgium; RDF, Bulgaria; Iron Will, Moldavia; Koninklijke Nederlandse Akademie Van Wetenschappen—KNAW, Netherlands; University of Bologna, Italy; Athena Research Centre, Greece; Laboratorio Nacional de Engenharia Civil, Portugal; The

Cyprus Institute, Cyprus; Idryma Technologias Kai Erevnas—FORTH, Greece; Istituto Centrale per il Catalogo Unico delle biblioteche italiane e per le informazioni bibliografiche—ICCU, Italy; Connecting Archaeology and Architecture In Europe—CARARE, Ireland; Michael Culture Association, Belgium; Institutul National al Patrimoniului, Romania; Universite de Tours, France; Leica Geosystems, Switzerland.

The 4CH project has been applied under the Work Programme Europe in a changing world— inclusive, innovative and reflective Societies (Call—Socioeconomic and Cultural Transformations in the Context of the Fourth Industrial Revolution—H2020-SC6-Transformations-2018-2019-2020).

4CH is a Horizon 2020 project funded by the European Commission under Grant Agreement n.101004468—4CH.

References

1. Maxwell, I., Drdácký, M., Vintzileou, E., Bonazza, A., Hanus, C.: Safeguarding Cultural Heritage from Natural and Man-Made Disasters. A comparative analysis of risk management in the EU. European Commission, © European Union (2018)
2. Machat, C., Ziesemer, J. (eds.): Heritage at Risk. World Report 2016–2019 on Monuments and Sites in Danger. ICOMOS, Hendrik Bäßler verlag, Berlin (2020)
3. Markham, A., Osipova, E., Lafrenz Samuels, K., Caldas, A.: World Heritage and Tourism in a Changing Climate. United Nations Environment Programme, Nairobi, Kenya and United Nations Educational, Scientific and Cultural Organization, Paris, France (2016). https://whc. unesco.org/document/139944. Accessed 29 Jul 2021
4. https://cordis.europa.eu/article/id/413473-how-digital-technologies-can-play-a-vital-role-for-the-preservation-of-cultural-heritage. Accessed 14 May 2021
5. Maietti, F., et al.: Documentation, processing, and representation of architectural heritage through 3d semantic modelling: the INCEPTION project. In: Bolognesi, C., Santagati, C. (eds.) Impact of Industry 4.0 on Architecture and Cultural Heritage, pp. 202–238. IGI Global, Hershey, PA (2020)
6. Di Giulio, R., Maietti, F., Piaia, E., Medici, M., Ferrari, F., Turillazzi, B.: Integrated data capturing requirements for 3D semantic modelling of Cultural Heritage: the INCEPTION Protocol. In: The International Archives of the Photogrammetry, Remote Sensing and Spatial Information Sciences, XLII-2/W3, pp. 251–257 (2017)
7. Amico N., Ronzino P., Felicetti A., Niccolucci F.: Quality management of 3d cultural heritage replicas with CIDOC-CRM. In: Alexiev, V., Ivanov, V., Grinberg, M. (eds.) Practical Experiences with CIDOC CRM and its Extensions (CRMEX 2013) Workshop, 17th International Conference on Theory and Practice of Digital Libraries, pp. 61–69 (2013)
8. https://ec.europa.eu/info/funding-tenders/opportunities/portal/screen/opportunities/topic-det ails/dt-transformations-20-2020. Accessed 29 Jul 2021
9. Cooperation on advancing digitisation of cultural heritage. Digital Day 2019, Brussels, Belgium (2019). https://ec.europa.eu/digital-single-market/en/news/eu-member-states-signcooperate-digitising-cultural-heritage. Accessed 14 Jun 2021
10. Apollonio, F.I., Gaiani, M., Sun, Z.: A reality integrated BIM for architectural heritage conservation. In: Ippolito, A. (ed.) Handbook of research on emerging technologies for architectural and archaeological heritage, pp. 31–65. IGI Global, Hershey, PA (2017)
11. López, F., Lerones, P., Llamas, J., Gómez-García-Bermejo, J., Zalama, E.: A review of heritage building information modeling (H-BIM). Multimodal Technol. Interact. 2(2), 21 (2018)

12. Jouan, P.A., Hallot, P.: Digital Twin: A HBIM-based methodology to support preventive conservation of historic assets through heritage significance awareness. Int. Arch., Remote Sens. Spat. Inform. Sci. **42**(2019), 609–615 (2019)
13. Brusaporci, S., Maiezza, P., Tata, A.: A framework for architectural heritage HBIM semantization and development. In: The International Archives of the Photogrammetry, Remote Sensing and Spatial Information Sciences, vol. XLII-2, pp. 179–184 (2018)
14. Bianchini, C., Ippolito, A., Bartolomei, C.: The surveying and representation process applied to architecture: non-contact methods for the documentation of cultural heritage. In: Brusaporci, S. (ed.) Handbook of research on emerging digital tools for architectural surveying, modeling, and representation, pp. 44–93. IGI Global, Hershey, PA (2015)
15. Bianchini, C.: Survey, modeling, interpretation as multidisciplinary components of a knowledge system. SCIRES-IT-Sci. Res. Inform. Technol. **4**(1), 15–24 (2014)

How Your Cultural Dataset is Connected to the Rest Linked Open Data?

Michalis Mountantonakis[1]([envelope]) [iD] and Yannis Tzitzikas[1,2] [iD]

[1] Institute of Computer Science, FORTH-ICS, Heraklion, Greece
{mountant,tzitzik}@ics.forth.gr
[2] Computer Science Department, University of Crete, Heraklion, Greece

Abstract. More and more publishers tend to create and upload their data as digital open data, and this is also the case for the Cultural Heritage (CH) domain. For facilitating their Data Interchange, Integration, Preservation and Management, publishers tend to create their data as Linked Open Data (LOD) and connect them with existing LOD datasets that belong to the popular LOD Cloud, which contains over 1,300 datasets (including more than 150 datasets of CH domain). Due to the high amount of available LOD datasets, it is not trivial to find all the datasets having commonalities (e.g., common entities) with a given dataset at real time. However, it can be of primary importance for several tasks to connect these datasets, for being able to answer more queries and in a more complete manner (e.g., for better understanding our history), for enriching the information of a given entity (e.g., for a book, a historical person, an event), for estimating the veracity of data, etc. For this reason, we present a research prototype, called `ConnectionChecker`, which receives as input a LOD Dataset, computes and shows the connections to hundreds of LOD Cloud datasets through `LODsyndesis` knowledge graph, and offers several measurements, visualizations and metadata for the given dataset. We describe how one can exploit `ConnectionChecker` for their own dataset, and we provide use cases for the CH domain, by using two real linked CH datasets: a) a dataset from the National Library of Netherlands, and b) a dataset for World War I from the Universities of Aalto and Helsinki.

Keywords: Linked data · Digital heritage · Cultural datasets · Connectivity analytics · Data integration · Data enrichment · Verification

1 Introduction

There is a high proliferation of publishers that decide to provide their data as digital open data, since such data can be a valuable asset for scientists and users, and this is also the case for Cultural Heritage (CH) domain [5,9,11]. However, given the high volume of data (e.g., see an example in CH domain [1]), it a strong requirement that the data are Findable, Accessible, Interoperable,

A. Moropoulou et al. (Eds.): TMM_CH 2021, CCIS 1574, pp. 136–148, 2022.
https://doi.org/10.1007/978-3-031-20253-7_12

and Reuseable (FAIR) [24], for easing their interchange, integration, preservation and management. Therefore, an emerging challenge is to link and integrate these data at large scale, for aiding users to find all the data about an entity, to discover relationships, answer queries and better understanding the past in general, and to estimate data veracity. This need is quite important for CH domain comparing to other domains, since cultural data cover various disciplines, i.e., digital libraries (such as Europeana [9]), archaeological data [1], museums and galleries [14], cultural databases for identifying images [22], visual collections for 3D reconstruction [13], and others.

One way to achieve this is by publishing the data in a structured way by using Linked Open Data (LOD) techniques [3], and a typical Data Publishing and Integration scenario is introduced in the upper side of Fig. 1. In particular, different providers produce data in many formats, e.g., CSV files, relational databases, and these data are usually transformed by using a specific model such as international standards like CIDOC-CRM [6] (see an example in [10]), for creating and publishing a central knowledge base as LOD. Existing approaches, such as FAST CAT [8] and Synthesis [7], can be exploited for performing the above process for cultural datasets. A further important step is to create links with existing LOD datasets, i.e., for enabling its publishing and connectivity to the popular LOD Cloud[1], which contains over 1,300 LOD Datasets (including over 150 datasets of CH domain), and for enabling the production of more advanced data access services.

However, due to the high and increasing number (and volume) of available LOD datasets and given the distributed nature of LOD, it is quite challenging to find all the datasets having commonalities with a given one. The major problems are that (i) it is inefficient and very time-consuming to discover and analyze every other LOD dataset (they can be even thousands), and (ii) publishers tend to use different URIs, names, schemas, languages and techniques for creating their data [19].

For tackling these difficulties, one can create cross-dataset relationships between entities and schemas, e.g., by using `owl:sameAs` relationships, however, it is not trivial since the `owl:sameAs` relationships a) model an equivalence relation and their transitive and symmetric closure has to be computed, and b) this presupposes knowledge of all datasets. For assisting this task at large scale, we have created `LODsyndesis` [16,17] knowledge graph, which has pre-computed the equivalence relationships among hundreds of LOD datasets (including 94 CH LOD datasets) and provides fast access to all the available information about an entity, through global scale entity-centric indexes and offers connectivity measurements for each underlying dataset. However, `LODsyndesis` contains a set of pre-collected manually fetched datasets, thereby it is not feasible to have access to such services for a new dataset before its actual publishing, although they can be an important asset for a dataset owner.

The key motivation (see the lower side of Fig. 1), is to connect the new dataset (e.g., a central knowledge base) to existing LOD datasets (through

---

[1] https://lod-cloud.net.

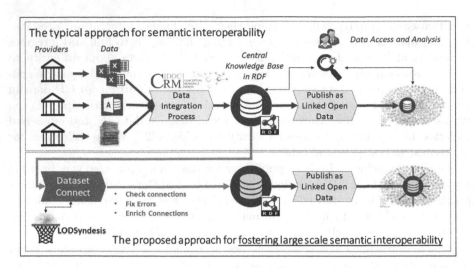

Fig. 1. The typical versus the proposed approach for fostering semantic interoperability

LODsyndesis) before its actual publishing, for ensuring its connectivity, for fixing possible connectivity errors, and for enriching its contents by discovering related datasets. For achieving this target, we introduce ConnectionChecker application, which extends LODsyndesis for providing such services directly at no cost for the dataset owner at real time. ConnectionChecker exploits the results of the transitive and symmetric closure of owl:sameAs relationships of LODsyndesis, for connecting the new dataset to LODsyndesis and for offering several measurements, visualizations and metadata for the input dataset, which can be exploited for evaluating its connectivity.

As a running example, suppose that in Fig. 2 we create a dataset containing data about "Jerusalem Old City Heritage" (JER), since we desire to perform an analysis about heritage sites, e.g., an analysis for "Holy Sepulchre" (e.g., see [1]). For making "JER" dataset more discoverable and reusable, we create links with one other CH dataset, say VIAF[2]. Our target is to connect "JER" dataset to LODsyndesis, for finding for each entity all its equivalent URIs (and their provenance), for enriching their information, and for discovering the top-K connected datasets to "JER" dataset.

Concerning our contribution, ConnectionChecker is accessible online[3], where one can easily check the connectivity of a dataset even in a few seconds for thousands of RDF triples. Moreover, we evaluate ConnectionChecker by using two real LOD datasets from CH domain, i.e., a) a dataset from the

---

[2] https://viaf.org.
[3] https://demos.isl.ics.forth.gr/ConnectionChecker/.

National Library of Netherlands[4], and b) a dataset for World War I [14] from the Universities of Aalto and Helsinki, Finland.

The rest of this paper is organized as follows. In Sect. 2, we give more details about Linked Data and LODsyndesis knowledge graph, and we present related approaches. In Sect. 3, we describe the ConnectionChecker application, and in Sect. 4 we evaluate ConnectionChecker through use cases from CH domain. Finally, Sect. 5 concludes the paper and discusses directions for future work.

2   Background and Related Work

Here, in Sect. 2.1 we provide background information about Linked Open Data and RDF, in Sect. 2.2 we describe LODsyndesis knowledge graph, whereas in Sect. 2.3 we present related approaches.

2.1   Background: Linked Data and RDF

"Linked Data refers to a method of publishing structured data, so that it can be interlinked and become more useful through semantic queries, founded on HTTP, RDF and URIs" [3]. The major principles of Linked Data, are the following: "(1) use URIs as names for things, (2) use HTTP URIs so that people can look up those names, (3) when someone looks up a URI, provide useful information, using the standards (RDF, SPARQL), and (4) include links to other URIs, so that they can discover more things".

Concerning RDF, it is a knowledge base that can be represented as a graph. It identifies resources with URIs (Uniform Resource Identifiers), e.g., the URI of "Holy Sepulchre" in German National Library (DNB) is http://d-nb.info/gnd/4073018-9. RDF describes resources with triples, where each triple is a statement of the following form: subject-predicate-object. A subject describes an entity, a predicate corresponds to a property of that entity, and an object to the value of that property for the entity occurring as subject, e.g., the upper left side of Fig. 2 shows an example with 4 triples. One triple is the following: "Holy Sepulchre, founder, Constantine the Great", where "Holy Sepulchre" is the subject, "founder" the predicate and "Constantine the Great" the object.

In the running example, the prefix of each URI (or node), i.e., the text before ":", indicates the provenance of each URI, e.g., "dbp" means that the provenance is DBpedia knowledge base [12]. Finally, owl:sameAs relationships are used for denoting that two URIs (or nodes) refer to the same real world entity, e.g., in the upper left side of Fig. 2, we connected the URI of "Holy Sepulchre" of "JER" dataset (i.e., "jer:Holy_Sepulchre") with the equivalent VIAF URI ("viaf:Holy_Sepulchre") through an owl:sameAs property.

---

[4] http://data.bibliotheken.nl.

2.2   Background: LODsyndesis Knowledge Graph

The current version of LODsyndesis[5] [16,17] contains over 400 million entities from 400 LOD datasets and two billion facts. It has pre-computed the transitive and symmetric closure of 44 millions owl:sameAs relationships among all the underlying datasets, for storing for each entity in global entity-centric indexes all its URIs, its triples and their provenance. The upper right side of Fig. 2 depicts the graph representation of LODsyndesis for "Holy Sepulchre" entity, e.g., LODsyndesis has computed all its equivalent URIs in all the datasets (see the nodes inside the big node) and has replaced all the URIs of "Holy Sepulchre" with a unique node (i.e., see the big node). It has also collected all its triples and their provenance (see the labels under each node in Fig. 2), e.g., the fact "Holy Sepulchre, style, Romanesque" occurs in DNB and DBpedia datasets.

By exploiting this knowledge graph the following services are offered [16,17,19]: (i) a service for finding all the available URIs, the provenance and all the facts about an entity (e.g., "Find all the URIs of Holy Sepulchre"), (ii) a fact checking service for estimating the veracity of a fact (e.g., "Is 335 AC the consecrated year of "Holy Sepulchre?"), (iii) Dataset Discovery services, for ensuring the connectivity of each dataset and for discovering the top-K relevant datasets to a given one, e.g., "Which are the top-K datasets having common entities with the National Library of France?". Moreover, it provides (iv) measurements among any subset of datasets, e.g., for finding the number of common entities among three datasets, e.g., "How many entities share VIAF, German and British Library?". Finally, it offers (v) several other services, e.g., machine-learning based services.

Limitation. The key limitation of LODsyndesis is that one is not feasible to add a new dataset before its actual publishing, e.g., for ensuring its connectivity, and for this reason we introduce ConnectionChecker application.

2.3   Related Work

There are several approaches focusing on data management for CH domain. [2] proposes an approach for making historical research data reusable according to the FAIR principles, through a collaborative ontology management environment. [5] introduces ArCo, a knowledge graph of Italian Cultural Heritage, which consists of several ontologies that model the CH domain. Furthermore, [25] presents an approach for enhancing knowledge management for Heritage Building Information Modeling (H-BIM) in CH domain through LOD techniques, whereas [11] presents a knowledge graph for Finland in the Second World War by using an infrastructure containing shared ontologies. [15] presents ARIADNE infrastructure for registering and connecting archaeological data and offers several data access services for the integrated resources. [4] introduces a framework for enriching the contents of CH datasets by using knowledge bases such as Wikidata [23], whereas [21] presents tools and methodologies for enriching and publishing CH

---

[5] https://demos.isl.ics.forth.gr/lodsyndesis.

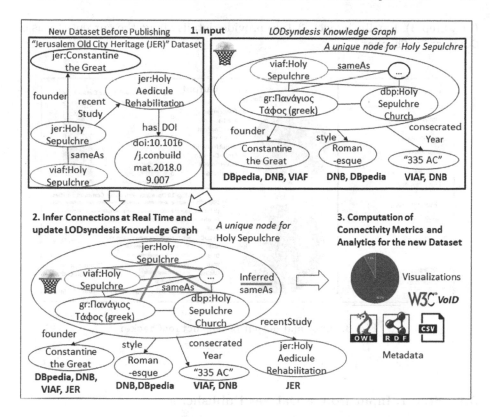

Fig. 2. Running example: Connecting the dataset "Jerusalem Old City Heritage" (JER) to the rest LOD Cloud before its actual publishing through `ConnectionChecker`

data through LOD techniques. Finally, [9] describes a workflow for aiding linked CH data analysis and integration and a case study for the Europeana network.

Novelty of `ConnectionChecker`. Comparing to the above approaches, to the best of our knowledge `ConnectionChecker` is the first research prototype that assists a data publisher (e.g., from CH domain) to evaluate the connectivity and to discover new connections for their dataset before its actual publishing. In this way, the data publishers can enrich (or verify) the contents of their dataset before publishing it to the LOD cloud.

3   The Steps of `ConnectionChecker`

The process of `ConnectionChecker` consists of there different steps. In particular, in Sect. 3.1 we describe how to receive the input from a dataset publisher (i.e., Step 1), in Sect. 3.2 we analyze how to infer new connections by using `LODsyndesis` (i.e., Step 2), and in Sect. 3.3 we describe how we compute the connectivity measurements and what analytics and visualizations are offered (i.e., Step 3). Finally, in Sect. 3.4 we provide details about the current status of ConnectionChecker.

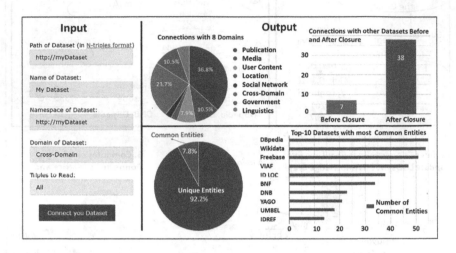

Fig. 3. Input and output of ConnectionChecker

3.1   Step 1. Input from a Dataset Publisher

The dataset owner fills a form about their dataset (see the left side of Fig. 3). Specifically, the user/publisher should provide a link containing the RDF triples in N-Triples format[6], the name of the dataset, its URL and its domain. Finally, for having a very fast overview for the connectivity of a given dataset, one can optionally select to perform the measurements for a smaller part of their dataset (e.g., for the first 10,000 triples).

3.2   Step 2. Inferring New Connections by Updating LODsyndesis

ConnectionChecker retrieves the dataset, and merges the LODsyndesis knowledge graph with the input dataset. In particular, it detects the equivalence relationships of the new dataset and computes the transitive and symmetric closure of equivalence relationships between the input dataset and the already existing datasets in LODsyndesis, for discovering inferred equivalence relationships. For instance, in the upper left side of Fig. 2, we can see that the URI "jer:Holy_Sepulchre" of "JER" dataset is connected with a owl:sameAs relationship with the corresponding URI of VIAF dataset, i.e., "viaf:Holy_Sepulchre". In LODsyndesis, i.e., see the upper right side of Fig. 2, the latter VIAF URI, is connected with several URIs from other datasets that contain information about

---

[6] https://www.w3.org/TR/n-triples/.

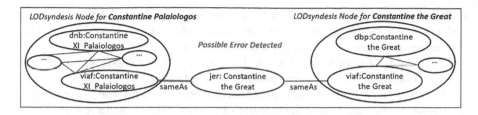

Fig. 4. Detect possible connectivity errors through `ConnectionChecker`

"Holy_Sepulchre" (e.g., see the connections with DBpedia and with a dataset in Greek language). By merging these relationships (see the lower left side of Fig. 2), we inferred new `owl:sameAs` relationships for the URI of "Holy_Sepulchre" in "JER" dataset (see the green thick connections), and we discovered commonalities with other datasets (except for VIAF). For example, we inferred that "JER" is connected with DBpedia dataset, since the URI "jer:Holy_Sepulchre" refers to the same entity as the URI "dbp:Holy Sepulchre Church".

By finding such connections, it is feasible to enrich and to verify the contents of a dataset. For example, in the lower left side of Fig. 2, a) we can enrich the contents of "JER" dataset about "Holy Sepulchre" from other datasets, e.g., the information about the style and consecrated year of "Holy Sepulchre" were not included in "JER" dataset, and b) we can verify the fact "Constantine the Great was the founder of Holy Sepulchre" from three other datasets.

3.2.1 Detecting Possible Errors.
`ConnectionChecker` can detect possible `owl:sameAs` errors by checking if an entity of the new dataset is connected with two or more real entities. For example, suppose that in Fig. 4 we have created the following `owl:sameAs` relationships (e.g., through an instance matching tool) for Constantine the Great: "jer:Constantine the Great `owl:sameAs` viaf:Constantine the Great" and "jer:Constantine the Great `owl:sameAs` viaf:Constantine XI Palaiologos". Since `LODsyndesis` has computed that "viaf:Constantine the Great" and "viaf:Constantine XI Palaiologos" refer to different entities, the user is informed that at least one of these `owl:sameAs` relationships is probably incorrect.

3.3   Step 3. Computation of Connectivity Measurements and Production of Analytics and Visualizations

`ConnectionChecker` exploits the updated `LODsyndesis` knowledge graph for computing content-based connectivity measurements (which are described in [18,20]), and for producing several connectivity analytics and visualizations, see the lower right side of Fig. 2. In brief, for the input dataset the following connectivity analytics and dataset discovery measurements are computed and visualized (examples of visualizations are shown in the right side of Fig. 3):

- The number of common entities, i.e., indicates how many entities of the new dataset can be found in at least one other LOD dataset, and the average number of datasets containing each common entity.
- The number of unique entities, i.e., how many entities exist only in the new (input) dataset, and the corresponding percentage.
- The number of inferred `owl:sameAs` relationships (and the corresponding increase percentage), and the number of possible `owl:sameAs` errors.
- The number of connections before and after connecting to `LODsyndesis` (and the corresponding increase percentage), i.e., for estimating the gain of transitive and symmetric closure of `owl:sameAs` relationships.
- The dataset ranking according to the number of connections in descending order, i.e., if the ranking of the dataset is 1, it means that it is the most connected dataset (it has more connections than any other LOD dataset).
- The top-K datasets having the most common entities with the entities of the new dataset (i.e., the most relevant datasets to the given dataset).
- The number of connections of the new dataset with each domain (e.g., how many connections exist with datasets from CH domain).
- The top K triads and quads of datasets with the most common entities that contain the input dataset, based on lattice-based measurements [16,20].

How to Exploit the Results. The user can either browse the above results through visualizations or export these results, all the inferred equivalence `owl:sameAs` relationships of each entity, the provenance of each entity, and metadata according to specific standards, i.e., in VoID[7] and CSV[8] formats.

3.4   The Current Status of `ConnectionChecker`

`ConnectionChecker` is an online web application[9]. It uses standard technologies, e.g., JavaScript and JAVA Servlets, and Google Charts[10] for creating the visualizations. A tutorial video for `ConnectionChecker` is accessible online[11].

4   Evaluation: Use Cases in Cultural Heritage Domain

We present use cases for two CH datasets for estimating their connectivity and for evaluating the gain of connecting them to `LODsyndesis` through `ConnectionChecker`. In particular, we use a) a subset of the dataset "Persons of National Library of Netherlands (*PNLN*)"[12], which contains the following data about persons (e.g., writers, historians): 3,000,000 triples (facts), 731,456 entities, and 535,407 `owl:sameAs` relationships. The initial dataset contains links to

---

[7] https://www.w3.org/TR/void/.
[8] https://en.wikipedia.org/wiki/Comma-separated_values.
[9] https://demos.isl.ics.forth.gr/ConnectionChecker/.
[10] https://developers.google.com/chart.
[11] https://youtu.be/vwKu5nVnjoM.
[12] http://data.bibliotheken.nl/doc/dataset/persons.

Table 1. Measurements for *PNLN* and *WW1LOD* datasets.

Measurement	Results for *PNLN*	Results for *WW1LOD*
# of unique entities (% wrt all entities of dataset)	582,234 (79.6%)	10,270 (92.6%)
# of common entities (% wrt all entities of dataset)	149,222 (20.4%)	825 (7.4%)
avg # of datasets containing each common entity	4.9	7.9
# of owl:sameAs relationships	535,407	547
# of inferred owl:sameAs relationships	615,813	2,172
Increase % of owl:sameAs relationships	115%	397%
# of possible errors in owl:sameAs relationships	0	0
# of connections before owl:sameAs closure	3	5
# of connections after owl:sameAs closure	38	29
Increase % of connections	1166%	480%
# of connections with CH datasets	15	12
Dataset ranking in connections (all datasets)	184 (out of 401)	212 (out of 401)
Dataset ranking in connections (CH datasets)	38 (out of 95)	43 (out of 95)

Table 2. Top-5 datasets having common entities with *PNLN*

Rank	Dataset having common entities with *PNLN*	Domain	Number of common entities
1	VIAF	Cultural heritage	148,756
2	Library of Congress	Cultural heritage	131,607
3	Germany National Library (DNB)	Cultural heritage	67,174
4	France National Library (BNF)	Cultural heritage	59,998
5	British National Library	Cultural heritage	42,861

three LOD datasets: *Wikidata* [23], *VIAF* and ISNI[13]. Moreover, we use b) the dataset "World War I as LOD (*WW1LOD*)" [14] from Aalto and Helsinki Universities, Finland, which contains data about World War I, i.e., 47,616 triples, 11,095 entities and 547 owl:sameAs mappings. The initial dataset contains links to five LOD datasets.

For the measurements, we used a single computer with 8 cores, 8 GB main memory and 60 GB disk space. For *PNLN* dataset, ConnectionChecker needed 45 min for computing the results (due to its high number of owl:sameAs relationships), whereas for *WW1LOD* it needed only 30 s (since it is much smaller in

---

[13] http://isni.org/.

Table 3. Top-5 connected triads of datasets including *PNLN*

Rank	Triad of datasets	# of Common entities
1	*PNLN, VIAF, Library of Congress*	131,578
2	*PNLN, VIAF, DNB*	67,173
3	*PNLN, VIAF, BNF*	59,914
4	*PNLN, DNB, Library of Congress*	55,458
5	*PNLN, Library of Congress, BNF*	54,586

size). The results of the measurements are accessible online[14]. Some indicative results are presented in Tables 1, 2 and 3 and are analyzed below.

4.1   Results for *PNLN* dataset

In the second column of Table 1, we can see that *PNLN* shares over 149,000 entities with at least one other LOD dataset, i.e., 20.4% of all entities of *PNLN*, whereas each of these entities can be found on average in 4.9 datasets. Moreover, the gain of connecting *PNLN* to LODsyndesis is obvious, i.e., we managed to infer 615,813 new owl:sameAs relationships (i.e., 115% increase), which resulted in 35 new "inferred" connections with other datasets for *PNLN* (i.e., 1166% increase). We identified that *PNLN* shares entities with 15 other CH datasets.

Table 2 shows the 5 datasets (and their domain) having the most common entities with *PNLN*. We can see that it shares thousands of entities with other CH datasets, indicatively 67,174 entities with *DNB*, although there were no connections between these two datasets in the initial *PNLN* dataset. Finally, Table 3 shows measurements among triads of datasets that include *PNLN*, e.g., we can see that *PNLN, VIAF* and *Library of Congress* share over 131,000 entities.

4.2   Results for *WW1LOD* dataset

In the third column of Table 1, we can see that *WW1LOD* dataset shares over 800 entities with at least one other dataset. Moreover, we inferred 2,172 new owl:sameAs mappings and we discovered 24 new connections for *WW1LOD*, whereas we found that it is connected with 12 CH datasets. Finally, the most connected dataset to *WW1LOD* is *Wikidata* with 792 commons entities, whereas the most connected dataset from CH domain is *VIAF* with 369 common entities.

5   Concluding Remarks

We presented a research prototype called ConnectionChecker, which exploits LODsyndesis for connecting any dataset, e.g., from Cultural Heritage

---

[14] http://islcatalog.ics.forth.gr/dataset/connectionchecker.

(CH) domain, to the rest Linked Open Data (LOD). In particular, ConnectionChecker can be exploited for ensuring the connectivity of a LOD dataset before its actual publishing, i.e., for discovering the most relevant datasets to this dataset, for better understanding the past, for enriching the information of its entities, and for estimating the veracity of its data.

Regarding evaluation, we introduced use cases from CH domain, e.g., for a dataset derived from the National Library of Netherlands. Indicatively, with ConnectionChecker we found that this dataset shares common entities with 38 other datasets, although the initial dataset included links to only 3 other datasets (i.e., 1166% increase). Moreover, we found that it shares even thousands of entities with several CH datasets (such as the National Library of France), although the initial dataset did not contain links to these datasets.

As a future work, we plan (a) to provide more connectivity measurements for an input dataset, e.g., for its schema elements and for its triples, (b) to describe all the technical details of ConnectionChecker, and (c) to evaluate its efficiency.

Acknowledgements. This work has received funding from the European Union's Horizon 2020 coordination and support action 4CH (Grant agreement No 101004468).

References

1. Alexakis, E., Kapassa, E., Touloupou, M., Kyriazis, D., Georgopoulos, A., Moropoulou, A.: Innovative methodology for personalized 3D representation and big data management in cultural heritage. In: Moropoulou, A., Korres, M., Georgopoulos, A., Spyrakos, C., Mouzakis, C. (eds.) TMM_CH 2018. CCIS, vol. 961, pp. 69–77. Springer, Cham (2019). https://doi.org/10.1007/978-3-030-12957-6_5
2. Beretta, F.: A challenge for historical research: making data FAIR using a collaborative ontology management environment (OntoME). Semant. Web 1(12), 279–294 (2021)
3. Bizer, C., Heath, T., Berners-Lee, T.: Linked data: the story so far. In: Semantic Services, Interoperability and Web Applications: Emerging Concepts, pp. 205–227. IGI Global (2011)
4. Candela, G., Escobar, P., Carrasco, R.C., Marco-Such, M.: A linked open data framework to enhance the discoverability and impact of culture heritage. J. Inf. Sci. 45(6), 756–766 (2019)
5. Carriero, V.A., Gangemi, A., Mancinelli, M.L., Nuzzolese, A.G., Presutti, V., Veninata, C.: Pattern-based design applied to cultural heritage knowledge graphs. Semant. Web 12(2), 313–357 (2021)
6. Doerr, M.: The CIDOC conceptual reference module: an ontological approach to semantic interoperability of metadata. AI Mag. 24(3), 75 (2003)
7. Fafalios, P., et al.: Towards semantic interoperability in historical research: documenting research data and knowledge with synthesis. In: Hotho, A., et al. (eds.) ISWC 2021. LNCS, vol. 12922, pp. 682–698. Springer, Cham (2021). https://doi.org/10.1007/978-3-030-88361-4_40
8. Fafalios, P., et al.: FAST CAT: collaborative data entry and curation for semantic interoperability in digital humanities. J. Comput. Cult. Herit. 14(4), 1–20 (2021)
9. Freire, N., Voorburg, R., Cornelissen, R., de Valk, S., Meijers, E., Isaac, A.: Aggregation of linked data in the cultural heritage domain: a case study in the Europeana network. Information 10(8), 252 (2019)

10. Karvasonis, I.: Study of the heterogeneity in cultural databases and transformation of examples from CIMI to the CIDOC CRM. Technical report, Citeseer (2001)
11. Koho, M., Ikkala, E., Leskinen, P., Tamper, M., Tuominen, J., Hyvönen, E.: WarSampo knowledge graph: Finland in the second world war as linked open data. Semant. Web **12**, 1–14 (2021)
12. Lehmann, J., et al.: DBpedia-a large-scale, multilingual knowledge base extracted from Wikipedia. Semant. web **6**(2), 167–195 (2015)
13. Makantasis, K., Doulamis, A., Doulamis, N., Ioannides, M.: In the wild image retrieval and clustering for 3D cultural heritage landmarks reconstruction. Multimedia Tools Appl. **75**(7), 3593–3629 (2016). https://doi.org/10.1007/s11042-014-2191-z
14. Mäkelä, E., Törnroos, J., Lindquist, T., Hyvönen, E.: WW1LOD: an application of CIDOC-CRM to world war 1 linked data. IJDL **18**(4), 333–343 (2017). https://doi.org/10.1007/s00799-016-0186-2
15. Meghini, C., et al.: ARIADNE: a research infrastructure for archaeology. ACM JOCCH **10**(3), 1–27 (2017)
16. Mountantonakis, M.: Services for Connecting and Integrating Big Numbers of Linked Datasets. IOS Press, Amsterdam (2021)
17. Mountantonakis, M., Tzitzikas, Y.: LODsyndesis: global scale knowledge services. Heritage **1**(2), 335–348 (2018)
18. Mountantonakis, M., Tzitzikas, Y.: Scalable methods for measuring the connectivity and quality of large numbers of linked datasets. JDIQ **9**(3), 1–49 (2018)
19. Mountantonakis, M., Tzitzikas, Y.: Large-scale semantic integration of linked data: a survey. ACM Comput. Surv. (CSUR) **52**(5), 1–40 (2019)
20. Mountantonakis, M., Tzitzikas, Y.: Content-based union and complement metrics for dataset search over RDF knowledge graphs. J. Data Inf. Qual. (JDIQ) **12**(2), 1–31 (2020)
21. Simou, N., Chortaras, A., Stamou, G., Kollias, S.: Enriching and publishing cultural heritage as linked open data. In: Mixed Reality and Gamification for Cultural Heritage, pp. 201–223. Springer, Cham (2017). https://doi.org/10.1007/978-3-319-49607-8_7
22. Valle, E., Cord, M., Philipp-Foliguet, S.: CBIR in cultural databases for identification of images: a local-descriptors approach (2008)
23. Vrandečić, D., Krötzsch, M.: Wikidata: a free collaborative knowledgebase. Commun. ACM **57**(10), 78–85 (2014)
24. Wilkinson, M.D., Dumontier, M., et al.: The FAIR guiding principles for scientific data management and stewardship. Sci. data **3**(1), 1–9 (2016)
25. Ziri, A.E., et al.: Cultural heritage sites holistic documentation through semantic web technologies. In: Moropoulou, A., Korres, M., Georgopoulos, A., Spyrakos, C., Mouzakis, C. (eds.) TMM_CH 2018. CCIS, vol. 962, pp. 347–358. Springer, Cham (2019). https://doi.org/10.1007/978-3-030-12960-6_23

The Naval Base of Navarino: Mapping the Fortifications of the Italians in Pylos

George Malaperdas[1]([✉]) [iD] and Dimitrios Panoskaltsis[2]

[1] University of The Peloponnese, Old Campus, 24133 Kalamata, Greece
envcart@yahoo.gr
[2] Tsiklitiras Street, 24001 Pylos, Greece

Abstract. October 28, 1940. The Greek-Italian war begins between Greece and the coalition of Italy and Albania after the former refuses to grant the Italian forces safe passage across the Greek borders. The occupation of Greece by both the Italians and Germans and the subsequent bloody events are often a field of controversy because of the brutality that these memories evoke.

The present paper deals with the above subject and presents one of the most important, if not the most, Italian naval base in the Peloponnese, which was called the base of Navarino (Pylos) and was characterized by the Italians themselves as the "first Italian temporary naval base" (prima base passegera) after Taranto, Italy.

The purpose of this paper is not to delve into the events, but to map and highlight the fortifications, especially in the major part of the Italian barracks, which was located south of Pylos, on Mount Agios Nikolaos. Thus, for the first time, scientific documents and photographic evidence from the bunkers and other fortifications reach the public eye, while a complete mapping of these sites is being made, thus contributing to the preservation of the memory of this distinct cultural heritage for a theme and an area that until our days very few people have looked at. To be sure, no one has so far entered the process of mapping it, thereby making the danger of full-fledged dissolution a probable scenario.

Keywords: Base of Navarino · Italian occupation · Mapping history · Pylos · GIS

1 Introduction (Historical Background)

1.1 The Entrenchment of the Italians in Pylos

At dawn on 28 October 1940, the Italian Ambassador in Athens, Emmanuel Grazzi, handed the Greek dictator Ioannis Metaxas, at his home in Kifissia, an ultimatum demanding the free passage of the Italian army from the Greek-Albanian border. After Metaxas' refusal, Italian military forces began military operations to invade Greece through the Greek-Albanian border. During the first days of April, alongside the beginning of the German offensive, the Italians launched a new attack from their part.

The Greek forces held out until 6 April 1941 when Germany attacked Greece. In early May 1941, the German forces arrived at the central square of Pylos, with twelve armored motorcyclists in search of British allied forces, who were considered as fugitives. They were welcomed by the President of Pylos Community[1], Anastasios Roidakis, and the constabulary squadron leader Nikolaos Anagnostopoulos, who replied that there were no fugitive allies in Pylos [1].

From the very first moment, all of Greece was under foreign occupation, but there was a Greek political administration which answered to the occupation authorities. The Italian army had overrun the villages and towns.

It was July 17, 1941 when a company of Italian infantry, under the command of the reserve officer Captain Domenico de Mouxie, settled in the castle of Pylos (Niokastro). The Italian forces continued to arrive, informed beforehand of the geostrategic importance of the location of Pylos, through descriptions in the earlier diaries of famous Italian travelers such as Collegno, who described Pylos as an important passage not only to Greek territory but to the whole Mediterranean [2].

Pylos is one of the largest natural harbours in the Mediterranean and the largest in the Peloponnese. The town and the port itself are surrounded and protected by the isle of Sfakteria and subsequently are protected from both natural disasters and hostile activities [3, 4].

It is no coincidence that the wise king Nestor chose the port of the prehistoric period of Pylos in these locations, nor is it a coincidence that Ancient Pylos, located in Koryphasium peninsula (nowadays under the second castle of Pylos, Paleokastro), occupied a fortified location that overlooked the entire passage of the Ionian Sea [5–8].

In this regard, it was no surprise that the Italian navy set up a large naval base at the harbour of Pylos. On September 1941, the 15,000-ton Italian battleship "Andrea Doria" (Fig. 1), arrived at the port of Pylos, accompanied by three destroyer ships, followed shortly after by two other transport ships, the "Tripoli" and the "Barbara", from which thousands of soldiers, sailors and their commanding officers disembarked [8].

Still enormous was the number of weapons, coastal artillery units, and anti-aircraft guns 'flaks', machine guns, personal armament as well as clothing and vehicles which was unloaded. In order to block the port of Pylos, empty barrels and anti-submarine nets were placed at the entrance of the port of Pylos as well as Yialova, in the so-called "Steno Sykias" or "Bouka".

Pylos was one of the most important bases of the Italians in the entire Peloponnese, who had a man power of nearly 15,000 men. The senior generals and heads of the task force were accommodated in the modern town of Pylos by commandeering entire blocks of land in the western part of the town. The exact locations of these Services are described in the book of Misirlis, who was an eyewitness to the events. The Services with which the Italians were burdened in Pylos were the garrison headquarters alongside its auxiliary

---

[1] According to the Hellenic Agency for Local Development and Local Government, since 21-04-1835 the Municipality of Pylos was established with its seat in Pylos (which exists until today), the only period in which the Municipality downgraded to Community was from 31-08-1912 to 26-09-1946, when it was reorganized as the Municipality of Pylos. It is worth mentioning, that many provinces, if not all with an exception of Kalamata, during the same period experienced a similar administrative downgrading from Municipalities to Communities including the most populated towns of Messenia Prefecture, such as Messini, Filiatra, Kyparissia etc. [16].

Fig. 1. Italian battleship "Andrea Doria" at Malta in 1943 [Source: Whitley, 1998].

services, the command post, the logistics, the management of the naval base and its port services, the police, the hospital, the infirmary, the dispensary and the officers' club [1].

On the other hand, the private foot soldiers settled the outskirts of Mount Agios Nikolaos. Italians also settled inside the fortress and destroyed part of the wall in order to build fortifications. As it also happened in other areas of occupied Greece, the occupiers built fortified positions and watchtowers, charted new roads, such as the one that was to remain until our days and connect Pylos with the southern Mount of Agios Nikolaos. In Agios Nikolaos, the four most powerful coastal artillery batteries were stationed, which were used for sea cover and under the fear of the Allied invasion.

Huge searchlights were placed at the same spot for maximum visibility for reconnaissance even at night. The Italians constructed concrete bases with circularly embedded pins to rivet the guns to the ground with large bolts. As for the reasons for choosing this particular location, it was chosen as it is very close to the town of Pylos, it has direct visibility to the town itself, while controlling all of the southern and western passages of the Ionian Sea to mainland Greece. Still because of its location and its heights, it was convenient for the development of telecommunications, with radio antennas being placed on the Mount of Agios Nikolaos, while further down in sheltered places (shelters), radio communications were operated (Fig. 2).

Thus, the port of Pylos and Sfakteria became the "Base of Navarino", the "first Italian temporal naval base" (prima de passegera) after Taranto in Puglia [9]. The Commander of the base was Count Ruggerio Ruggeri. The Navarino Base was the venue where the Italians repaired the auxiliary ships that supplied their forces in Africa, which had been damaged by allied submarines torpedoes [1].

In fact, as the Italian officer Herme Filipponio mentions in his book Gira La Giostra, recounting his memories of the Italian occupation of Pylos, three cruisers "Duca D'Aosta", "DucaDegliAbbruzzi" and "Garibaldi", six destroyers, the repair ship "Quariaro", some escort ships and a large number of submarines were permanently stationed in the port (Fig. 3).

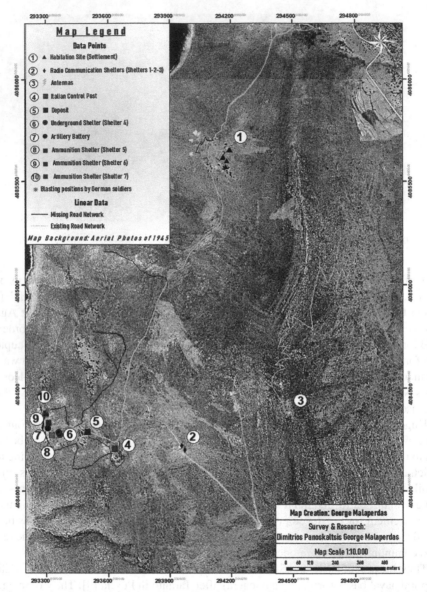

Fig. 2. Mapping the fortifications of the Italians in Agios Nikolaos (background: aerial photos of 1945).

He also adds, that in August 1942 the Italians staying in Navarino had a terrible workload as the ships leaving from Taranto to supply the troops in Africa, stopped at Navarino Base, not only for fuel and material supplies, but also in order to repair the damages caused by bombs and English torpedoes.

As he continues, not a day went by during that period that a cargo ship was not docked without being hit on its side. Among them were the "Monyiso", "Enrichetta",

Fig. 3. The Italian 8th Cruiser Division in Navarino, Greece, summer 1942. In the foreground, cruiser Duca d'Aosta with destroyer Bersagliere; farther away, cruiser Duca degli Abruzzi with destroyer Mitraglier.

"Nino Bixio" and the "Sebastiano Veniero", which was docked off the coast of Methoni carrying English prisoners from Libya.

At that time, the Navarino Base had become a huge shipyard for the repair of the Italian ships and one of the most important ports for the supply of the African troops [1, 10, 11].

Nevertheless, the German allies of the Italians, in their letters to their superiors and for the purpose of evaluating the Italian naval bases in general, often expressed their strong dissatisfaction. The cases found on the internet are dozens, indicative of which is the letter of General Rintelen, probably to Rommel himself, which clearly describes the desperate situation facing the Italian naval and air forces in the central Mediterranean. He mentions Malta as ineffective, while for the bases of Souda and Navarino he states that their air protection is considered ineffective and calls for their immediate reinforcement to improve their operation [12], while the Italians themselves refer extensively to the repeated bombardments of their naval bases in the Mediterranean, with dozens of references to the naval Base of Navarino [13, 14].

1.2 The Positions of the Italians in the Broader Area of Pylos

While the main Italian positions in Pylos and Agios Nikolaos have already been noted, their activity is hardly limited there.

Outposts, such as the one at Kainourgio Chorio, which is the main passage from Pylos to Methoni, appear at key locations; Artillery batteries, initially placed at the centre of Yialova, due to the advanced levels of soil moisture during winter time, were moved to a higher ground in Yialova, named "Dapia".

To control the passage of wheeled vehicles on the public roads to Methoni, Kalamata and Kyparissia, two fortified manned checkpoints were set up; backed up with anti-tank obstacles, made of stone walls and large iron rods. The first was near the present-day chapel of Agios Nektarios (driving from Pylos on the road to Methoni), over which they mounted an artillery battery. And the second one was in the small village of Palionero, which they almost cleared of its inhabitants in order to accommodate an additional Italian company and another artillery battery.

The third checkpoint block was placed at the location named "Mytikas" directly outside the last northeastern houses of Pylos, this time in the direction of Kalamata, before the location named "Miden", while a little further down the road, they set up an artillery battery. At a distance of about 700 m northern from the previous position, they placed large searchlights and a telephone installation. At the same position, but at an altitude about 50 m higher, a support artillery battery was set up, while another one was set up 300 m lower at, the location "Kanoni". Taking into account the bulk of the aforementioned arguments, we can easily infer that Pylos was an extremely important town for the Italians, and it was so well armoured that nothing could get in or get out without the knowledge of the Italians.

While all roads for cars were closed, inside Niokastro, a cannon and a machine gun were placed on the Acropolis of the Castle, and a second one on the eastern tower of Agios Patrikios. Another cannon was placed on the walls, of the "Megali Verga" watchtower, as well as an observation post, while two large concrete cannons were set up, one at the city hospital and the other at the "Spilies" location inside Pylos. In the courtyard of Pylos's old commercial bank, were placed two large land-based guns, while the building itself functioned as the gunners' barracks. Two other smaller guns were located outside the Roussopoulos Hotel[2] (on the coastal road) and another one could be found in the grove of Pylos. In the basements of many houses there were cannon nests, while many rooftops hosted machine guns.

In this way a huge defensive cordon with 312 guns of every type had been placed, while the occupation troops reached 15,000 men, preventing passage both by land and by sea. However, as mentioned before, the air defense was far from effective.

On the isle of Sfakteria, they also built a road from one end to the other, while they also placed artillery batteries there and built water tanks and observation posts with radios [1].

1.3 The Liberation of Pylos

On 3 September 1943, five days before the announcement of the Italian capitulation, the Italians surrender the base. The occupation was continued by the Germans. The Italian soldiers form the large naval Base of Navarino left on boats or on foot to Kalamata. The materiel of the Italians was handed over to the Germans and the Niokastro castle, became the headquarters of the German conquerors. The rich Italian stores of food and clothing were loaded into more than 400 trucks to reinforce the German forces [1, 15].

---

[2] It is reported that the Germans, aided from Roussopoulos Hotel, targeted without success the monument of the Italian Philhellene Santarosa, who fell at Sfakteria on 26 April 1826 [15].

On their departure however, the Italians marked their stay with bitter memories as they removed the carved snakes from the temple of the Church of Sotiros in Niokastro, as well as from the Church of the Cemetery of Ayios Ioannis inside Pylos, but in this case they were fortunately found and repositioned in the temple of the Ayios Ioannis church[3]. From a chapel on the river Xerias, they took a head of Christ from an old fresco, a work made by the famous painter Moschos. They also took 12 large iron cannons, keepsakes of the glorious naval battle of Navarino (1827), from the isle of Sfakteria, below the place called "Kokkinovrachos". The rest of the cannons were thrown into the sea.

A year later, on September 2 1944, Pylos was liberated, after the Allied invasion of French Normandy and the fatal retreat of the Germans towards their threatened homeland. But German brutality left its mark on the entire region. The Germans, after driving off what supplies they could redeem, they blew up their forts and dismantled the magnificent naval base set up by their Italian allies.

From the Italian guns which were set up to the west side of Ayios Nikolaos Mount, they aimed and blew up the lighthouse. The house of the lamplighter sat the entrance of the harbour, at Tsichli – Baba, which since 1873 had been operating peacefully bidding wishes for a safe journey to the ships entering or leaving this great harbour. After a while, they eventually blew them up too. Finally, the Germans had set up dynamite all over the Pylos quay, to get back at the Greeks and make a spectacular exit by blowing up the whole pier of Pylos. Fortunately, local residents[4] caught up and picked up the cables thus preventing an unimaginable disaster for the historical town of Pylos [1, 10].

2 Methodology and Results

The research for the mapping of the fortifications of the Italians in Pylos includes a field work visit to the points of interest. At the first stage all these points of interest were marked in a cartographical background of Quickbird Satellite Images of the 20.01.2008 for the wider study area. The fieldwork combined with the sources, bibliographical references, provided us with a thorough study which contains empirical knowledge by collecting primary data and scientific documentation by collecting secondary sources.

The field survey was conducted primarily to obtain the exact coordinates of the sites and also to collect photographs and to identify and record the current condition of the sites. For the accuracy of the measurements, the geodetic GPS station of the Laboratory of Archaeometry of the University of The Peloponnese was used (measurement accuracy ± 10 mm), while the projection system used is the Greek Geodetic Reference System

---

[3] Both the Church of Sotiros in Niokastro and the Church of Ayios Ioannis in the Cemetery of Pylos, show the same technique in the iconostasis with carved snakes on either side of the Cross.

[4] Due to the great dynamism of the occupying forces in Pylos, a large resistance network developed. It is speculated that members of this network prevented by blowing up of the pier of the port of Pylos, while at the same time they transmitted information by radio about the movements of the Axis forces, such as the large huge bombardment of the fortification tower of "MegaliVerga" at Niokastro inside Pylos, which was used as an ammunition depot back in 1943.

(EGSA'87), which is the most common and uniform reference system for the entire Greek territory and must be used in all topographic projects carried out in Greece.

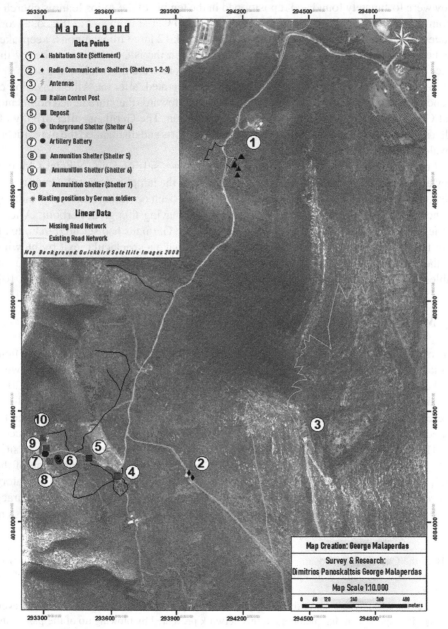

Fig. 4. Mapping the fortifications of the Italians in Agios Nikolaos (background: Quickbird satellite images date of receive 01.20.2008).

With this primary data collected, the database for the fortification works in Agios Nikolaos was created. The database in turn was imported into a Geographic Information Systems (GIS) environment and converted into a point vector layer of geospatial information in shapefile (*.shp) format. At the same time, for the presentation of the locations on maps and also for their creation, it was decided to use as a background, in addition to the aforementioned satellite images, aerial photos of the year 1945 (very close in time to the period we are referring to), for the identification of the sites at that time. Indeed, the 1945 aerial photos show the Italian roads, among other information, which were digitized as linear vector information files and inserted into the maps. In this way it is possible to compare the road network built by the Italians in 1945 and the changes appearing nowadays.

Finally, it is speculated that the roads that existed in 1945 were built to lead to sites of Italian infrastructures that were subsequently destroyed and a second targeted visit to these sites may be needed to identify possible remains on the ground (Fig. 4).

2.1 The Fortifications of the Italians in Agios Nikolaos

The area of Agios Nikolaos, where the bulk of the soldiers resided, numbered around 10–12,000 soldiers [1]. For their accommodation, they created an entire town on the outskirts of Agios Nikolaos with both stone and wooden buildings. The buildings were destroyed by the inhabitants after the liberation of the area. Their stones were used for the construction of dry stone terraces and for the delimitation of its fields. Throughout the area, the stones testify to the occupation of the place (Fig. 5). One of the few, if not the only surviving building contains the so-called Italian mural (graffiti), depicting a flower on the left side of the wall, and three young wolves on the right side (Fig. 6). The Italians often used the art of mural painting and decorated their buildings as recently revealed by the example of the Italian occupation in Leros [17]. Even the Ministry of Culture has recently highlighted the historical murals (graffiti) of the prisoners of the Italian and German occupation inside the fortress of Pylos [18].

Fig. 5. The stones of the houses of the Italians, after the war, were used to built terraces for the fields of the local inhabitants.

Fig. 6. Ruins of an Italian building in the area of Agios Nikolaos with preserved fresco.

In the same place the Italians had created water supply and sewage systems. The deposits, the laundry and the watering trough for the animals of the Italian soldiers can still be seen today (Fig. 7).

Fig. 7. Infrastructures: (a) deposit, (b) general view, (c) watering trough, (d) deposit and laundry.

Continuing towards the top of the mount, there were antennas for telecommunications (no longer preserved). A little further down the radio shelters are located. They are named so as this is the location where both the radio communications and the radio operators were sheltered. These are also known as the twin shelters, which for the purpose of this

Fig. 8. (a) The twin Shelters: shelter 1 on the left, Shelter 2 on the right, (b) Shelter 3: the most inaccessible as the entrance has been destroyed by rockfalls.

research were named by the authors of the article as Shelter 1 and Shelter 2. A few dozen metres further up the mount there is another radio shelter, named Shelter 3 (Fig. 8).

Both Shelter 1 and Shelter 2 are spacious and keep their main entrance open. They are easily accessible. The outer entrance still has the iron bars used to secure the door. Names and possible battalion numbers are still engraved on the outside. The third in the order (Shelter 3), presents a different situation as its entrance is almost gone. Its access is impossible as all that is fitting is only the photographer's hand for the photographic documentation of its interior. Some objects made by wood can still be seen inside, probably from benches and beds used by the Italian soldiers for resting. All evidence shows that Shelter 3 has been closed for decades, so it is most likely that objects from that period could be found, as it seems that nothing has been confiscated, like the other shelters (Fig. 9).

Fig. 9. Interior: (a) shelter 1, (b) shelter 2, (c) shelter 3.

Descending to a lower position, the most powerful artillery batteries were placed in order to cover the seafront. The first site is an old military outpost of which only the outer walls survive until today. A few metres further there is another large deposit for the hydration needs of the Italian soldiers (Fig. 10).

Fig. 10. (a) and (b) visibility from the site where the Italians covered the sea front, (c) deposit

Continuing to the west, there is another underground shelter with possible use as a dwelling (Shelter 4). It has two entrances, the north and south, which are connected by a narrow corridor. In the interior there are two large rooms. It is generally preserved in a very good condition, while it is also very well covered by the local vegetation of the area (Fig. 11).

Once again and continuing to the west, the first of the two possible artillery batteries described by Misirlis [1], for which the base is preserved is located. Regarding the second one, the base no longer exists (Fig. 12).

Fig. 11. (a) The northern entrance of Shelter 4, very difficult to detect as the natural vegetation of the area is ideal for its concealment, (b) the northern entrance through the Shelter, (c) the southern entrance through the Shelter, (d) the stairs of the northern entrance can be seen, as well as the west facing rooms.

Fig. 12. The base of the artillery battery in Agios Nikolaos.

Walking to the south from the position of the artillery battery is the first ammunition shelter of the Italians (Shelter 5), while further north and closer to the base of the artillery battery is a second ammunition shelter (Shelter 6). In those years this site was directly connected with the artillery battery by an underground passage. The passageways as well as the shelters were blown up by the Germans when they left. The last station on this route is the northernmost of the ammunition shelters (Shelter 7), where the main entrance has been covered by rocks and impossible to approach (Fig. 13).

In the area, the positions where the German soldiers blew up their shelters during their departure are still recognizable, while small objects can be found all over the landscape, which testifies to the occupation image of Agios Nikolaos in Pylos (Fig. 14).

Fig. 13. Ammunition Shelters: (a) Shelter 5 entrance, (b) Shelter 6 entrance, (c) Shelter 7 entrance, (d) Shelter 5 interior, (e, g, h) Shelter 6 interior.

Fig. 14. (a) The northernmost of the German blasting positions, (b) the second German blasting, (c) small objects that testify to the passage of the Italian occupation forces from the mount of Agios Nikolaos of Pylos.

3   Conclusion

During the Italian occupation, Pylos functioned as one of the most important strategic positions for the Italian forces. This is where the large naval Base of Navarino was established; a base that served as an intermediate transshipment station for the Italian interventions in North Africa. The second important function of the base was its use as a repair yard for Italian ships, which were constantly being through back and forth to Navarino Bay to repair damages they had suffered either from enemy actions or from weather conditions. Still, as a modern town at that time, with large streets and squares, beautiful and clean, it functioned as an attraction for the Italian conquerors in their choice of a place to live.

The fortifications of the Italians are monumental cultural resources that constitute the cultural heritage, which is regulated and protected by law no. 3028/2002. They are distinguished in newer monuments on the basis of their definition "as newer monuments are understood the cultural heritage that are later than 1830 and whose protection is required due to their historical, artistic or scientific importance" (Government Gazette 153/A/2002). The European Commission has been working on the digitization and accessibility of cultural resources since 2000. Over the last decade, significant steps have been taken, in order to coordinate digitization activities in the European area, with the adoption of common guidelines and best practices in key areas; relating to digitization, documentation and the dissemination of results at European level.

This paper uses topography and Geographical Information Systems to map the fortifications of the Italians in Agios Nikolaos of Pylos. Based on the bibliographical references, a field survey was carried out and resulted not only in the mapping, but also in the publication of primary photographical material, which is displayed for the first time.

In this regard, the contribution of this paper is vital for the preservation of the historical memory of the occupation and its related events in the region of Pylos. To be sure, the landscape has already undergone a year to year alteration (transformation); the natural environment is being degraded, while the site itself, and in a very short distance from the ammunition depots, has become a dumping ground for the Municipality of Pylos since the 1960s. This fact could be seen as another indication that the local authorities sought to erase the memories of the occupation of their territories by the Axis forces; by burying them with their garbage there by ignoring the words of the German historian Wofgang Bent who argued that "memorial sites should not be treated as places of emotions, but as places of moral and political reflection. That is why they should be highlighted and have a central place, not only in annual commemorations, but also in political culture".

Acknowledgements. The authors would like to thank Dr. Georgios Rigas and Dimitrios Mitsos for the corrections to the translation and the interesting remarks they introduced to the original text.

This project was implemented within the scope of the "Exceptional Laboratory Practices in Cultural Heritage: Upgrading Infrastructure and Extending Research Perspectives of the Laboratory of Archaeometry", a co-financed by Greece and the European Union project under the auspices of the program "Competitiveness, Entrepreneurship and Innovation" NSRF 2014–2020.

References

1. Misirlis, I.: Pylos, to the Path of the Centuries. Editions Papadimas, Athens (2003)
2. Collegno, G.: Diario dell'assedio di Navarino memorie di Giacinto Collegno precedute da un ricordo biografico dell'autore scritto da Massimo D'Azeglio. In: Pelazza Tipografia Economica. Via Della Posta, Torino (1857)
3. Mpaltas, C.: Pylos, Navarino, Niokastro, Nestor's Palace. Unknown Editions, Athens (1987)
4. Papathanasopoulos, G., Papathanasopoulos, T.: Pylos-Pylia. A Journey Through Space and Time. Archaeological Receipts Fund, Athens (2000)
5. Marinatos, S.: Excavation of Pylos: Coryphasium. In: PAE 1958, Athens 1965, pp.184–187 (1958)
6. Yialouris, N.: The Hellenistic Cemetery of Yialova-PalaioNavarino (Coryphasium) AD, vol. 221, pp. 64–165 (1966)

7. Korres, G.: Navarino Bay. Installation Memories from Prehistoric Era. Messenian Flash J. **131**, 48–50 (2000)
8. Papachatzis, N.: Pausanias Messenia - Ileia. Athenian Publishing House, Athens (2009)
9. Rohwer, J.: Chronology of the War at Sea 1939–1945: The Naval History of World War Two, 3rd edn. Naval Institute Press, Annapolis (2005)
10. Kaldis, V.: A journey to Modern Pylos. Unknown editions, Athens (1978)
11. Filipponio, H.: Gira la giostra!...: ricordi e meditazioni in terra straniera. ELI, stampa, Milano (1961)
12. Homepage: https://rommelsriposte.com/2014/02/10/a-most-sombre-assessment/. Access 7 Jun 2021
13. Homepage. https://issuu.com/rivista.militare1/docs/diario-vol-viii-tomo1-testo. Access 7 Jun 2021
14. Biagini e Frattolillo: Diario Storico del Comando Supremo Vol VIII Tomo 1 – Parte Prima. dal 1.9.1942 al 31.12.1942 -DIARIO- Edizione Ufficio Storico (1999)
15. Chatzigewrgiou, O.: Pylos during the Italian occupation. In: Handwritten memoirs (1960)
16. Homepage: https://www.eetaa.gr/metaboles/dkmet_details.php?id=269. Access 7 Jun 2021
17. Homepage: https://www.ertnews.gr/eidiseis/ellada/kinonia/822630-2/. Access 7 Jun 2021
18. Homepage: https://www.culture.gov.gr/el/Information/SitePages/view_announcement.aspx?nID=3091#prettyPhoto. Access 7 Jun 2021

Documentation of Cultural Heritage Monuments, by Introducing New Surveying Technologies

Implementation in Sarlitza Pallas, in Thermi Mytilene

Garoufos George, Ioannidou Stefania⬤, Kanellopoulos Nikolaos⬤, and Pantazis George(✉)⬤

School of Rural, Surveying and Geoinformatics Engineering, National Technical University of Athens, 15780 Athens, Zografos, Greece
gpanta@central.ntua.gr

Abstract. Visualization in 3D is an effective way to analyze and represent the environment of a building, especially if it's Cultural Heritage. Technology development of standardized methods can be very motivating for researchers of different sciences to integrate 3D modeling in their jobs. A key question is if it is possible for these methods to reach or maybe exceed the accuracy of classic geodetic methods and specifically those that are using total stations. Digital documentation combined with innovative analytical techniques and digital tools can be an effective strategy to support transdisciplinary documentations and modeling aimed at conservation, enhancement and preservation of Cultural Heritage. This paper presents the comparison between the two methods of documentation, classic and digital. Research object is Sarlitza Pallas, a small, historical and noted hotel which is based from 1909 in a small village called Thermi in Mytilene, Greece.

A geometrical documentation has been done (elevations, floor plans, cross-sections), by using a conventional reflectorless total station. As regards the digital documentation and the 3D model of the hotel, have been produced by using a modern Multi-Station.

The result was the documentation of Sarlitza Pallas with two different methods and their comparison, in order to assess the overall time and accuracy of derivative product and the capability of Multi-Station autonomous use in similar studies of Cultural Heritage monuments.

Keywords: 3D visualization · Multi-Station · Documentation · Cultural heritage · Sarlitza Pallas · Dense point cloud · Orthophoto/rectified image

Abbreviations

EDM Electronic Distance Measurement
GCP Ground Control Points
IATS Image Assisted Total Station
MS Multi-Station
TBC Trimble Business Center
TS Total Station

A. Moropoulou et al. (Eds.): TMM_CH 2021, CCIS 1574, pp. 164–173, 2022.
https://doi.org/10.1007/978-3-031-20253-7_14

1 Introduction

Conservation and preservation of cultural heritage assets is nowadays a serious issue that concerns not only the scientific community but also the people around the world. Current studies have shown that there is an approach concerning the architectural and geometric documentation, creating textured three-dimensional (3D) models or two-dimensional (2D) plans with high accuracy. (Delegou et al. 2019).

In addition, the historical buildings, in order to be properly highlighted and restored, have to be documented in three ways (Haddad and Akasheh 2005):

- The written documentation which includes the architectural description and all the results and reports of all investigations.
- The graphic documentation which is based on conventional surveying and includes plans, elevations and cross-sections (2D information).
- And the photographic documentation which uses photography, photogrammetry, and 3D laser scanner, so as to create 3D models or present textures and optical details.

During the years, different geometric methods of documentation have been utilized and implemented. Each of them has both advantages and disadvantages, concerning not only the use but also the required accuracy. On the other hand, over the last decade, due to the development of technology, Multi-Station is an innovation which combines features and provisions of the above methods.

In this paper, after the analysis of the existing geometric methodologies of documentation in buildings, a detailed presentation about Multi-Stations is made. Their capabilities will be explained and tested, and new possibilities can arise. In the end, there is also an implementation, of Sarlitza Pallas in Mytilene, Greece, using both known methods and Multi-Station technologies.

2 Geometric Methods of Documentation

"Geometric documentation is the action of acquiring, processing, presenting and recording the appropriate data for the determination of the position and the actual existing form, shape and size of an object in the three-dimensional space at a particular moment." (Stylianidis and Georgopoulos 2017).

Four principal methods are used to compile metric data each of them is following described, so as to figure out its positive and negative aspects. By now, it's well accepted that different methods are more accurate and describe the overall study better than one method. So selection and integration of the following survey techniques are used in order to preserve and conserve historical monuments.

2.1 The Traditional Manual Method

The traditional manual method, is one the most ancient methodologies that used in monument documentation. It determines dimensions by measuring angles and distances using flexometers, plumb lines, poles, squares, measuring tapes, and manual laser distance meters.

Even if it is a low cost method (<3.000$), it needs trained people and a small area to be documented. Furthermore it is time-consuming and the accuracy in locating points is above ±5 cm. Also, the collected data are without spatial connection and the results are simple paper plans and not in digital format (Arias et al. 2006).

2.2 The Topography Method

This method is also known as the geodetic methodology, and is one of the most famous methods in geometric documentation with a cost 3.000$ to 12.000$. It is based on calculating three-dimensional coordinates of specific points of an object in order to establish its geometry (Arias et al. 2006).

The main equipment is a total station which is effective over a great range of scales and have an accuracy at around ±1 mm. Polar coordinates' measurements (horizontal/vertical angle and slope distance) from fixed points provide horizontal and vertical information respectively.

Using a geodetic control network, georeferenced point regions are created, and after processing, the points are projected so as to be digital2D plans, elevations and cross-sections.

2.3 The Photogrammetry Method

Additionally, classical and close-range photogrammetry methods are also well-known in monument documentation at a cost of <3.000$ and >12.000$ respectively. The greatest advantage of them is that they are faster in measuring than the others, but the processing (office work) is more complicated.

Overlapping photographs, due to image matching, are aligned and a dense point cloud is created. In order to reproduce true position and scale, geodetic support is needed, by assigning coordinates to a set of points on the photographs of the object (Bastonero et al. 2014).

The final result can be 2D orthophotos and detailed 3D models with texture, which contains surface or other optical details. The accuracy, depends on the uncertainty of the geodetic points and the processing algorithms and it is between ±1 mm to ±5 cm (Arias et al. 2006).

2.4 The Scanning Method

The last method using in monument documentation is the scanning, which is a combination between geodetic and photogrammetric method by an accuracy between ±1 mm to some cm and cost higher than 12.000$.

A Terrestrial Laser Scanner, using polar measurements, creates dense point clouds of the monument. These clouds need cleaning, alignment and georeference so as to be correct in scale and size, and finally a 3D model without texture is created.

Although method's accuracy is high, it has time-consuming processing, and may have difficulties on some material surfaces (Bastonero et al. 2014).

3 Presentation of Multi-station Technique

In many cases, Multi-Station (MS) tends to be the best alternative solution of Total Stations' (TS) measurements, thanks to the very high acquisition rate of points and the possibilities of deeper processing at the software level. Due to faster and more accurate sensor technology, MS is proven to be a reliable solution for high accuracy for 3D surveying and documentation of natural and technical infrastructure.

The up-to-date Multi-Station (SX10 of Trimble), is a geodetic instrument combining high accuracy 3D scanning and Image Assisted Total Stations (IATS) functionalities. SX10 released in October 2016, as a part of a wider instrument category of Multi-Stations that are multiplex and innovative multi-sensor systems (Lachat et al. 2017).

Most Multi-Stations have three cameras: one wide and two with smaller optical frames, called: overview, primary and telescope, depending on the manufacturer (Fig. 1). The first two are located parallel to the EDM axis with an offset. The third is placed in the measurement axis and is used for enlargement. All of them depict the reality on the screen of the controller-tablet, while it does not have a real/virtual telescope or screen. Furthermore, it creates panoramic images, and by choosing a region, MS captures several overlapping pictures in the horizontal and vertical direction (Lachat et al. 2017).

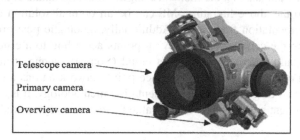

Fig. 1. Inside view and cameras of a Multi-Station (https://surveying.org.au/)

It is planned to be an innovative instrument merging the capabilities of TS with these of a Laser Scanner (LS). With this MS instrument, it is possible to get a dense point cloud of a scene in a very short time. Also, there is the opportunity to get a dense point cloud in full-dome mode. About the point cloud density there are four options: coarse (±10 mm), standard (±5 mm), fine (±2 mm), and superfine (±1 mm). A remarkable advantage is the capability of a real-time visualization of data in the field.

After the acquisition of the measurements, Trimble Business Center (TBC) contains all the post-process functions needed in order to analyze, inspect, correct, improve and produce the final digital documents.

According to previous studies, in building facades and road bridges, when using Trimble SX10, the longer the distance of the object is, the lower is the density of the point cloud (Lachat et al. 2017). About the georeference methods (direct and indirect methodologies) higher 3D standard deviations are presented in direct method, in areas where the density of the point cloud is lower and incidence angles are big, causing bigger noise. As a result the direct georeferencing method is very convenient but it is not always the best solution for the creation of a high accuracy model (Lachat et al. 2017).

There is not a single method that constitutes the perfect solution and a combination of methods seems to be the best idea. Therefore, the question posed is what will be more effective, cost-reducing, and time-saving when using different methods independently or a combination of them (Scherer 2002).

Multi-Station can be considered as a hybrid solution. Except for the capabilities mentioned before as a Laser Scanner, also belongs in the category of Total Stations. Some important advantages are the capability of object documentation with images, the capturing of georeferenced point clouds and panoramas or the originality which is based on the absence of a telescope (Lachat et al. 2017).

It has the ability of acquisition very high point density and large spatial coverage, with high measurement accuracy, in a short time. Moreover, a MS enables 3D visualization of an object or scene which allows users to interact with it from different angles and directions (Slob and Hack 2004). The quality of independent points, in a point cloud, is not yet well understood because of its impact on the simple steps of post-processing procedure, such as the point cloud registration and segmentation.

Scanned point quality is affected by four significant factors: instrument mechanism, atmospheric conditions, object surface properties, and scan geometry. Therefore, it is very important to mention that the local geometry depends on the distance between object and scanner and also on the incidence angle (Soudarissanane et al. 2011).

According to the above literature, MS can be an optimal solution considered the fact of the implementation framework. Additionally, automatic post-processing often is realized during the capture, e.g. removing points according to a criterion that may also affect the quality of the overall point cloud (Soudarissanane et al. 2011). MS's process is much correlated with the reference point network and as a consequence, a lot of attention must be given to the implementation methodology. It is a high-cost new generation instrument but can be an added value factor in surveying studies or jobs.

4 Implementation

Multi-Station SX10 of Trimble has been used for the digital documentation of a small, historical and famous hotel, which is called Sarlitza Pallas, and it is located at Thermi in Mytilene, Greece (Fig. 2). The research study refers to the creation of the hotel's digital model, vertical plans and facades, in order to be compared with those using classic methods. In this section, data acquisition and processing for generating the final products are analyzed.

4.1 Data Acquisition

In order to do the scans for the digital documentation of Sarlitza Pallas, nine points with known coordinates (from a geodetic network) had been used. Each station measured both the previous and next station for its orientation. The reference system used was arbitrary and it was founded by assigning local coordinates to the first point. Scanning procedure of the object took place with a standard point density (±5 mm).

The described implementation was done for the acquisition of necessary data using MS SX10. It is clear from the measurement procedure that the MS has many capabilities either like a Total Station or Laser Scanner.

Fig. 2. Front and back view of Sarlitza Pallas at Thermi in Mytilene, Greece

4.2 Data Processing

This section describes the process to create the orthophotos of facades of Sarlitza Pallas, which are essentially the final product of this study. Data processing has been done with TBC.

Loading the point cloud to a computer, an initial check for gross errors took place through a general inspection of the point cloud to assess the quality of its completeness. Another check took place to confirm basic surveying information (by checking the angles and distances report) for the station points.

The process continues with cleaning of the point cloud from noise and vegetation. All the data that were out of the polygon, defined by the scanner stations, were cleaned up automatically. On the other hand vegetation is done manually and it is time-consuming, and not simple. During the study of Sarlitza Pallas, big quantities of vegetation had to be discarded. After this procedure, a general inspection of the point cloud is done especially on the building corners which was hidden by vegetation (Fig. 3).

Fig. 3. Before and after the cleaning of vegetation

The next step refers to the georeferencing of the station points. After these procedures a recomputing of the project is necessary. With this functionality, possible error flags appear in the project. These errors have to be corrected so as to complete the georeference procedure with the proper results (Fig. 4).

Then, it is necessary to do a geometric check as well as errors may appear in the surveying (e.g. wrong distances between the point stations). Their correction can be done

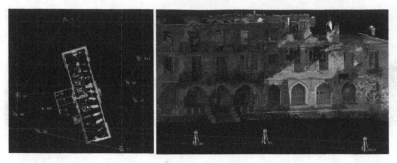

Fig. 4. Error flags in georeferencing and final georeferenced point cloud in 3D

with the definition of a threshold. The georeference procedure ends after the manual correction of these errors and a general inspection.

Subsequently, the coordinates of specific points on the hotel's facades calculated from the MS scanning procedure, were checked and also compared with the coordinates of corresponding points in the classical surveying method. Moreover, some significant distances were measured, like the general dimensions of the building, dimensions of specific windows, etc.

A very important part of the process is the definition of planes to which the final products will be referred to. After the definition, the following procedure is the creation of orthophotos that is particularly the final product of this study (Fig. 5). Through an option in TBC software, a cut was done with the definition of a vertical plane from two points of the point cloud. Then, the selection of the pixel size is done carefully to follow the corresponding point density from the acquisition (standard: ±5 mm). Pixel size selection procedure is trial and error. It is essential that the pixel size must be the same in all the orthophotos of building facades to be uniform.

Fig. 5. Orthophoto of the front view of Sarlitza Pallas

After the creation of the orthophotos for each different façade, the point cloud and the photos are exported from the TBC software. These products are then inserted in AutoCAD to rectify their geometry and to carry out specific geometric checks. In the same layer are also facade points of the classical geodetic method. This is a reliable way to do a complete check on the final products (Fig. 6).

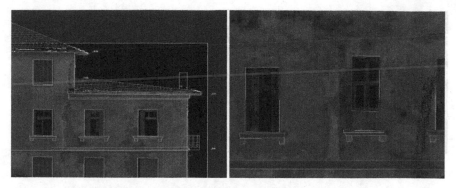

Fig. 6. Orthophotos and classical geodetic method in AutoCAD

5 Discussion and Conclusions

Nowadays, when technology is growing rapidly, more and more companies are creating hybrid measurement instruments that are able to combine different methodologies in only one station. Multi-Stations combine the Geodetic and Image Assisted total stations with the 3D laser scanners, in order to create 2D and 3D models of an object.

On the other hand, digital documentation is necessary in conservation and preservation of cultural heritage, and combines many methodologies for the final decision.

When using a Multi-Station in digital documentation of historical buildings, an immediate modern solution is offered. It is possible to check the scans from the tablet to identify any problems before starting data processing. Even if the measurements are faster than other classical methods, the processing is time-consuming and not simple, especially at point cloud cleaning.

According to the final products, the MS and its methodology mentioned above, offers both vector and raster (textured) details of the building. It may be plans, 3D models or orthophotos. If it is used under special conditions, the same accuracy, with the well-known methods, will be obtained.

Regarding the coordinates' differences, obtained from the MS and the classic methods, they fluctuate from $\leq\pm1$ cm to ±10 cm. A representation of the residuals calculated between the values of coordinates' obtained from each method, is made at Fig. 7. Various points from one of the facades have been picked in order to examine the overall accuracy and proper implementation of the documentation.

Specifically, with cyan hue are represented the points which residuals don't exceed ±5 cm, with green hue the ones that fluctuate from ±6 cm to ±10 cm and with the orange color the points, whose coordinates differ between the two methods by ±10–15 cm.

A total number of 170 check points were used for the differences evaluation. From this dataset only three points (Fig. 8) refer to the $\geq\pm10$ cm boundary and 95% of the remaining points refer to minimum differences.

Finally, according to the advantages or disadvantages, Multi-Stations can be used as a new multi-sensor system, depending on the expectations required by the project. It can meet the needs of common topographic tasks and enlarges the users' choice for a smart, hybrid surveying instrument.

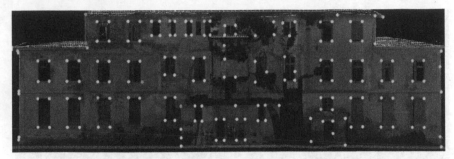

Fig. 7. Residuals between the points obtained from MS and classic methods

Fig. 8. Check points with higher residual values (orange color) (color figure online)

Conflicts of Interest. The authors declare no conflict of interest.

References

Arias, P., Ordóñez, C., Lorenzo, H., Herraez, J.: Methods for documenting historical agro-industrial buildings: a comparative study and a simple photogrammetric method. J. Cult. Herit. **7**(4), 350–354 (2006)

Bastonero, P., Donadio, E., Chiabrando, F., Spanò, A.: Fusion of 3D models derived from TLS and image-based techniques for CH enhanced documentation. ISPRS Ann. Photogramm. Remote Sens. Spat. Inf. Sci. **2**(5), 73–80 (2014)

Delegou, E.T., Mourgi, G., Tsilimantou, E., Ioannidis, C., Moropoulou, A.: A multidisciplinary approach for historic buildings diagnosis: the case study of the Kaisariani monastery. Heritage **2**(2), 1211–1232 (2019)

Haddad, N., Akasheh, T.: Documentation of archaeological sites and monuments: ancient theatres in Jerash. In: Conservation of Cultural Heritage in the Arab Region, pp. 64–71. ICCROM – International Centre for the Study of the Preservation and Restoration of Cultural Property (2005)

Stylianidis, E., Georgopoulos, A.: Digital surveying in cultural heritage: the image-based recording and documentation approaches. In: Ippolito, A., Cigola, M. (eds.) Handbook of Research on Emerging Technologies for Digital Preservation and Information Modeling, pp. 119–149. IGI Global (2017)

Lachat, E., Landes, T., Grussenmeyer, P.: Investigation of a combined surveying and scanning device: the trimble SX10 scanning total station. Sensors **17**(4), 730 (2017)

Landes, T., Lachat, E., Grussenmeyer, P.: First experiences with the trimble SX10 scanning total station for building facade survey. The Int. Arch. Photogrammetry, Remote Sens. Spat. Inform. Sci. **42**, 405 (2017)

Slob, S., Hack, R.: 3D terrestrial laser scanning as a new field measurement and monitoring technique. In: Hack, R., Azzam, R., Charlier, R. (eds.) Engineering Geology for Infrastructure Planning in Europe, pp. 179–189. Springer, Heidelberg (2004)

Soudarissanane, S., Lindenbergh, R., Menenti, M., Teunissen, P.: Scanning geometry: Influencing factor on the quality of terrestrial laser scanning points. ISPRS J. Photogramm. Remote. Sens. **66**(4), 389–399 (2011)

Scherer, M.: Advantages of the integration of image processing and direct coordinate measurement for architectural surveying-development of the system total–JS 28. Integration of technics and corrections to achieve accurate engeneering survey. In: FIG XXII International Congress. Washington, D.C. USA (2002)

Virtualand: An Immersive Virtual Experience for Cultural and Natural Heritage Sites

Christos Bellos[1] ⓘ, Ioannis Fudos[2]([✉]) ⓘ, Angeliki Kita[1], Spyridoula Kolovou[2],
Vasileios Nitsiakos[3], Dafni Patelou[2], Konstantinos Stefanou[1] ⓘ,
and Georgios Stergios[1]

[1] LIME Technology IKE, Ioannina, Greece
[2] Department of Computer Science and Engineering, University of Ioannina,
Ioannina, Greece
fudos@uoi.gr
[3] Department of History and Archaeology, University of Ioannina, Ioannina, Greece

Abstract. The cross-border area of Greece and Albania is characterized by a rich and diverse cultural heritage in a unique natural beauty setting that could form the basis for tourism development. Cultural heritage has been preserved in various printed and audiovisual material (aka Cultural Heritage Objects - CHOs for short) that are stored in libraries across this area. However, many of such CHOs that are part of the history, tradition and culture of the two nations, are being stored behind glass showcases or in the basement of the libraries with no access to visitors due to their sensitive condition or significance.

The overall objective of this work is: (i) to identify, protect and preserve cultural heritage of the area through highlighting content included in rare, old, significant assets in the libraries. (ii) to act as a novel touristic concept that will result to an innovative attraction pole for all tourists visiting the area. The central feature is to provide tourists the opportunity to live an in-depth experience with tangible and intangible assets and better understand the traditions, history and culture of the CB area.

To this end, VirtuaLand delivers a Virtual Reality (VR) interactive platform, where selected CHOs are converted to cultural and touristic scenarios.

Users not only browse the assets of interest, but experience life into another era, become acquainted with the living conditions of that period and interact with characters of the era.

VirtuaLand has produced a library of 3D objects and an open VR platform, that will be used by librarians and tourism professionals with limited programming skills to create their own VR stories.

Keywords: Immersive · Virtual Reality · Cultural heritage

A. Moropoulou et al. (Eds.): TMM_CH 2021, CCIS 1574, pp. 174–185, 2022.
https://doi.org/10.1007/978-3-031-20253-7_15

1 Introduction

The cross-border (CB) Greece-Albania area, where the activities of the VirtuaLand project are located, is characterized by a unique and diverse cultural heritage that could form the basis for tourism development. Cultural heritage has been preserved in books, magazines, letters and other printed or audiovisual material that are stored mainly in public Libraries across this area. However, many of those Cultural Heritage Objects (CHOs) that comprises the history, tradition, and culture of the two nations sharing the CB area, are being stored in closed showcases or in special rooms of the libraries with no or limited access to visitors. This is due to many factors, such as physical aging, poor quality of the original book and increased significance of those CHOs. Also, due to poor quality, often it is cumbersome to digitize those assets in acceptable quality. On the other hand, in the CB area, the recent economic crisis in Greece, drove the local economy into a recession on the Greek part and slowed down growth rates on the Albanian part.As the Albanian government has recognized that the country is a promising tourism destination (based on an increase in international arrivals) and that tourism is "a key area" for economic development, the need for tourism research for developing and adopting innovative tourism strategies has been identified. Thus, this leads to an opportunity to use significant cultural assets, in an innovative way to promote tourism in the CB area.

To address these challenges, VirtuaLand delivers a Virtual Reality (VR) interactive platform, where selected CHOs are being converted to virtual cultural and tourist browsing scenarios. In this pilot program the CHOs will be mainly acquired from the University of Ioannina Library and the Folklore Museum that hold rare essays and objects as well as assets from the University of Gjirokaster Library and the Central Public Library of Konitsa all with increased significance for the CB area. The visitor will be able not only to understand the content, but also to experience interactive living in the era and the environment associated to the cultural assets. Visitors will be able to view the emotions of a soldier writing a letter during the World War II, helping farmers cultivating their fields, reading letters from local landowners to Ali Pasha, shopping at the interwar open market of Ioannina etc. Besides the VR scenarios, VirtuaLand is developing a library of 3D objects and an open VR platform, where librarians, tourism professionals or individuals with limited programming skills will be able to create their own VR stories. The platform is also connected to existing Digital Libraries, created through previous Interreg Greece-Albania initiatives, (for example Balkaneana and Exploral).

This enhancement of conventional touristic information with valuable information acquired from oral and written sources, will result to transforming the VR scenarios to a reference point for all tourists in the area, while the VR demonstration could be included in touristic packages.

2   Related Work

"Tholos" [1] is a dome-shaped Virtual Reality "Theatre" of the Foundation of the Hellenic World, which hosts the digital collections of the Foundation which include "Hagia Sofia: 1500 years of History", "A Walk Through Ancient Miletus", "Interactive Tour at the Ancient Agora of Athens", "Interactive Tour of the Acropolis of Athens (circa 5th century B.C.)" and other productions. Since these works are designed for showings in large theaters they have limited interactivity. Furthermore, a group of computer graphics engineers is required to develop and optimize the computer graphics part.

Lithodromos VR have developed an app called "Athens in VR" [2] that offers an interactive tour of Athens. Furthermore, they have created 3D models of Acropolis, Parthenon and the Athenian Agora and therefore the user can have an immersive experience and browse these building of unique architectural significance in the modern landscape. However, the interactivity is again limited and the user cannot have an interactive virtual experience of that era.

There are several lines of research work on using immersive VR technology for cultural heritage collection (see e.g. [3–5]). Multifragment rendering technologies have also been used for rendering cultural artifacts [6,7]. Finally, CAD-based approaches have been used successfully for reconstructing traditional jewelry [8].

3   Project Methodology

The following end user groups have been identified:

1. Tourists, who can get in depth knowledge for the area and get familiar not only with the sightseeing, but also with the cultural and historical heritage and feel more like locals.
2. Visitors of the libraries could benefit from the VR infrastructure and get an interactive experience.
3. Citizens that want to have access to the content of the libraries to acquire in depth knowledge for the CB area of interest and its cultural and historical framework. Especially, people that have origins from the CB area would like to look back into their roots.
4. Researchers and historians that want to explore the content acquired through oral sources to study the common culture and history of the area.
5. However, the beneficiaries of VirtuaLand include, also tour operators and tour agents as well as tourism professionals in general. Such professionals can exploit the VirtuaLand open platform and create additional VR scenarios and cross-border touristic packages to clients, targeted to culture or history highlighting the common heritage and resources and probably the common local people memories on historical or cultural events.

The overall objective is to:

(i) Identify, protect and preserve cultural heritage of the cross-border area through highlighting content that exists in rare, very old, significant assets included in the Libraries.

(ii) Act as part of an attractive touristic package and as a common reference point for all tourists visiting the area that will have an in-depth experience with tangible and intangible assets and better understand the traditions, history and culture of people living in the area.

The proposed methodology is implemented in six work packages. The first work package concerns administrative, financial and managerial activities as well as the project coordination.

The second work package handles the dissemination activities, such as workshops, publicity events, project's multilingual website (in Greek, Albanian and English), and publicity through social media that is of much interest of the project goals.

The third work package "International Project Promotion and Publicity Activities" includes dissemination and promotional activities outside the cross-border area and participation to international exhibitions and conferences. The fourth work package "VirtuaLand Content Library and 3D objects" includes activities related to the identification of the oral and written content as well as the cultural tangible and intangible assets that will be transferred to the virtual worlds by the development of VR scenarios. Also, the environment will be captured as well as the living conditions highlighting issues that should be reflected to the VR objects and scenarios. During this work package, the assets will be explicitly defined and the required content will be determined and collected (i.e. oral tradition, description, images, videos and other multimedia content).

Work package five includes activities related to the development of the VR environment and platform that should be integrated to the content specified during work package four. This workpackage includes also the development of a game-like scenario, where visitors could test their knowledge acquired through their tour on the VR world. The platform, developed in this work package, will be made available to public to be utilised after the end of the project to create new VR experiences.

Finally, wor kpackage six includes additional promotion events to local authorities, tourists and tourism professionals, such as two press and fam demonstration trips and two VR Infrastructure demonstration activities (one at each country). Also, two VR hotspots will be implemented during this work package and will include several different types of VR equipment available to the public so that anyone can have a complete immersive experience of the scenes revived by the project.

In terms of technical contributions, the aim of this project is to automate the process of creating an immersive virtual reality experience once all objects and characters have been created or reverse engineered.

Fig. 1. Photos of Liampei Alley during interwar. Liampei Alley was one of the alleys where the open market of Ioannina was hosted from the 18th century until the 1970s.

4 An Example Case: Reviving the Interwar Ioannina Open Market

During the process of developing a recreation of the open market of Ioannina, several graphics tools where used. Namely, Blender, Unity 3D and MakeHuman. Blender [9] is a free, open-source software for 3D graphics. It is mainly used for modeling, rendering and animation. Unity 3D [10] is a widely known game engine, used for developing games and other applications. Lastly, MakeHuman [11] is a free, open-source software that is used for creating photorealistic humanoid 3D models.

To build the scene of the application, the first step is to create all individual 3D model parts necessary for the final composition. That includes the buildings, the human characters acting as sellers, the products being sold and the furniture

Fig. 2. Current situation of Liampei Alley.

Fig. 3. Reconstructing Liampei Alley as it was during the interwar period.

used for the benches. In particular with regards to the architecture, the inspiration is drawn from a traditional alley of Ioannina, Liampei Alley, that has, to a degree, preserved its appearance through centuries (see Fig. 1). Other traditional alleys and buildings were also used as sources to add details to the open market scene.

The modeling of the alley was carried out using Blender and the entire process was performed in parts. Each building front was modeled individually and later on they were all combined to create the final 3D model. The building fronts are very similar to one another, as that was the look of the alley back in the day. The doors and windows were, also, created separately at first and are based on real doors and windows that are still found around town at traditional houses and stores in the area where the market was. In the final model, besides the building fronts, more things were added to create whole alley. Those include the ground, arches on each end, pavement and road made of cobble stones and more building fronts to represent shops across the street from the alley. Figure 2 shows the alley as it is today and Fig. 3 illustrates the 3D model of the reconstructed alley of the interwar period.

The next step was to create the 3D models of the humans characters that shall act as merchants. These models had to resemble people during the interwar period, so we made them as accurate as possible. Their hair, facial hair and clothes were based on photographs the era. The basis for all the models was a rigged body for each character, made with MakeHuman. The facial features and body proportions were randomly generated from the software until the final result was satisfactory. Makehuman also offers different choices for armature and from them we have chosen to use one with many bones so as to have more degrees for freedom during the animation. The rigged models were then imported into Blender for further editing. A significant task to enhance realism was to create clothes, for which 3D models found on the internet were mainly used and changed their materials based on folklore archives to look more appropriate for the time. An example of a 3D model of a human character of the interwar era is shown in Fig. 4a. Once the models were finished,, short animation sequences were created for each model. More specifically each human has two animation sequences, an idle and an interaction sequence. Idle sequence is used to model a very subtle movement, when a model is mainly staying still, such as blinking, moving the head and slightly moving the rest of the body. The interaction sequence is specific to each human and it incorporates interaction with something from their counter or with a client.

Subsequently we have organized the merchants into counters to take the form of a market. Thus, a total of six counters were created. The shoemaker counter, the weaver counter, the silverware counter, the fruit and vegetable counter, the fisherman counter and the leather counter. The above professions were chosen because they were the main occupations of the people at that time. Each counter has the corresponding items on it which were appropriately placed with respect to each other using Blender. After building the individual parts of the scene, all models were added to the main scene in Unity. First of all, the model of the

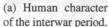

(a) Human character of the interwar period.

(b) Immersive virtual reality application main menu.

Fig. 4. Snapshots of the immersive VR application.

Fig. 5. Highlighting an object for selection.

alley was imported and then the counters in a zigzag pattern to facilitate the user movement through the scene. Lastly, the human models were added, each vendor at their respective counter and the narrator at one end of the alley. At this point, a very important step was the customization of the materials for each object. To render the materials of the objects as realistically as possible, appropriate shaders were used. To achieve realistic rendering, all values for the local illumination model (e.g. metallic, roughness, reflection etc.) where appropriately adjusted for each individual material. In addition to this, for a better user experience, the narrator of the scene, upon user request, may start a short tour of the

Fig. 6. Browsing a selected object.

(a) Photo of actual object in its current form.

(b) 3D model of reverse engineered object.

(c) Photo of actual object in its current form.

(d) 3D model of reverse engineered object.

Fig. 7. Reverse engineering cultural heritage objects.

Fig. 8. Moving around in the virtual scene using teleporting.

market. That is, the narrator stops at each counter and shares some information about the products of that counter. This tour can also be done individually for one counter if the user chooses to do so. The application starts with a main menu which is illustrated in Fig. 4b). From there one can choose to start the application, to see relevant information about Ioannina open market or a manual for using the application. While using the application the user has the option to pause the application and then either continue, go to the main menu or exit the application.

Another functionality that offers a complete user experience is the item inspection. The user has the ability to select a cultural heritage object to take a closer look at it. These items appear as highlighted when the user hovers a pointer over them (see Fig. 5). After selecting an object, the user can rotate it and view it from any perspective (see Fig. 6).

Finally, market sounds have been incorporated into the scene. More specifically, a synthesis of various sounds that one can hear in flea markets, such as the sound of a hammer hitting, crowd sound effects, and general noise, were added to the scene. These sound clips were made by individual artists and are provided according to a creative common license.

A big part of the creation process was modeling the cultural heritage objects such as silverware and woven products. It was very important to recreate these objects as accurately as possible so that the final app can be used as a reliable source of information. To achieve that, photos were used as reference for both the shape and the materials of the objects. These photos were mainly from the Metsovo Folk Art Museum and from the University Folklore Museum of Ioannina. The creation of these 3D models was performed in Blender. The modeling process creating the shape from scratch, starting from a simple mesh, e.g. a circle or a plane and building the final mesh step by step. Slight imperfections were added both through the materials used and by deforming the mesh in parts. These slight imperfections are crucial to create a more realistic 3D model of an object that is handcrafted. For their materials, textures from open repositories were used, alongside with the corresponding maps, i.e. normal, metallic, roughness and ambient occlusion. The combination of these textures and maps is commonly used to create PBR (Physically Based Rendering) materials. Some examples of the reference photos in Figs. 7a and 7c are shown in comparison to the final 3D model in Figs. 7b and 7d. An exception to this were some objects with, very specific and difficult to recreate, engraved details. For these objects, the reference photo was actually used as a texture with the combination of a normal map. This method was also used for the woven products.

In addition to the cultural heritage objects created entirely from scratch, some ready-made objects from various 3D model repositories [12–15]. These models have been edited in size, shape and material to fit the scene needs. In regards to the movement, the user has the option to move in two ways in the scene. Firstly, the user can move freely, i.e. walking around the room while using the app and wearing VR glasses. However, because of the possible lack of space and the difficulty for the user to synchronize his actual movement with the movement in the scene, the teleport option is also available. The user using the controllers and pressing the corresponding buttons aims at the point that wishes to move to and teleports (Fig. 8). Both ways of moving were implemented with tools offered by Unity which are differ according to the virtual reality headset used. We have used HTC Vive and Oculus quest.

For the implementation of the VR functionalities, ready-made packages from the Unity asset store were used. From these packages, the prefab of the user was used to move the user and the camera attached to the user, which renders the scene. In addition, from these packages, scripts were also used, with minor changes, to implement the teleportation. Finally, teleport point prefabs were placed in front of each counter, to help implement the narration. For the HTC Vive implementation, specifically, the final outcome is quite photorealistic in regards to materials and environment because it is compatible Unity HDRP (High Definition Render Pipeline) render pipeline. This pipeline provides several shaders, from which we have used the Lit shader. In the Lit shader texture as well as maps can be added to recreate the PBR materials that are used for the 3D models in Blender. When it comes to the environment, HDRP volume profiles were used to create as much of a realistic sky as possible. More specifically, a 360° photo of the sky was used as a Skybox and also, fog and dust were added to make the entire scene more realistic.

5   Conclusions

We have reported on the implementation of project "Virtualand" that aims at delivering a software plugin for Unity3D (asset) that will facilitate users with basic knowledge of programming or computer graphics to create an engaging, immersive and interactive virtual reality application that will promote and preserve tangible and intangible cultural heritage. A case study has been described, in which the open market of Ioannina during interwar was revived into an immersive, interactive tour.

Acknowledgments. This work has been co-financed by the European Union (European Regional Development Fund- ERDF) and Greek national funds through the Interreg Greece Albania 2014–2020 Program (project VirtuaLand).

References

1. Foundation of the Hellenic world, tholos VR showings. http://www.tholos254.gr/en/index.html
2. Lithodomos VR, Athens in VR. https://play.google.com/store/apps/details?id=com.LVR.agora&hl=en&gl=US
3. Eftaxopoulos, E., Vasilakis, A., Fudos, I.: AR-TagBrowse: annotating and browsing 3D objects on mobile devices. In: Paulin, M., Dachsbacher, C. (eds.) 35th Annual Conference of the European Association for Computer Graphics, Eurographics 2014 - Posters, Strasbourg, France, 7–11 April 2014, pp. 5–6. Eurographics Association (2014)
4. Yiakoumettis, C., Doulamis, N., Miaoulis, G., Ghazanfarpour, D.: Active learning of user's preferences estimation towards a personalized 3D navigation of geo-referenced scenes. GeoInformatica **18**, 27–62 (2014). https://doi.org/10.1007/s10707-013-0176-0
5. Doulamis, A.D., Doulamis, N.D., Makantasis, K., Klein, M.: A 4D virtual/augmented reality viewer exploiting unstructured web-based image data. In: Braz, J., Battiato, S., Imai, F.H.(eds.) VISAPP 2015 - Proceedings of the 10th International Conference on Computer Vision Theory and Applications, Volume 2, Berlin, Germany, 11–14 March 2015, pp. 631–639. SciTePress (2015)
6. Rossignac, J., Fudos, I., Vasilakis, A.: Direct rendering of boolean combinations of self-trimmed surfaces. Comput. Aided Des. **45**(2), 288–300 (2013)
7. Adamopoulos, G., Moutafidou, A., Drosou, A., Tzovaras, D., Fudos, I.: A multifragment renderer for material aging visualization. In: Proceedings of the 39th Annual European Association for Computer Graphics Conference: Posters, EG 2018 (Goslar, DEU), pp. 27–28. Eurographics Association (2018)
8. Stamati, V., Antonopoulos, G., Azariadis, P.N., Fudos, I.: A parametric feature-based approach to reconstructing traditional filigree jewelry. Comput. Aided Des. **43**(12), 1814–1828 (2011)
9. Blender online community, blender - a 3D modelling and rendering package. Blender Foundation, Stichting Blender Foundation, Amsterdam (2018). http://www.blender.org
10. Haas, J.K.: A history of the unity game engine (2014)
11. MakeHuman Community, MakeHuman: open source tool for making 3D characters. MakeHuman Community. http://www.makehumancommunity.org/
12. CG Trader, 3D Models for VR / AR and CG projects. https://www.cgtrader.com/
13. Sketchfab, Publish and find 3D models. https://sketchfab.com/feed
14. Turbosquid, 3D models for professionals. https://www.turbosquid.com/
15. 3D warehouse, the place to share and download SketchUp 3D models for architecture, design, construction, and fun. https://3dwarehouse.sketchup.com/?hl=en

Digitizing Mystras: The Palace Complex

Vayia V. Panagiotidis[✉] and Nikolaos Zacharias

Laboratory of Archaeometry, University of the Peloponnese, Old Camp, 24133 Kalamata, Greece

Abstract. The city of Mystras is situated at the foot of Taygetos mountain west of the city of Sparta and is considered the best-preserved Byzantine city in Greece. Also called the "Castle City of Mystras" (culture.gr) it was founded in 1249 by Frank commander William II of Villehardouin in order to control the Valley of Evrota where he built a castle fortress on top of Myzithra Hill. The city expanded outside the Acropolis walls quickly after its surrender to the Byzantines in 1259. Mystras' location and ties to the Byzantine capital of Constantinople boosted the city's development. The Castle city has been extensively studied but due to its nature has room for research and development in a number of fields (Arvanitopoulos 2004).

Contributing to the study of Mystras an overall approach to the digitization of the landscape and structures has been made. Using an unmanned aerial vehicle (UAV), a GPS GNSS receiver and control points for georeferencing, the city has been recorded through extensive photographing. The collected data, photographs and GCP coordinates are used to create an orthophoto of the city. The orthophoto in turn is used as the basemap for the subsequent analysis via Geographic Information Systems (GIS) for creating a geodatabase of the archaeological and historic information concerning the study area, buildings, churches, fortification etc. This paper presents the palace complex of Mystras. The structures, built on the plateau at the north end of the Upper City, constitute a number of additions to the initial building A from the thirteenth century until the beginning of the 15th c. The study of the structural evolution of the Palace as well as the supportive buildings surrounding the complex are particularly intriguing. The complex includes bulky two-storey and three-storey buildings with terraces and galleries, functional lavatories, storage facilities, cisterns and chapels (Sinos, St. (2009). Through the digitization project the layout is presented by type, period of construction and usage while depicting any relations between them using modern spatial technologies in the recording, study and preservation of cultural heritage.

Keywords: UAV photogrammetry · Mystras · GIS · Cultural heritage management · Digital applications

1 Introduction

Geographic Information Systems (GIS) in collaboration with location-based application software provide a friendly, digital platform for the management and enhancement of archaeological and cultural heritage environments. The goal of this research project is

A. Moropoulou et al. (Eds.): TMM_CH 2021, CCIS 1574, pp. 186–206, 2022.
https://doi.org/10.1007/978-3-031-20253-7_16

to present the multidimensional development of Mystras through a spatial presentation. This analysis includes political, economic and spatial parameters. The spatial presentation of the Acropolis included the multifaceted development distinguished based on the political situation of the city into ultimately three periods. In the case of the Palatial complex situated on the plateau at the NW edge of the city the approach varied from that of the Acropolis. Specifically, the point of the initial study of the Palatial complex is to not only present its evolution chronologically but also include additional information to its connection with the buildings surrounding it and not part of the Palace itself. Available data regarding architecture, building usage, art etc. is provided in the geodatabase.

The city of Mystras was founded in 1249 by the Frankish Prince of Achaia following the three-year siege of the castle of Monemvasia on an island off the east coast of the Peloponnese. The conquer of Monemvasia in 1246 was one of the few remaining territories of the Peloponnese that had not yet fallen during the Fourth Crusade during which Constantinople was also conquered for the first time in 1204 by the Franks and Latins. While dividing the territories of the Empire, the Peloponnese was granted to the Villehardouin house which in turn continued their march to subjugate the rest of the peninsula along with Lacedaemonia, Medieval Sparta, in 1207 and most of the Laconia prefecture excluding the lands of the Tsakonians in Parnon and the Slavic Milingans in the Taygetos mountain range as well as Monemvasia. It was on the Franks return from Monemvasia in 1249, when William II built the Castle of Mystras, in a key position to control the valley of Evrotas, six kilometers southwest of Sparta, the emblematic fortress at the top of Myzithra Hill. Structurally, the fortress is divided into three sections, the exterior wall, the interior wall and a large building within the second enclosure. The Frankish citadel is the main fortification complex in the overall organization of the city (Georgiadis 2002).

In 1262 Mystras was surrendered to the Byzantines following William II's capture during the Battle of Pelagonia in 1259. During the negotiation for his release, he bestowed the castles of the Great Maina, Monemvasia and Mystras to Michael VIII Palaeologos, the Byzantine Emperor (Kalonaros 1940). Regardless though of the Franks agreement with the Byzantines, William II maintained his interest in Mystras. His continuous claim on the city created tension for the local populations of Lacedaemonia (Chatzidakis 1992). The Byzantines quickly begin their campaign over the total of Lacedaemona. It was at this time that the population of Lacaedomonia began to resettle on the hillside of Myzithras under the shadow of the Acropolis. The resettlement in Mystras was reinforced when the Christian Orthodox Bishop established his seat in the city after his expulsion from Lacaedemonia transferring the Metropolis of Lacaedemonia to the newly constructed church of Saint Demetrios at the lowest part of the city. Saint Demetrios essentially defined the lower border of the city (Sinos 2009).

As Mystras grew in population and area over Myzithras hill summit, the city experienced a number of phases. Following the battle of Makryplagi in 1262 Chora of Myzithras was established and fortified below the Castle (Chatzidakis 1992). During the first Byzantine Period from 1259 to 1348, Mystras became the seat of the Byzantine General, titled "Sevastocrator". The Sevastocrator ruled the entire Peloponnese and was replaced yearly (culture.gr).

The next phase, 1349–1383, during the reign of the Dynasty of Kantakouzenos, Mystras was upgraded to a Despotate, becoming one of the most important provinces of the weakened Byzantine Empire. The city experienced great prosperity during this period and played an important role in Byzantium until the fall of the Empire (Sinos 2009). Emperor Ioannis Kantakouzenos VI, founded the Despotate of Morea with Mystras as its capital by appointing Manuel, his second son, as Despot of Mystra. The city's expansion and evolution into the Despotate of Mystras made it the epicenter of Byzantine power in the Peloponnese.

Mystras was surrendered to the Ottoman Turks in 1460 following extensive pressure from their presence and occupation of the northern Peloponnese. During the period of Ottoman occupation, 1460–1821 Mystras held an important position in the Ottoman Empire and was one of the most important silk production centers in the Eastern Mediterranean (Sinos 2009) (Runciman 1986). The Ottoman period of Mystras was interrupted in 1687 until 1715 when the Peloponnese was occupied by the Venetians. During the Venetian period significant part of the Greek population was killed or forced to leave (Arvanitopoulos 2004).

After the establishment of the Greek State in 1834, the new city of Sparta was founded and a large part of the inhabitants of Mystras left the Castle City situated on Myzithra Hill. The Castle city was declared in 1921 a prominent Byzantine monument, the last inhabitants finally left Mystras in 1953. The archaeological site was included by UNESCO in the list of World Cultural Heritage sites (UNESCO) in 1989, making it the best-preserved Byzantine state of Greece (culture.gr).

2   Case Study: The Palatial Complex

The goal of this research project is to present the multidimensional development of Mystras through a spatial presentation. This analysis includes political, economic and spatial parameters. Throughout the study of Mystras the same chronological presentation is maintained. The classification is determined be significant changes either political or economic. Specifically,

I.   Period of Latin occupancy 1249–1262
II.   Late–Byzantine I 1262–1348 (seat of the Byzantine General)
III.   Late–Byzantine II 1348–1384 (Reign of Kantakouzenos)
IV.   Late–Byzantine III 1384–1460 (Reign of Palaeologos)
V.   Post–Byzantine 1460–1821

The temporal presentation assists in the spatial representation of the phases from the first building A as early as the period of Latin occupancy including the Post Byzantine period during which the Palace includes the structural development of the Palace and surrounding buildings from 1249 to 1821. The Palace complex went through extensive development with additions, alterations and changes in use. These fluctuations are displayed through the geodatabase.

3 Methodology

The declared by UNESCO archaeological site of Mystras covers more than 540 acres (54.43 hectares), which in combination with the extensive vegetation and the morphology of the area, extending on a sharp slope in some parts, means that detailed mapping of the entire archaeological site should be carried out using advanced technological equipment (Forte et al. 2020). In this study the Palatial complex was photographed using a DJI Mavic 2 Pro unmanned aerial vehicle (UAV). Ground Control Points (GCPs) where set over the study area and their exact coordinates measured using a Top Con GR5 geodetic station in order to ensure high accuracy for georeferencing the images. All data was collected in the Greek coordinate system EGSA'87.

The images for the photographic overview of the Palatial complex were captured with the UAV at a relative altitude of 100 m from the takeoff point in the east court in front of the entrance to building [E]. Ground Control Points (GCPs) were placed on site in order to be visible from the UAV (Fig. 1).

Fig. 1. GCPs Mystras_A, Mystras_B, Mystras_C, Mystras_CC1, Mystras_DDD, Mystras_E, Mystras_III, Mystras_K, Mystras_L, Mystras_M, Mystras_J, Mystras_K, Mystras_L, Mystras_M, and Mystras_N

The UAV, navigated using the Litchi application, one of the top applications for drone navigation (expertphotography.com) followed a grid flight pattern (Fig. 2) while maintaining 75% overlap of the attained images. Waypoints as well as altitude, image capture frequency and speed were determined before flight (Gutiérrez 2016).

Overall, in order to record the Palatial complex 320 photos from the UAV with a resolution of 5472 X 3648 pixels and 14 GPCs were used. The images were transferred from the UAV to a computer and processed using the photogrammetry software Agisoft

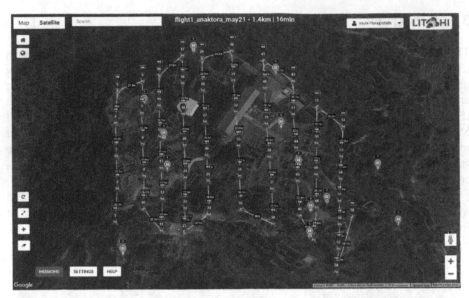

Fig. 2. Litchi application screenshot UAV flight plan

Metashape, the best all-around drone mapping software (coptrz.com). The spatial resolution of the generated orthophoto mosaic from the 320 overlapping images is ~ 3 cm for a flight at 100 m.

Images are imported to the open workspace and the first part of processing includes image (camera) alignment, which translates into the software finds the camera position

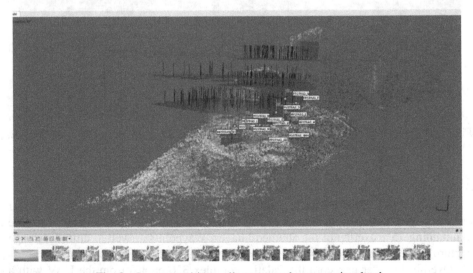

Fig. 3. Camera positions, alignment and sparse point cloud

and orientation for each photo. This positioning creates a rough three-dimensional model of the space in the form of a sparse point cloud (Fig. 3).

In order for the software to accurately define the model's (in reality each camera's) position GCPs are necessary. The coordinates measured with the Top Con GNSS GPS for the 14 GCPs are imported directly to the workspace as a csv file. The software identifies the coordinates as markers and automatically adds them as so to the model. The position of the markers in each image must be adjusted separately to confirm the correct placement above the visible GCPs within each image. This procedure ensures better georeferencing results compared to using only the UAV's GPS. Following optimization, a dense point cloud of the study area is generated. The dense point cloud creates a detailed three-dimensional model of the examined area is created (Fig. 4).

Fig. 4. 3D perspective of Palatial complex [screenshot Agisoft Metashape]

The dense-point cloud produces the study area's digital elevation model (DEM) from which in turn the high resolution orthophoto of the Palatial complex is produced (Fig. 5).

Fig. 5. Study area's Orthophoto

The aspects examined in this particular unit of the city are construction phases in correspondence to the political changes in the city, building types and usage as well as an individual examination of additions made to the main buildings of the Palace ([A], [B], [Γ], [Δ], [E], [Z], [I]). Using the available bibliography from the archaeological study of Mystras the general categorization of the remains within the vicinity of the Palace is shown in Table 1 (Arvanitopoulos 2004; Sinos 2009; Chatzidakis 1992; Georgiades 2002; Runciman 1986). During the short period of Venetian rule of the city there was no reconstruction or intervention work regarding the fortifications (Arvanitopoulos 2004) therefore the specific period, 1687–1715, is excluded from the timeframe (Table 2).

Table 1. Palace remains categorization

Structure	Code	Time Period	Description
Building [A]–The Frankish Building	[A]	1249–1262	[A] was possibly used after 1262 as a public space with administrative centers of the Despotate on the first level (first floor) and living spaces on the second level (second floor). Until the beginning of the 15th century senate sessions most possibly took place on the 2nd floor

(continued)

Table 1. (*continued*)

Structure	Code	Time Period	Description
Tower A1 Building [A]	A1	1262–1348	Rectangular, at least three-storeys, the same width with the main building but much shorter. Two constructional phases, at least, as the main building [A]. Spaces of the upper three levels were suitable for services regarding the autonomous province of Mystras along with lower level of [Z] & SW ground level room of [Δ]
Building [B]	[B]	1262–1348	The First Byzantine extension. Built a few meters north of [A] also at least in two different phases. Actually, a complex of three smaller trapezoid shaped two-storey buildings, [B], [B1] and tower [B2]. [B] is a narrow long structure parallel to [B1] under the ground floor of which two cisterns where built K6. J1. The upper level of [B] possibly worked as living quarters until the beginning of the 15th century
Building [B1]	[B1]	1262–1348	[B1] the oldest of the three in a similar condition today as [A1]
Tower B2	[B2]	1262–1348	Cistern of the ground level, washing rooms on the upper level and living quarters for the family of the Despot on the second level (third floor)
The Stairway Building	[Γ]	1384–1460	Four storey, 1st & 2nd staircase and 3rd & 4th used as a guest space for ambassadors & distinguished visitors of the Despot and Emperor
The Manuel Kantakouzenos Building	[Δ]	1348–1384	The upper level of [Δ] possibly worked as living quarters for the Despot families until the beginning of the fifteenth century. The Despot's guard most possibly resided on the ground level of building [Δ]

(*continued*)

Table 1. (*continued*)

Structure	Code	Time Period	Description
Building [Z]	[Z]	1262–1348	The ground level possibly worked for services regarding the autonomous province of Mystras along with [A1] & SW ground level room of [Δ]. The two upper levels (at least) of building [Z] worked as living quarters until the beginning of the 15th century. The first level also included the cloakroom of the Despotate
The West Wing	[E]	1384–1460	Built in one constructional phase, most prominent the throne hall at the third level (second floor) and spaces for secondary uses on the lower two, the West Wing of the Palace was built during the Palaeologos reign. The West Wing composes of 7 spaces, compartments under the eight transverse vaults on the ground floor. The ground level contained the Palace stables, the first level sleeping quarters for the servants and at times kitchens. The second level comprised the throne hall where meetings, officials' reception, trials etc. under the ruling of the Despot of Emperor took place as well as official meals
Building [Θ]	[Θ]	1384–1460	Finely built the structure is well preserved. Findings from the internal surfaces indicate that the structure was a cistern. The addition adjacent the north side is most possibly post Byzantine
[H]	[H]	1384–1460	Three-storey irregularly shaped. Characterized by the 5 continuous tall arches of the front
[I]	[I]		Adjacent to building [Z], the three–storey building [I] is of similar length but much small width than [Z]. The vaulted first level is mostly underground now

(*continued*)

Table 1. (*continued*)

Structure	Code	Time Period	Description
[K]	**[K]**	**1460–1821**	Post-Byzantine structure of low significance

According to S. Sinos the latest investigation of the palatial complex gives indications of a previous phase on the plateau where the Palace is situated that belonged to an early settlement, possibly Roman mid-fourth century B.C., around building [A] that later constituted the core of the Palace complex (Fig. 6). The first phase of the construction of the Palace a simple structure [A] at a lower level is built, above it a vault with a door to the north (Sinos 2009).

During the first Byzantine phase of Mystras, Late-Byzantine I, the Palace developed to the west of the initial core [A]. During this second phase, a tower was erected to the north, A1. The first Byzantine expansion includes also buildings [Z] and unit [B]. During this phase large houses, mansions are built in the vicinity of the Palace, e.g., small palace A (Sinos 2009) (Fig. 7).

During the next phase, Late–Byzantine II, the renewed Byzantine settlement begins to grow marking significant changes in the city's architecture which is clearly influenced by Byzantine tradition. With the reign of the Kantakouzenos family during the second Late Byzantine phase the first expansion of the Palace is continued with building [Δ] and the Monastery of Saint Sophia dedicated to the "wisdom of God" is built as the church for the Palace (Sinos 2009) (Fig. 8).

In the last Byzantine period of Mystras, Late Byzantine III, a new phase of construction marks the monuments through radical changes to the form of the Palace and its surroundings. The staircase building [Γ] is erected along with building [E] containing the majestic throne hall. It is [E] that transforms the shape of the Palace complex into an L that creates a Palace square, the forum (Fig. 9).

In the overall examination of the Palatial unit's evolution comparison with historical maps were created using the topographical diagram of the city by G. Millet (Fig. 10). Millet's plan of the city was scanned and imported to ArcGIS 10.8, the GIS package used in this study. The digitized map is referenced by recognizing elements of the current landscape as reference points and scale matching. In the case of Millet's plan, the Castle fortress is visible as well as a number of other buildings, the Palace, Pantanassa Monastery etc. in order to create the matching reference points to the basemap generated from Agisoft's Metashape. Each collection of data is created in separate layers in the ArcGIS environment, thus composing a database of historical information (Anagnostakis et al. 2014).

Table 2. Structural changes to the main palatial complex

Code	Time Period	Structure	Description
A	1262–1348	3-storey	Small palace, complex of 5 buildings, the largest of the city
A10	1348–1384		Semi-circular tower part of the tower cage of the palace complex
A11	1348–1384		Square tower part of the tower cage of the palace complex
A12	1348–1384		Square tower part of the tower cage of the palace complex
A5			Rectangular tower
A6			Small square tower
B	1384–1460	2-storey	Wide faced with a 3-storey tower to the E, adjacent to b. 124 &123
Γ	1384–1460	4-storey	Only four-storey building in the city
Δ		2-storey	Later addition to b. 62, narrow faced dated in the fourteenth century
E	1384–1460	2-storey	Wide faced building, later to b. 87
E4			Nauplia Gate, actually a system of two arched gates
O1	1460–1821		Cubed shaped Mosque
O2	1460–1821		Possible bathing house
Π21			Chapel Π21
X	1384–1460		Chapel X was the Palace chapel built in the LBII period
61		3-storey	Small sized, three-storey, trapezoid shaped building
62		2-storey	Large, two-storey structure adjacent to b. Δ built parallel to the elevation line possibly an earlier structure to Δ
63		3-storey	Wide face, three-storey, adjacent to b. Δ & 62
64		2-storey	At least two-storey structure later to its adjacent b. 63
65		2-storey	At least two-storey, small sized building
66			Adjacent to b. 67 & 68, later to both
67		2-storey	At least two-storey, small sized building adjacent to b. 66 & 68
68		3-storey	Two tangent buildings (a) & (b), wide faced, three-storey buildings. The first to the W (a) the oldest and later to the b. 67
69		2-storey	Two-storey building of which the N segment is based on a cave like natural feature
70		2-storey	Wide faced at least two-storey structure
71		3-storey	West side of the structure rebuilt during the post-Byzantine period
72			Small sized possibly trapezoid shaped structure

(*continued*)

Table 2. (*continued*)

Code	Time Period	Structure	Description
73		2-storey	Small sized, parallel to the slope possibly two-storey
74		2-storey	Small sized, at least two-storey almost square shaped structure
75			Small sized structure parallel to the slope
76			Only the S wall is visible today as well as a few segments of the E and W
77		2-storey	At least two-storey particularly narrow and long building, part of a unit. Access was through the courtyard between b. 77, tower A6 & b. 78
78			Access as in the case of b. 77 was through their common courtyard and a very meticulously decorated overhead lintels to the gate
79	1384–1460	2-storey	The building indicates at least two constructional phases. The first possibly late–Byzantine although the later post–Byzantine. It is possible that the interior did not exist but only to hide the natural rock at that particular location and was indeed built during the post–Byzantine period
80			In the area enclosed by the rampart, E of tower A12, a unit of three tangent structures. The first to the S a subterranean vaulted, small sized structure, almost triangle shaped covered the area between the E wall of A12, the continuing wall after the tower and the curved projection the fortification within which b. 84 was erected. The second small sized, rectangular, covered by a semi-cylindric chamber, tangent to the first and tower A12 and outer wall of b. 84. Substantially larger than the first two is the transverse to the former
81		2-storey	Small sized, at least two-storey
82			Complex of three tangent spaces. The one further to the S was semisubterranean and vaulted. The second rectangular with a small semi cylindric chamber adjacent to the former space and tower A12 as well at the outer wall of b. 84
83	1460–1821	2-storey	Small sized trapezoid shaped possibly two-storey building
84			Small trapezoid shaped space covered with a cruciform and continuous to the north irregular vault
85		2-storey	Narrow face, particularly large sized building at least two-storey
86	1460–1821		

(*continued*)

Table 2. (*continued*)

Code	Time Period	Structure	Description
87			Overall structure where two spaces are distinguishable. The first square shaped, to the W, adjacent to tower A13 and the a second adjacent to (a) and E. The two spaces did not communicate
88		2-storey	Wide front, later to adjacent b. 89 & 98, two-storey building
89		2-storey	Small almost square two-storey building
90		3-storey	Wide face adjacent to b. 89 three-storey building
91	1460–1821	2-storey	Narrow long, wide face building adjacent to b. 98. The addition of the second level was implemented during the post-Byzantine period
92		2-storey	Small narrow face building later to b. 98
93			Small sized, narrow face, adjacent to b. 92 & 94, building. Possibly with an addition of a second level or built parapet
94		3-storey	Almost square shaped, three-storey building adjacent to b. 92, 93, 95 & 97. In the SE corner of the first level a lavatory was located similarly in the E area of the mid-level. The third level indicates the existence of a balcony
95		3-storey	Narrow long, large sized, three-storey building adjacent to b. 94 & 97, later than both. Similar to the one in b. 94, near the NE corner of the first level a lavatory was located
96			Adjacent to b. 96 & 97
97		2-storey	Wide face, large sized, two-storey structure later to b. 88 & 98. On the ground level two semisubterranean vaulted chambers cover the E side of the unit without communicated between themselves. The S segment included a cistern and the N to the first initially had the same use
98		3-storey	Wide fronted, large sized, three-storey building adjacent to earlier b. 89 & 90
99	1460–1821		Possibly Post Byzantine quite long building, transverse to the slope, just south of the mosque
100	1384–1460		Two constructional phases the second clearly post-Byzantine while the SE corner suggests an earlier Late Byzantine phase
101			Almost square small building, b. 102 later was built adjacently to the W
102	1460–1821		Adjacent to b. 101 post-Byzantine
103		2-storey	Transverse to the slope at least 2-storey building

(*continued*)

Table 2. (*continued*)

Code	Time Period	Structure	Description
104	1460–1821		Exterior characteristics place the structure in the post-Byzantine period
105	1460–1821		Post-Byzantine structure with clear indications of timber circumferential binding on the exterior
106		3-storey	Three-storey parallel to the slope built in contact with the natural stone wall to the W. The S side on the 2nd level maintains a hearth while indications on the 3rd level refer an additional hearth on the S wall
107		2-storey	Very small structure at least two-storey built later on the S wall of b. 106. B. 107 & 106 communicated through a narrow door on the S wall of b. 106
108		2-storey	Very small structure adjacent to b. 107 at least two-storey parallel to the slope. Access was through b. 107 and a door on the first level as well as from the main road (mesi)
109		3-storey	Gamma shaped, three-storey structure. The steep stone slope remained raw on the W side of the ground floor making it semisubterranean. The floor plan of the internal corner of the gamma structure reveals the existence of a square tower built in front of the N end of the vaulted corridor upon which Saint Paraskevi's sanctuary is built. The corridor was used as that until the tower was built reducing its width and probably leading to the change of its use into an ossuary
110			Long corridor which connects the narthex of Saint Paraskevi and the road that lead to the forum
111	1460–1821	3-storey	Transverse to the slope, three-storey post–Byzantine structure
112	1460–1821	2-storey	West of Saint Nikoloas adjacent to b. 111 maintains its W wall
113			Parallel to the slope small structure
114	1460–1821		A tall wall originating from the W exterior wall of Aghios Nikolaos with a N orientation slightly bends W and again N only to turn E transverse to its original orientation reaching the outside section of the W wall of b. 119. The larger part of the possibly four leveled and multiple chambered structure is post-Byzantine (timber circumferential binding) while the lower part of the W wall, as well as the openings of the second chamber indicate a previous late-Byzantine phase
115	1460–1821		Adjacent to the SE wall of b. 116 post-Byzantine structure
116		3-storey	Wide-fronted, three-storey, small building SW of the palaces

(*continued*)

Table 2. (*continued*)

Code	Time Period	Structure	Description
117		2-storey	Parallel to the elevation curve small sized two-storey structure. Remains indicate that b. 117 and 119 are built as a unit, the ground level is used for storage while the E side where a wide corridor exists it was most probably used a public pass way. Above the vaulted corridor possibly worked as a balcony. Later, post-Byzantine, b. 116 is built adjacent and gradually the ground level is converted to vaulted pass ways
118	1460–1821		Adjacent to b. 243
119	1384–1460	2-storey	Two-storey parallel to the elevation curve building. Part of the ground level possibly used as pass way. Well-built structure with similarities at a smaller grade as b. [E]
120		2-storey	Long and narrow, at least two-storey building
121	1460–1821		
122		3-storey	Wide faced, three-storey building near Saint Sophia, parallel to the slope. The ground level is almost fully covered by the natural stone while on the E side towards the road two openings are formed. Balconies are formed on the third level on both the S and E sides
123		2-storey	Two-storey later to b. B adjacent to b. B's tower to the N
124	1384–1460	2-storey	At least three level building adjacent to b. B
125			Only the S wall is visible probably the only part of the building maintained to a small height
126	1384–1460	2-storey	At least two-storey large building transverse to the slope
127			Adjacent structure to b. 126
135	1460–1821		Adjacent to b. 134 large structure built transverse to the slope

The digitization of the phases, structural and temporal is presented overlapping Millet's historical topographical plan offering unique perspective in relation to the archaeological study and the remains that exist today (Fig. 11a). Millet's plan clearly depicts the Palace and its surrounding buildings and structures many of which have been identified on the orthophoto of the area today. Specifically, the main buildings [A], [B], [Γ], [Δ], etc. as well as the structures in the surrounding areas such as the buildings west of the main building [E], those outside the Palace square south, and south east such as buildings A, B, Δ etc. From the orthophoto structures beyond the wall northwest of the Palace

Palace Complex - Latin Occupancy 1249 - 1262

Fig. 6. Depiction of the palace complex during the latin occupancy phase 1249–1262.

are visible most probably what F. Vasieur mentions in the eighteenth century survey as the Jewish Corner (Sinos 2009). Figure 11a offers a clear depiction of the geodatabase information overlaying Millet's plan while maintaining a view of the orthophoto in the background. Similarly, comparing the database to Millet's diagram offers an alternative view for studying the city remains (Fig. 11b).

Palace Complex - Late Byzantine I

Fig. 7. Depiction of palace complex during the late Byzantine I phase 1262–1348.

Through the spatial visualization of Mystras, unknown to the public areas and aspects of the urban fabric area revealed. In the case of the Palace a large part of the surrounding area is off limits to visitors for over a decade due to the intensive restoration work. Hopefully the application of the geodatabase will offer incentive with the upcoming opening of the restored Palace for further study of the surrounding buildings to the Palace and through the process highlight an additional socioeconomic aspect of the Late Byzantine city.

Palace Complex - Late Byzantine II

Fig. 8. Depiction of palace complex during the late Byzantine II phase 1348–1384

4 Future Aims

The work presented in this study is part of an ongoing research effort for the mapping and high-resolution depiction of the archaeological site of Mystras including a detailed geodatabase of all the structures of the city. Through the overall presentation of the medieval city via GIS and the developed geodatabase users have the opportunity to study the site depending on their research interests through a centralized application containing a significant segment the published research data regarding Mystras. The database layers can be used in a variety of additional applications from AR and VR applications, to 3D visualization projects, educational games and digital smart guides. Future aims include the continuation of the development of the geodatabase in English

Palace Complex - Late Byzantine III

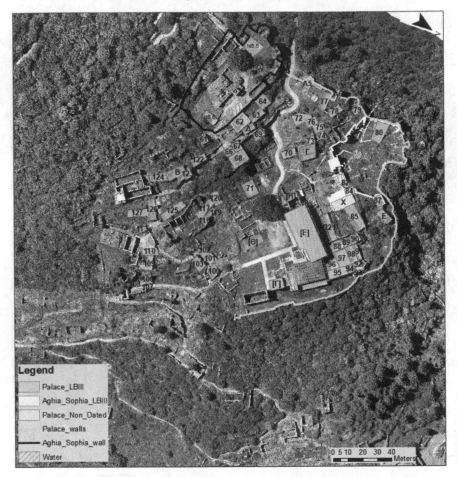

Fig. 9. Depiction of palace complex during the late Byzantine III phase 1384–1460

and enhanced information. Additionally, the archaeological site will be scanned using LIDAR technology in order to obtain a better view of the site surface which is covered by the extensive vegetation over Myzithra hill.

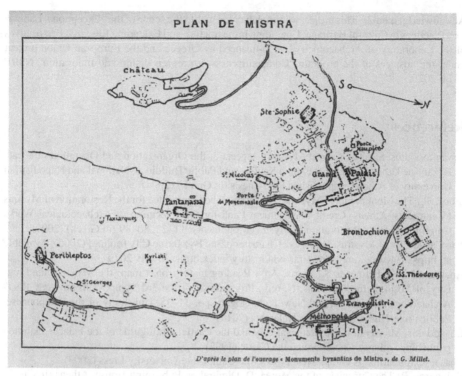

Fig. 10. Plan of mystras [plan de mistra, monuments byzantine de mistra, de G. Millet]

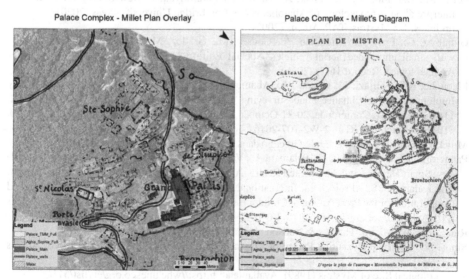

Fig. 11. Overlaying the database to Millet's diagram (a) left and (b) right

Acknowledgements. This project was implemented within the scope of the "Exceptional Laboratory Practices in Cultural Heritage: Upgrading Infrastructure and Extending Research Perspectives of the Laboratory of Archaeometry", a co-financed by Greece and the European Union project under the auspices of the program "Competitiveness, Entrepreneurship and Innovation" NSRF 2014–2020.

References

Arvanitopoulos, St.: The City of Mystras: Aspects of the Organization and Operation of a Late Byzantine Urban Complex Based on Sources and Public Buildings. National and Kapodistrian University of Athens, unpublished PhD Thesis (in Greek) (2004)

Sinos, St.: The Monuments of Mystras, The work of the Committee for the Restoration of Mystras Monuments. Athens: Credit Management Fund for the Execution of Archaeological Works Committee for the Restoration of Mystras Monuments, 11–22, 80–89 (in Greek) (2009)

The Castle City of Mystras: History & Character of the Byzantine City [online] (2005). Available at: https://www.culture.gr/mystras-edu/history/index.html. 20 July 2019

Anagnostaki K., Petmezas S., Sarris, A.p.: Reading history on a map: the Venetian land registry of Vostitsa. In: Zacharias, N. (ed.) Proceedings of the 3rd Symposium on Arch_RNT-Archaeological Research and New Technologies, pp. 31–38. University of the Peloponnese, Publications Humanities Series, Kalamata (2014)

Chatzidakis, M.: Mystras the Medieval City and the Castle, a full guide of the Palaces. Athinon publishing, Athens, Churches and the Castle (1992)

Chase, K.: Firearms: A Global History to 1700. Cambridge University Press (2003)

Kalonaros, P.: The Chronicle of the Morea. D. Dimitrakou Publishing House, Athens (in Greek) (1940)

Forte, M., Danelon, N., Marciniak, A.: Drones At Çatalhöyük: A New Survey for Landscape Interpretation, Archaeology of Anatolia, vol. 3. Cambridge University Press (2020)

Georgiades, N.: Mystras. TAP, Athens (2002)

Gutiérrez, G., Erny, G., Friedman, A., Godsey, M., Gradoz, M.: Archaeological topography with small unmanned aerial vehicles. Special Edition Drones in Archaeology. The SAA Archaeological Record **16**(2) (2016)

Meouche, R.El., Hijazi, L., Oncet, PA., Abumemeh, M., Rezouge, M.: UAV Photogrammetry Implementation to Enhance Land Surveying, Comparisons and Possibilities, Vol XlII-2/W2, 11th 3D Geoinfo Conference, 20-21 October 2016. Athens Greece (2016). https://doi.org/10.5194/isprs-archives-XLII-2-W2-107-2016

Millet, E.: Gabriel Millet. L'Ecole Grecque dans Γ architecture Byzantine, Paris (1916)

Panagiotidis, V., Malaperdas, G., Palamara, E., Valantou, V., Zacharias, N.: Information Technology, Smart Devices and Augmented Reality Applications for Cultural Heritage Enhancement: The Kalamata 1821 Project, 1st International Transdisciplinary Multispectral Modelling and Cooperation for the Preservation of Cultural Heritage. Springer Nature Switzerland AG, Athens (2019). https://doi.org/10.1007/978-3-030-12957-6_15

Runciman, St.: Mistra. Thames & Hudson, Athens (in Greek) (1980)

Sinos, St.: The Late Byzantine Palace of Mystras and its Restoration. Kapon Editions, Athens (2021)

Archaeological Site of Mystras (1989). Available at: https://whc.unesco.org/en/list/511/

Best Drone Photography Apps, Expert photography (2020). Available at: https://expertphotography.com/best-drone-apps/. Accessed 10 September 2020

Top 5 Drone Mapping Software for 2020, Commercial Drone Experts. https://www.coptrz.com/top-5-drone-mapping-software/. Accessed 10 September 2020

An Approach to Facilitate Visitors' Engagement with Contemporary Art in a Virtual Museum

Christina Tsita[1]([✉]) [iD], Charalabos Georgiadis[1], Maria Zampeti[2], Evi Papavergou[2], Syrago Tsiara[2], Alexandros Pedefoudas[1], and Dionysios Kehagias[1] [iD]

[1] Information Technologies Institute, Centre for Research & Technology Hellas, 57001 Thermi, Greece
{tsita,ch.georgiadis,alexandrospedefoudas,diok}@iti.gr
[2] Metropolitan Organisation of Museums of Visual Arts of Thessaloniki, Kolokotroni 21, Stavroupoli, 00000 Thessaloniki, Greece
{maria.zampeti,education.modern,director.contemporary}@momus.gr

Abstract. In recent years, the exhibition of digitized Cultural Heritage in Virtual Museums has increased, while Cultural Heritage institutions are trying to align with current trends regarding their communication with the audience. In VMs created with 360° panoramas; web 3D VMs and 3D virtual exhibitions created with authoring tools, the visitor-exhibit interactions are usually limited to display information about an exhibit. On the other hand, in Virtual Reality museums visitors get involved in more complex hands-on activities with educational potential. In this paper, we present a theoretical and practical approach that aims to support a deeper understanding of contemporary art for a wide audience. To this end, we suggest a virtual reality museum setting with different types of interactions and experiential activities that highlight the artwork's main message, and increase the experience's educational value. The suggested set of activities can be used to create experiences in any virtual museum setting. We present the pedagogical framework of the study and how it is applied in the case of the 2gether VR museum.

Keywords: Virtual museum · Virtual reality · Contemporary Art · Experiential learning · Animations

1 Introduction

Recently, there has been a great effort in the digitization of Cultural Heritage (CH) to support needs such as conservation of artefacts, modernization of exhibitions, reaching a wider audience, increase visitors' engagement, etc. First, the immerging novel methods for reconstruction of CH sites and artefacts highlight the importance of rigorous 3D representation of CH [1, 2] not only for the study of the monuments and artefacts but also for their preservation in digitized version. The (re)use of such digitized artefacts are useful for CH institutions to support their preservation, conservation, and restoration work [3] and to communicate their work to the public [4].

CH institutions, through Virtual Museums (VMs) [5] and other digital applications, not only keep in touch and renew the interest of the existing audience but also reach new

A. Moropoulou et al. (Eds.): TMM_CH 2021, CCIS 1574, pp. 207–217, 2022.
https://doi.org/10.1007/978-3-031-20253-7_17

groups of remote digital audiences. Pandemic conditions boosted CH institutions to keep up, by opening or expanding their digital doors to the public, whereas their physical doors remained closed. The current status indicates that what has started during the pandemic is here to stay and new challenges begin to emerge. Visitors are keen on digital experiences offered by CH institutions around the world, via a variety of technological means and applications. The threshold of the users' satisfaction from a CH digital experience will keep rising, as more and more people are being familiarized with new media and devices, and seek more meaningful experiences with added cognitive, psychomotor and affective value.

VMs can be either replicas of physical museums or representations of spaces that do not exist in the real world. Three-dimensional (3D) representations that do not correspond to real museums can be created from scratch with any specifications regarding the exhibition's shell. Moreover, these spaces can host digitized objects from different real-world museums. In this context, there are infinite possibilities in terms of the structure and content of exhibitions that can be created in a digital 3D setting. This allows CH institutions to communicate a story that would require more resources to be told in a physical museum context. Additionally, VMs can host digitized objects, the originals of which are impossible or very difficult to be displayed in a real-world museum, due to safety restrictions (e.g. cannot be exposed due to age/maintenance work, there is no suitable/sufficient space for their exhibition, etc.). In a VM such CH objects are not only displayed in safety but also can be enriched with interactions that strengthen their meaning and make their stories easier and more fun for the visitors to extract and understand. Although it seems ideal to be able to design an exhibition without the physical space limitations, in reality such freedom brings new challenges to the museological design, whereas the shell of the museum needs to be designed as well. In addition to this, more things need to be considered when designing the visitor's experience in a VM, as the latter comprises not only a museum but also a digital application.

Virtual Reality (VR) brings new possibilities to the VMs, where the level of immersion and sense of presence are increased [6]. Moreover, Head-mounted devices (HMDs) offer the possibility to the users to interact with 3D objects inside the virtual environment e.g. via touch controllers. Hands-on activities overcome the limitation of touching an artefact in a physical museum. The feeling of being part of a photorealistic 3D environment, combined with handling objects activities, can raise the pedagogical value of the whole VM experience especially when they are designed to promote experiential learning [7]. This approach is also aligned with modern museology, which encourages visitors to form their own interpretations about the museum objects [8–10]. Furthermore, the visual stimuli from the 3D world can contribute to the user's understanding of the exhibition's content [11]. In this context, visual activities can offer the possibility to the users to practice their photo-visual skills and understanding visual messages from artworks [12].

Offering VM experiences that not only represent a typical physical museum visit raises the usefulness of such applications in users' perception, as well as their satisfaction in terms of entertainment and learning in a VM setting. In the context of finding ways on creating meaningful experiences in a VM that can enhance understanding of visual culture [13], our research focuses on increasing the pedagogical value of such experiences via the use of VR technology. Thus, instead of offering VR experiences that their main strength is the use of VR technology itself to trigger the interest of the audience, we try to reinforce the motivation of the users to explore the studied cultural heritage theme of the application. More specifically, we aim to create not a simple walk-and-watch VR exhibition with simple click-interactions, but a rich-in-stimuli VR exhibition that integrates experiential activities for users who interact with the artefacts in order to promote higher-order cognitive skills [14, 15] and reinforce a positive attitude towards museums and cultural heritage in general.

2 Related Work and Contribution

The VMs developed in recent years highlight the plethora of options available in terms of technologies, navigation, interactions, and scenarios that exist to serve different VM dissemination and communication needs [16, 17]. A well-known service to create a VM is Google Arts & Culture, which allows CH institutions to display their exhibitions digitized with 360° panoramas via Street View tours [18]. The user navigates in a digital replica of a museum and remotely observes the exhibits in their current location. Although 360° panoramas can be used to provide remote cost-effective access to an exhibition, the immersion is relatively low and the user can view the flattened 3D objects only from a single point of view. On the other hand, 3D VMs can offer richer experiences, with exhibitions that usually exist only in the digital world. In a 3D setting, usually created with game engines (e.g. Unity3D), the user can walk through the space and observe a 3D object from all sides. A VM like this allows the user to navigate in a 3D exhibition area and display some information about the exhibits [19].

3D VMs developed in VR, offer an increased level of detail and immersion for the user. In such museums, the visitor usually wears an HMD to navigate and interacts with the CH objects e.g. via touch controllers. In the Anthropology VM [20] an integrated 3D viewer allows the user to observe CH objects with related multimedia content and interact via multiple-choice questions. The Scan4Reco VM offered in desktop and VR, allows the users to inspect CH objects via a 3D viewer, where there is textual information about the object, and research metadata related to specific areas on the object [21]. The user can also change the texture of 3D objects to display different time instances. Another VM hosts the Antikythera Mechanism, an ancient artefact found in the shipwreck of Antikythera sparred in fragments [22]. This VM is a characteristic example of exhibiting a highly fragile CH object in the safety of the virtual environment. The visitors can grab and observe the fragments from a very short eye distance. They can also enter the geometry of each fragment to view gears and inscriptions hidden inside the fragment mass via a CT scans viewer. This is an example of an activity that is impossible or very difficult to be executed in the real world by a wide audience and exploits the possibilities of VR technologies.

More than ten years ago, the benefits of creating dynamic virtual exhibitions had been highlighted [23]. DynaMus is a 3D VM framework that is used to create virtual exhibitions with content from open data web images resources and supports 3D objects display as well [24]. VIRTUE system allows curators to set up VM exhibitions of static and dynamic 2D (paintings, photographs, videos, etc.) and 3D artefacts. Curators can add an unlimited number of rooms, which can be adjusted. Visitors may navigate through the virtual rooms, inspect the artefacts and display information about them [25]. The Invisible Museum platform allows the curators to create virtual exhibitions available in both web 3D and VR [26]. Deep learning mechanisms facilitate the users to present textual narratives based on the socio-historic context of the artworks. Curators create VMs by adding images, videos, and 3D objects in the 3D virtual space.

To sum up, 3D VMs offer a variety of experiences. One can have a quick remote visit to a real-world exhibition via 360° panorama or can visit an exhibition that exists only in a 3D digital form. In 3D virtual exhibitions, the experience of the user usually includes a walk around a room and simple interactions to view textual information. More complicated activities are integrated into VR settings with various interactions and activities according to needs. Finally, the complexity of the exhibitions that can be created with VM authoring tools is increasing.

Furthermore, for the creation of VMs we need to take into account their educational potential [27], as well as the importance of providing meaningful experiences through them [28]. Being inspired by existing VR museums and utilizing the possibilities of VR settings, we suggest an approach that can facilitate the VM users to understand the exhibition's content and trigger them to get more interested in artefacts, contemporary art, and CH in general. In this study, a set of interaction and activity types is presented that can be used in any VM for 2D and 3D CH objects. Through these interactions and activities, the users can practice their photo-visual skills, meaning their ability to understand visual messages from artworks. We aspire to make this set useful for future VM authoring tools willing to introduce more sophisticated types of activities in their exhibitions and raise the experiences' educational value, as well as the visitors' satisfaction in terms of entertainment and learning.

In the context of the "2gether" project, the aim is to establish a technological and conceptual framework that allows a deeper understanding of contemporary art by a wide audience. To this end, a crowdsourcing platform and a VR environment are the main components of the system. We are developing a 3D VM in VR to explore more sophisticated interactions and activities for the users by a) increasing the pedagogical value of such experiences and b) allowing the users to practice their photo-visual skills and their understanding of contemporary art in a VM setting. In addition to the VM, a crowdsourcing web platform is being developed not only for the curators but also for the artists to upload their artworks and create their own 3D virtual exhibitions, which is not described in detail as it is out of the scope of this paper.

This study offers an approach that VM developers and museum experts can use to create meaningful experiences in VR museum settings with high educational value. More specifically, the users can practice their photo-visual skills, increase their knowledge in a deeper level than information retention (understanding) [7] and reinforce their positive perception about museums and cultural heritage in general.

The paper is organized as follows: In Sect. 3, the methodology is described. Next, in Sect. 4, the pedagogical approach is presented including interactivity and activity types that can be used in a VR museum to support learning. In Sect. 5, we describe how this approach is applied to the 2gether virtual exhibition and the VR museum application. Finally, Sect. 6 consists of the discussion and the conclusion of this research.

3 Methodology

After a review on 3D VMs and the interactions they support, we found different techniques that CH institutions use in their sites or social media channels to animate their artefacts to increase their audience's engagement. Then we classified the techniques that we could apply to 2D and 3D CH digitized objects in a VR environment. Afterwards, a generic exhibition shell was designed to support the user's explorative behavior [11], together with some activities that can facilitate learning [29] for any kind of exhibit in a VM. In parallel, a museological study was conducted to define the theme of the prototype digital exhibition. At a later stage, our team selected the artworks for the exhibition, defined the learning content and objectives for each artwork [29]. Then we selected the animation techniques that would be better to use for each object and designed the animation/activity scenarios. Based on the scenarios we proceeded to the implementation phase, which is currently in progress.

4 Pedagogical Approach

Initially, the design of the VM space should support the museological goals of the CH institution and be aligned with its educational policy. Our main objective is to encourage the explorative behavior of the visitors inside the digital exhibition and facilitate the users to understand the learning content for the artworks, via various interactions that highlight their concepts.

The suggested types of interactions that can enhance artefacts meanings in a VM setting are presented in Table 1, for 2D and 3D digitized objects. In the first column, one can view the interaction type. The second and the third column show the interactivity and immersion level, respectively. The fourth column presents what needs to be created for each interaction type to work from a technical point of view. The fifth column shows the intended User Experience (UX) for the visitors. In a 2D animation interaction the user views a painting hanging on the wall with a 2D animated texture and interacts with the artwork only to trigger the animation to play. The interaction level is low compared to a hands-on activity, in which the user grabs and manipulates parts of the artwork. Furthermore, in a 3D animation interaction where a 2D painting is being transformed into a 3D scene, the user enters the painting canvas. Thus, the immersion is higher with respect to a 2D animation interaction.

In an experiential activity (hands-on) the user forms a hypothesis on how to complete successfully a task regarding an artefact. Then, the user tests the hypothesis, by interacting with the artefact and receives feedback from the environment. According to the feedback, the user alters the previous hypothesis and tests something else until the riddle is solved [7]. In practice, the user has to execute a task with a specific goal. Once the user completes the task, an animation can be triggered as a reward/ feedback on the successful execution of the task. The task can foster the user to observe structural elements of the artwork, perform synthetic or analytical thinking regarding the artwork, form meanings and understand key messages and visual choices of the artist. The animation that follows the completed task can validate the hypothesis of the user by enhancing the key message derived from the learning objectives set for the specific artwork.

Table 1. Interaction types for 2D and 3D digitized CH assets

Interaction	Relative interactivity level	Relative immersion level	Implementation	Intended User Experience
Digitized 2D artwork e.g. painting	-	-	3D canvas model with still image texture	Observes the artwork
2D animation	Low	Low	3D model with 2D animated texture (video)	Observes the artwork and its 2D animation which demonstrates the key message
3D animation	Medium	High	3D scene with animated elements of the painting	Observes the artworks' structural elements and levels. Feels like being inside the painting
Hands on activity and animation	High	Medium	Mixed	Observes the artwork and its structural elements with a targeted goal. Synthesizes part of the artwork
Digitized 3D artwork e.g. sculpture	-	-	3D model	Observes the artwork
3D animation	Low	High	Animated 3D model	Observes the artwork and its animation which demonstrates the key message
Hands on activity and animation	High	High	Mixed	Observes the artwork and its structural elements with a targeted goal. Synthesizes part of the artwork

In addition to the interaction types that can be applied in 2D/3D digitized CH objects in a VM, a set of activities can be applied horizontally for all exhibits to facilitate learning in a VM [29]. Firstly, an embodied virtual agent may present information about the artworks, as it would happen to a real-world exhibition tour. Secondly, a Points of Interest (PoIs) activity can be available for the visitors that want to delve into a deeper level of information about an artefact. When the user is successfully motivated to learn more about an artefact should be able to view more information about it. Specifically, the user can view PoIs on the artwork and select one to learn more about it. This activity resembles the real-world process of pointing at a specific area on the artwork to explain a specific visual detail on a 2D or 3D CH asset e.g. a form/shape/color, a characteristic feature of the artist/artistic movement, a visual choice of the artist, etc. Finally, to strengthen the VM effectiveness in terms of learning, we suggest to set the learning content and learning objectives of the artefacts from the very beginning in order to achieve consistency among the design, production, and assessment phase of the VM [30].

5   The "2Gether" VR Museum

The aforementioned approach was used to create the "2gether" VR museum. The virtual exhibition is about the human body and how is perceived and visualized in contemporary art. We brought together artworks from different geographical regions to exploit the possibilities of the digital exhibition. The virtual exhibition consists of both 2D (e.g. paintings) and 3D (e.g. sculptures) artworks that allow us to try different animation techniques and interactions. The decisive factor for the selection of the artworks was the acquisition of appropriate licenses by the artists or their families. Regarding the exhibition shell, we aim to encourage free exploration and support the positioning of the artefacts in chronological order.

For each artwork, we defined the basic learning concept, with which we deal in interactions and activities e.g. for Edgar Degas's "Little Dancer of Fourteen Years" we focus on the ballerina's pose, while in Liubov Popova's "Portrait study" we focus on the cubo-futurismo artistic expression (see Fig. 1). Then we described the learning content [29] limited in a few sentences: the information one needs to know to understand the basic concept (e.g. main message and/or artist/ artistic movement, socio-historical context, techniques, etc.). Then we defined the learning objectives: what we expect from the visitor to gain in terms of learning through the interactions with the artwork. For example, Aleksandr Rodtchenko's "Construction on White (Robot)" (see Fig. 1) learning objectives are: the user to recognize the male and female figures; construct part of the human figure out of geometrical shapes; understand that the geometrical visualization of the couple emphasizes their mechanical – robotic relationship. Then we selected the interaction type of Table 1 for each art piece and the specific scenarios for the animations and hands-on activities. To do so we considered a) the learning content and learning objectives; b) the opportunities that the VR environment and various 2D and 3D animation techniques can offer to the artwork, in terms of enhancing its meaning; and c) any limitation immerged from a museological perspective and/or license issues. It was also specified that when the animation of the artwork is playing or when the visitor executes an activity to interact with the artwork, it should be clear that this is an intervention on the artist's work and not the original art piece. For this reason, visual elements indicate and distinguish the original piece from its interventions, and a relevant informative text shows up at the beginning of the experience. Finally, we also included a short description of how we expect the user to approach the learning content through the interactions and activities.

We also suggest a PoIs activity that will be available for all artworks to facilitate the visitors to focus on visual elements on the art pieces and form related meanings. These PoIs have been defined for each artwork together with the preliminary information that the user will be able to view in each PoI (see Fig. 2). Another activity available for all artworks is the embodied virtual guide who introduces basic information about the artworks to the visitor (see Fig. 3).

Fig. 1. Images of a) Edgar Degas: Little Dancer of Fourteen Years © Vassilis and Eliza Goulandris Foundation Collection, b) Liubov Popova: Portrait study © Metropolitan Organisation of Museums of Visual Arts of Thessaloniki (MOMus)[1], c) Aleksandr Rodtchenko: Construction on White (Robot) © MOMus.

Fig. 2. Visualization of PoI activity on a 3D digitized asset (mockup). The user selects a PoI on the digitized asset to view more information. Artwork: Alex Mylona: Angel II © MOMus.

Until now, most of the artworks have been digitized with photogrammetry and/or polygon modeling to be integrated into the game engine. The VM is a work in progress and is being developed with Unity High-Definition Render Pipeline (HDRP) to pursue high graphical realism. The VM will be available in VR with HMD (Oculus Quest) and touch controllers. To increase the learnability and usability of the system, we designed a tutorial at the beginning of the VM experience to familiarize the user with the system. We intend to reduce the cognitive load needed to explore the VM and make easier to focus on the CH content and the tasks.

---

[1] https://www.momus.gr/en.

Fig. 3. The embodied guide presenting a 2D digitized asset. Artwork: Aleksandr Rodtchenko: Construction on White (Robot) © MOMus.

6 Discussion and Conclusions

3D VMs offer a variety of experiences and can meet various CH institutions and audiences' needs. From 360° panoramas to 3D digital exhibitions and VMs derived from authoring tools, there are various ways for the users to interact with the digitized CH assets, which are usually limited to displaying textual information. On the other hand, 3D VR museums offer more complicated interactions that can have additional educational value with hands-on activities and rich stimuli. We can utilize the possibilities of the VR technologies to create VMs with more sophisticated interactions and activities that a) are not possible to be executed in a physical museum (touch CH objects, interact, experiential activities, etc.), and b) enhance learning aspects of the whole VM experience (e.g. knowledge: understanding of the CH contents, affective: increase engagement, trigger/retain/increase motivation to explore more about the CH content, skills: photo-visual, analysis, synthesis, form own interpretations, etc.).

We presented a set of interaction and activity types that can be applied in 2D and 3D digitized assets in VMs. Our pedagogical approach focuses on experiential learning and visual stimuli to understand art pieces and highlights the importance of defining the learning content and objectives for the artworks scenarios. This approach aims to facilitate users to increase their knowledge regarding the content of a specific VM in a substantial way: information retention level, understanding and beyond. In parallel, the goal is the users to practice their photo-visual skills, which are useful for any museum setting, digital or physical, so as to transfer their knowledge outside our application. We also aspire to strengthen visitors' confidence in forming their interpretations about the art pieces and increase their interest in the artworks, contemporary art and CH in general. The assessment of user experience will provide us with insights about the usefulness and appropriateness of the interactions and activities, as well as the effectiveness of the whole experience, in terms of user satisfaction, entertainment and learning (skills, knowledge, attitude). Finally, in our future work we foresee incorporating a classification of sophisticated interactions and activities in VM authoring tools that already tend to offer more complicated and adjustable virtual exhibitions.

Acknowledgements. This research was funded by the General Secretariat for Research and Innovation, Greece, under the call "Special Actions AQUACULTURE - INDUSTRIAL MATERIALS

- OPEN INNOVATION IN CULTURE" (24485–28/2/2020) with a project name "2gether" (http://www.2gether-project.gr/).

References

1. Papachristou, K., Dimitriou, N., Drosou, A., Karagiannis, G., Tzovaras, D.: Realistic texture reconstruction incorporating spectrophotometric color correction. In: 25th IEEE International Conference on Image Processing (ICIP), pp. 415–419. IEEE (October 2018)
2. Doulamis, A., Voulodimos, A., Protopapadakis, E., Doulamis, N., Makantasis, K.: Automatic 3d modeling and reconstruction of cultural heritage sites from twitter images. Sustainability 12(10), 4223 (2020)
3. Papadopoulos, S., Dimitriou, N., Drosou, A., Tzovaras, D.: Modelling spatio-temporal ageing phenomena with deep Generative Adversarial Networks. Signal Processing: Image Communication 94, 116200 (2021)
4. Doulamis, A., Liarokapis, F., Petridis, P., Miaoulis, G.: Serious games for cultural applications. In: Intelligent computer graphics 2011, pp. 97–115. Springer, Berlin, Heidelberg (2012)
5. The ViMM Definition of a Virtual Museum: https://www.vi-mm.eu/2018/01/10/the-vimm-definition-of-a-virtual-museum/. Last accessed 21 July 2021
6. Jung, T., tom Dieck, M.C., Lee, H., Chung, N.: Effects of Virtual Reality and Augmented Reality on Visitor Experiences in Museum. In: Inversini, A., Schegg, R. (eds.) Information and Communication Technologies in Tourism 2016, pp. 621–635. Springer, Cham (2016). https://doi.org/10.1007/978-3-319-28231-2_45
7. Kolb, D.A: Experiential learning: Experience as the source of learning and development. FT press (2014)
8. Falk, J.H., Dierking, L.D.: Learning from museums. Rowman & Littlefield (2018)
9. Mairesse, F., Desvallées, A.: Key concepts of museology. International Council of museums (2010)
10. Black, G.: The engaging museum: developing museums for visitor involvement. Psychology Press (2005)
11. Tsita, C., Satratzemi, M.: A VR serious game for understanding cultural heritage. In: Helin, K., Perret, J., Kuts, V. (eds.) The application track, posters and demos of EuroVR: Proceedings of the 16th Annual EuroVR Conference - 2019. pp. 98–101. VTT Technical Research Centre of Finland. VTT Technology No. 357 (2019). https://doi.org/10.32040/2242-122X.2019.T357
12. Eshet, Y.: Learning with technology: the way we think in the digital ERA. In: International Conference Cognition and Exploratory Learning in Digital Age (CELDA), pp. 305–310 (2004)
13. Hooper-Greenhill, E.: Museums and the interpretation of visual culture. Routledge (2020)
14. Krathwohl, D.R.: A revision of Bloom's taxonomy: an overview. Theory into Practice 41(4), 212–218 (2002)
15. Bloom, B.S.: Taxonomy of educational objectives, vol. 1: Cognitive domain. McKay, New York (1956)
16. Sylaiou, S., Liarokapis, F., Kotsakis, K., Patias, P.: Virtual museums, a survey and some issues for consideration. J. Cult. Herit. 10(4), 520–528 (2009)
17. Schweibenz, W.: The virtual museum: an overview of its origins, concepts, and terminology. The Museum Review 4(1), 1–29 (2019)
18. Google Arts and Culture: https://artsandculture.google.com/. Last accessed 21 July 2021
19. Skamantzari, M., Kontogianni, G., Georgopoulos, A., Kazanis, S.: Developing a virtual museum for the Stoa of Attalos. In: 2017 9th International Conference on Virtual Worlds and Games for Serious Applications (VS-Games), pp. 260–263. IEEE (2017)

20. Anastasovitis, E., Ververidis, D., Nikolopoulos S., Kompatsiaris, I.: Digiart: Building new 3D cultural heritage worlds. In: 2017 3DTV Conference: The True Vision - Capture, Transmission and Display of 3D Video (3DTV-CON), pp. 1–4 (2017). https://doi.org/10.1109/3DTV.2017. 8280406

21. Tsita, C., et al.: A configurable design approach for virtual museums. In: GCH 2018 - Eurographics Workshop on Graphics and Cultural Heritage (2018). https://doi.org/10.2312/gch. 20181349

22. Anastasovitis, E., Roumeliotis, M.: Virtual museum for the antikythera mechanism: designing an immersive cultural exhibition. In: Adjunct Proceedings - IEEE 2018 International Symposium on Mixed and Augmented Reality (2018). ISMAR-Adjunct. https://doi.org/10.1109/ISMAR-Adjunct.2018.00092

23. Walczak, K., Cellary, W., White, M.: Virtual museum exhibitions. Computer **39**(3), 93–95 (2006)

24. Kiourt, C., Koutsoudis, A., Pavlidis, G.: DynaMus: A fully dynamic 3D virtual museum framework. J. Cult. Herit. **22**, 984–991 (2016)

25. Giangreco, I., et al.: Virtue: a virtual reality museum experience. In: Proceedings of the 24th international conference on intelligent user interfaces: companion, pp. 119–120 (2019)

26. Zidianakis, E., et al.: The invisible museum: a user-centric platform for creating virtual 3D exhibitions with VR support. Electronics **10**(3), 363 (2021)

27. Taranova, T.N.: Virtual museum technologies and the modern educational process. ARPHA Proceedings **3**, 2513 (2020)

28. Perry, S., Roussou, M., Economou, M., Young, H., Pujol, L.: Moving beyond the virtual museum: Engaging visitors emotionally. In: 2017 23rd International Conference on Virtual System & Multimedia (VSMM), pp. 1–8. IEEE (October 2017)

29. Tsita, C., Satratzemi, M.: Conceptual Factors for the Design of Serious Games. In: Gentile, M., Allegra, M., Söbke, H. (eds.) GALA 2018. LNCS, vol. 11385, pp. 232–241. Springer, Cham (2019). https://doi.org/10.1007/978-3-030-11548-7_22

30. Tsita, C., Satratzemi, M.: A Serious Game Design and Evaluation Approach to Enhance Cultural Heritage Understanding. In: Liapis, A., Yannakakis, G.N., Gentile, M., Ninaus, M. (eds.) GALA 2019. LNCS, vol. 11899, pp. 438–446. Springer, Cham (2019). https://doi.org/10.1007/978-3-030-34350-7_42

Enhancing Archaeological Sites. Interconnecting Physically and Digitally – InterArch

Eleni Maistrou, Konstantinos Moraitis, Yanis Maistros, Katerina Boulougoura[(✉)],
Amalia-Maria Konidi, and Karolina Moretti[(✉)]

National Technical University of Athens, Patision 42, 10682 Athens, Greece
boulougoura.k@gmail.com, amkonidi@gmail.com,
kanel8car@hotmail.com

Abstract. InterArch is a research program that is running since September 2020.
It involves mutual collaboration between academic and cultural institutions, and
the contribution of an IT applications development company. It aims at the design
of a site-based digital application, for archaeological visits and guided tours. The
proposed application will run as a pilot project for the Archaeological site of
Ancient Messene.

The applied research program integrates an interactive approach to the natural
environment, aiming at a manifold sensory experience. The project also embraces
storytelling processes, by engaging an interdisciplinary approach, that familiarizes
the user to multiple semantic interpretations and free associations with cultural
descriptions. Management of huge amount of data -historical, cultural, geospatial
and environmental- will be applied. This research integrates scientific fields, such
as archaeology, architecture, topography, computer and network engineering in a
holistic approach. Featuring the city's distinct landscapes, all treated as equally
important, a directed graph is elaborated to emphasize this approach, illustrating
the ways different data are associated with different perspective views of narration,
engaging multimodal storytelling.

Keywords: Archaeological · Natural · Multi-sensory · Digital · Semantics

1 Introduction

InterArch is a design research project based on digital representation, supporting Virtual
and Augmented Reality (VR, AR) technology. Multiple senses are engaged, through the
processes of storytelling, while the proposed application takes into account the physical
features of the archaeological site, by enabling different levels of interaction with the
digital contents and archaeological data, as well as with the natural surroundings. Aiming
at app customization, the application is also addressed to people with visual or hearing
impairments. A digital learning Game is especially developed for school students and
children.

The research proposal was designed by an NTUA research team, submitted for
evaluation in 2019, with the contribution of the Ephorate of Antiquities of Messenia,

the Society of Messenian Archaeological Studies and the IT applications development company Diadrasis. The program is running since September 2020, to be completed 2023 and is co-financed by the European Regional Development Fund of the European Union and Greek national funds, through the Operational Program Competitiveness, Entrepreneurship and Innovation, under the call Research – Create – Innovate for the period 2014–2020 (project code: T2EΔK-01659).

2 Scope Description

Project Initiation. Cultural institutions around the world, acknowledge the importance of digital technologies in the maintenance, conservation, documentation, and revitalization of cultural heritage. As far as Greece is concerned, there is an on-going research supporting digital guided tours, mainly inside museums and interior spaces.

Nonetheless digital outdoor guided tours that combine virtual visits to excavation sites and the relevant museums, are not fully developed. Applying augmented reality in places of such historical value, also encounters important geospatial and environmental issues, along with the landscape's fluidity.

Research Objective. Archaeological sites are important landmarks of significant cultural, historical, and educational value. They are often located in places of outstanding natural beauty. In contrast to museum exhibitions, being organized and structured, archaeological sites enable visitors to associate more freely with the physical environment. Archaeological visits are significant on their own right, combining cultural and historical data, with the constantly evolving natural landscape of the archaeological excavation.

Presently, mobile applications, specifically developed for archaeological guided tours, include mere historical descriptions of the site monuments and archaeological findings. However, there is limited reference to the ways the site monuments are associated with their natural and cultural surroundings. At the same time augmented reality-based mobile applications give priority to visual information (systems of virtual reality and 3Dobject representation), diminishing partially the multisensory character of the actual visit.

InterArch involves the design of a site-based digital application, for archaeological visits and guided tours. Our applied research program integrates an interactive approach to the natural environment, aiming at a manifold sensory experience. This project also implements story telling processes, by engaging an interdisciplinary approach, that familiarizes the user to multiple semantic interpretations and free associations with the cultural descriptions.

Interacting with knowledge and space may yield to rich cultural experience. Implementing ubiquitous computing by using sensors and actuators, that seamlessly blend with their surroundings, visitors may explore and discover freely the archaeological site. In addition, this project aiming at personalization, enables visitors to freely associate with the available information. Exceeding the physical boundaries of the archaeological site, the visitors engage semantically with the cultural content provided, supporting multiple interpretations and associations, that connect historical data to the present time.

The proposed application will run as a pilot for the Archaeological site of Ancient Messene and will be implemented for visitors on-site, for validation, so that it will be available for adaptation to other archaeological sites and cultural environments.

2.1 Research Methodology

The fundamental stages of the research involve:

1. Analysis of the guiding principles for the preservation and revitalization of cultural heritage sites. Evaluation and use of existing documentation standards for the recording of cultural data and information management systems.
2. Spatial analysis and data collection. Optimization of the existing technology. Elaborating and testing the initial user scenario (0 scenario).
3. Design of multiple user scenarios. Appropriate readjustment of the technological tools for Augmented Reality, for outdoor guided tours and app development.
4. Implementing and testing the application for visitors on-site.

Further elaboration follows, describing the stages of the present research.

3 The Case Study

Ancient Messene is referred to, amongst the most important archaeological sites in Greece. The city's remains are situated almost intact, having not been destroyed by more recent settlements. The ongoing excavation works over the past thirty years, have brought to light an impressive ensemble of public buildings, sanctuaries, houses, public spaces, fortifications, and tombs. The extensive archaeological findings in an environment of outstanding natural beauty of 200 acres, along with the systematic restoration works and monument reconstruction, by the Society of Messenian Archaeological Studies [1] and the Ephorate of Antiquities of Messenia, establish a comparative advantage for the city of Messene, as one of the most visited archaeological locations.

The physical configuration of the landscape, along with the building assemblages, divide the city into three distinctive functional zones that form its religious, political and commercial centers: a. The Ancient Agora and the Ancient Theatre b. The Asklepion and its adjacent public buildings c. The Stadium and the Gymnasium. Furthermore, a multi layered cultural landscape of Hellenistic, Roman and Byzantine structures outline the morphological character of the city, with its Hippodamian plan. The distinctive morphological features of the ancient city and its explicit spatial structure became the primary field of research [2].

The design of a site-based digital application requires the collection and further analysis of the spatial data, as well as the detailed evaluation of the extensive archaeological findings and historic records. In addition, an in-depth elaboration of the semantic relations that could be collected by different narratives and interpretations of the City's history, is almost necessary, in order to develop next stages of the research.

4 Research Description

4.1 The Guiding Principles for the Recording, Preservation, and Revitalization of Cultural Heritage

In 1996, the 11th general assembly organized by ICOMOS sets out guiding principles, 'for the recording of the cultural heritage', to ensure the 'maintenance and conservation of monuments, historical buildings and sites of heritage value'. This process involves the documentation of tangible as well as intangible evidence. Recording should be 'appropriate to the nature of the heritage and the cultural context', while the purpose of the records should be clearly defined, emphasizing the need to document all physical structures at risk, due to natural destruction [3].

The recording of heritage becomes even more essential and challenging in the late '90s, based on digital technologies and information systems and the Semantic Web development. The need to safely store the continuously increasing information, leads to the development of high-quality standards, specifying the ways cultural contents are organized, interpreted, documented, and digitized for the dissemination and preservation of the related heritage [4].

The research on the implementation of established international standards for the project's objectives, is described below:

Digital Cultural Heritage Management in Greece. Following the guiding principles and criteria, for the recording of cultural heritage, one of the main tasks of the research program is the careful examination and listing of all the existing digital or non-digital records and archives, about the archaeological site of Ancient Messene. An in-depth indexing involves the scrupulous work carried out by the Ephorate of Antiquities of Messenia, the Society of Messenian Archaeological Studies, as well as the Archaeological Museum of Ancient Messene.

The project also investigated the work accomplished by several cultural institutions throughout Greece, including the Ministry of Culture and the National Documentation Center, actively involved in the technological upgrading of digital systems, initiating projects such as the Ongoing Catalogue of the Listed Archaeological Sites and Monuments [5], the Searchculture project [6], as well as the Work of the Directorate National Archive of Monuments and the digital repository Odysseus etc.

International Documentation Standards. Several models supporting representation of cultural content metadata are examined, including the European Data Model (EDM), the CIDOC conceptual reference model [7] for formalized knowledge and cultural documentation, the SKOS model supporting knowledge organization systems [8] and the RDF model (Resource Description Framework) for data merging and integration [9]. These standards are developed based on the consensus of the cultural community, of mutual academic, library and museum collaboration, setting up a core semantics for Web-based resources. They provide semantic interoperability for cultural heritage, by transforming localized information sources into a coherent global resource, that allows for the data exchange.

Digitizing cultural content and managing data on the semantic Web using network technologies, enable users for enhanced search and data retrieval. Archaeological excavation 'involves the recovery of several types of data' tangible and intangible evidence, including artifacts, features, ecofacts, etc. Archaeological and historical data mingle, linking information from various semantic relations, engaging multiple associations that allow multifaceted interpretations, affecting thus the ways historical descriptions are presented and re-used.

From this point of view, generating multiple interpretations of the digital records, also entails a certain awareness regarding the impact of the existing cultural tendencies, on the ways semantic relations are structured across the Web. Depending on the historical and cultural conditions, the semantics of descriptions relate intrinsically, to the ways knowledge is perceived, understood, and explained, affecting decisively contemporary design practices.

4.2 Approaching InterArch

Cultural reference Scope. The research outlines the archaeological site's tangible and intangible characteristics, depicting its physical structures and monuments, its natural surroundings, and archaeological findings, as well as any evidence documenting human activity, connected with the socio-political, economic religious and cultural everyday life of the city [10]. These complementary perspectives of the historical narrative about the Ancient city of Messene, engages the mind into a zooming in and zooming out, both on a physical and nonphysical scale. The political and ethical standards encountered not only in Ancient Messene, but also in similar cultural environments throughout the world, allows us to travel in space and time cognitively, using multiple associations and semantic relations.

Complex queries such as the following: "What urges the Dutch Painter Isaac Walraven in the 18th century, to encapsulate the death of Epaminondas?" [11] or "Why does the British explorer Richard Francis Burton claim that the myth describing Aristomenis' escape from his capture by the Spartans, with the help of a fox that shows him a passage to the outside, became the inspiration for the fourth voyage of Sinbad the Sailor, in the Book of the Thousand Nights and a Night?" [12] provide a multidimensional approach for cultural associations, that exceed the physical and geographical borders of the archaeological site. In this sense, Ancient Messene could potentially become a special point of interest and a place of cultural reference on a global scale. The storytelling is rattled abruptly, by the unexpected integration of nonlinear information, highlighting new semantic interpretations and interrelations, that exceed the mere descriptive characteristics of the city's history, disrupting thus, the logical sequence of the narrative.

Different perspectives of narration may also reveal:

- Various views of the city's urban and architectural structure, following the Hippodamian plan, highlighting the different levels of socio-political, economic and cultural co-relations.
- Alternate views of the landscape's morphology and a site-oriented analysis of the archaeological findings. The documentation of the archaeological site follows a topological approach, revealing the organizational structure of the landscape and its diverse

perspectives, along with the archaeological data. This type of projection is extended, as a possible comparison of two perspectives placed side by side; the natural space surface morphology, with that of Hellenistic sculptures representing an intense sense of movement. These two images simultaneously placed together, extend perception of depth and scale, enhancing the sensory experience with the natural surroundings (Fig. 1).

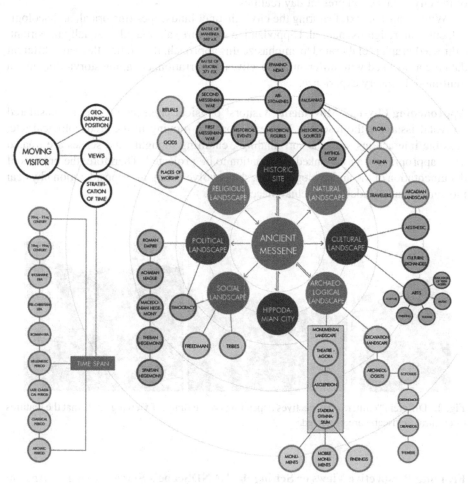

Fig. 1. Multidimensional aspects of ancient messene as a rolling undirected/directed graph.

- The essential part of body exercise and physical fitness in Ancient's Messene' s everyday life, is emphasized through the meticulous depictions produced in sculpture and architecture. Ancient Greeks believed that physical fitness coincides with mental clarity. Entire building assemblages, including the Gymnasium along with the Stadium, as well as small-scaled buildings, are committed for the purpose of everyday exercise, as a vital part of the social, cultural and religious life of city's inhabitants.

Highlighting the significant values and the multidimensional aspects of Ancient Messene, in a holistic overall approach of multiple narrations, becomes vital to this research. Enabling the multiple semantic associations with the use of different data (historical, cultural, artistic, architectural etc.) also emphasizes the influential character of the city's impact on present-day realities.

Within this context, featuring the city's distinct landscapes (historical, archaeological, cultural, religious, natural, Hippodamian structure) all treated as equally important, a directed graph is elaborated to emphasize this approach, illustrating the ways different data are associated with different perspectives of narration, engaging storytelling into a multimodal sensory experience.

Approaching Physical Movement. Visitors' physical presence on site, is considered a pivotal issue for the research. While visitors are moving in the archaeological site, possible interactions with the surroundings, entailing thoughts and senses are treated as an appropriate way for linked Information to be projected. Therefore, the process of documentation of the archaeological site, shall evolve taking into consideration physical movement and wandering in actual place (Fig. 2).

Fig. 2. Different "camera" perspectives depending on the range of viewing angle that the features of cultural landscape are projected.

Framing Perspective Views or Setting the LANDScape's Stages. Using Ancient Messene as a case study, the analysis of the site formation is based on the visitors' flows and aims at an assessment framework on the correlations generated, in terms of physical wandering and projected views of the landscape. Accordingly, categories of landscape attributes are suggested and linked to specific locations of the archaeological site, where given information can be highlighted by these attributes.

Thus, setting the landscape's stages is pursued, so as to enhance the narrative tours/wanderings.

   As a common example, one could mention the special conditions of sightseeing, during a hot sunny day, in the extended area of Ancient Messene, where its shaded parts are already naturally annotated and can be used as "portals" to various narrations and historical information. Nevertheless, while spatial characteristics are further clarified, particular locations in the archaeological site are classified into three categories, depending on the range of the particular viewing angle, where different features of the cultural landscape are projected, facing: a) wide angle view, b) view of focused area and c) highlighted spot.

   As a result, different "cameras" are set up in place, so as that the relevant features of the cultural landscape can trigger senses, thoughts and narrations. Furthermore, by using these "cameras", physical features are related to the archaeological ones, and the natural environment is considered present, while cultural information is perceived. On the next level, the different perspective views are combined with the ways archaeological findings are physically approached each time, activating wider areas as distinctive functional fields, where the suggested information, aims to influence the physical movement in different ways. For example, there are (Fig. 3):

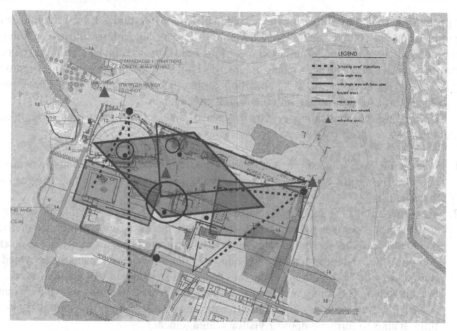

Fig. 3. Spatial analysis of the theatre-agora area - encoding the landscape.

– areas where many possible ways are emergent, so visitors' movement can be redefined. The dilemma can be managed, according to the ways information is projected, by using the landscape's features assessment framework.
– classified areas regarding visitors' accessibility where vague space becomes distinct.

– areas where dynamic views can create "crossing over" transitions, both physically and cognitively or mentally. In these areas, the offered information can refer to a challenging topic, so that visitors may reflect beyond usual approaches. Depending on the given information, "crossing over" transitions can also be used to "create" direction in a vague space.
– focused areas depending on the scale, density and proximity of archaeological findings. In these areas the configuration of visitors' movement concerns a more limited space and is usually formed in a radial way that links the different points of interest.

So far, an initial encoding formula proposes different ways of connecting information to the archaeological findings and the landscape. Presently, a primary conceptual framework is applied for assigning historical descriptions to archeological findings, and natural features of the landscape. However, the multifaceted character of the emerging information about the archaeological site, does not only concern setting up landscape sceneries, that apply a certain rhythm on perceiving information and narration, but also evolves through the basic principles set by the application itself. These basic principles are described below.

Application Tools Creating an Interactive Multimedia System. Basic principles of gamification are applied, namely by integrating gaming algorithms into non-gaming procedures. These techniques are used in various fields (marketing, education, distance training, social media, business management, tourism, etc.) for the design of information systems and applications, by using specific features that make a game attractive, so as to enhance the user interaction with the digital environment.

Developing the application so far, 3 types of interactive movements have been identified. More specifically:

1. Free action. Free choice of action, so as to specify interaction according to visitors' interest. The visitor is free to choose the type of information he prefers e.g. read a historical text.
2. Triggered action. The action is activated under certain circumstances, that are usually spatial ones. As visitors approach a specific area or a certain monument of the archaeological site, the emotion of surprise is triggered. For example, as visitors approach the Arsinoi Fountain, the sound of running water is instantly activated. Simultaneously information and choices relevant to the monument are displayed.
3. Forced action. The action is activated as an outcome of a previous one, e.g., when a particular free action is chosen, or after staying in a place over a certain period of time. It aims to further empower visitor's engagement.

5   Conclusions

InterArch project involves the design of a digital application that highlights the multi-dimensional character of Ancient Messene. It combines the physical and non-physical characteristics of the archaeological site, into a holistic design approach, featuring the city's different landscapes, not only on a natural and historical level, but also on the level of social, political, and cultural reference.

This research is interdisciplinary and requires the expertise of several scientific fields, such as archaeology, architecture, topography, computer, and network engineering. As already described in the previous chapters, our main goal is to integrate different data typologies within the spatial environment of the archaeological site, depending on the different levels of granularity and specification of information.

For this purpose, additional data will be acquired, with the use of 3D modeling techniques, combing image-based (photogrammetry) and laser scanning methods, as well as three dimensional recontractions of selected monuments and artifacts [13]. Recording visitors' trajectories and the ways they engage cognitively and emotionally with their surroundings, is also vital to this research and could provide us with a spatial framework, appropriate to trace the different ways historical and cultural descriptions could emerge. Incorporating spatial and temporal data regarding visitor's interaction with the archaeological findings on-site, may provide us time and space varying dynamic maps [14]. This also involves:

- The use of GPS locators tracking visitors' itineraries, throughout the archaeological tour [14].
- Questionnaires implemented with the use of selected key words, in the form of volunteer survey, that will help us obtain statistically useful feedback, for the recording of visitors' archaeological experience [15].

The data obtained will enable us to associate specific locations of the site, to relevant information, for the elaboration of multiple user scenarios and storytelling processes. The primary goal of this research, is to engage visitors in a multimodal sensory experience that enhances the physical connection with the landscape and at the same time, stimulates their imaginary, enabling an overall cognitive experience with knowledge.

Acknowledgements. Warm thanks to P. Themelis for his rich and constructive cooperation, but above all, for his contribution to our country and the global culture related to the now excavated Ancient Messene.

This research has been co-financed by the European Union and Greek national funds through the Operational Program Competitiveness, Entrepreneurship and Innovation, under the call RESEARCH – CREATE – INNOVATE (project code: project code: T2EΔK-01659)

EPAnEK 2014-2020
OPERATIONAL PROGRAMME
COMPETITIVENESS
ENTREPRENEURSHIP
INNOVATION

European Union
European Regional
Development Fund

Partnership Agreement
2014 - 2020

Co-financed by Greece and the European Union

References

1. Society of Messenian Archaeological Studies: Monument restoration (2007). https://www.snf.org/en/grants/grantees/s/society-of-messenian-archaeological-studies/monument-restoration/
2. Themelis, P.: Ancient Messene. Kapon Editions, Athens (2019)

3. ICOMOS: Principles for the Recording of Monuments. Groups of Buildings and Sites, pp. 1–3 (1996). https://www.icomos.org/charters/archives-e.pdf

4. Europeana pro: Mission: Brief History (2020). https://pro.europeana.eu/about-us/mission

5. National Documentation Centre: SearchCultrure.gr: Culture in the Digital Public Space (2022). https://www.searchculture.gr/

6. Ministry of Culture: Ongoing Catalogue of the Listed Archaeological Sites and Monuments (2021). http://nam.culture.gr/portal/page/portal/deam/erga/catalogue. Last accessed 08 July 08

7. CIDOC CRM: Special Interest Group: Definition of the CIDOC Conceptual Reference Model. Version 7.1 pp. i-viii, March 8 (2021). http://www.cidoc-crm.org/sites/default/files/CIDOC% 20CRM_v.7.1%20%5B8%20March%202021%5D.pdf

8. SKOS: Simple Knowledge Organization System Reference (2009). https://www.w3.org/TR/ skos-reference/

9. RDF/XML: Syntax Specification (Revised) W3C Recommendation. (no date [2004]). https:// www.w3.org/TR/REC-rdf-syntax/

10. Themelis, P.: The Economy and society of messenia under roman rule. In: Rizakis, A.D., Lepenioti, C.L.E.: (eds.) Roman Peloponese III, pp. 89–110. Research Institute for Greek and Roman Antiquity, Athens (2010)

11. The historian shut: The Death of Epaminondas. Painted By Isaac Walraven (c. 1686–1765) (2021). https://thehistorianshut.com/2021/02/03/the-death-of-epaminondas-painted-by-isaac-walraven-c-1686-1765/

12. Kalimniou, D.: Sinbad the Greek (2008). http://diatribe-column.blogspot.com/2008/01/sin bad-greek.html. Last accessed 08 July 2021

13. Georgopoulos, A., Tapinaki, S., Makris, G.N., Stefanakis, M.I.: Innovative Methods for Digital Heritage Documentation: The archaeological landscape of Kymissala in Rhodes. ICOMOS General Assembly and International Symposium, Florence, November (2014). http://openar chive.icomos.org/id/eprint/2020/

14. Evgenikou, V., Georgopoulos, A.: Investigating 3d reconstruction methods for small artifacts. In: ISPRS Archives, Volume XL-5/W4, pp. 101–108. WG V/4, CIPA - 3D-Arch (2015). https://www.int-arch-photogramm-remote-sens-spatial-inf-sci.net/XL-5-W4/101/2015/isprsarchives-XL-5-W4-101-2015.pdf. http://www.int-arch-photogramm-rem ote-sens-spatial-inf-sci.net/XL-5-W4/101/2015/isprsarchives-XL-5-W4-101-2015.pdf. Last accessed 06 October 2021

15. Doulamis, A. et al.: 5D modelling: an efficient approach for creating spatiotemporal predictive 3D maps of large-scale cultural resources. In: ISPRS Annals of the Photogrammetry, Remote Sensing and Spatial Information Sciences (2015). https://www.researchgate.net/ publication/282521303_5D_Modelling_An_Efficient_Approach_for_Creating_Spatiotem poral_Predictive_3D_Maps_of_Large-Scale_Cultural_Resources

Preservation, Reuse and Reveal of Cultural Heritage Through Sustainable Land Management, Rural and Urban Development to Recapture the World in Crisis Through Culture

Sustainable Management of Cultural Heritage. The Science of Conservation in the Transition Towards a Global Sustainable Model

Eleftheria Mavromati[1]($\boxtimes$) (iD) and Anna Karatzani[2] (iD)

[1] Conservator of Antiquities and Works of Art - Archaeologist, West Attica University, 3 Paridi str. Polygono, 11476 Athens, Greece
`teripieri@gmail.com, elmavromati@uniwa.gr`
[2] Textile Conservator, Department of Conservation of Antiquities and Works of Arts, University of West Attica, Ag. Spyridonos Str, Egaleo, 12243 Athens, Greece
`karatzani@uniwa.gr`

Abstract. Sustainability is a moral principle. Programming on behalf of societies, in the individual areas of human growth, becomes necessary in order to ensure their sustainable function and to achieve aligned and controlled growth. To achieve the principles of sustainable development, humans are constantly developing tools trying to manage the ever-changing information about the planet, the human community and technology and to define strategies that support the sustainable development and consumption of goods. Conserving cultural heritage for the next generations concerns the viability of our planet and is necessary for the smooth progress of technological development in ways that do not disrupt the future survival. The protection of the natural/anthropogenic environment is closely linked and the responsibility corresponding to the field of cultural heritage conservation, in terms of local/environmental level, has not yet been investigated thoroughly. Environmental protection through options and strategies is a new issue in Conservators' Community.

Keywords: Sustainability · Cultural heritage · Sustainable conservation and materials · Collections management sustainability · Future preservation · Sustainable standards

1 Introduction

Sustainability is a moral principle. The concept of sustainability emerged in the 1990s [1] and takes various forms through science, society and technology. Since then, there has been an urgent need to preserve all human achievements and the survival of the planet as well as the natural and anthropogenic environment. Nowadays, societies have understood that planning in all sectors of human development is needed in order to achieve their sustainable operation and their aligned and controlled development. In this context, the ecological footprint in the field of Cultural Heritage Preservation and Conservation for its impact on the local and environmental level and the formulation of sustainable proposals for the future has not yet been sufficiently explored and environmental protection through choices and strategies remains a new issue for the conservation community.

2 Relation Between Environment, Culture and Conservation. The Protection of Cultural Heritage Through Sustainability

The social responsibility and participation of those involved in the global development of the 21st century, including private or public bodies, as well as institutions and companies is the objective to protect and promote cultural heritage.

The natural and anthropogenic environment form an inseparable unity, which interact with each other and the imbalance of the first from the uncontrolled human activities[1] leads to a reduction in physical reserves and consequently to the incapability to support human life and the built environment. Climate change and its negative impacts degrade the ability of all countries to achieve sustainable development. Our experience[2] has shown that the disconnection of natural from cultural environment leads to the inefficiency of the states' actions and creates many problems regarding the cooperation of the involved and co-competent services. However, the main issue is the proper balance between the anthropogenic and the natural environment, given the current degree of development of western and western-style societies, the planning of cities, the scales of urban development, the choices made in recent years for the renovation of historic centers and the preservation and promotion of culture heritage of a region support the principles of cultural sustainability and their transmission to future generations [4].

Cultural sustainability includes the preservation of all the elements of the past in cities, villages, settlements, monuments and archeological sites, historical / mythical sites[3] and also embraces all forms of intangible culture and their values, all the values that accompany the material culture of each place and region [4], since the choices of the inhabitants influence the environment and shape the cultural content of that society. The protection of cultural heritage is an issue that has engaged the scientific community for at least 90 years and is beyond the scopes of this article. Cultural sustainability and its contribution towards the increased relations between countries, improvement of the life quality and the transfer of cultural heritage to the future generations have been of particular concern to the scientific and political community the past years. Museums integrated with society should co-create cultural capital to improve the quality of life, holistically, for both current and future generations [5].

The principle of subsidiarity [6] is part of the cultural sector, which on one hand is a strong and important pillar in the preservation of cultural goods for future generations, on the other hand, a guarantor of progress, development and sustainability. Sciences are called to apply new technologies and change data, adopting sustainable practices, as part of their effort to create conditions for sustainable, inclusive and sustained economic growth and shared prosperity, considering different levels of national development and capacities in its three dimensions – economic, social and environmental – in a balanced

---

[1] Such as mining activities, the indiscriminate exploitation of natural resources, the excessive use of chemicals and pesticides, the pumping of water until the aquifer is depleted [2, 3].

[2] The Greek Ombudsman has long been concerned with the protection of cultural heritage and has proposed the cooperation of the relevant ministries, identifying problems and possible solutions for the creation of a grid of logistics for the cultural stock of Greece (reports on Thission and the Historic Center of Athens).

[3] L. 3028/2002, 2nd article.

and integrated manner, the effort for sustainable protection of cultural heritage[4] is also included [7–9].

The conservation of the cultural heritage for future generations applies to the sustainability of our planet and is necessary for the smooth evolution of technological development in ways that do not disrupt the ability to survive in the future. [4, 10]. In the agenda of 2031[5] UNESCO is working in a similar context, urging the creation of sustainable cities emphasizing on their cultural elements. The documentation and protection of cultural heritage are linked to technological development and strategies adopted to achieve sustainable goals [4, 10].

In Greece, the protection provided by the provisions of Law 3028/2002 concerning the cultural heritage of the country and combines the protection of the cultural man-made environment with the protection of the natural environment, emphasizing the equal importance of both parameters[6].

3 Conservation at the Services of Sustainability

Fig. 1. Essential parameters for cultural sustainability. (Mavromati Eleftheria – Karatzani Anna, all rights preserved 2021).

The Chart of Venice, the Dublin Declaration, the Oslo Symposium and the 1997 Thessaloniki Declaration highlighted the need to combine environmental and sustainable development issues. Sustainability in conservation science becomes functional and connected to society and culture [6, 11–14]. To this end, appropriate public education and awareness, should be recognized as one of the pillars of sustainability along with legislation, economy and technology [6, 13, 15].

In the 2016 Paris Convention, the conservation of global natural and cultural heritage was incorporated and great importance of the term was given. A few years later, in the Amsterdam Declaration, the science of conservation emerged as a key factor in the preservation of cultural monuments that are important to humans [16]. The conservation

---

[4] See the Greek Ombudsman's documents, professors of NTUA and other universities efforts. The importance of sustainability and protection of cultural resources for future generations and the proposal to manage the collections in the light of the holistic treatment of monuments, with the contribution of available technology engaged an ongoing doctoral research by Mavromati Eleftheria, entitled *"Conservation study and proposals of sustainable management for the masks at the National Theatre of Greece"*, supervised by Karatzani Anna, University of West Attica.

[5] The 11th goal of the 2030 agenda refers to the creation of sustainable cities and environment.

[6] Law 3028/2002, articles 1 to 3 et seq., In which the protection refers both to the protected culturally monuments and to their surrounding area.

in all aspects of natural resources, the atmosphere and the restoration of environmental quality depend worldwide on choices made in a variety of areas of human activity and conservation science is seeking ways to incorporate sustainability in practice and education [6, 12, 13, 15] (Fig. 1).

3.1 Good Practices of Sustainable Conservation

The integration of the concept of sustainability in conservation science is certainly a fact that experts in many countries have not yet taken notice of. However, several European and American universities and institutions for the management and conservation of cultural monuments, follow rules that lead to a more rational organization of goods and materials in order to preserve cultural and other monuments with the smallest possible energy and environmental footprint [6, 12, 17]. The flow and quality of information on the environment, the factors affecting it and their negative impacts become known, with the aim of choosing alternative practices and options with the least negative impact on the natural and man-made environment possible [15].

Knowledge of options follows: a) the optimal use of the available data for sustainable outcomes, b) the choice of personal and scientific steps leading to the change in the data currently available, c) the discovery and adaption of new fields that lead conservation science into new areas, d) the implementation of good practices[7] the use of natural resources (water, energy and materials) [18, 19], e) the use of circular waste management systems in museums, collection and management (tools and materials for second use, waste collection and management [15, 18, 20], f) the development of websites and a platform for the provision of data[8] [21], g) the creation of a network for dialogue, exchange of views and provision of information and advice[9].

Regarding the creation and disposal of materials, Life Cycle Assessment, already applied to the recycling of materials for cars, industrial products, etc., is also applied to museums and conservation laboratories. Environmental impacts arise at every stage,

---

[7] At California Academy of Sciences for example, the green living roof of the institution provides the building excellent insulation, which reduces energy needed for heating and cooling; it captures the excess rain water, which reduces pollutants carried into the ecosystem and turns carbon dioxide into oxygen. The roof is also bursting with native plants that provide an ecosystem for birds and insects. Similarly, universities in Northern Europe are looking for alternative sources of deionized water and find solutions by melting snow or purifying water with the help of the sun [15]. At the National Theatre of Greece, where the PhD research on theatrical masks is carried out, they reuse props, masks and garments, with appropriate alterations, thus reducing the overconsumption of materials, the mismanagement of human resources and the waste of materials and objects. Typical examples of alternative materials can also be found in the article by Balliana et al. [18].

[8] The STiCH platform which is being prepared, will provide data on the energy footprint of materials, their composition and various data with which the Conservator will be able to choose the most environmentally friendly material [17].

[9] A network called "Sic: Sustainability for Conservation" has been set up in Europe, which aims to inform and train students and scientists to use their knowledge in the environment where they work, study and act. Volunteer conservators also become ambassadors to bring the concept and sustainable practices to the community.

from the manufacture, purchase, use and disposal of materials as well as recycling or reuse [12, 18]. Consequently, safety specifications are given for each material, the environmental footprint is controlled at each stage of the life cycle and is expected and the multiple environmental impacts resulting from each stage of the maintenance process are ensured in such a way that they do not constitute shifting loads from one impact to another. All stages are reexamined and lead to decisions on the policies to be followed. The cycle therefore follows the subsequent chain, during which supplementary chains are interconnected [15]: 1) decision-making, action, sustainable material productions and use, 2) product manufacturing with green impact, 3) inform, use and distribution of the ecofriendly product, 4) recycling or disposal when its circle is finished.

For conservation science, the selection of pure/specific materials, with precise quality and manufacturing performance specifications, ex. in the field of textile or paper conservation, including environmental footprint control, is part of the process and adoption of good sustainable conservation practices. Focusing on the protection of the natural environment through the selection of materials with the least negative impact inevitably leads to the challenge of maintaining a balanced cultural and natural heritage [12, 19, 20].

A good example of sustainable management in the field of conservation concerns the packaging of monuments for storage or transport. Throughout the process, consideration and decision making, selection of materials, alternatives are explored, standards and available sustainable materials are considered, reassessment is made, if necessary, with the aim to protect monuments and natural resources alongside [17, 20]. The same happens during the conservation of stone monuments, for which the use of supporting and filling materials is chosen for their interior and exterior, after taking into consideration a number of factors such as a) toxicity and air pollutants for the visiting public and workers, conservators, archaeologists, etc., b) the impact on the natural environment in various ways, c) the ratio between the quantity of material and the negative impact on the environment, d) the preservation of the flora and fauna of the area, in the case of archaeological sites[10], e) the source of the materials and the damaging effect of the construction on animals, plants and humans [17].

3.2 Sustainable Management Using Computer Systems. The Example of the Theatrical Masks at the National Theatre of Greece

According to the contemporary archiving data, for the preservation of cultural heritage objects, collection, digitization, categorization, electronic storage and remote access are compulsory [22, 23]. The Greek National Theater has created a digital archive[11] (Fig. 2), containing the performance programs, newspaper clippings, photographic material, audio documents (since 1950), video recordings (since 1994) and musical scores.

---

[10] Typical examples of archaeological sites where the flora and fauna of the surrounding area of the monuments is protected are the Acropolis in Athens and the archaeological site of Eleusis.

[11] The project was implemented under the calls 65 and 172 of the Information Society and was co-financed by the European Regional Development Fund (80%) and by national resources (20%). The Digitized Archive of the National Theatre of Greece includes its collections from 1932 to 2005, with rare and sometimes unique material.

Additionally, in the context of the collaboration with the Ministry of Culture and Sports, a large number of costumes and ten (10) masks have been recorded and have been declared as monuments of contemporary culture.

In the context of the sustainable collection management and through this ongoing doctoral research for the conservation and preservation of the mask collection from the Historic Cloakroom (declared or not), which have both historical and artistic value, either in their material form or as entries in the NT digital archive and other sources, the following actions are proposed and gradually implemented: a) Gathering and addition of all the masks in the digital archiving system, b) creation of spreadsheets in the form of electronic condition survey cards for each mask that include the object information and documentation images[12], c) creation of graphs and diagrams and the inference of statistical data for the masks of the Historical Cloakroom, d) 3D documentation of the masks with a 3D modeling program [23], e) data input and archiving of the masks following specific criteria in combination with their common characteristics, f) formatting and integration of the data collected into the digitized archive of the NT or on a separate digital platform, g) provision of descriptive, structural and managing metadata of 3D modeling through the digitized NT file, [23], e) key words and criteria searching of each mask, emergence, study and ability to print digital information.

Fig. 2. Digital archive of the Greek National Theatre, accessed on 28.10.2021, http://www.nt-arc hive.gr/.

4   Proposals for Aiming the Goals of Sustainability at the Scientific Area of Conservation

A comprehensive approach to a sustainable conservation program is a matter of study, administrative coordination and successful implementation of recycled and environmentally and human-friendly materials. In the context of sustainable management of natural resources[13], private and public as well as university conservation laboratories should

---

[12] Mask information, condition, performance title and actors, materials, conservation actions, etc.
[13] Such as soil, water, natural areas and coastal zones.

work towards exploring ways of reducing the consumption of natural resources, materials and objects that have a negative impact. Achieving green conservation requires sensitivity, knowledge and strategy.

In particular, it is proposed to: 1) rational management of materials and available resources used in the protection of cultural heritage and choice of eco-labelled materials, materials with reduced environmental impact or materials labelled "green"[14]; 2) revision of traditional practices for obtaining raw materials from the environment and selection of alternative materials in order to preserve its integrity. We need to make decisions about the sustainability of monuments so we need to be aware of their origins, their history their values as well as the conservation materials[15], for deciding about their condition and how to treat them in the present and how to sustain them in the future; 3) integrated control of all stages in conservation science regarding the pollution caused (atmospheric, water or soil), holistic management of pollutants, research into cleaning, recycling, reuse and the creation of standard procedures for the final disposal of conservation waste (Fig. 3) [20]; 4) compliance with EU Directives in order to reduce the environmental footprint; 5) improving infrastructure and technical means, selection of 'green' technologies and machinery and comparative economic control, which determines choices through long-term planning and economic payback, while ensuring environmental benefits; 6) using renewable energy sources and reducing energy consumption in museums and conservation workshops; 7) design and selection of materials and conservation practices with a positive impact on the environment[16]. 8) comparative study between single-use and multi-use materials and selection of those with the least negative environmental impact; 9) selection of materials that are friendly to cultural monuments[17], which can be removed and allow reversibility to a certain extent and rework ability, i.e.re-intervention on cultural monuments by future conservators [24, 25]; 10) choice of materials that are friendly to conservators, with low toxicity and an increased rate of safe use and replacement of traditional materials [18, 19, 26, 27]; 11) actions to promote and preserve cultural heritage [28, 29] while protecting the overall natural and cultural landscape [23, 25]; 12) re-using the man-made landscape and use of the built environment (housing estates, listed buildings, monuments, industrial sites) and their natural environment through the process of conservation, in order to make sustainable use of the historic cultural heritage [19, 30]; 13) dissemination to the scientific and local community of environmental information and good practices[18] by creating electronic information tools (platforms

---

[14] Green materials have been extensively discussed in the article by Balliana et al. [18] → 18. Also, ICCROM recommends the sustainable dimension through which actions for the preservation of cultural heritage should be carried out, by reducing the energy footprint of cultural institutions, seeking alternative renewable energy sources, environmentally sustainable building design, passive climate control, LED-lighting technology and use of green chemistry [12] → 12.

[15] Indirect background: linked industrial processes, economic models, national resource etc.

[16] It can be applied at all stages of conservation, in the selection of conservation materials, conservation tools, storage and display of cultural objects. Biocides for example must follow the lines of the REACH Regulation and the principles of prevention and precaution. The aim is human and environmental sustainability and sustainable development.

[17] See the article by Sousa M. et al. [35].

[18] In Balliana et al. [18], it is proposed to inform conservators about "green" alternative products and their protocols and the holistic approach of any restoration project.

etc.), sustainable material and process standards (ISO) and data provision, which help to make common, more efficient and rational decisions for the environment and the cultural heritage of the planet [31]; 14) development of strategies by museums, universities and public institutions, which are urged to play a leading and dominant role in the science of conservation [15, 28, 32, 33]; 15) integration in academic programs of courses on sustainability and holistic management of materials and monuments. In particular, a critical role will be played by training young archaeologists, conservators, engineers, etc. from the very beginning of their studies, in green technology, familiarizing them with sustainable materials and seeking new methods of preserving cultural heritage that are compatible with the natural environment and are enhancing the quality of human-made structures [21]; 16) creation of data libraries with these tools and uploading on the websites of cultural and academic institutions the actions that have been applied and tested and can be adopted by the global community to achieve sustainable results, 17) a communication channel between consultants, representatives and institutions (private and public) in the cultural sector and environmental policy representatives of the EU Member States, collaboration between leadership, organizers, partners, suppliers, contractors, and participants [12], in order to share responsibility, partnership and implementation of sustainable measures and practices effectively.

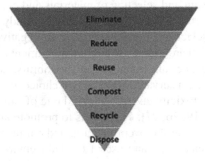

Fig. 3. Zero waste by ICCROM, https://www.iccrom.org/resources/going-zero-waste-promoting-sustainable-consumption-and-production-cultural-heritage, available online, accessed on 22.05.2021.

5   Opportunities and Perspectives of Sustainable Conservation (Conclusions)

Achieving sustainability in all scientific fields of human activity is the challenge that all nations, governments [29] and institutions are urged to take up in order to meet the goals of a sustainable future for the planet. To achieve the principles of sustainable development, nations are constantly developing tools and defining strategies that support sustainable development and consumption of goods. Action plans are developed for rapid and radical change in behaviors and lifestyles, including changing patterns of production and consumption, reforming their laws and institutions to achieve maximum global warming reduction, upgrading ecosystems and protecting biodiversity and cultural heritage.

The science of conservation in conjunction with the environment, cultural monuments and sustainable protection is not incidental and conservation is an integral part of the dual action to protect the natural and cultural environment[19], emphasizing the equal importance of both parameters in parallel [34]. Conservation is supported by specific educational, legislative and political practices aiming at safeguarding world culture in perpetuity, with the participation of the younger generations in particular. Conservation should then be viewed through the lens of a process, and not merely an end goal to succeed environmental sustainability. We have to think creatively, determine our personal choices, and create new paths to scientific behavior, ethics and practices. We may be the last to have the opportunity of saving the planet and preserving cultural remains is one way to sustainable future.

Acknowledgments. We are thankful to Ifigeneia Sagia, Lawyer LLM Master 2, Human Rights and Humanitarian Law, Université Paris 2 Panthéon-Assas, for her contribution to the article translation, ifigeneia.sag@gmail.com.

References

1. Kalaitzidis, D.: The vision of Sustainability (n.d.). http://www.aeiforum.eu/index.php/el/taf totita/to-orama-tis-aeiforias. Last accessed 11 April 2021
2. Mavromati, E.: Management and protection of the island of Chryssi at Ierapetra, Crete, report which was posted on the website of the Ombudsman (2017). https://www.synigoros.gr/?i= quality-of-life.el.epemvaseis_oikosysthmata.450037
3. Mavromati, E.: Protecting Wetland estuary Aposelemis Crete Heraklion River, report which was posted on the website of the Ombudsman (2016). http://www.synigoros.gr/?i=quality-of-life.el.epemvaseis_oikosysthmata.389116
4. Andreopoulos, A.: Cultural sustainability: the preservation and promotion of our cultural heritage. Social and cultural sustainability. In: Papavasileiou, V., Fokiali, P., Nikolaou, E., Matzanos, D., Kaila, M. (eds.) Postgraduate program on Environmental Education. University of Aegean, Rhodes (2017)
5. Xydakis, N.: Speech of the Deputy Minister of Culture given at the ICOM Greece in the event of the celebration of the International Day of Museum 2015 "Museums for a Sustainable Society (2015). 18-05-2015. https://www.culture.gov.gr/el/information/SitePages/view.aspx? nID=1375. Last accessed 07 March 2021
6. Commission of the European Communities: Objective the Sustainability. Brussels Vol. II (1992). https://eur-lex.europa.eu/legal-content/EL/TXT/PDF/?uri=CELEX:51992PC0023& from=EN. Last accessed 11 April 2021
7. Mavromati, E., Stamatiou, E., Chrysaeidis, L., Astaras, K.: Improving the Geometric Documentation of Cultural Heritage: Combined Methods for the Creation of an Integrated Management Information System in Greece. In: Moropoulou, A., Korres, M., Georgopoulos, A., Spyrakos, C., Mouzakis, C. (eds.) TMM_CH 2018. CCIS, vol. 962, pp. 3–21. Springer, Cham (2019). https://doi.org/10.1007/978-3-030-12960-6_1

---

[19] Articles have been published the Last 20 years for the parallel protection of natural/cultural environment and their conservation, available if requested.

8. Moropoulou, A., Korres, M., Georgopoulos, A., Spyrakos, C., Mouzakis, C. (eds.): Transdisciplinary Multispectral Modeling and Cooperation for the Preservation of Cultural Heritage, First International Conference, TMM_CH 2018. Revised Selected Papers, Part II, «Communications in Computer and Information Science book series. Springer, Heidelberg (2019). https://doi.org/10.1007/978-3-030-12957-6

9. Liritzis, I., Korka, E.: Archaeometry's role in cultural heritage sustainability and development. Sustainability 11(7), 1972 (2019). https://doi.org/10.3390/su11071972

10. UNESCO: Culture for Sustainable Development. https://en.unesco.org/themes/culture-sustainable-development. Last accessed 25 April 2021

11. Pottgiesser, U., Fatoric, S., Hein, C., de Maaker, E., Roders, A.P. (eds.): LDE HERITAGE CONFERENCE on Heritage and the Sustainable Development Goals Proceedings. TU Delft Open. https://books.bk.tudelft.nl/press/catalog/view/781/892/860-2 (2020). Last accessed 25 April 2021

12. ICCROM: Going "Zero Waste": promoting sustainable consumption and production in cultural heritage training. https://www.iccrom.org/resources/going-zero-waste-promoting-sustainable-consumption-and-production-cultural-heritage. Last accessed 25 April 2021

13. The Thessaloniki Declaration: http://www.edc.uoc.gr/~mkalaitz/odigos/promitheas/mmlab.uoc.gr/promitheas/pe/thesalonikis.htm. Last accessed 07 March 2021

14. Vasilakis, K., Tzamberis, N.: Evaluation of the school building with criteria of environmental and social sustainability. In: Papavasileiou, V., Fokiali, P., Nikolaou, E., Matzanos, D., Kaila, M. (eds.) Postgraduate program on Environmental Education. University of Aegean, Rhodes (2017)

15. Styx, L.: Museums and the art of environmental sustainability (2020). https://www.museumnext.com/article/museums-and-the-art-of-environmental-sustainability/. Last accessed 23 May 2021

16. The Amsterdam Declaration (1975). http://www.library.tee.gr/digital/techr/1976/techr_1976_8_9_70.pdf. Last accessed 07 March 2021

17. Eckelman, M., Nunberg, S., Sunchez, S., Sutton, S.: Webinar, STiCH Sustainability Tools in Cultural Heritage Preservation, AIC and FAIC Learning (2021)

18. Balliana, E., Ricci, J., Pesce, C., Zendri, E.: Assessing the value of green conservation for cultural heritage: positive and critical aspects of already methodologies. Int. J. Conserv. Sci. 7(SI1), 185–202 (2016)

19. Mavromati, E.: Environmental concerns and sustainable approach to the design and operation of the ancient city. In: 2nd International Conference EMAET "Ancient Greek Technology" TEE-EMAET. War Museum, Athens (2005)

20. A Sustainable Development Guide for Canada's Museums, ch. 8 Waste management, https://www.museums.ca/document/1148/Chapter_8.pdf. Last accessed 23 May 2021

21. Mavromati, E.: Two chapters entitled "Access to environmental information" and "Protection of Biodiversity" in the Guide for citizens issued by the Ombudsman and the WWF (2008). http://www.synigoros.gr/?i=quality-of-life.el.pzevents.33452

22. Jeffery, S.R., O'gwen, G.L., Hornsby, B.A., McBryde, K.E., Powell, W.C., Rizk, T.A.: U.S. Patent No. 6,957,384. U.S. Patent and Trademark Office, Washington, DC (2005). https://www.google.com/patents/US6957384. Last accessed 19 April 2021

23. Pavlou, K.: The theatrical poster in Cyprus. Archiving digital files of the theatrical posters, Lemessos (2016). https://ktisis.cut.ac.cy/bitstream/10488/12824/1/%CE%A0%CE%B1%CF%8D%CE%BB%CE%BF%CF%85%20%CE%9A%CE%AC%CE%BB%CE%B9%CE%B1.pdf

24. Stamatiou, El., Mavromati, E., Petousi, T.: Landscape architecture: Harmonization of man-made and natural environments. Evolution in the Hellenic space, provisions, questions and perspectives. In: Ananiadou-Tzimopoulou, M., Tsakalidis, I. (eds.) Conference Proccedings

"Landscape Architecture. Education, Research and Practice", pp. 165–175. Thessaloniki, Aristotle University Vol. III. Ziti publications (2006)

25. Mavromati, E.: Byzantine and Post-Byzantine architectural landscape and natural environment - Harmony Link or enforcement, 25th Symposium of Byzantine and Post-Byzantine Archaeology and Art, Christian Archaeological Society, Byzantine and Christian Museum, Athens, Abstracts & Announcements Program, pp. 109–110. Publications ChAE (2005)

26. Macchia, A., Luvidi, L., Prestileo, F., La Russa, M.F., Ruffolo, S.A., (eds.). Aim, International Journal of Conservation 7(1) Special Issue in Green Conservation and Cultural Heritages Article (ijcs.ro) Last accessed 22 May 2021

27. Green Conservation of Cultural Heritage: https://www.researchitaly.it/en/events/green-conservation-of-cultural-heritage/#null. Last accessed 22 May 2021

28. McGhie, H.: Free guide: How can museums support the Sustainable Development Goals? (2019). https://curatingtomorrow236646048.wordpress.com/2019/08/21/how-can-museums-support-the-sustainable-development-goals/. Last accessed 05 June 2021

29. Speech by the Minister of Culture E. Venizelos in an open discussion on the subject: Role of Higher Education and Research on Sustainability. https://www.culture.gov.gr/el/SitePages/searchresults.aspx?#k=%CE%B1%CE%B5%CE%B9%CF%86%CE%BF%CF%81%CE%AF%CE%B1. Last accessed 07 March 2021

30. The Paris Declaration: (1972). https://www.law-archaeology.gr/index.php/el/diethnes-dikaio2/unesco-unidroit. Last accessed 27 April 2021

31. Katsigianni, A., Katsigianni, B.: Local knowledge as an expression of the cultural dimension of sustainability: its connection with local management systems and education. Postgraduate program on Environmental education, University of the Aegean, Rhodes, Social and cultural sustainability (2017)

32. Antoniou, C.: Sustainability, environment and culture in education through actions in museums: teachers' views, challenges and prospects, PhD thesis, Department of Multimedia and Graphic Arts, Cyprus University of Technology (2016). https://ktisis.cut.ac.cy/handle/10488/9067. Last accessed 25 April 2021

33. City of Westminster, Institution Waste Management. https://cleanstreets.westminster.gov.uk/institutions-museums-waste-management/. Last accessed 23 May 2021

34. Mavromati, E.: Museum objects: materials pollutants and protection -the issue of air pollution, 24 Letters publication, Athens (in Greek) (2020)

35. Sousa, M., Melo, M.J.: The art of CO2 for art conservation: a green approach to antique textile cleaning. Green Chem. **9**, 943–947 (2007). https://doi.org/10.1039/b617543k

Cultural-Oriented Mobile Game Application and the Gamification of Tourism

Ioannis Rallis[1]([✉]), George Kopsiaftis[2], Ilias Kalisperakis[2], Christos Stentoumis[2], Dimitris Koutsomitsos[3], and Vivian Riga[1]

[1] Heraklio Travel, N. Iraklio, Greece
rallisioannis88@gmail.com
[2] up2metric, Athens, Greece
[3] Tamasenco, Marousi Athens, Greece

Abstract. This paper briefly presents the overall concept of an "advergame" which aims to reproduce complete processes of the touristic sector using Augmented Reality, Virtual Reality and Photogrammetric techniques. A realistic game experience will be used as the basis for both entertainment and educational purposes. The mobile game application will be developed in a six phase process, which will include the implementation of state-of-the-art Image Processing and Computer Graphics techniques to create accurate 3D background and the development of an efficient game engine. The sub-systems and individual components of the game engine will be designed in such a way that will allow the reproduction of several real-world scenarios, which will represent a complete touristic experience, including a significant number of services and products.

Keywords: Tourism · Photogrammetry · Mobile game · Cultural heritage

1 Introduction

In recent years, mobile games have drawn great attention from different aspects, encompassing healthcare, education, sports, culture and tourism. Due to the fact that many mobile games are released every year, the effectiveness of the mobile games has been decreased and marketers have sought more attractive techniques to engage users. One of these advertisement tools is the mobile "advergame". This term refers to games which are developed by companies to promote their products, brand identity or services. The game developers in order to differentiate their work from the competition include more interactive features, which allow them to enhance the users' experience and address a personalized advertisement. Mobile games for Cultural Heritage (CH) applications can significantly improve user experience through the implementation of immersive and enhanced 3D representations.

© The Author(s), under exclusive license to Springer Nature Switzerland AG 2022
A. Moropoulou et al. (Eds.): TMM_CH 2021, CCIS 1574, pp. 242–251, 2022.
https://doi.org/10.1007/978-3-031-20253-7_20

Nowadays, in a lot of new mobile games, Augmented Reality (AR), Virtual Reality (VR) and Photogrammetric techniques are adopted to enhance users' experience. 3D textured models are applied from different approaches (Procedural content generation, Structure from Motion, Laser Scanning) in order to create accurate 3D representations that will be employed to the graphic engine of the games. Photogrammetric techniques are boosting the game development pipeline. These techniques provide an added value to graphic engine of the games increasing the granularity level of the games' representations.

Gamification is also adopted by marketing researchers to improve customer loyalty by bringing dynamic interactions between users and rewards [27]. With the fast development of new technology, tourist marketers are seeking mobile applications, which require a deeper engagement and an immersive experience. To that end, they form scenarios based on real-life business procedures, which utilize reward mechanisms. Although research on gamification is continuously emerging, its use in the sectors of tourism and CH is still restricted [7,10]. The utilization of gamification for motivating users' behaviour and supporting marketing practices is tremendously spreading [21]. Business simulation games are also known as tycoon games. Financial processes, usually in the form of a business, try to retain the player's attention using creative graphics. The interest in these games lies in the precise simulation of real-world or business-oriented procedures. In [10], the authors declare that gamification acts as an essential factor for tourism marketing.

This paper analyzes (i) the concept of tourism games with respect to photogrammetric features, (ii) the game design elements, (iii) the implementation of these element to the game engine.

2   Previous Works

The utilization of gamification [14] is evident in many domains such as health industry [24], education applications [4,13,30], marketing [22] business sector [8] and tourism industry [1,9]. Especially in the tourism context, gamification is gaining ground, increasing brand awareness [19] and users' loyalty.

Since gamification is a relatively new trend in the touristic sector, the related literature is limited [9,16,20,25]. In [20], the authors declare that gamification could provide enhanced experiences for tourists, while in [27], the authors proposed that the gamification of tourism can foster more interactions, increase brand awareness and even the satisfaction of travellers. Other researchers focus on the influence that gamification could have on tourists' experiences related to certain attractions such as cultural heritage sites [16] and performances [23].

A considerable amount of effort has been made towards the enhancement of tourist experience [3,7] users' engagement and the improvement of customer loyalty or advertisement strategies. These mobile games usually exploit VR/AR capabilities to create an immersive environment [11,28]. However, they can not visualize precisely real cultural heritage monuments or cultural heritage terrains as part of the mobile game scenario. In addition, these games do not take into consideration the local economy, which could be achieved by providing a rewarding system for the local businesses.

The main idea of the TTGR framework is to develop an innovative Business Simulation advergame, which will concern the management of a travel agency activities and will be based on a digitized map of Greece. The aim of this study is to present the multidisciplinary role of gamification as a support in tourism, cultural heritage and marketing sectors.

3   TTGR Proposed Methodology

3.1   TTGR Objectives

For the implementation of the business oriented TYCOON TRAVEL Game (TTGR), a methodical approach is followed, in order to minimize the risks and to achieve timely and qualitatively optimized results during the implementation. This approach includes the utilization and development of existing techniques and algorithms which are widely used in Photogrammetry, Remote Sensing and Computer Vision [2,5,6,15,17,18,29]. The prime objective of TTGR is the promotion of Cultural Heritage assets and the gamification of Tourist/Cultural resources considering the business operation of a travel agency. The sub-objectives of the proposed framework could be summarized as follows:

- Complete simulation of the business-model of a travel agency using gamification.
- 3D capturing of Cultural Heritage (CH) sites in the area of Greece. Development of an integrated 3D system for capturing CH monuments and artifacts and the geospatial terrain.
- Creating a marketplace and ticketing system that connects the simulation game with resources and benefits of real economy. In this platform, the users will be rewarded with privileges or discounts from local stores/businesses.
- Commercialization, dissemination and exploitation of results.

3.2   TTGR Concept

In order to achieve the aforementioned objectives, the proposed architecture of the TTGR application is based on two axes. The first one considers the collection and combination of multi-modal data from heterogeneous sources. These data encompasses geographical location of specific monuments or points of interests, location of hotels, digitized maps and recommendation with respect to local businesses. The second axis concerns the achievement of a level of flexibility and scalability so that the proposed architecture can encompasses new requirements and use case scenarios. To that end, advanced photogrammetric techniques are employed to decrease the computation cost, without decreasing the visualization granularity level.

The TTGR framework could be divided in four discrete modules a) the visualization interface module, which consists of the user interface for the game platform, b) the game engine module which processes the spatio-temporal data, employs the photogrammetric algorithms and applies the game scenario, c) the multi-modal database module responsible for the game engine, the back-end solutions, the overall platform logic, the storing mechanism and the related processes and d) the TTGR e-portfolio. Specifically, the three modules are described with more details below:

- **Visualization interface:** This is the top level module which provides the game interface. It is responsible for the user's interaction by offering realistic graphics and representations of terrains related to Greek cities with touristic interest. The access to the TTGR idle game is granted using authentication process.
- **Game engine:** This module is the middle-ware level between the visualization level and the multi-modal database. This layer encompasses all the photogrammetric solutions enhanced by Machine Learning techniques (SLAM [12], such as CNNs [26]) that TTGR game exploits in order to provide realistic graphics. The proposed terrain will provide several textures of different resolution to ensure realism to the Game Experience according to the user's needs. These textures will be created using data from various sources, such as geophysical maps, satellite images, photorealistic elements, or photographic texture from unmanned aerial vehicles (UAVs). Regarding the touristic sites, the reconstruction of 3D models will be based on ready-made RGB color capturing sensors, suitable panoramic lenses and economical depth sensors, which will facilitate the fast 3D capturing of points of interest.
- **Multi-modal database:** This module refers to the database of the TTGR framework. This database consists of the 3D digitized cities, 3D digitized artefacts, the geo-location of the points-of-interest (hotels, local businesses) and the respective metadata. Open geospatial databases will be utilized to create two main components of the game: i) the cartographic background, e.g., a 3D map of Greece and ii) the points of interest, e.g., touristic and CH sites. Furthermore, the database will incorporate the methodology for creating game content considering the users' reactions, such as tourist attractions and hotel reviews.
- **TTGR e-portfolio:** This portfolio includes the financial benefits of the users after specific achievements during the game scenario. TTGR will create a local business network that will accept coupons. For the implementation of the system coupon issuance uses a pseudo-unique identifier (i.e., QR code) corresponding to privileges in the Marketplace. The platform will support the marking of the pseudo-unique identifier with the description of privileges.

Figure 1 presents schematically the overall architecture of the TTGR.

4   TTGR Workflow

The TTGR will be developed in six phases. These phases are briefly described as follows:

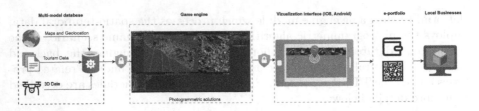

Fig. 1. TTGR overall architecture

Phase 1: Definition of Functional and Technical Specifications of Travel Tycoon Game. Phase 1 could be further divided in the following steps:

1. *Analysis and definition of Operational Specifications*: the analysis takes into consideration several factors, such as user needs and technological trends, competing products world-wide, the results of previous related research efforts and relevant projects. In addition, this work will determine the extent and volume of content that will be included in the world of the game (game world and game engine).
2. *Defining Technical Specifications of the Game*: this task will define the operating system, devices, distribution platform (i.e., Steam), the graphics quality (i.e., resolution, image refresh rate), but also the game's internal geometry, such as communication files.
3. *Analysis of the current state-of-the-art*: this step includes a thorough review of the current technological level in games and specifically in tycoon games, with emphasis in the 2D/3D representation techniques of the cartographic background (terrain) and the virtual navigation methods in this background.

Phase 2: Development of Methodology for the Definition, the Structure and the Content of the TRAVEL TYCOON Game. Phase 2 could be divided in the following:

1. *Recording and creating a travel agency operating model*: initially, the operation of the travel agency will be analyzed in detail and then it will be formalized.
2. *Creating a Tourism Resource Platform*: at this state, the travel services database will be customized to provide prices with selected markups in a database to be used by the game for the functions of virtual travel agency.
3. *Geo-spatial data collection*: the creation of the three-dimensional map of Greece and the 3D representation of the tourist resources.
4. *Manage and synchronize different resources with the Travel Tycoon game engine*: the software that will manage and synchronize the Tourism Resource Platform with the basic 2D will be developed background and kernel of the Game, while at the same time it will support the multiple languages of the game.

Phase 3: Efficient Virtual 3D Representations (Terrain and Digitized Cultural Heritage Artifacts. Phase 3 includes the following steps:

1. *Development of an algorithm for cross-referencing and texture rendering from heterogeneous data in the 3D geo-spatial background*: this terrain will have different high-resolution textures providing realistic game experiences.
2. *Development of a system for three-dimensional reconstruction of models of Tourism Resources*: for this purpose, data from different calibrated sensors, will be imported in specialized software for 3D reconstruction and texture rendering based on modern optical descriptors, 3D descriptors, stereoreconstruction algorithms and simultaneous algorithms detection and reconstruction, such as COLMPAP and LSD-SLAM.
3. *Background/Foreground Optimization Methodology*: techniques from Image Processing and Computer Graphics will be used to make 3D models according to the requirements of the Game.
4. *Management and synchronization software*: a software engine will be developed to manage the 3D background in relation to the remaining game subsystems. In addition, the artistic curation of the background and the 3D representations of the tourist resources will be completed.

Phase 4: Development of the Game Software (Front and Back End). Phase 4 consists of the following steps:

1. *Design and development of the TTGR game engine*: design and development of the game engine, consisting of the Game Logic Subsystems, the Game Mechanisms, Game States/Flow and Player Actions.
2. *Design and implementation of an internal game economy model*: design and implementation of an Internal Economy Model of the Game.
3. *Design and artistic display of graphical user interface*: artistic display of touristic resources, Design and Artistic display of Graphic User Interface (GUI), Artistic Development and Narrative and Character Illustration.

Phase 5: Development of e-portfolio. Phase 5 could be divided as follow:

1. *Marketplace Development*: creation of a virtual market within TTGR, where the user has the ability to buy/offer products and services.
2. *Creating Agreements and Original Content*: expansion of the market to real-world products and services to provide greater realism in the player experience. In this context, agreements are concluded with companies/providers of these items (hotel services, shops, etc.) in order to offer existing products and services with discount.
3. *Development of the Electronic Wallet Platform*: creation of the system of distribution (issuance) and control of coupons.

Phase 6: Trials, Test, Improvements and Final Evaluation of the Game. The final phase of the workflow includes the following:

1. *Testing, evaluation and improvements*: alpha version, covering all the basic game subsystems and integration of the implementation of Automatic Graphic Quality Adjustment depending on the level of equipment the game is running.
2. *Beta version*: this version represents the integrated marketplace function. The different variants of the Game will be tested through different Games Modes (campaign mode, skirmish mode, business mode). Finally, the evaluation of the artistic illustration of a travel agency will be performed and the available game options will be finalized.
3. *Final test*: during this step several components of the game will be tested, such as the multiplayer support system and the Internal Economy Model. Extensive testing will be performed regarding not only the software but also the minimum specifications of the hardware system which could support the game.
4. *Socioeconomic evaluation*: the concept of Social Life Cycle Assessment (SLCA) has emerged in recent years with the aim to integrate the social impact and benefits of the products and provided services.
5. *Evaluation of proposed methodology*: monitoring business and social response information based on the RAMS (reliability, availability, maintenance and security) analysis of the system will increase the overall reliability of the game. The evaluation process, which will be conducted along the entire life cycle of the game, will weigh all possible configuration changes that will allow the system to meet the specific RAMS requirements and to achieve the best possible active involvement of stakeholders in the decision-making process. The development of innovative business plans will also be considered between the private and public sectors.

Figure 2 includes screenshots from the preliminary steps of the game's graphical user interface, as well as indicative results from the geo-spatial data process. In particular, this figure illustrates the main screens of the game. Each character is related to a specific job of a tourist business. The user should unlock all characters and all point of interests to complete the advergame experience. Each point of interest is depicted in a real 3D map including specific actions that each user should fulfil. The scenario of this idle game is that each user should unlock specific touristic areas and to create a business chain with various business approaches. In order to create the realistic graphics, UAVs have digitized specific touristic areas and terrains. These 3D data are ingested to the graphic engine using algorithms and techniques (i.e., SLAM, ORBIT, Isomap, PCA, Kernel PCA, Factor Analysis, Linear Discriminant Analysis) to reduce their complexity. The aforementioned procedure is utmost important due to this advergame is created for mobile devices.

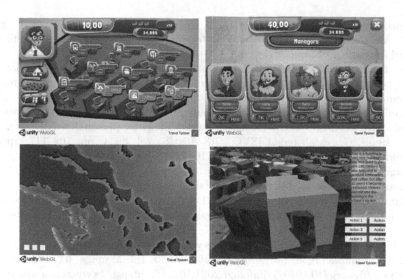

Fig. 2. TTGR overall architecture

5 Conclusions

This paper describes the development of an "advergame" which aims to realistically reproduce an overall touristic experience from both the customer's and the service provider's side. The TRAVEL TYCOON Game will utilize state-of-the-art techniques from virtual 3D representation and gamification sectors. It should be noted that the proposed gamification approach could be expanded into most cultural heritage related services and become a valuable tool for the improvement of the visitor/customer experience.

Acknowledgment. This research has been co-financed by the European Union and Greek national funds through the Operational Program Competitiveness, Entrepreneurship and Innovation, under the call RESEARCH - CREATE - INNOVATE (project code: T1EDK-05315).

References

1. Abou-Shouk, M., Soliman, M.: The impact of gamification adoption intention on brand awareness and loyalty in tourism: the mediating effect of customer engagement. J. Destination Mark. Manag. **20**, 100559 (2021)
2. Bakalos, N., Rallis, I., Doulamis, N., Doulamis, A., Protopapadakis, E., Voulodimos, A.: Choreographic pose identification using convolutional neural networks. In: 2019 11th International Conference on Virtual Worlds and Games for Serious Applications (VS-Games), pp. 1–7. IEEE (2019)
3. Corrêa, C., Kitano, C.: Gamification in tourism: analysis of brazil quest game. In: E-review of Tourism, vol. 6 (2015)

4. Domínguez, A., Saenz-de Navarrete, J., De-Marcos, L., Fernández-Sanz, L., Pagés, C., Martínez-Herráiz, J.J.: Gamifying learning experiences: practical implications and outcomes. Comput. Educ. **63**, 380–392 (2013)
5. Doulamis, A., et al: 5D modelling: an efficient approach for creating spatiotemporal predictive 3D maps of large-scale cultural resources. ISPRS Ann. Photogram. Remote Sens. Spat. Inf. Sci. (2015)
6. Doulamis, N., Yiakoumettis, C., Miaoulis, G., Protopapadakis, E.: A constraint inductive learning-spectral clustering methodology for personalized 3D navigation. In: Bebis, G., et al. (eds.) ISVC 2013. LNCS, vol. 8034, pp. 108–117. Springer, Heidelberg (2013). https://doi.org/10.1007/978-3-642-41939-3_11
7. Egger, R., Bulencea, P.: Gamification in Tourism: Designing Memorable Experiences. BoD-Books on Demand, Norderstedt (2015)
8. Hammedi, W., Leclercq, T., Poncin, I., Alkire, L.: Uncovering the dark side of gamification at work: impacts on engagement and well-being. J. Bus. Res. **122**, 256–269 (2021)
9. Hsiao, C.H., Tang, K.Y.: Who captures whom - pokémon or tourists? A perspective of the stimulus-organism-response model. Int. J. Inf. Manage. **61**, 102312 (2021). https://doi.org/10.1016/j.ijinfomgt.2021.102312, https://www.sciencedirect.com/science/article/pii/S0268401221000050
10. Huotari, K., Hamari, J.: Defining gamification: a service marketing perspective. In: Proceeding of the 16th International Academic MindTrek Conference, pp. 17–22 (2012)
11. Ioannides, M., Magnenat-Thalmann, N., Papagiannakis, G.: Mixed Reality and Gamification for Cultural Heritage, vol. 2. Springer, Heidelberg (2017). https://doi.org/10.1007/978-3-319-49607-8.pdf
12. Kalisperakis, I., et al.: A modular mobile mapping platform for complex indoor and outdoor environments. Int. Arch. Photogrammetry, Remote Sens. Spat. Inf. Sci. **43**, 243–250 (2020)
13. Kalogiannakis, M., Papadakis, S., Zourmpakis, A.I.: Gamification in science education. a systematic review of the literature. Educ. Sci. **11**(1), 22 (2021). https://www.mdpi.com/2227-7102/11/1/22
14. Krath, J., Schürmann, L., von Korflesch, H.F.: Revealing the theoretical basis of gamification: a systematic review and analysis of theory in research on gamification, serious games and game-based learning. Comput. Hum. Behav. **125**, 106963 (2021)
15. Kyriakaki, G., et al.: 4D reconstruction of tangible cultural heritage objects from web-retrieved images. Int. J. Heritage Digit. Era **3**(2), 431–451 (2014)
16. Lee, B.C.: The effect of gamification on psychological and behavioral outcomes: implications for cruise tourism destinations. Sustainability **11**(11), 3002 (2019)
17. Rallis, I., Doulamis, N., Doulamis, A., Voulodimos, A., Vescoukis, V.: Spatiotemporal summarization of dance choreographies. Comput. Graph. **73**, 88–101 (2018)
18. Rallis, I., Doulamis, N., Voulodimos, A., Doulamis, A.: Hierarchical sparse modeling for representative selection in choreographic time series. In: 2018 25th IEEE International Conference on Image Processing (ICIP), pp. 1023–1027. IEEE (2018)
19. Shi, S., Leung, W.K., Munelli, F.: Gamification in OTA platforms: a mixed-methods research involving online shopping carnival. Tour. Manage. **88**, 104426 (2022)
20. Sigala, M.: The application and impact of gamification funware on trip planning and experiences: the case of TripAdvisor's funware. Electron. Mark. **25**(3), 189–209 (2015). https://doi.org/10.1007/s12525-014-0179-1

21. Sigala, M.: Gamification for crowdsourcing marketing practices: applications and benefits in tourism. In: Garrigos-Simon, F.J., Gil-Pechuán, I., Estelles-Miguel, S. (eds.) Advances in Crowdsourcing, pp. 129–145. Springer, Cham (2015). https://doi.org/10.1007/978-3-319-18341-1_11

22. Simanjuntak, M.: Designing of service dominant logic and business model canvas: narrative study of village tourism. Golden Ratio Mark. Appl. Psychol. Bus. 1(2), 73–80 (2021)

23. Tan, W.K.: Gamification in aquarium context: intention to play game that imparts knowledge and promotes marine animal conservation. Inf. Technol. People (2018)

24. Van Gaalen, A., Brouwer, J., Schönrock-Adema, J., Bouwkamp-Timmer, T., Jaarsma, A., Georgiadis, J.: Gamification of health professions education: a systematic review. Adv. Health Sci. Educ. 26(2), 683–711 (2021). https://doi.org/10.1007/s10459-020-10000-3

25. Vella, K., et al.: A sense of belonging: pokémon go and social connectedness. Games Cult. 14(6), 583–603 (2019)

26. Voulodimos, A., Doulamis, N., Doulamis, A., Protopapadakis, E.: Deep learning for computer vision: a brief review. Comput. Intell. Neurosci. 2018 (2018)

27. Xu, F., Buhalis, D., Weber, J.: Serious games and the gamification of tourism. Tour. Manage. 60, 244–256 (2017)

28. Xu, F., Tian, F., Buhalis, D., Weber, J., Zhang, H.: Tourists as mobile gamers: gamification for tourism marketing. J. Travel Tour. Mark. 33(8), 1124–1142 (2016)

29. Yiakoumettis, C., Doulamis, N., Miaoulis, G., Ghazanfarpour, D.: Active learning of user's preferences estimation towards a personalized 3D navigation of georeferenced scenes. GeoInformatica 18(1), 27–62 (2014). https://doi.org/10.1007/s10707-013-0176-0

30. Yildiz, İ, Topçu, E., Kaymakci, S.: The effect of gamification on motivation in the education of pre-service social studies teachers. Thinking Skills Creat. 42, 100907 (2021)

A Web and a Mobile Application to Explore the Cultural Heritage in the Greece-Albania Cross Border Region

Christos Bellos[1]([⊠]) [iD], Konstantinos Stefanou[1] [iD], Georgios Stergios[1],
Thanos Kotsis[2], Georgia Tsamadia[2], Angeliki Kita[3], Persefoni Ntoulia[3],
Vasileios Nitsiakos[2], and Ioannis Fudos[2] [iD]

[1] Lime Technology IKE, Ioannina, Greece
cbellos@lime-technology.gr
[2] University of Ioannina, Ioannina, Greece
[3] Public Central Library of Konitsa, Konitsa, Greece

Abstract. There is a significant interest, from an ethnographic, cultural, and historical perspective, to record testimonies from oral sources in the cross-border area of interest. In the regions of Permet, Gjirokastra and Konitsa we can discover different sides of history and traditions and identify and promote common cultural characteristics that are associated with the areas of interest. Legends, folk tales and oral history testimonies were collected in the regions of Gjirokastra and Konitsa and were connected to the archive of the Library of Konitsa. The content of those oral sources is being used to enrich and transform the perception of the environment in the region and has an inherent additional social value by contributing to the social cohesion, dynamic evolution, and durability of the local cultural heritage.

Thus, this connection of the touristic information with valuable information acquired from oral and written sources, not only would result to transforming the Library, in its physical or digital form, to a reference point for all tourists in the area but to create a sustainable tourist product for the region as well.

Keywords: Cultural heritage · Mobile application · Digital library · Oral history · Testimonies

1 Introduction

Cultural heritage is considered one of the most important assets of tourism. It is an economic activity that promotes the socio-cultural objects in the context of sustainable tourist development [1]. This kind of tourism encloses traditional and social customs, local history, art and cultural events. Finally, the cultural heritage tourism is based on the nostalgia and the desire of the tourist to experience a variety of cultural landscapes [2]. The aforenamed point of view led to the creation of the project EXPLORAL.

The project EXPLORAL builds on the successful project Balkaneana funded under the IPA Cross-Border PROGRAMME "Greece – Albania 2007–2013" that delivered a multimodal digital library with content from the Central Public Library of Konitsa and the Municipal Library of Gjirokaster. The overall objective of the project was twofold: to transform libraries into a reference point for all tourists visiting the cross-border area and to identify and promote the common heritage of the cross-border region through the study and analysis of the oral history and tradition and their interconnection to the written sources.

To this end, the EXPLORAL Digital Library is developed since digital libraries [3] and computational methods [4] are considered in general, as important tools towards the preservation of cultural heritage. The EXPLORAL Digital Library holds a treasure of cultural information in the form of text (PDF), sound and video and is offered to the users in a mobile application that serves as a mobile online documentary. This cultural information is stored to the project database.

The mobile application that was developed within the framework of the project gives users the opportunity to enjoy a mobile online documentary of the Greek-Albanian cross border area witnessing the cultural treasures of these neighboring lands. The mobile application offers an easy and enjoyable way to browse through them and have the chance to listen to oral testimonies of people that lived events of the previous century and many more.

2 Materials and Methods

In this work we will present the EXPLORAL project, including a web and a mobile application, interconnecting each other, and sharing a common and online digital library that has been populated with cultural assets of the Greece-Albania cross border region. The aim is to explore the cultural heritage in this area of interest and link the oral history with written Cultural Heritage Objects (CHOs). The mobile app is user-friendly, targeting the visitor in the area and is built using open-source technologies, capable to access and parse data from the online digital library. On the other hand, the web application is more expert-specific, providing to users advanced search capabilities, based on metadata and in-text search. In addition, the web application has a backend interface for administrators to upload new CHOs and manage the existing assets of the digital library, while the Optical character recognition (OCR) is, also, enabled to admins.

In Fig. 1 the information flow of the EXPLORAL project is displayed, linking the mobile app, the Database of the Digital Library and the web platform.

The EXPLORAL project exploits the digitized material of the finished Balkaneana project, stored in the digital library, while in the framework of the project, interviews were designed and conducted in Greece and Albania, towards the acquisition of oral history and linkage to the digital library. In total, 30 interviews were conducted, ranging from twenty minutes to one and a half hours.

2.1 The Interview Methodology

More specifically, from July 4 2019 to September 20 2019, 3 missions were made to Greece and Albania. The research methodology was defined as ethnographic field research, while the interviews were freely structured with emphasis on the life stories,

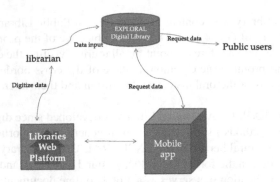

Fig. 1. Information flow of the EXPLORAL project

utilizing methodological tools from literary folklore, oral history and social anthropology, focusing on modern approaches to qualitative social research. The main themes of the interviews were related to World War II, to Civil War incidents, to personal stories around the border and to post-war circumstances in Greece and Albania, as well as to myths, legends and historical folk songs based to locations.

In Greece, interviews were held in the province of Konitsa, with residents from various villages in the wider area, sometimes in Konitsa, where most now live regardless of their origin and sometimes in the surrounding villages. Specifically, we visited Konitsa, Ganadio, Amaranto and Heliorachi. Nevertheless, in Konitsa we recorded stories of residents who come from the villages of Vourbiani, Peklari, Theotokos, Distrato, Lykomoro and Derveni.

In Albania, two research missions were carried out in the area of the Greek minority in the villages of Upper and down Dropolis in the prefecture of Argyrokastro, and in the village of Aliko in region of Saranda. Specifically, in Dropoli we visited the villages of Kosovitsa, Sellio, Vodino, Dervitsani.

2.2 The Backend Functionalities of the EXPLORAL Digital Library

A powerful backend web system has been developed in order to add functionalities to the Digital Library, as depicted in Fig. 2. The technology we used at this stage of development was PHP 5.4.33 along with HTML5, CSS and JavaScript.

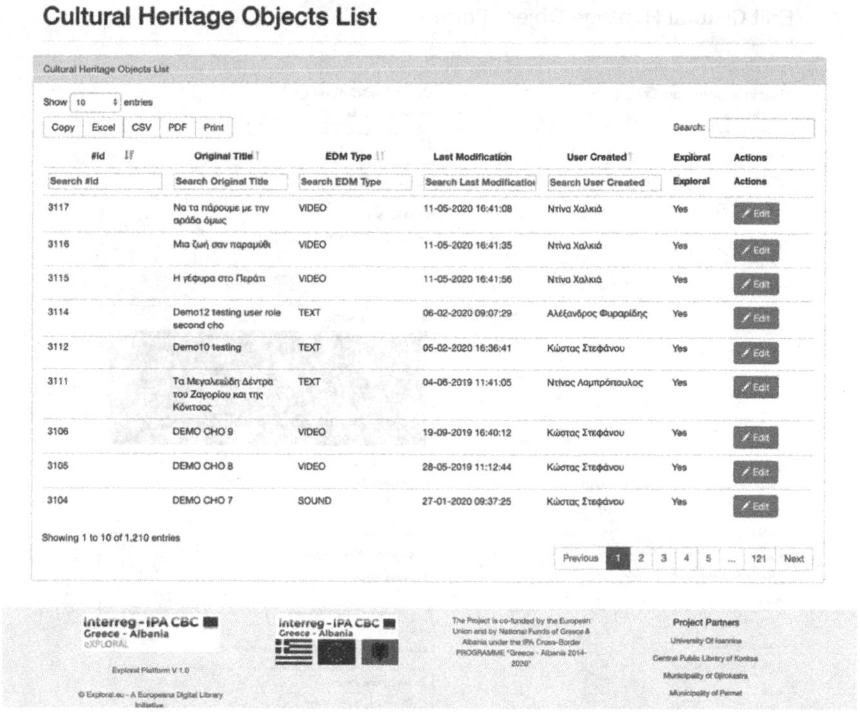

Cultural Heritage Objects List

Fig. 2. Backend interface with the view of the CHO list page

In order to insert a new Cultural Heritage Object or edit an existing one, the Dublin Core Metadata Initiative [5] is used, as displayed in Fig. 3.

2.2.1 Recommender System

Recommender systems aim to predict users' interests and recommend product items that quite likely are interesting for them. They are among the most powerful machine learning systems that online retailers implement to drive sales. Recommendations typically speed up searches and make it easier for users to access content they're interested in, and surprise them with material they would have never searched for.

EXPLORAL uses a content-based recommender system in order to provide the users with useful and correct recommendations.

The basis of this mechanism is to provide a right model for the user-item interactions. In EXPLORAL, we have a lot of criteria to choose from (title, type, language, creator, contributor, publisher, place, place of reference, date, date of reference, motif, reference items, etc.).

For this reason, we planned and organized round-table meetings with the experts (IT and librarians) to define which criteria should be included in our model and which not. After a round of careful requirements analysis, we reached the conclusion that 2 of these criteria are the most significant ones and should be used in the EXPLORAL

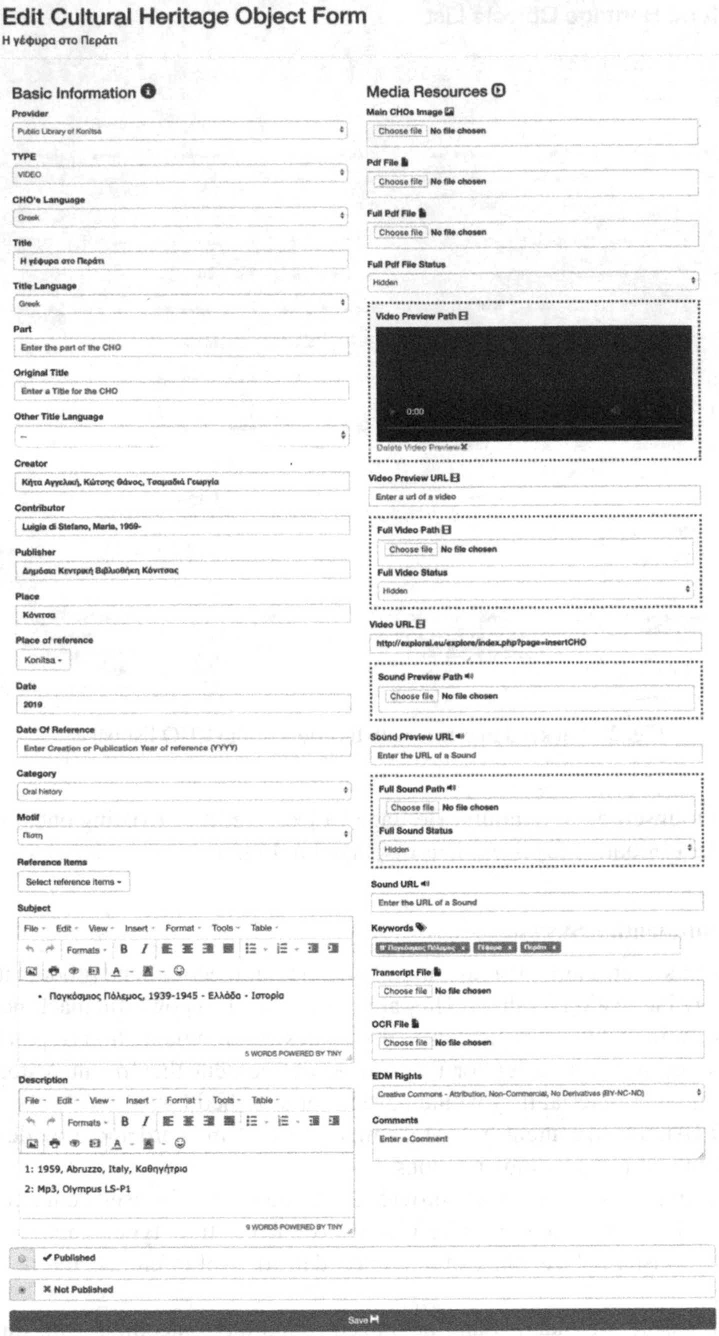

Fig. 3. Edit interface of an existing CHO

recommendation mechanism, namely the place (location) of the searched CHO and the reference item of the searched CHO.

2.2.2 Optical Character Recognition (OCR) Functionality

The technology that we used was the Google Cloud Vision API (https://cloud.google.com/vision/) along with the Google Cloud Storage API (https://cloud.google.com/storage). The combination of the above APIs provided us with a complete suite of development options to provide a concrete OCR functionality for the EXPLORAL platform (Fig. 4).

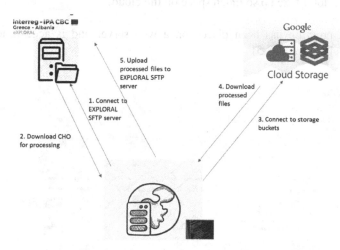

Fig. 4. Information flow for the OCR task

The information flow that was designed for the OCR task consists of i) the setup of the EXPLORAL SFTP server, ii) the setup of the Google Cloud storage buckets and iii) the programming part, which acts as a glue between the server and the buckets.

i)   The EXPLORAL SFTP server was set up in the premises of University of Ioannina in a secure manner, allowing a secure authentication mechanism using a username and a password for the users. This server holds all the CHOs that were utilized for the OCR process.

ii) The setup of the Google Cloud storage buckets required a registration process where the project related credentials were handed to us as a JSON file, which should be safely stored and explicitly declared while programming in the later part. In this cloud platform, we created two buckets as you can see below, the 'exploral-imagebucket', where we would upload all images to be processed and the 'exploral-textbucket', where we would export the OCR results.

iii) The program that we developed for the purpose of the OCR task consists of many parts and makes heavy use of the Google Cloud Vision and Storage API endpoints.

•   At first, the program, connects to the EXPLORAL SFTP server and downloads the requested CHO as a PDF file.

- This file is then uploaded to the 'exploral-imagebucket' storage bucket using the Google Cloud credentials provided to us by Google.
- Then the file is being processed in the cloud and its outputs are transferred to the 'exploral-textbucket' storage bucket.
- The generated files are in JSON format and we cannot process them any further without converting them to TXT files. This step is performed by our algorithm which takes as input the JSON files and outputs the TXT files.
- The final step is to upload the newly generated TXT files to a specific folder to the EXPLORAL SFTP sever so that the indexing procedure can initiate.
- Finally, the objects that were uploaded to the 'exploral-imagebucket' are deleted so that we don't take up so much space on the cloud.

The OCR program has been placed on a web server and is accessible via the EXPLORAL platform (Fig. 5).

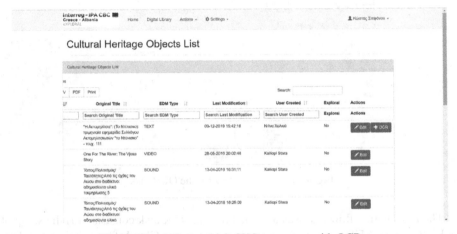

Fig. 5. User selects which CHO to process with OCR

2.3 The EXPLORAL Mobile Application

In Fig. 6 is depicted graphical representation of the connection between the web server and the mobile application towards the real time process and visualization of the Cultural Heritage Objects (CHO).

The EXPLORAL app is developed both in Android and iOS. In the following screenshots, the functionalities of the mobile app are displayed (Fig. 7).

The technology we used at this stage was the cross-platform Apache Cordova environment (https://cordova.apache.org/), which gives developers the ability to develop apps in Android, iOS and Windows Phone. Apache Cordova is an open-source development environment for mobile apps. It allows for the use of standard web technologies – HTML5, CSS3 and JavaScript for cross-platform development. The apps are executed within wrappers targeting each platform and depend on bindings so that they have access

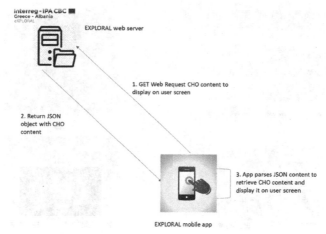

Fig. 6. A graphical representation of the connection between the web server and the mobile application

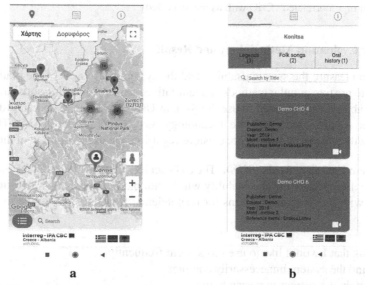

a   b

Fig. 7. (a) The map with the available CHOs locations. (b) A list of CHOs from a specific location that have the "Legend" category

to each device's capabilities, like sensors, data, network, etc. The code reusability feature that we accomplish with Cordova gives us the choice to reuse many code parts that are written for one platform to be used for other platforms as well, a fact that is welcome during the development procedure. The code written for the EXPLORAL app is a mix of HTML/JavaScript/CSS, and converted to an app via a native container for all platforms, while the full functionality is exposed via a unified JavaScript API (Fig. 8).

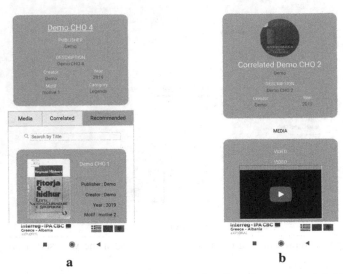

a   b

Fig. 8. (a) The information of a selected CHO with a list of recommended CHOs. (b) The information of a "correlated" CHO with its media (video)

2.4 User Evaluation Methodology and Results

In order to measure the system usability and the system usefulness of the platform, we proposed to use two popular methods of quantitative measure regarding software. For the system usability, we proposed to use the System Usability Scale (SUS) and for system usefulness, we proposed to use the Technology Assessment Model (TAM). These two methods will assist us in making conclusions regarding the users' opinion of the system.

The System Usability Scale (SUS). The SUS scale, that provides a "quick and dirty", reliable tool for measuring the usability will be adopted. It consists of a 10-item questionnaire with five response options for respondents; from Strongly agree to Strongly disagree:

1. I think that I would like to use this system frequently.
2. I found the system unnecessarily complex.
3. I thought the system was easy to use.
4. I would need the support of a technical person to be able to use this system.
5. I found the various functions in this system were well integrated.
6. I thought there was too much inconsistency in this system.
7. I would imagine that most people would learn to use this system very quickly.
8. I found the system very cumbersome to use.
9. I felt very confident using the system.
10. I needed to learn a lot of things before I could get going with this system.

We had 12 filled questionnaires the results of which can be shown in the following table. Each row shows the answer of each filled questionnaire (questionnaires from 1 to

12, answers from 1 to 5) and each column represents the number of the question (10 in total).

	1	2	3	4	5	6	7	8	9	10
1	5	2	5	1	4	1	4	2	5	1
2	4	1	4	2	5	1	5	1	5	2
3	4	2	5	2	4	2	4	2	5	1
4	4	1	5	1	5	2	4	2	4	1
5	4	1	5	2	5	1	4	1	4	2
6	4	1	5	1	4	2	4	1	4	1
7	4	2	5	2	4	2	5	1	4	1
8	5	2	5	2	4	2	5	1	4	1
9	5	1	5	1	5	1	4	1	5	1
10	5	2	4	2	5	1	5	2	5	2
11	4	2	4	2	4	2	4	2	4	2
12	5	2	4	1	5	1	5	2	4	3

We now translate these answers to points as shown below.

	1	2	3	4	5	6	7	8	9	10	Score	Score in 100 basis
1	4	3	4	4	3	4	3	3	4	4	36	90
2	3	4	3	3	4	4	4	4	4	3	36	90
3	3	3	4	3	3	3	3	3	4	4	33	82,5
4	3	4	4	4	4	3	3	3	3	4	35	87,5
5	3	4	4	3	4	4	3	4	3	3	35	87,5
6	3	4	4	4	3	3	3	4	3	4	35	87,5
7	3	3	4	3	3	3	4	4	3	4	34	85
8	4	3	4	3	3	3	4	4	3	4	35	87,5
9	4	4	4	4	4	4	3	4	4	4	39	97,5
10	4	3	3	3	4	4	4	3	4	3	35	87,5
11	3	3	3	3	3	3	3	3	3	3	30	75
12	4	3	3	4	4	4	4	3	3	2	34	85
												1042,5
											Final result	86,875

We notice that the final result is 86.875 which is way higher than 68, which is considered above average for the usability of the system.

The Technology Assessment Model (TAM). TAM is one of the most influential extensions of Ajzen and Fishbein's theory of reasoned action (TRA) in the literature. It was developed by Fred Davis and Richard Bagozzi. The TAM is an information systems theory that models how users come to accept and use a technology. The model suggests that when users are presented with a new technology, a number of factors influence their decision about how and when they will use it. In TAM, participants are asked to provide their level of agreement on a 7 point scale (1 = strongly disagree and 7 = strongly agree). Here are the 10 usefulness items:

1. Using this software improves the quality of the work I do.
2. Using this software gives me greater control over my work.
3. This software enables me to accomplish tasks more quickly.
4. This software supports critical aspects.
5. This software increases my productivity.
6. This software improves my job performance.

7. This software allows me to do more work than would otherwise be possible.
8. This software enhances my effectiveness on the job.
9. This software makes it easier to do my job.
10. Overall, I find this software useful in my job.

	1	2	3	4	5	6	7	8	9	10			
1	7	7	7	7	6	6	7	7	6	7		67	0,95714286	95,71429
2	7	6	7	6	6	7	6	6	7	7		65	0,92857143	92,85714
3	7	7	6	6	7	7	6	7	7	6		66	0,94285714	94,28571
4	6	6	6	7	6	7	7	7	6	7		65	0,92857143	92,85714
5	7	7	6	6	7	7	6	7	7	6		66	0,94285714	94,28571
6	6	6	7	6	7	6	6	6	7	7		64	0,91428571	91,42857
7	7	7	7	6	5	6	5	6	6	6		61	0,87142857	87,14286
8	6	7	7	5	6	6	6	6	7	6		62	0,88571429	88,57143
9	7	7	7	6	5	5	7	6	7	7		64	0,91428571	91,42857
10	6	6	6	5	4	5	6	5	6	6		55	0,78571429	78,57143
11	7	7	7	7	7	7	7	7	7	7		70	1	100
														1007,143
													Final result	91,55844

We had 11 filled questionnaires the results of which can be shown in the following table. Each row shows the answer of each filled questionnaire (questionnaires from 1 to 11, answers from 1 to 7) and each column represents the number of the question (10 in total). We notice that the final result is 91.55844 which is a great result for the usefulness of the system.

3 Conclusions

The COVID-19 pandemic and the necessary physical and social isolation made clear the increasing need for more digital content in the frame of cultural heritage. Namely, in mountainous and isolated areas where not so many museums or art galleries exist, the digital content is something extremely promising. Even if authenticity is partially lost after digitalization, through EXPLORAL, a visitor can experience new cultural landscapes, ´meet´ the locals, hear their stories and engage with their culture [6, 7]. All these result to the transformation of the tourist product according to the guidelines of cultural heritage tourism. The project has great potentials and all the functionalities that are included can be improved through artificial intelligence [8]. This is one of the priorities of the team to work on the next years and us artificial intelligence to extend and improve the EXPLORAL OCR, recommender and functionality of linking oral history assets to written CHOs.

Acknowledgements. This study has been co-financed by the European Union (European Regional Development Fund – ERDF) and Greek national funds through the Interreg Greece-Albania 2014–2020 Program "EXPLORAL".

References

1. Nilsson, P.A.: Impact of cultural heritage on tourists: the heritagization process. Athens J. Tour. **5**(1), 35–54 (2018). https://doi.org/10.30958/ajt.5.1.3

2. Packer, J., Ballantyne, R.: Conceptualizing the visitor experience: a review of literature and development of a multifaceted model. Visit. Stud. **19**(2), 128–143 (2016). https://doi.org/10.1080/10645578.2016.1144023
3. Kioussi, A., et al.: A knowledge JSON-based database for integrating multiple disciplines in cultural heritage. In: Osman, A., Moropoulou, A. (eds.) Nondestructive Evaluation and Monitoring Technologies, Documentation, Diagnosis and Preservation of Cultural Heritage. SPM, pp. 121–132. Springer, Cham (2019). https://doi.org/10.1007/978-3-030-25763-7_9
4. Kioussi, A., et al.: A computationally assisted cultural heritage conservation method. J. Cult. Herit. **48**, 119–128 (2021)
5. Available online: https://dublincore.org/
6. Stamati, V., Antonopoulos, G., Azariadis, P.N., Fudos, I.: A parametric feature-based approach to reconstructing traditional filigree jewelry. Comput. Aided Des. **43**(12), 1814–1828 (2011)
7. Eftaxopoulos, E., Vasilakis, A., Fudos, I.: AR-TagBrowse: annotating and browsing 3d objects on mobile devices. In: Paulin, M., Dachsbacher, C. (eds.) 35th Annual Conference of the European Association for Computer Graphics, Eurographics 2014 – Posters, Strasbourg, France, April 7–11, pp. 5–6. Eurographics Association (2014)
8. Voulodimos, A., Doulamis, N., Doulamis, A., Protopapadakis, E.: Deep learning for computer vision: a brief review. Comput. Intell. Neurosci. **2018**, 1–13 (2018). https://doi.org/10.1155/2018/7068349

Computer Aided Design for the Preservation of Cultural Heritage: The Case of Mavrogiorgiannika in Kythera, Greece

Anastasia Vythoulka[1], Ekaterini Delegou[1], Costas Caradimas[2], and Antonia Moropoulou[1]([envelope])

[1] Laboratory of Materials Science and Engineering, School of Chemical Engineering, National Technical University of Athens (NTUA), 9 Iroon Polytechniou Street, Zografou Campus, 15780 Athens, Greece
amoropul@central.ntua.gr
[2] School of Architecture, National Technical University of Athens, Athens, Greece

Abstract. Sustainable development is linked with the preservation and revealing of cultural heritage via practices of adaptive reuse. Adaptive reuse of cultural assets could provide various benefits to the local communities: environmental, economic and social. An important goal of these practices is the attraction of external economies in order to ensure the financial viability of monuments but also to succeed the prosperity of the residents. This study is focused in Kythera, a Greek isolated island. Information collected by local archives, communication with local bodies and in situ observations were combined with spatial data about the island's settlements, road and trail network and cultural reserve. This process permitted the creation of thematic maps that led to the configuration of Kythera's potentials and threats. Thus, the proposal scheme focuses on the abandoned neighborhood, Mavrogiorgianika of Karavas, a traditional settlement in the less prominent northern part of Kythera. The proposal suggests the restoration and reuse of the abandoned housing stock as agro tourism facilities in the context of a comprehensive circular economy program. The aim of the proposal scheme is to promote the natural environment, local products and local agricultural practices, with the active participation of residents and agricultural cooperatives of the island. The proposal of the rehabilitation of the neighborhood is combined with the reuse of the old agricultural school in the village, the watermills and the developed network of trails on the island.

Keywords: Circular economy · Traditional settlements · Cultural heritage · Kythera

1 Background and Literature Review

1.1 Circular Economy, Sustainable Development and Cultural Heritage

As outlined by the European Commission, the adaptation of a circular economy development model demands a shift from the "supply, production, consumption and disposal" model to a model based on the fourfold "reuse, repair, renovation and recycling" [1]. The adaptive reuse of cultural heritage fits to this framework, being in the center of regional sustainable development. The benefits provided by these practices of revealing cultural heritage are environmental, social and economic. The environmental gain is related to the energy saving of reuse instead of new constructions [2]. The social benefits are educational and symbiotic for the local communities when the economic benefits are related to external economies, such as tourism. Especially in remote areas, the contribution of cultural heritage to the regional financial growth is essential [3].

In this context, the management of cultural heritage assets should ensure the maximum performance of the potential benefits above mentioned. Thus, the choice of the proper management model for each case is not unambiguous. The new use proposed should be compatible with the characteristics of the monument, ensuring its financial viability and acceptance by the local community [4]. The combination of financial models and the involvement of both public and private stakeholders could achieve the success of a revealing project, related to the overall sustainable regional development plans. In this process the contribution of local government is crucial in order to regulate the participation of the different stakeholders involved, engaging the local communities [5].

1.2 Computer Aided Design for the Preservation of Cultural Heritage

Revealing and management of cultural heritage consist of a complex issue, including various aspects. The interdisciplinary approach is necessary in order to achieve the sustainable preservation of cultural heritage [6]. The integrated design of this process demands the collection, evaluation and combination of a large quantity of different data in order to obtain a detailed documentation of the study area. In the next step, different scholars of various scientific fields should combine their research consumptions in order to set the basis for the proposals [7, 8]. The participation of local communities and bodies should be integrated as well, in order to achieve the social approval of the proposed scheme. Thus, the contribution of computer aided design is crucial for the proper elaboration of a revealing model. Computer-aided design and drafting (CAD) software programs permit the 2 or 3 dimensional design of historic buildings and sites. The drawing program is essential to every step of the study, from documenting existing conditions to designing interventions [9]. The program is also useful for presenting all that information to project team members, as well as keeping records of any treatments for future generations of conservators. In terms of presentation, the use of CAD could incorporate non-quantitative elements, providing a complex yet understandable image of the proposal. The combination of various software programs in terms of drawing (2D and 3D), combining information (GIS, BIM) with images, texts and testimonies could serve in the formation of o cohesive preservation plan [10]. Another aspect of the contribution of computer-aided design in cultural heritage conservation is the integration of the social aspect in the project. The design, distribution and data analysis of special questionnaires, addressing to various stakeholders of revealing programs could be easier and quicker with the use of special and free software programs (Google forms).

2 Methodology

The study area analysis was conducted through research of local archives, communication with local bodies and residents and in situ observations, providing information about Kythera's history, cultural and natural assets, social and economic organization. In addition, research in open data bases such as Island Geospatial Information Infrastructure, Archeological Candastre, Kythera Trails Network, Google Maps, provided spatial data of the study area in kml files.

Through Google My Maps application, the different kml files where inserted into a cohesive map containing various data about Kythera. This map was converted in a CAD file when information, spatial and arithmetic, was organized, classified and presented in different thematic maps. The results of the analysis, led to the choice of Karavas as a field of intervention. Especially the proposal focuses in Mavrogiorgiannika, an abandoned neighborhood of the village crossed by trail M49 of Kythera Trails Network (Fig. 1).

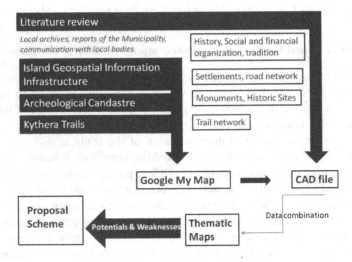

Fig. 1. The methodology of the study

3 The Case Study of Kythera

3.1 Study Area Analysis

Kythera, is the further southern island of Ionian Islands complex. It's capital is Chora and 62 settlements are developed over its surface (Fig. 2). Kythera's key geographical position attracted various conquerors to the island over the years. English, French and Venetian conquerors disembarked on the island over the time, influencing Kythera's cultural identity [11]. The vicinity of Kythera with Crete and Peloponnese also influenced the island's architecture as well as the frequent pirate raids that imposed a fortress building construction. Under these terms, the traditional architecture of Kythera is a blend of English and Venetian simplified forms (public buildings and infrastructure) combined with elements of traditional forms from Crete (southern Kythera) and Peloponnese (northern Kythera) [12]. The monuments of Kythera date back to Prehistoric and Ancient Age, to Byzantine and post-Byzantine period while monuments of the Venetian and English occupancy of the island stand as important landmarks [13, 14, 15] (Fig. 3).

The total permanent population of the Municipality of Kythera amounts to approximately 3,900 residents. However, this number is to be decreased. The main reasons of

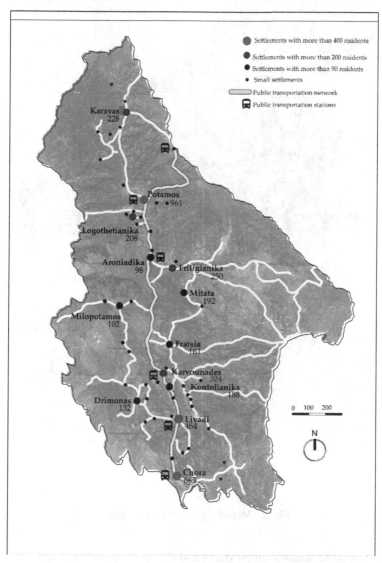

Fig. 2. Map of Kythera's settlements, road and transportation network

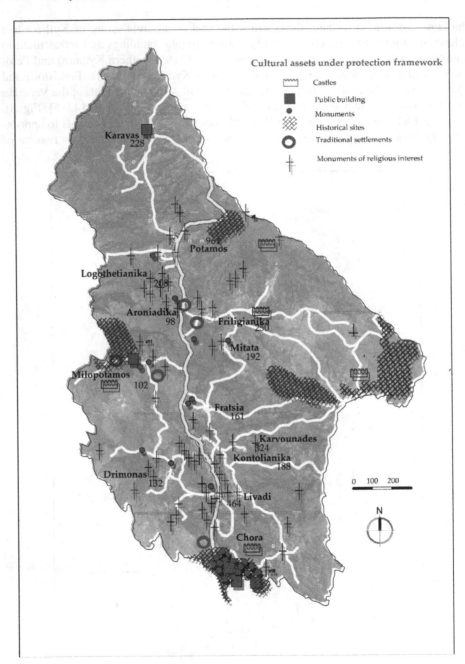

Fig. 3. Map of Kythera's cultural assets

this prediction is the seasonal employment and residence, the island's remote nature and the problematic inland transport, as well as the general phenomenon of abandonment of

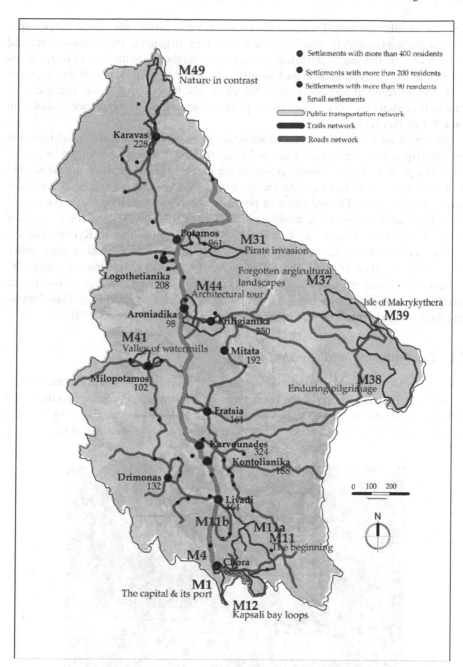

Fig. 4. Map of Kythera's trail

the province that is observed throughout Greece [16]. Kytherians are mainly engaged in the primary sector (agriculture, beekeeping, animal husbandry, etc.), trade and, in the summer months, tourism. Transportation remains quite problematic even today, especially in the winter, with limited ferry and air services. In general, the island has retained its local identity to a satisfactory degree and this is mainly due to the love of its residents for their place, the geographical location of Kythera and the limited tourist development [13]. The agricultural activity is small but stable and high quality, while organic agriculture is constantly evolving. The island produces several products that are available in the local market [16].

In a traditionally rural island, infrastructure such as watermills and windmills, the special irrigation system, terraces and paths are still important elements of the landscape [17]. The paths in Kythera were opened in the past by the residents of the island and in many cases functioned as main roads to inaccessible destinations, or as shortcuts between main roads. The reduction of population and the corresponding reduction of agricultural activity caused the abandonement of many of them. The official network of trails, 'Kythera Trails', consist of an initiative of the Municipality of Kythera and the foundation of Kythera's Culture and Development, including 11 thematic routes, with a total length of 100 km (Fig. 4). The trail network of Kythera was the first in Greece with a specialized brand, website and use of QR codes. Innovations continue as two routes recently became the first in Europe to be certified under the Green Flag Trails brand, and the first Via Ferrata climbing trail was integrated into the network [18].

3.2 The Settlement of Mavrogiorgiannika

This study focuses on the abandoned settlement "Mavrogiorgiannika", in the village of Karavas (Fig. 5). Karavas is the most northern organized settlement of Kythera and consists of ten sub-neighborhoods, one of which is Mavrogiorgiannika (Fig. 6). The famous springs of Amir Ali, which are an attraction for Kythera are situated there, while

Fig. 5. Mavrogiorgianika in Karavas

Karavas is the starting point of many mountaineering and hiking trails. The character of the settlement is rural, mainly with crops of olive and almond trees while due to the strong presence of the liquid element the area is flooded with plane trees and all kinds of vegetation. The neighborhood of Mavrogiorgiannika is uninhabited, and consists of dilapidated or semi-dilapidated houses, which maintain in very good condition the traditional character of the architecture of Kythera. The migratory currents of the 20th century resulted in the abandonment of the settlement. The buildings, although were built two centuries ago, retain their original building form and elements useful for understanding the lifestyle of their former residents (…). In general, they have large storage spaces for the needs of agriculture [19]. The property regime is very complex since many of these houses belong to Kytherians who immigrated to Australia and Egypt. Based on the data available in the real estate offices of Kythera, a process has begun to investigate ways to reuse them (*a specific complex of 4 houses in Mavrogiorgiannika is sold for 75,000 euros for restoration and reuse*). The houses of the settlement are arranged in two main neighborhoods and in three independent buildings. In the upper neighborhood, the houses are densely built with partitions, creating two linear groups of houses, parallel to the elevation curves. In the second group the ground is smoother, the houses are also denser, more square, with access from many sides [17].

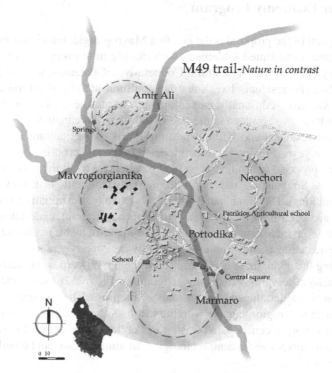

Fig. 6. Map of Karavas in Kyther

3.3 Potentials and Threats

Kythera is an island with a very dense and rich cultural and environmental reserve. Initiatives such as "Kythera Trails" could strengthen the revealing process of the island's cultural heritage but also the traditional rural practices and constructions. The population of Kythera is mainly occupied in agriculture and tourism, activities that could be combined with a sustainable development model in terms of which cultural and environmental assets are a core issue. In this framework, the need of the elongation of touristic period, the increase of permanent residents and the revealing of the least permanent settlements in the island could be answered by a model of sustainable tourism. The distribution of declared monuments, the transportation network and the current development model of the island, set the northern settlements of Kythera as a less prominent area. Thus, adaptive reuse of the island's abandoned housing stock in Karavas, a village of rural tradition and natural beauty could be beneficial for the preservation of Kythera's cultural heritage but also for the local economy.

4 The Restoration and Reuse of the Abandoned Houses as Agrotourism Hostels in the Context of a Comprehensive Circular Economy Program

The starting point of the proposal is the fact that Mavrogiorgiannika is not inhabited but is located within a residented settlement, with mainly rural everyday life. The village is located very close to the Agricultural Cooperative of Potamos, gathers many small producers while the residents have important cultural activity (Cultural Association "Portokalia" Karava). Additionally, the settlement is located next to the gorge of Karavas, with the abandoned watermills and the traditional watering canals that are restored on the initiative of residents and KIPA, while the Patrikios Agricultural School used to operate there for years. Finally, Karavas is located in the less prominent northern part of the island, so a proposal to promote it would be beneficial to all the northern villages.

According to Sougiannis, "the only solution to save the settlement is its overall declaration as traditional. The Municipal Authority should have the initiative, responsibility, coordination and control for the implementation of this program, undertaking to inform the owners and convince them of the need to save the settlement. In this way the settlement will be treated as a unity and arbitrary individual interventions will be avoided" [17]. Following this plan, there is no need to merge the properties, the restoration process can be subject to various financing programs while in most cases the changes in the interior are limited to the addition of sanitary facilities. The configuration of a road that will connect Mavrogiorgiannika with the rest of Karavas, ending in parking lots, is crucial. Water supply, electricity and wastewater collection must be addressed through an underground network and a central biological treatment plant can be built at the foot of the settlement.

The clarification of properties in the village is an important issue as well. In any case, whether after these procedures the reuse of Mavrogiorgianika is purely private or if the Municipality buys the properties, the coordination of the old owners is necessary so that the settlement is treated as a unity. Finding private funding is essential, so the

Municipality must work to set strict conditions on how to rehabilitate and then operate the settlement.

All the above, contributed to the idea of creating a complex of agritourist accommodation [20] in Mavrogiorgiannika, in the configuration of which the elements of rural tradition of the village will play a key role. Starting from the very neighborhood of Mavrogiorgiannika, their adaptive reuse as agritourist accommodation requires the use of only the upper floor spaces, which are accessible by external stairs and properly lit and ventilated. As can be seen in the following drawings (Fig. 7, Fig. 8), these are thirty-three houses and three detached houses, resulting sixty-eight rooms. The rooms are not equivalent in area and space, which allows the project to be addressed in different holiday scenarios but also to guests of different financial levels [21].

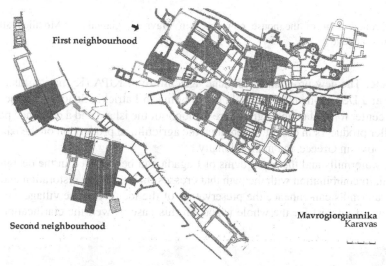

Fig. 7. The house complexes in Mavrogiorgiannika – Modified after Ch. Sougiannis' archive

The ground floors can be used as seminar spaces for residents and visitors on traditional agricultural practices and principles of organic farming, as folklore exhibition spaces, which could even accommodate some of the objects and constructions located today in Mavrogiorgiannika or as storage areas for cultivated products. Their use as points of promotion of local products could also be compatible as well as the formation of information points on the initiatives of the Municipality for programs similar to the "Kythera Trails". Finally, some of the spaces could accommodate the needs of the local cultural association, the agricultural cooperative or the ancillary needs of the accommodation, such as shared kitchens or dining rooms. In any case, the intention is for these spaces to be open to the local community and its activities and to be an incentive for the creation of new initiatives and movements.

The building and the orchard of the Patrikia Rural School (Fig. 9) are proposed to be used as a new school for the local producers, with which the visitors of the village will be able to come in contact. New experimental crops, sustainable beekeeping and organic farming courses, community gardens are some of the activities that could be hosted

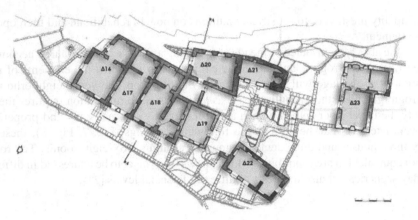

Fig. 8. Ground floor of the house complexes in Mavrogiorgiannika – Modified after Ch. Sougiannis' archive

on the site. The new program for organic agriculture of KIPA (Kytherian Institute for Culture and Development) [19] could find a home in Patrickia School with the aim of being a center for sustainable agriculture throughout the island and a reference point for all smaller producers in order to strengthen the agricultural production on the island and its promotion in Greece and internationally.

The watermills and the small dams of Lagada can be included in the design of the proposal, in combination with the path that crosses it. The proper restoration and reveal of the watermills can enhance the preservation of the identity of the village, creating a new point of interest for the whole island. In this case as well the clarification of the

Fig. 9. Patrikios Agricultural School of Karavas

Fig. 10. Restoration of arrogation canals in Karavas

Fig. 11. Watermill in Karavas

properties will be a guide in shaping the proposal, offering new important development opportunities (Fig. 10, Fig. 11).

5 Conclusions

The methodology flow followed in this study permitted the identification of Kythera's most important development potentials and weaknesses. Kythera is an island with a very dense and rich cultural and environmental reserve. Initiatives such as "Kythera Trails" could strengthen the revealing process of the island's cultural heritage but also the traditional rural practices and constructions. The population of Kythera is mainly occupied in agriculture and tourism, activities that could be combined with a sustainable development model in terms of which cultural and environmental assets are a core issue. In this framework, the need of the elongation of touristic period, the increase of permanent residents and the revealing of the least permanent settlements in the island could be answered by a model of sustainable tourism. The distribution of declared monuments, the transportation network and the current development model of the island, set the northern settlements of Kythera as a less prominent area. Thus, adaptive reuse of the island's abandoned housing stock in Karavas, a village of rural tradition and natural beauty could be beneficial for the preservation of Kythera's cultural heritage but also for the local economy.

The proposal for the reuse of Mavrogiorgiannika has an economic, environmental and social aspect since it is part of a model of cultural heritage management based on the circular economy. The economic aspect has to do with the attraction of external economies in Karavas that could influence all the northern settlements of the island. The environmental aspect is served by the revealing of the tradition rural activities and construction and the promotion of sustainable farming. Finally, the social impact of the proposal is the strengthening of the local community by suggesting participatory activities to the residents, setting Karavas in the center of a sustainable agrotourism model.

References

1. Lavouta, V.: Circular and sharing economy-principles and criteria. In: World Standards Day Event: "Standards for Sustainable and Smart Cities", Greek National Documentation Center, Athens (2017)
2. Gravanguolo, A., De Angelis, R., Iodice, S.: Circular economy strategies in the historic built environment: cultural heritage adaptive reuse. Resour. Conserv. Recycl. **152**, 104507 (2020). https://doi.org/10.1016/j.resconrec.2019.104507
3. Foster, G.: Circular economy strategies for adaptive reuse of cultural heritage buildings to reduce environmental impacts. Resour. Conserv. Recycl. **152**, 104507 (2020). https://doi.org/10.1016/j.resconrec.2019.104507
4. Moropoulou, A., Delegou, E.T.: Innovative technologies and strategic planning methodology for assessing and decision making concerning preservation and management of historic cities In: Proceedings of the 7th International Symposium of the Organization of World Heritage Cities, Rhodes, Greece, 23–26 Sep 2003

5. Pickard, R.: Funding the Architectural Heritage: A Guide to Policies and Examples. Council of Europe Publications, Strasbourg Cedex, France, pp. 12–20 (2009). ISBN: 9287164983

6. Lobovikov-Katz, A., Martins, J., Ioannides, M., Sojref, D., Degrigny, C.: Interdisciplinarity of cultural heritage conservation making and makers: through diversity towards compatibility of approaches. In: Ioannides, M., et al. (eds.) EuroMed 2018. LNCS, vol. 11196, pp. 623–638. Springer, Cham (2018). https://doi.org/10.1007/978-3-030-01762-0_55

7. Kioussi, A., Karoglou, M., Labropoulos, K., Moropoulou, A.: Integrated documentation protocol providing with new cultural heritage documentation procedures. In: Proceedings of the 12th International Conference on the Deterioration and Conservation of Stone, New York, USA, 21–25 Oct 2012

8. Kioussi, A, Labropoulos, K., Karoglou, M, Moropoulou, A., Zarnic, R.: Recommendations and Strategies for the Establishment of a Guideline for Monument Documentation Harmonized with the Existing European Standards and Codes. Prague, Czech Republic, XXIIIrd International CIPA Symposium (2011)

9. Akboy-Ilk, S.: The nature of drawing in the changing culture of architectural documentation. J. Archi. Plann. Res. 33(1), 29–44 (2016). http://www.jstor.org/stable/44113126

10. Pocobelli, D.P., et al.: BIM for heritage science: a review. Herit. Sci. 6, 30 (2018). https://doi.org/10.1186/s40494-018-0191-4

11. Koukkou, E.: History of the Ionian Islands from 1797 until the British occupation, p. 16, pp. 32–40. Papadima Publications, Athens (1983). ISBN: 9789602064504

12. Filippidis, D.: Greek Traditional Architecture – Kythera, pp. 3–24. Melissa Publications, Athens, Greece (1983). ISBN: 9602041366

13. Eghorios Periousia website. Available online: https://www.eghorios.gr/. Accessed on 23 Oct 2021

14. Dodouras, S., Liratzaki, E.: Recording and evaluation of the cultural characteristics of Kythera and Antikythera, pp. 9–14, 72–76. Medina, Athens, Greece (2017). Available online: https://med-ina.org/wp-content/uploads/2021/01/Kythera-Cultural-Rapid-Assessment.pdf. Accessed 11 Oct 2021

15. Bury, J.B., Meiggs, R.: A History of Greece, Greek Translation, p. 84, pp. 420–423, p. 436, pp. 441. Kardamitsa Publications, Athens, Greece (2011). ISBN: 0333154932

16. Municipality of Kythera, Strategic planning of the Municipality of Kythira, Kythera (2011). Available online: http://kythira.gr/oldsite/downloads/Strat_sxed.pdf. Accessed 11 Oct 2021

17. Sougiannis, Ch.: Principles of protection of modern monuments-the example of the traditional settlement Mavrogiorgiannika in Karavas, Kythera. In: Proceedings to the 1st International Conference Myth & Reality, Kythera, 2000, obtained after personal communication with the author

18. Kythera Trails website. Available online: https://kytheratrails.gr/. Accessed 23 Oct 2021

19. Kythera institution of culture and development homepage (KIPA). Available online: kipa-foundation.org. Accessed 11 Oct 2021

20. Ciolac, R., et al.: Agritourism-a sustainable development factor for improving the 'health' of rural settlements case study Apuseni Mountains area. Sustainability 11, 1467 (2019). https://doi.org/10.3390/su11051467

21. Scuttari, A., Della Lucia, M., Martini, U.: Integrated planning of sustainable tourism and mobility: an exploration study. J. Sustain. Tour. 21, 614–637 (2013)

Cretan Cultural Landscapes: Using Virtual Reality to Promote the Marine and Mountainous Environment of Mirabello. The Experience of the Research Project DIATOPO in Crete

Nikos Papadopoulos[1], Katerina Konstantinou[2(✉)], Georgia Moschovi[3],
Theotokis Theodoulou[4], Nikos S. Papadopoulos[1], Christina Tsigonaki[5],
Gianluca Cantoro[6], and Dimitrios Oikonomou[1]

[1] GeoSat ReSeArch Lab, IMS-FORTH, Rethymno, Greece
nikos@ims.forth.gr

[2] Department of Social Anthropology, Panteion University of Social and Political Sciences,
Athens, Greece
k.konstantinou@panteion.gr

[3] Ephorate of Antiquities of Lasithi, Ministry of Culture and Tourism, Crete, Greece

[4] Cretan Section of the Ephorate of Underwater Antiquities, Ministry of Culture and Tourism,
Crete, Greece

[5] Department of History and Archaeology, School of Philosophy, University of Crete, Crete,
Greece

[6] Institute of Heritage Science, Italian National Research Council, Rome, Italy

Abstract. This paper aims to present "Cretan cultural landscapes over the time: promoting marine and mountainous environment of Mirabello – DIATOPO" (hereafter DIATOPO) a multidisciplinary research program exploring and documenting the cultural heritage of Elounda and its surrounding landscapes. DIATOPO's primary goal is to develop novel, suitable, and effective methods for the application of different and diverse cultural heritage documentation practices as well as ways of promoting marine and mountainous heritage landscapes and raise awareness for cultural and natural heritage preservation. Focusing on eastern Mirabello gulf, the program gathers all kinds of archaeological and historical resources, produces knowledge and reinforces deeper understanding of the landscape and its multiple past and present uses. Drawing from the content produced through archaeological and historical research, analysis of the environmental conditions of the archaeological sites, documentation and mapping sites through geoinformatics methods and practices (aerial photography, underwater documentation, geophysical mapping, 3D landscape and architectural representations) DIATOPO designed four heritage routes that connect Elounda and its marine antiquities to the byzantine heritage site on the mountain of Oxa. Within its scope, DIATOPO combines all relevant resources in a virtual reality application in an effort to creatively disseminate scientific knowledge concerning the natural and cultural landscape of the region and experiment with state-of-the-art digital means.

Keywords: Cultural heritage documentation · Virtual reality application · 3D landscape representation

© The Author(s), under exclusive license to Springer Nature Switzerland AG 2022
A. Moropoulou et al. (Eds.): TMM_CH 2021, CCIS 1574, pp. 278–284, 2022.
https://doi.org/10.1007/978-3-031-20253-7_23

1 Research Context

1.1 Goals and Objectives

The idea of DIATOPO was developed on the basis of recent scholarship concerning the ways in which cultural heritage documentation can become relevant to the public [17] and meaningful for local communities, tourists and the society at larger scale (among others [11]). The context of Mirabello gulf provided a great case study for this research. Elounda, the village located on the southern side of the gulf, is today a world famous tourist destination. Attracting most of the tourism attention, Elounda is considered to be the center of the region of Mirabello, thus overshadowing other sites of interest. Oxa, an outstanding mountainous landscape centred around the Timios Stavros byzantine church is one of them. What is today known as the ancient Olous, the underwater site which is being investigated by a team of marine archaeologists in the bay of modern Elounda and around the so-called island of Kolokytha, along with the peak of Oxa have been our two major focal points. Our multidisciplinary team has been researching these two sites as well as sites of historical interest such as the salt pans of Elounda and aspects of the natural environment.

East Crete, due to eustatic and tectonic processes, appears to have several submerged sites, seven of which are found in the Elounda bay. This phenomenon is expected to gradually increase risk caused by climate change and its negative impact on the natural and built environment according to the European Environment Agency 2012 report [5]. At the same time, the mountainous environment is equally at risk. Peak of Oxa is facing the multi-sided issue of desertification in the same way as other Mediterranean mountains and regions [4]. Dealing with these growing challenges that make cultural heritage documentation and public engagement with its management difficult, DIATOPO team works towards devising new methods by applying practices from different disciplinary fields and combining diverse modes to support creativity and transform research material into a digital experience of the mountainous and marine landscape of Mirabello for the public.

Further, taking into account the local community's turn of interest the project will promote sustainable tourism and will compile directions to protect, preserve and present cultural heritage assets hitherto unknown to massive tourism. Thus the main goals of DIATOPO will try to respond to social and environmental needs including the following:

- Document and promote sites of cultural interest in Elounda (Ancient Olous) and Oxa through digital topographic and geometric documentation by applying the most advanced methods of geoinformatics.
- Implement a GIS database to organize the collected amount of information. This database will be of use for the local and government stakeholders as well as for the tourist industry.
- Define hazards and impact on cultural heritage sites.
- Design heritage routes that bring together marine and mountainous landscape. Emphasis was placed on the urban center of the submerged ancient Olous, salt pans of Elounda, the island of Kolokytha and the fortified site on the top to Oxa mountain.

- Design and implement an interactive narrative application combining video, virtual reality, historical information and 3-D models of archaeological sites. This application aims at providing ways to attract interest in geoarchaeological trails and routes that connect land and off-shore archaeological and historical sites of Crete.
- Enhance and empower cultural and environmental education through easily usable and reliable information about the history of the place and the formation of its natural landscape.
- Disseminate new knowledge produced through the combination of the collected amount of information by three groups involved in the research: scientists, local communities and tourists.
- Attract tourists' interest and increase tourism through enhancing high quality tourist products of the region.
- Draw from the experience of designing and implementing the interactive application to compile good practices for the preservation and promotion of heritage sites, the engagement of local communities and tourism.

2 Working Together Across Disciplines

2.1 Transdisciplinarity and Novel Approaches in Heritage Studies

As a digital heritage project, DIATOPO aims at bringing together diverse understandings of the natural and cultural landscape of Mirabello. Archaeological, historical, anthropological and environmental data concerning sites of interest within our research field were listed in a registry containing visual and textual forms of information providing proper documentation. In this part of the documentation process, team members arranged all sorts of bibliographical references from previous research in Mirabello and combined them with newly produced knowledge through archaeological and anthropological fieldwork.

In parallel, geoinformatic technologies were put into use to map terrestrial and submerged sites of historical and archaeological significance. These methods were not only aimed at documenting sites and spatializing knowledge produced through archaeological and historical research but also at adding into efforts of preserving the landscape and promoting its cultural assets. As it has been pointed out by many scholars, geoinformatic methods and practices provide efficient ways of documenting cultural heritage and thus protecting and promoting it (among others [1, 16, 8]).

Geoinformatic documentation technologies have been extensively applied in mapping terrestrial archaeological sites. In marine archaeology, interpretation of geophysical recordings has been used especially for spotting deep-water shipwrecks [15]. A major effort of DIATOPO was put into implementing and assessing non-destructive geophysical methods to explore and document shallow submerged archaeological finds in the gulf of Mirabello. To do so, and in order to improve practices of capturing underwater sites, the team of geophysicists brought in the experience of different case studies in the eastern Mediterranean into a comparative account recently published by Nikos Papadopoulos [13] (Fig. 1).

Based on the use of two different technologies and two devices i.e. a 360-degree camera and a 3D laser scanner, a set of 3D representations of natural and urban landscapes

Fig. 1. Underwater research in ancient Olous

were produced by the team of DIATOPO. These representations are associated with other relevant multimedia material, such as objects and soundscapes, in ways that provide manifold potentials and possibilities in producing meaning through linking things together [10]. Enriching 3D representations with a variety of historical and archaeological information, either it being 2D or 3D elements of cultural heritage, renders it meaningful for people. Introducing time-based data in 3D representations has been analysed and evaluated in recent scholarship regarding the ways in which relating techniques provide comprehensive approaches of heritage both for scholars and the various publics [14]. In terms of research, the so-called 4D reconstructions in cultural heritage expand methods and practices of collecting heterogeneous data and presenting them in meaningful ways [3].

The end product of DIATOPO is a web interactive virtual reality application for the transformation and dissemination of the scientific knowledge acquired through our landscape survey in Mirabello, which comprises a major challenge of the project. It demands to convert analog information into digital multimedia, combine diverse research material, find associations between manifold types of knowledge, and make it relevant to different sorts of publics. For this, DIATOPO members have been involved in reviewing and considering digital research infrastructures, disciplinary boundaries, and methodological frontiers.

3   A Technology-Enhanced Landscape Experience

DIATOPO web application is designed and implemented to provide remote access to the landscapes of the gulf of Mirabello. It is expected to increase interest towards the natural and cultural landscape surrounding Elounda, influence leisure activities [6] or even inspire innovative guided tours or other physical experiences offered by tourism professionals. The digitized environment of Mirabello is to facilitate discovery of the place beyond its most known tourist attractions but also beyond what is physically accessible. The overall effort is in line with the emerging sustainable tourism and economy. Experience and knowledge produced throughout the research serves to inform the development of an application where users can "walk" through heritage trails, "meet" scholars and researchers, listen to locals and view various sites that aren't easily accessible.

Cultural and heritage trails and routes as a means to attract local attention and tourism interest in less known sites and their intangible aspects have been widely used in empirical studies aimed at proposing new experiential activities and increasing our understanding of the multiple dimensions of landscapes (see for example [2, 18]). DIATOPO's heritage trails are informed by several development models that have been put forward by scholars and heritage practitioners in Greece and abroad (among other Greek case studies [7]). Yet, heritage trails are most often designed to connect sites of interest in physical space. Moving into the abstract and digital space while trying to exploit possibilities and resources offered by cutting-edge interactive technologies is one of the main challenges of DIATOPO.

Our goal, concerning this part of the project, is to design and efficiently implement an interactive experience of the landscape of Mirabello that will go beyond mere reproduction of accurate images and detailed maps. In our effort to expand visitor's experience of heritage sites, we are working on the production of rich content and multimedia material that will enhance views and perceptions of the landscape. The virtual reality application that we are working on is based on a simulation of the world around us which is possible through the use of advanced technological equipment. That also has been tested and assessed in various applications which make use of virtual and augmented reality in several heritage sites around the world (see for example [9] as well as other publications, projects and exhibitions by Sarah Kenderdine). To move a step beyond that, DIATOPO application is trying to bring in narrative aspects of the landscape. Narrative engagement is expected to be triggered by site-specific video and audio material intertwined with three-dimensional representations of heritage sites that remain inaccessible to the public such as the shallow water ancient remains in Elounda bay.

4 Preliminary Remarks

Although the overall research was intended to meet the needs of the so-called digital heritage tourist [12], its outcome couldn't be more timely, as the demand for digital experiences and digitized activities is considerably increasing due to the Covid-19 pandemic. Pressing conditions of the current pandemic along with parameters that affect cultural heritage such as mass tourism, climate change and loss of interest have been advancing needs for documentation and dissemination as well.

DIATOPO research has been developing for the past two years on two major pillars. The one being the practice and assessment of cultural heritage documentation through technological means and geoinformatic technologies and the other to design and implement a virtual reality application combining digital objects and multimedia material in a three-dimensional environment. Both parts of the research have been faced with challenges and have provided fertile ground for advancements as well as considerations regarding the ways in which digital heritage production can be integrated in multidisciplinary research.

Acknowledgements. The project "Cretan cultural landscapes over the time: highlighting the marine and mountainous environment of Mirabello" – DIATOPO is part of the Priority Axis "Strengthening the competitiveness, innovation and entrepreneurship of Crete" of the OP. "Crete" 2014–2020 and co-financed by the European Regional Development Fund.

References

1. Barrett, B.: The challenge of conserving cultural resources on a landscape scale. Living Landscape Observer. https://livinglandscapeobserver.net/the-challenge-of-cultural-resources-on-a-landscape-scale/ (2018). Accessed 09 July 2021
2. Boyd, S.: Editorial: heritage trails and tourism. J. Herit. Tour. **12**, 417–422 (2017). https://doi.org/10.1080/1743873X.2016.1265972
3. Doulamis, A., Doulamis, N., Protopapadakis, E., Voulodimos, A., Ioannides, M.: 4D modelling in cultural heritage. In: Ioannides, M., Martins, J., Žarnić, R., Lim, V. (eds.) Advances in Digital Cultural Heritage. LNCS, vol. 10754, pp. 174–196. Springer, Cham (2018). https://doi.org/10.1007/978-3-319-75789-6_13
4. Dubost, M.: Desertification of Mediterranean and Mountainous Regions, pp. 185–196. Springer, Berlin, Heidelberg (1997)
5. EEA. Climate Change, Impacts and Vulnerability in Europe. European Environment Agency. https://www.eea.europa.eu/publications/climate-imp (2012)
6. Han, D.-I.D., Tom Dieck, M.C., Jung, T.: Augmented Reality Smart Glasses (ARSG) visitor adoption in cultural tourism. Leisure Stud. **38**(5), 618–633 (2019). https://doi.org/10.1080/02614367.2019.1604790
7. Kanellopoulou, G.: "Participatory cultural mapping as a methodological tool for the development of the Ecomuseum of Petritis in South Corfu" [Η συμμετοχική πολιτισμική χαρτογράφηση ως μεθοδολογικό εργαλείο για την ανάπτυξη του «Οικομουσείου Πετρίτη και Νότιας Κέρκυρας»]. In: Σιμπόνιας, Κ., Καπετάνιος, Α. (eds.) in Corfu's Coastal Environments, Cultural Heritage & Local Communities [Παράκτια περιβάλλοντα της Κέρκυρας, Πολιτιστική κληρονομιά και τοπικές κοινωνίες,], pp. 1–20. Corfu (2020) (in Greek)
8. Karle, S., Carman, R.: Digital cultural heritage and rural landscapes: preserving the histories of landscape conservation in the United States. Built Heritage **4**(1), 1–17 (2020). https://doi.org/10.1186/s43238-020-00006-6
9. Kenderdine, S.: Hemispheres. In: Lewi, H., Smith, W., vom Lehn, D., Cooke, S., Lewi, H., Smith, W., vom Lehn, D., Cooke, S. (eds.) The Routledge International Handbook of New Digital Practices in Galleries, Libraries, Archives, Museums and Heritage Sites, pp. 305–318. Routledge (2019). https://doi.org/10.4324/9780429506765-27
10. Kyriakaki, G., et al.: 4D reconstruction of tangible cultural heritage objects from web-retrieved images. Int. J. Heritage Digit. Era **3**(2), 431–451 (2014). https://doi.org/10.1260/2047-4970.3.2.431
11. Fernández Martín, J.J., García Fernández, J., Delgado del Hoyo, F.J., Finat Codes, J.: Preliminary ideas for a project on cultural heritage: "Heva"-digital resources optimization for the enhancement of cultural heritage. Int. J. Heritage Digit. Era **1**(1_suppl), 43–48 (2012). https://doi.org/10.1260/2047-4970.1.0.43
12. Navarrete, T.: Digital heritage tourism: innovations in museums. World Leis. J. **61**(3), 200–214 (2019). https://doi.org/10.1080/16078055.2019.1639920
13. Papadopoulos, N.: Shallow offshore geophysical prospection of archaeological sites in Eastern Mediterranean. Remote Sens. **13**(7), 1237 (2021). https://doi.org/10.3390/rs13071237

14. Rodríguez-Gonzálvez, P., et al.: 4D Reconstruction and visualization of cultural heritage: analyzing our legacy through time. Int. Arch. Photogram. Remote Sens. Spatial Inf. Sci. **XLII-2/W3**, 609–616 (2017). https://doi.org/10.5194/isprs-archives-XLII-2-W3-609-2017
15. Sakellariou, D.: Remote sensing techniques in the search for ancient shipwrecks: how to distinguish a wreck from a rock in geophysical recordings. Bull. Geol. Soc. Greece **40**(4), 1845–1856 (2007). https://doi.org/10.12681/BGSG.17145
16. Sarris, A.: Best Practices of GeoInformatic Technologies for the Mapping of Archaeolandscapes. Archaeopress, Oxford, United Kingdom (2015)
17. Simon, N.: The art of Relevance. Museum 2.0 (2016)
18. Timothy, D.J., Boyd, S.W. (eds.): Tourism and Trails: Cultural, Ecological and Management Issues. Channel View Publications, Bristol (2015)

Author Index

Printed in the United States
by Baker & Taylor Publisher Services

Printed in the United States
by Baker & Taylor Publisher Services